D1526315

STATE CONTROL IN SOVIET RUSSIA

CHALLENGE OF THE SOVIET EMPIRE

The Party Leaders in 1934
Back row: A.S. Enukidze, K.E. Voroshilov, L.M. Kaganovich, V.V. Kuibyshev.
Front row: G.K. Ordzhonikidze, I.V. Stalin, V.M. Molotov, S.M. Kirov.

State Control in Soviet Russia

The Rise and Fall of the Workers' and Peasants' Inspectorate, 1920–34

E.A. Rees

St. Martin's Press   New York

First published in the United States of America in 1987

Printed in Hong Kong

ISBN 0–312–00767–1

Library of Congress Cataloging-in-Publication Data
Rees, E.A.
State control in Soviet Russia.
Bibliography: p.
Including indexes.
1. Russian S.F.S.R.   Narodnyĭ komissariat
   raboche-krest ianskoĭ inspektsii — History.
2. Soviet Union—Politics and government—1917–1936.
3. Soviet Union—Economic policy—1917–   .
I. Title.
JN6524.R44   1987   947.084′1   87–4777
ISBN 0–312–00767–1

For my father, Gwynfor Meredydd Rees, and my mother, Elizabeth Jane Rees

'NKRKI . . . a sort of permanent super-commission for audit and control: it is continually combing the other state departments for traces of graft, bureaucratism and other abuses. The Rabkrin has a far flung net; its inspectors look into everything, from the management of the Moscow Art Museum to the building of a new industrial plant, from civil service qualifications of the officials in Daghestan to the conditions of the peasant farms in the Kuban.'

W.H. Chamberlin, *Soviet Russia* (London, 1930)

'NKRKI. What tremors these five letters cause in Russia today, an Industrial Scotland Yard. The first example the Soviet Union has set the world . . . a new departure, watching the Industries of the Union, with its spies in every part of the country working hand in glove with the OGPU . . . The huge building hums with activity at all hours . . . couriers come through its portals hurriedly, its officials know no fixed hours of work. Their high powered motor cars stand waiting to be summoned at a moment's notice, all kind and class of people come and go on all kinds of business.'

J.R. Westgarth, *Russian Engineer* (London, 1934)

'The USSR Commission for Workers' and Peasants' Inspection came to have no fewer than five assistants, each at the head of a considerable department – so true is the common Russian joke that the only remedy for bureaucracy is the creation of more bureaucracy.'

S. Webb and B. Webb, *Soviet Communism: A New Civilization?* (London, 1935)

'It is much to be hoped that, even should the Russians relax their fierce repression of the now unpopular social classes, they will not lightly abandon their institution of Workers' and Peasants' Inspection. Undoubtedly the price of this meddlesome interference of the rank and file into affairs of which they must, in ninety-nine cases out of a hundred, understand nothing at all is a considerable sacrifice of efficiency. But, even at that price, it may be argued that the safeguard which it affords against the odious vulgarities of class distinction is well worth having.'

B. Wootton, *Plan or No Plan* (London, 1934)

Contents

Contents

List of Illustrations

List of Plates

List of Tables

Preface and Acknowledgements

The 1920s remains one of the most fascinating periods in Soviet history, a period of innovation and experimentation, a period of political and intellectual ferment, in which the direction and course of the October revolution was debated and resolved. In the fields of politics, economics and culture and other areas of intellectual endeavour the Soviet Union in this period was a pioneer. The attraction of this period derives from the vital interaction of intellectual debate and practical difficulties besetting a revolutionary regime, an interaction mediated through the prism of political and ideological struggles between individuals and factions for control of the party and for the direction of the revolution. The 1920s is a bridge between the October revolution and Stalinist authoritarianism of the 1930s, and the debate concerning the elements of continuity, between the Leninist and the Stalinist eras is a matter of great controversy, and remains a central issue for understanding the political development of Soviet society.

This period is also the most extensively researched by Western historians, and any attempt to follow in the wake of such monumental studies as E.H. Carr's *History of Soviet Russia* deserves some explanation and justification. The present work examines the history of one people's commissariat – the People's Commissariat of Workers' and Peasants' Inspection (Rabkrin) – during these momentous years. The purpose of this study is to examine the political development of the Soviet regime – the growth of the party-state apparatus, the management of policy-making, the conduct of factional struggles within the party – through the work and activity of this agency. Rabkrin as an instrument of state control provides an excellent vantage point from which to view these processes, through its close connections with the leading party and government organs, and its responsibility for exercising direct oversight over the state administration and economy. As will be seen the commissariat itself was a major actor in the drama, playing a decisive role in determining the course of political events.

This work provides an in-depth study of one people's commissariat and one previously only examined peripherally in Western literature. In contrast Soviet historians have paid much more attention to this curious hybrid organization, whose centrality to the development of the Soviet political system they have more fully appreciated. The present work straddles the disciplines of history and political science. It draws heavily on the works of Western theorists of administration, particularly the works of A. Downs and V.A. Thompson, to illuminate the central issues underlying the operation of control agencies entrusted with the task of monitoring large complex organizations. Central to this study is the dilemma of control, the advantages and disadvantages associated with different control strategies, and the implications which different control systems carry not only for the practical functioning of the institutions involved but also for the management of policy-making.

The present work has been in preparation over many years. It has developed out of a PhD thesis written whilst a postgraduate student attached to the Centre for Russian and East European Studies, Birmingham University. It was submitted in 1982, entitled 'Rabkrin and the Soviet System of State Control 1920–1930.' The present work follows the history of Rabkrin up to its abolition in 1934. Although mainly concerned with Rabkrin, the principal agency of state control in this period, the study of necessity has also to deal in part with the work and organisation of the Central Control Commission (TsKK), the main agency of party control, which from 1923 until 1934 was organizationally joined to Rabkrin.

In writing this work I have incurred various debts and I should like to record my gratitude to those who have assisted me. My chief debt is to Professor R.W. Davies, my supervisor at CREES, who provided great assistance and advice, carefully reading and criticising initial drafts, and providing encouragement to bring the work to fruition. I should also like to record my thanks to Professor M. Lewin, who supervised the work in its early stages. I owe a debt also to former and present members of CREES who provided such a stimulating environment within which to work, whose researches I have drawn on, but whom I hope I have fully acknowledged in my references and footnotes. I should also like to express my thanks to Jenny Brine, ex-librarian at the Baykov Library, CREES, who was unfailingly helpful in offering advice and assistance.

In undertaking this research I was fortunate to receive assistance from the British Council and under their auspices I was able to undertake two visits to the Soviet Union in 1975 and 1984. These visits were invaluable for the opportunity they provided to carry out research in the main libraries in Moscow and to gather material unobtainable in the West. On my first visit I received useful advice and assistance from the Soviet historian S.N. Ikonnikov, whose two books on the history of Rabkrin provided an important starting-point for my own research.

In preparing the work for publication I received assistance from Dr R.J. Service of the School of Slavonic and East European Studies, London, who read several of the chapters and made many useful suggestions for their improvement. Dr P. Lester also read many of the chapters and helped to make the text more comprehensible. The arduous work of typing successive drafts of the book was done with great efficiency and good humour by Kim Pickerill.

As always, the author bears full responsibility for whatever errors or shortcomings there are in the text, and for the interpretation put on events.

Keele E.A. REES

Introduction: Aspects of State Control

The central issue in the study of all political systems is the nature of the state, and central to the state is the issue of its control and accountability. The October revolution inaugurated the first attempt by a Marxist regime to tackle these complex problems. The issue of state control had long preoccupied the tsarist government and its people, even inspiring Gogol's famous comedy *Revizor* (The Inspector General). The Bolsheviks – as a revolutionary, modernizing party – encountered particularly stubborn difficulties in the realm of state building and state control. The regime's future course was determined to a large extent by the party's response to these problems. [1]

This work examines the development of the Soviet system of state control in the period 1920–34. It provides a history of the principal state control agency – the People's Commissariat of Workers' and Peasants' Inspection (*Narodnyi kommissariat raboche-krest'yanskoi inspektsii*, known also as NKRKI and by its acronym Rabkrin). The study of state control provides a vantage point from which to study Bolshevik policies of state building, the party's efforts to combat bureaucratization and to bind the state to the society. It affords an insight into policy-making in this period of dramatic and momentous change – and provides also an analysis of the major political struggles that occurred. NKRKI stood at the heart of these events and controversies. The importance of state control in the Soviet context highlights some of the distinctive characteristics of the Soviet state. The response to the problem of control set the regime apart from the western liberal tradition of the state – the Russian word 'kontrol' means to check, verify, monitor, survey, regulate, inspect or audit. All political systems operate a multiplicity of control levers to levers to regulate the state machine, at the heart of this question is the problem of accountability and the central dilemma – *quis custodiet ipsos custodes* (who is to guard the guardians)?

Max Weber's 'ideal type' of bureaucratic organization provides a convenient starting point for our discussion of control within administrative systems.[2] 'Bureaucracy' was seen by Weber as the most developed and technically most efficient system of administration, an integral part of a political system based on 'rational legal authority'; its growth was part of a general rationalizing process shaping modern history. The Weberian ideal type envisaged a single, clearly-defined administrative hierarchy, a monistic or monocratic system which abjures the existence

1

of parallel or competing agencies on grounds of efficiency. It pictures a highly specialised structure, with clear demarcation of function, based on strict hierarchy and control. A clear flow of command passes from top to bottom of the hierarchy and a clear line of accountability flows in the reverse direction. The work of the bureaucracy is pervaded with impersonality.

Weber feared that the task of controlling these expanding, increasingly complex, powerful and stifling bureaucracies would pose an intractable problem for governments. Under socialism, he envisaged that state bureaucracy would flourish, with the enlargement of state activity and the elimination of autonomous centres of power which capital and labour provided under capitalism. He urged various strategies to check the power of the bureaucracy, including collegial management of agencies and systems of legislative oversight. Despairing of the effectiveness of such controls he argued the need for charismatic political leaders, backed by mass parties, as the only real hope for avoiding the dangers of bureaucratic domination.

Weber was unduly pessimistic regarding the dangers of bureaucratization and underestimated the effectiveness of alternative control strategies. Moreover, his monistic model corresponds only partly with the reality of administrative work – not all tasks can be categorized and routinized. The Weberian model, in emphasising impersonality, regularity and predictability, underplays the importance of flexibility, initiative and responsiveness for effective administration. This requires a certain devolution of authority within the bureaucracy. It requires an understanding of the complex interplay of administrative and political consideration at different levels. Reliance on single administrative hierarchies to perform functions may also exacerbate the problems of central control. This suggests the need for a fuller understanding of administrative behaviour, and of the different devices whereby the bureaucracy can be controlled and energised.[3]

In western countries the main controls over the state apparatus derive from the three main branches of government – the executive, legislature and judiciary. Furthermore, regular elections, the influence of public opinion and the pressure from interest groups provides some link between the state and the wider society. Within the state administration itself there operate internal departmental control agencies. The selection, promotion and training of officials provides another mechanism of control. These control systems all carry implications for administrative efficiency, for the organisation of policy making and policy implementation.[4]

The use of separate monitoring agencies is one of the most widespread devices for controlling large, complex governmental bureaucracies, where the tensions between politicians and administrators are often acute.[5] Independent control agencies, A. Downs argues, have various advantages: they multiply the direct surveillance capabilities of top-level officials; they form redundant channels of communications – as a counter to the distortions of the official channels; they permit the by-passing of administrative levels for the insertion of instructions and the extraction of data; and they create a rival to the operative bureau. Control agencies and operative bureaux have conflicting interests regarding the exposure of defects. This tension can be utilised by top-level officials to maximize control and stimulate initiative. However, control agencies develop their own departmental interests. Aggrandizement by monitoring agencies, Downs argues, produces the 'law of ever-expanding control'.

Operative bureaux may respond by complying with the orders issued or may try to undermine the loyalty of controllers by cultivating a client relationship. They may conceal defects in their work or pressurize their superiors to reduce the amount of monitoring they are subjected to on the grounds that it is detrimental to efficiency.

Effective control requires close collaboration between controllers and operatives. To prevent monitors being subverted by the officials, top-level officials may employ various methods: (i) separating the monitoring hierarchy from the operative hierarchies; (ii) providing high rewards to monitors for zealous performance of their duties; (iii) reducing close or prolonged contracts between monitors and operators; (iv) creating positive hostility between monitors and operators. Monitoring groups can be turned into 'elite corps', selected for their political reliability or chosen from ethnic or social groups hostile to the operating officials.

Downs outlines three different tactics which top-level officials can employ to control the monitors. First, they can set another bureau to monitor the monitors. This may merely shift the problem and further complicate the power relations involved. Second, they can use redundant channels of communications, by-pass strategies, and overlapping jurisdiction devices with both operating and monitoring bureau. Third, they can use operating bureaux to check on monitoring bureaux. This, however, may weaken the effectiveness of the monitoring agency. The problem of 'guarding the guardians', Downs argues, has no satisfactory or final solution.

The dilemma associated with independent monitoring bureaux is summarised by H. Simon:

Unless the overhead control organisations are just as extensive and specialised as the organisations they seek to control they will understand only meagrely the administrative decisions they seek to control and in most cases the power of initiative will not be with them. If they are just as extensively organised duplication will result and the cost of administration will be enormous. But more important who will then control the controllers? If overhead units enforce responsibility upon lower echelons of the hierarchy to whom or what will the overhead units themselves be accountable?

Kassof's concept of the 'administered society' and the work of Meyer both emphasise the usefulness of western theories of public administration and organisation in studying the Soviet system as an alternative to the totalitarian model.[8] The usefulness of employing such approaches is clearly demonstrated by Granick's and Berliner's studies of Soviet industrial organisation, Hough's study of the regional party's role in economic management, and Rigby's history of Sovnarkom.[9] The study of the role of 'interest groups', pioneered by Skilling and Griffiths, has also highlighted the complexity of decision-making in the Soviet system.[10]

The study of developmental administration in the emergent nations of the world has stimulated much debate concerning the appropriateness of different models for these countries.[11] The Weberian model, V.A. Thompson argues (based on the experience of the developed countries), is 'fixated on control' and reflects the relative stability of the environment in which these systems developed. This 'morbid preoccupation with control' relfects an 'ideal of perpetual stability'.[12]

In opposition to the 'control-orientated' model Thompson posits an alternative 'adaptation-orientated' model of administration. Development administration, Thompson argues, requires flexibility, a creative and imaginative approach in dealing with difficult and unexpected problems, a willingness to experiment, to take chances, to innovate. Innovation is facilitated by 'group administrative effort dominated by a professional outlook', by 'programme or subject matter uncertainty accompanied by personal security', by 'a nonhierarchical climate, especially a nonhierarchical communication structure' and by 'loose organisation in general'. This, Thompson argues, should undermine a narrow, departmental approach to problem-solving and encourage greater creativity, seriousness and responsibility. Policy-making and implementation should be closely integrated, with operative officials involved in setting policy goals.[13]

The Weberian monocratic model of administration, emphasizing hierarchy, discipline and order, may foster 'bureaupathology', with irresponsible officials refusing to display initiative and slavishly adhering to directives and precedents. Bureaupathology, Thompson argues, stems from excess control and the adoption of administrative methods which foster insecurity amongst officialdom. This insecurity can result from 'the existence of an arbitrary, non-rational and unpredictable authority at the very top as in the case of an authoritarian, single party political system'. It can result also from impatience and inability of high authority figures to wait for the results of 'development planning'.[14]

Excess control may inhibit rational decision-making by constraining or unbalancing discussion of contentious issues. Decision-makers themselves become the victims of the system – subordinates submit information and advice tailored to suit their superiors' known preferences. Unfavourable information or advice is filtered out of the system. To avoid these dangers the policy-making process must itself be carefully managed. Reliance on limited sources of information and advice may restrict the options open for consideration and distort perceptions of reality.

Thompson argues that the 'adaptation-orientated' model of administration 'will achieve more development more quickly and with less human cost, with more imagination, with more attention to more values, and therefore with greater benefit'.[15] Notwithstanding its purported advantages it is clear that the model is compatible only with a gradualistic, consensual strategy of economic development. Forced economic development, which places a major strain on the state apparatus and on the society itself, necessitates a control-centred model of administration. Thompson's model requires of political leaders a willingness to involve experts in decision-making, and a tolerance of administrative abuses, errors and corruption that may be difficult to achieve where there is intense distrust between politicians and administrators.

These issues were hotly debated in the Soviet Union in the 1920s. Thompson's thesis was anticipated by L.B. Krasin who advanced a similar 'production-centred' model of administration and warned of the dangers of a control-dominated system.[16] The control-centred model was central to the Stalinist system of government. The characteristics of 'totalitarianism' as a species of development administration are discussed by M. Fainsod.[17] This system, whilst appearing to confirm Weber's worst fears regarding modern bureaucracy was, however, by no means an inevitable outcome.

Marx's analysis of the state, with its rejection of western liberal assumptions about the state and state-societal relations, provided the theorectical framework within which the Bolsheviks after 1917 sought to grapple with the problem of state building. Lenin's classic study *The State and Revolution* offers a clear exposition of Marx's ideas on the class nature of the state and the more problematical question of the future of the state in the transition to socialism.

Lenin envisaged the destruction of the bourgeois state machine and its replacement by a new state apparatus, modelled on the Paris Commune, embodying 'the dictatorship of the proletariat'. He rejected western 'bourgeois' models of state organization with their separation of powers, checks and balances. 'Socialist democracy' would be a form of direct, party-guided, participatory democracy eradicating the dichotomy between state and society, transforming the specialist functions of professional administrators into relatively simple tasks of control and accounting which could be performed by all. All that was required was to introduce measures to democratize the state machine, and curb bureaucracy.[18]

Marxists have concerned themselves mainly with the question of the class nature of the state, generally neglecting technical and practical problems of state management and control. Only where Marxist parties have taken power and had to confront these difficulties has the problem of state control been studied and theorized.[19]

The problem of ensuring political control of the state assumed a new dimension and significance in Russia after 1917. The Bolsheviks – as a minority party which encountered fierce opposition – relied on the centralized state machine to ensure its survival and to enforce its policies. In the aftermath of the revolution the conflict between politicians and administrators was intense. The adaptation of the state for the novel purpose of socialist construction and its enlargement (consequent on the nationalisation of the economy) further complicated the issue of control. The Bolshevik's inexperience of government, their lack of qualified cadres, the general disorder of a post-revolutionary society, the disruption of communications, the fragmentation of political authority, greatly exacerbated the problem.

The strategies developed to deal with these intractable difficulties imparted to the regime much of its distinctive character. In the organisation of the state three general systems of control were developed: (i) party control, (ii) state or governmental control, (iii) social control.[20]

Party control (*partinnyi kontrol'*) has two aspects. Firstly, it refers to internal party control, the enforcement of party discipline. Secondly, it refers to party control over other bodies – either state or mass social organisations. In this second sense, it concerns the maintenance of party supremacy, the regulation of party–state relations through political appointments (*nomenklatura*) and direct supervision of subordinate bodies.[21] The term state control (*gosudarstvennyi kontrol'*) in the Soviet context embraces what in the west is understood as 'executive control'. Formal controls comprise internal departmental control (*vnutrennyi* or *vnutrivedomstvennyi kontrol'*) and control by external agencies (*vneshnii kontrol'*). Judicial control and police surveillance constitutes one important aspect of this latter mechanism.[22] In the economic sphere control functions are performed by financial, planning and data-gathering agencies.[23]

Social or popular control (*narodnyi, obshchestvennyi* or *massov yi kontrol'*) as part of the system of direct, participatory, socialist democracy was a major innovation in state administration in Russia after 1917.[24] It grew out of the workers' control movement of 1917–18 and the flowering of the soviets, factory committees and trade unions as agencies of mass democracy in that period. It sought the direct participation of the population in state administration, creating a new type of state based on popular power (*narodnovlastie*), a state more accountable to the society as preparation for the transition to a stateless Communist society organised on the principle of the self-administration of the people.[25]

State building in all socialist systems has excited intense controversy between political traditions which emphasise the centrality of the state's role and those which stress popular initiative and the autonomous power of social organizations. This can be seen as a conflict between a centralized statist and a decentralised libertarian conception of socialism. That division, although overdrawn, reflects a real tension between distinct ideological tendencies. In Russia it surfaced in the political debates of 1917–21. The same issues have arisen in other socialist systems: Hungary (1956), Czechoslovakia (1968) and Poland (1980). Other attempts to resolve the problem vary from the Yugoslavian experiments in worker self-management to the Chinese cultural revolution. The debate on the nature of the state is inseparable from the debate over control and the balance between party, state and popular control.

A unique feature of the Soviet experience of the 1920s was the attempt to combine together party, state and popular control within the same organisation. The study of control provides a means of analysing the development of the Soviet state and the problem of bureaucratization.[26]

NKRKI became a major institutional interest group within the system. Its role within the party–state apparatus is examined with particular reference to the formation of economic policy, highlighting the problems of control for a revolutionary regime which embarks on the path of economic modernisation.

10

BBC Hulton Picture Library
Plate I   I.V. Stalin (1879–1953): narkom RKI (February 1920–April 1922)

Novosti Press Agency
Plate II   A.D. Tsyurpa (1870–1928) Narkom RKI (May 1922–May 1923)

1 The Institutionalization of State Control (1919–22)

The Bolsheviks assumed power in Russia in 1917 with no experience of government and only the vaguest ideas about practical problems of state building. The theoretical problem of the state and the proletarian revolution had been extensively aired. After the October revolution the party faced the complex task of reconciling its ideological commitments with the practical problems of state administration and management. The issue was hotly debated, raising as it did the most basic questions concerning the meaning of socialism – in which the model of state socialism was counterposed to an alternative libertarian model. The debate on the organisation of state control was a vital part of this controversy. It culminated in the establishment in February 1920 of the new People's Commissariat of Workers' and Peasants' Inspection (Rabkrin, NKRKI or RKI – pronounced er-ka-ee) as the most novel Bolshevik experiment in state building.[1]

STATE, DEPARTMENTAL AND WORKERS' CONTROL (1918–19)

Lenin's *State and Revolution* encapsulated the Bolsheviks' view of the state. The socialist revolution was to smash the 'bourgeois' state and institute the 'dictatorship of the proletariat' which itself was to be a state in the process of dissolution. Socialism would abolish the state as a coercive instrument of class rule, and transcend the dichotomy between state and civil society. State functions would be progressively assumed by social organizations (through social control and accounting) preparing the way for a self-governing, classless Communist society. Lenin rejected on principle the western model of parliamentary government with its checks and balances and separation of powers, and aimed to model the new Soviet state on the experience of the Paris Commune of 1871.[2]

After the October revolution the Bolsheviks moved quickly to consolidate their power. Within the party the Central Committee remained the leading authority but power was progressively concentrated in the Politburo under Lenin's leadership. The Council of People's Commissars (Sovnarkom), under Lenin's chairmanship, took over the work of government, operating within the guidelines of party directives and subject to party control. The Central Executive Committee (VTsIK) of the Congress of Soviets, to which Sovnarkom was nominally accountable, was never allowed to develop as a strong legislative body and under Ya. M. Sverdlov's chairmanship its role was closely circumscribed.

The party, which had pledged to smash the centralised, bureaucratic tsarist state machine, took over the old apparatus almost *in toto*, adapting its procedures and methods.[3] The existing ministries were renamed 'people's commissariats', with party members, and briefly Left SR members, appointed to head them. Elsewhere reconstruction was more substantial with the creation of the Cheka and the Red Army, into which thousands of party members were drafted. Establishing party control over the state apparatus posed enormous difficulties. The former tsarist civil servants viewed the new regime with either hostility or antipathy, and sought to sabotage and obstruct its works. The party's lack of experienced administrators and technical specialists further compounded the problem. The huge increase in government activity in industry, transport and trade expanded the state apparatus and made effective control more difficult. Serious economic and administrative dislocation only added to these problems.

Party control over the state apparatus, and the efficient working of the latter, was obstructed by the fragmentation of authority. The soviets strongly resisted the encroachment of central government into their affairs. They remained the real power in the localities and looked to VTsIK to defend their autonomy. The trade unions, under the All-Russian Central Trade Union Council (VTsSPS), fought to secure control over industry and stubbornly resisted attempts to establish a system of state industrial management.

The transition from the dictatorship of the proletariat to Communism, outlined in Lenin's *State and Revolution*, provided a common standpoint for the party. The problem of interpretation and practice exposed major division in its ranks between distinct ideological tendencies. Crucial in this controversy was the speed with which the transition was to be effected and the powers of the state institutions transferred to the representative institutions in society. The ability of the proletariat to assume responsibility for socialist construction and the way this could be organised lay at the centre of the conflict.

These debates took place against the background of a tempestuous mass movement. The Bolsheviks came to power on the slogans of 'all power to the soviets' and the demand for workers' control (or supervision) of industry. The party's own power base lay in the soviets and in the factory committees and the trade unions. The challenge for the regime was to reconcile these demands with the needs of efficient government.

The tsarist regime's system of state control survived the period of the Provisional Government intact. A special department of control had been set up as early as 1811 as the Chief Administration for the Revision of State Accounts (*Glavnoe Upravlenie Revizii Gosundarstvennykh Otchetov*). This was renamed the department of State Control (*Gosudarstvennyi Kontrol'* or GosKontrol) in 1836. In 1905 when the Council of Ministers was formed the state controller was included in its composition with ministerial rights.[4]

GosKontrol was responsible for financial control, auditing the accounts of ministries and departments which were in receipt of budgetary revenue. It performed a similar function to the *Cour des comptes* in France, the *Rechnungshof des Deutschen Reichs* in Germany and the Comptroller and Auditor General's Office in Britain. However, major institutions connected to the tsar's court fell outside its purview and attempts by the Duma to reform it along west European lines failed. It also had responsibilities for improving the organisation of the state apparatus. The agency's competence extended to the localities through a network of local offices. After the Revolution, this agency was regularly condemned as bureaucratic and antiquated.

The need for effective accounting and control of administration became one of Lenin's major preoccupations.[5] GosKontrol, like most of the tsarist ministries, was taken over by the Bolshevik government. This was fiercely resisted by its conservative officials, resulting in a prolonged strike. In November 1917 VTsIK appointed E.E. Essen to lead the department's work.[6] Sovnarkom on 5 December 1917 approved two decrees, one establishing a collegium to lead its work, and the second granting the agency representation in Sovnarkom.[7]

Sovnarkom on 18 January 1918 approved a decree 'Concerning the Central Control Collegium' in a first attempt to establish a new unified control system. The collegium was to be responsible for reorganising GosKontrol and was to link this agency with 'accounting control collegia' attached to the local soviets and 'control commissions' in the factories and insitutions.[8]

Alongside this system of government control the spontaneous movement for workers' control which had arisen in 1917 continued to gain momentum, legitimised by the Sovnarkom decree 'On Workers' Control' of November 1917.[9] This movement was organized through the factory committees and control commissions. In 1918 it was brought progressively under trade union direction. In the spring of 1918 the movement provided the driving force behind the wave of industrial nationalisation. Attempts were also made to transform workers' control – in the sense of workers' supervision – into a syndicalistic form of workers' self-administration of industry.

The seriousness of this challenge to party policy was underlined with the emergence of the 'Left Communists'. This group supported workers' self-administration of industry, organised through the factory committees and the trade unions, and also defended the rights of local soviets against central authority.[10] The defeat of the Left Communists coincided with the intensification of the civil war in the summer of 1918.

'War Communism' from 1918 to 1921 saw an unprecedented extension in the power of the state. Trade was brought under strict government control and industry was subject to wholesale nationalization. The Supreme Council of the National Economy (Vesenkha) took over the management of industry through cumbersome and highly centralised glavki. The experiments in workers' control were cast aside. One-man management was introduced in industry, bourgeois specialists were re-employed, and the influence of the trade unions over management decisions curtailed.

A new attempt to centralize state control was made in May 1918 when the old tsarist GosKontol was renamed the People's Commissariat of State Control (NKGosKon). K.I. Lander was appointed People's Commissar (*narkom*). NKGosKon was based on the old tsarist agency and concentrated on financial control and auditing.[11] The Central Control Collegium was abolished. NKGosKon's responsibilities were extended to the newly nationalised industries, and, during the civil war control was tightened up. In November 1918 Sovnarkom approved a detailed degree on NKGosKon's work of financial control[12] and the commissariat's staff in this period grew rapidly.

NKGosKon failed, however, to cope with the vast scale of control work. In 1918 individual commissariats set up their own departmental control agencies. Vesenkha created an Inspectorate to supervise industry and individual glavki established their own bodies. The Red Army set up its Higher Military Inspectorate.[13] These bodies were founded by the departments with trade union participation.

The chaos created by the civil war in industry, transport and food supply also spawned a new system of popular or mass control – the workers' inspectorates set up by the trade unions. In December 1918 the Council of Defence appointed a commission to examine how control work could be made more effective. It proposed that NKGosKon's activities be supplemented by worker's inspectorates to be established by the trade unions in conjunction with the commissariats.[14]

VTsSPS established various workers' inspectorates, such as the Workers' Food Supply Inspectorate attached to the People's Commissariat of Supply (NKSnab), and the Railway Workers' Inspectorate attached to the People's Commissariat of Transport (NKPS). Another inspectorate, the Moscow Workers' Inspectorate, attached to the Moscow Soviet, was set up by the trade unions.[15] These agencies involved thousands of industrial workers in the direct supervision of production, transport, food shipment, and rationing as inspectors and guards. These volunteers exercised the same powers as NKGosKon's inspectors.

By the end of 1918 three different control systems co-existed – NKGosKon, the departmental control agencies, and the workers' inspectorates – each seeking to regulate the lumbering and inefficient state machine.

Sovnarkom met great difficulty in managing the state administration and in regulating the local soviets and the trade unions. These difficulties were compounded by the absence of an unified control system. Fragmentation of control, it was later argued, fostered a 'subjective' departmental approach 'to the detriment of the general interests of the State'.[16] The presidium of VTsIK on 20 December 1918 proposed establishing a new Supreme Control Inspectorate to direct and co-ordinate existing agencies. A commission, chaired by Sverdlov, was appointed to examine this scheme.[17]

The deteriorating military situation gave added urgency to this task. A major report which I.V. Stalin and F.E. Dzerzhinskii presented to the Central Committee in January 1919, on the capture of Perm by the Whites, castigated the disorganisation in the party and state administration. The report, outlining its main recommendation, noted:

> the absolute necessity for the establishment of a Control and Inspection Commission, under the Council of Defence, for the investigation of the so called 'defects in the machinery' of the People's Commissariats and their local departments in the rear and at the front.[18]

This report was drawn to the attention of the VTsIK commission and its authors appointed to the commission.

The commission rejected all proposals to create new control agencies. Instead it proposed that NKGosKon should become the supreme agency of government control. The departmental control agencies and the workers' inspectorates were to be subordinated to it, NKGosKon was to be responsible both for financial control and for improving state administration. Sovnarkom was thus to be provided with a powerful instrument for regulating the apparatus. The plan, despite Lenin's endorsement, met strong opposition.[19]

The second trade union congress in January 1919 severely criticized NKGosKon's failure to involve workers in control work. It proposed establishing VTsSPS's own organ of workers' control to supervise industry.[20] VTsSPS's presidium criticized the separation of state control from workers' control and insisted that NKGosKon's functions in industry be transferred to the trade unions.[21] VTsSPS's plenum proposed strengthening the trade union control commissions and urged the establishment of production control departments. NKGosKon, it proposed, should work through the trade union organs in industry.[22]

Moscow, a stronghold of the left, provided the main opposition to NKGosKon. In February and March 1919 NKGosKon came under a hail of criticism from *Vechernie izvestiya*, the paper of the Moscow Soviet.[23] The agency's activities, it was argued, seriously disrupted administrative work. The system of preliminary financial control operated by NKGosKon was bitterly criticized.[24]

In drafting its proposals, the Politburo had to tread warily. On 8 March 1919 Lenin in Sovnarkom advanced an important revision to VTsIK's limited scheme to revamp the bureaucratic NKGosKon. Attached to NKGosKon, he proposed, there should be established 'central and local organisations of workers' participation'[25] which were to transform the agency and its style of work. Through these bodies NKGosKon's influence would be extended throughout the apparatus.

G.E. Zinoviev broached the subject at the VIII Party Congress in March 1919. He stressed the need to reconstruct NKGosKon in order to create:

A commissariat of socialist control that will control all the units of our Soviet mechanism, pushing its feelers into all branches of Soviet construction, and have a special section concerned with the simplification and perfection of our machine.[26]

The plan was coolly received. The scheme to combine within NKGosKon both state and popular control was viewed with scepticism and hostility. It was seen by some critics as a Politburo stratagem to emasculate the soviets and trade unions by amalgamating their control agencies with the arch-bureaucratic NKGosKon. The old NKGosKon was derisively dismissed by one congress delegate as an 'antediluvian institution, which carries on with all its old officials, with all kinds of counterrevolutionary elements etc.'.[27] The congress resolution was non-committal, noting the need for a genuine system of factual socialist control, to be administered principally by the party organs and the trade unions.[28]

The trade unions fought to capture control over industry and wrested a major commitment from the party. The party programme, adopted by the congress, conceded the principle to the trade unions, declaring:

> The organisational apparatus of socialized industry must be based primarily on the trade unions . . . the trade unions must proceed to the actual concentration of their own hands of all the administration of the entire economy, as a single economic unit . . . The participation of the trade unions in economic management and their drawing of the broad masses into this work constitutes also the chief method of struggle against the bureaucratisation of the economic appartus.[29]

The timetable for implementing this provision was not specified, and generated heated controversy between the unions and the party leadership. Trade union demands threatened the government's role in industry and were strongly resisted by the Politburo.

After the congress, VTsIK on 31 March 1919 appointed Stalin as narkom of NKGosKon and strengthened the inspectorate's collegium.[30] Stalin's appointment increased NKGosKon's power and status, linking it directly with the Politburo and Orgburo. Government and party controls over industrial administration were to be stiffened as a check on the ambitions of the trade unions.

The Politburo's determination to force through the NKGosKon reform incensed the trade unions and was seen as a breach of the commitment made in the party programme. A Soviet historian writes:

> In the working out of the draft reorganisation of NKGosKontrol an incorrect position was adopted by the VTsSPS presidium, which spoke out against the amalgamation of the organs of GosKontrol and workers' control, and demanded the speedy removal of control over industry from the hands of NKGK and its transfer to the trade unions.

The reform was also opposed by the soviets. The II All-Russian Congress of Provincial (guberniya) Soviet Executive Committees in March 1919 stressed the need to safeguard the rights of the soviets from the encroaching central state apparatus.[32] Particular emphasis was placed on the need to retain the system of dual subordination in the organisation of the local control organs, both to the local soviets as well as to NKGosKon.

Stalin on 9 April 1919 presented the draft decree to VTsIK. In his report, he stressed that 'the existing workers' control bodies should be united into a single whole and all the forces engaged in control should be incorporated in the general State Control'. This reorganisation was 'to democratize GosKontrol, and to bring the mass of workers and peasants more closely into its work'.[33] NKGosKon, he noted, was the only commissariat not to have been purged and reconstructed since 1917.

VTsIK approved the decree. NKGosKon was to assist Sovnarkom in its work and was to supervise 'all the people's commissariats, provincial departments, and all organs of the Soviet government (*vlasti*) generally'.[34] The commissariat was to exercise financial control and, in addition, lead the work of improving the state administration. It was to check the implementation of governmental decrees and party directives, expose cases of illegality, and to develop proposals for the simplification of the apparatus, eradicating 'parallelism, mismanagement and bureaucratic red tape'.

The workers' inspectorates were to be merged with NKGosKon in order to 'renew and transform' it and:

to draw it fresh forces from the workers' control-revision organisations, to give it new tasks of real factual control, to involve in its work the broad strata of workers and peasants so that GosKontrol from an organ of formal control is transformed into an organ of popular socialist control (*narodnyi sotsialisticheskyi kontrol'*), accumulating experience of socialist construction and constantly improving the whole mechanism of the Soviet government.[35]

All workers and peasants were to participate in control work. The need to strengthen the regime's links with the society were re-emphasised.[36]

Whilst NKGosKon and the workers' inspectorates were to be merged, the commissariats were to retain their own control bodies. Instructions were issued to NKGosKon to determine precisely its rights and responsibilities in relations with other commissariats' and 'strictly to delimit revision – control functions from inspection functions, so that inspection is retained in the respective commissariats'.[37]

The decree retained the principle of dual subordination for local control agencies in order to appease the soviets. In the summer of 1919 NKGosKon pressed the party to abandon this principle in favour of an

unitary command structure of control. This proposal, strongly opposed
by the local soviets, was rejected.[38]

Limited attempts were made in 1919 to unify the different agencies
under NKGosKon.[39] The decree of April 1919, however, remained a
dead letter. In December 1919 all the old control agencies remained in
being, still operating independently with no effective co-ordination.

ESTABLISHMENT OF RABKRIN (1919–20)

In the autumn of 1919 soviet and trade union opposition to government
centralisation intensified. Within the party, discontent gave rise to two
new leftist groups – the Workers' Opposition (committed to the transfer
of industry from the state to the trade unions) and the Democratic
Centralist group (pledged to restore the power of the local soviets and
revive soviet democracy).[40] At the VII Congress of Soviets (in December
1919) Menshevik leaders criticized the congress's decline, the concentration of power in the VTsIK presidium, the growth of Sovnarkom, and
the atrophy of the soviets. The congress resolution demanded measures
to revitalise VTsIK and safeguard the powers of the soviets.[41]

At the VIII Party Conference (the same month) I.P. Fedeneev of the
Moscow Workers' Inspectorate advanced a scheme aimed at neutralis-
ing NKGosKon.[42] He proposed extending the work of the volunteer
workers' inspectorates which had sprung up in the previous eighteen
months. These local bodies of mass control established by the unions
and soviets, he argued, should be co-ordinated nationally through a new
'Workers' and Peasants' *Soviet* Inspectorate'[43] (emphasis added). This
body was to be wholly independent of NKGosKon and was to be
attached to VTsIK, with local inspectorates attached to the local soviets.

The conference reaffirmed the rights of local soviets 'to control and
revise the activities of all governmental institutions' within their
jurisdiction. It also referred the draft of the Moscow Workers'
Inspectorate for consideration to the VII All-Russian Congress of
Soviets.[44]

At the Congress of Soviets, Fedeneev argued the need to improve the
economic apparatus by purging it of bourgeois specialists and
proletarianizing its ranks. Mass control was to be extensively developed
as a check on bureaucracy. The workers' and peasants' inspectorate was
to be a real organ of people's power (*narodnovlastie*) bridging the chasm
between state and society, and ensuring that the regime did not 'lose
touch with the toiling masses'.[45]

Fedeneev's proposals were well received. Resentment against NKGosKon was strong, with local soviets clamouring for its abolition. L.M. Kaganovich amongst others urged that NKGosKon should be done away with.[46] The congress instructed VTsIK to work out proposals for the organisation of the Workers' Inspection, 'the necessity of which the congress recognises to be urgent'.[47]

The presidium VTsIK on 12 December 1919, set up a commission to work out a thesis on this question, comprising A.S. Kiselev (VTsIK), M.P. Tomskii (VTsSPS) and V.A. Avanesov (NKGosKon).[48] Kiselev, a leader of the Workers' Opposition, and Tomskii were outspoken defenders of trade union and soviet rights. Representatives of the Moscow Workers' Inspectorate and the Railway Workers' Inspectorate also attended the sessions of the commission.

The commission considered three alternative theses. One was submitted by NKGosKon, a second was presented jointly by the Railway Workers' Inspectorate and VTsSPS, and a third by Moscow Workers' Inspectorate.[49]

NKGosKon's thesis, backed by the Politburo, was a re-working of the VTsIK decree of 9 April 1919. NKGosKon was to be the sole agency of state control and the workers' inspectorates and departmental control agencies were to be merged with it. State control would remain firmly in Sovnarkom's hands. Workers' inspectorates were to be attached temporarily to NKGosKon in order to train proletarian cadres for the commissariat. Once this task was completed the inspectorates were to be dissolved. No provision for popular involvement in control work was advanced.[50]

The VTsSPS thesis in sharp contrast advocated a new control system, a Workers' Inspectorate, independent and superior to NKGosKon. It noted that:

> The workers inspectorate will be *an independent department of VTsIK*, and its local organs will be departments of workers' inspection, attached to the guberniya and uezd executive committees[51] (emphasis added).

The inspectorate was to be headed by a representative of VTsIK and two deputies nominated by VTsSPS. Local inspectorates were to be organized on similar lines. The inspectorate was to have wide powers for controlling the state administration. A central feature was to be popular participation in control work, with candidates being nominated by 'the trade unions, political parties and other organisations'. VTsSPS condemned NKGosKon's scheme which, it argued, would bureaucratize and stifle the workers' control movement.

The unification of the workers' inspectorates with state control cannot lead to the speedy revitalisation of GosKon, at the same time it may lead to the isolation of the worker inspectors from the proletarian mass and the adoption by them of the habits of routine, formalism and other bureaucratic deficiencies associated with the cadres of GosKon.[52]

The third thesis presented by the Moscow Workers' Inspectorate received little publicity and limited support. Like the VTsSPS thesis, it envisaged a new 'Workers' and Peasants' Soviet Inspectorate' attached to VTsIK. The powers of this body, however, were to exclude 'directing or administrative rights'.[53]

The two main theses presented irreconcilable approaches. The majority of the commission, Tomskii and Kiselev, supported VTsSPS's radical proposals.[54]

A Politburo directive on 23 January 1920 condemned the VTsSPS thesis and tacitly endorsed NKGosKon's plan. It charged the presidium of VTsIK and NKGosKon to observe the Central Committee's ruling:

Not to create new institutions in any field of state administration but to improve the existing People's Commissariats.[55]

Workers' inspectorates were to be retained but were to concentrate on proletarianizing NKGosKon. These inspectorates were to recruit their members *only* from amongst 'the unqualified, and mainly women'. A Workers' and Peasants' Inspection (RKI) was to be attached to NKGosKon, a draft on which was to be prepared with the participation of Avanesov.

Lenin in a note to Stalin on 24 January 1920 expressed his intention 'to rework all three projects into one' on the basis of the Politburo's directive. The RKI was to be a temproary section (*otdel*) of NKGosKon with the task of introducing 'workers' and peasants' inspection into all sections of GosKon'. Once achieved RKI was to be abolished as a separate unit. The object was 'to pass the whole of the toiling masses, both men and particularly women through participation in the workers' and peasants' inspection'. The NKGosKon 'bureaucrats' were to involve the workers in all their investigations.[56]

The Politburo discussed the matter on 28 January 1920 and adopted a resolution on NKGosKon's future organization which was approved by the Central Committee three days later.

VTsIK was assigned the task of editing the decree. To appease the Moscow Soviet the main report was presented by one of its delegates. The party fraction of VTsIK made two changes to the draft. A separate 'workers' and peasants' inspection' should not be attached to NKGosKon but the commissariat itself should be immediately reorganised to enable its departments to organize popular control. NKGos Kon was also to be renamed the People's Commissariat of Workers' and Peasants' Inspection (NKRKI).[57]

Formally the scheme was presented as a means for involving the people in the work of state administration as part of the transition to Communism. The state was to be transformed and proletarianized. In more mundane terms, it was intended also to overcome the regime's isolation, broaden its base of support, and instil in the masses an understanding of the problems of government. Mass involvement was also a means of controlling the sprawling state bureaucracy through a mechanism of social control directed by the government. It was also a means of harnessing and directing the volatile and unpredictable popular movement.

Lenin wished to use NKRKI as a counterweight to the trade unions and soviets. It was to organize the disorganized elements in society and raise their political consciousness. As such, it was intended as a check on the organized activists and as a means of bridging the gap between these disparate social elements. It was also a device to temper leftist influence entrenched in the trade unions and soviets.

VTsIK on 7 February 1920 approved its decree 'On the Workers' and Peasants' Inspection' based on the decree of 9 April 1919, which transformed NKGosKon into NKRKI. NKRKI became the pre-eminent agency of control with the subordination to it of the workers' inspectorates, inheriting from its predecessor the functions of budgetary and financial control and responsibility for improving the organization and work of the apparatus. It was empowered to exercise control over 'all the organs of state administration, the economy, and social organizations'.

NKRKI was assigned extensive responsibilities: supervising policy implementation and evaluating its effectiveness; fighting 'bureaucratism and red tape'; verifying observance of Soviet laws; receiving and processing complaints from the public concerning official crimes and abuses; preparing proposals for simplifying and streamlining the state administration; involving the populace in control work, preparing and training them for the task of 'managing the state apparatus'. NKRKI was given extensive powers to investigate the work of the state institutions, to attend their meetings, to demand documents and to request reports from responsible officials, but was denied powers of compulsion. Disputes between it and the institutions were to be referred to Sovnarkom for resolution.[58]

Lenin campaigned vigorously to win support for the reform, emphasizing NKRKI's role as an instrument of popular control. In a speech to non-party workers in February 1920 he declared:

> It is necessary that the workers go into all the state institutions so that they can control the entire apparatus and this must be done by the non-party workers who must elect their representatives at non-party conferences.[59]

Addressing the Moscow Soviet the following month he proposed recruiting into NKRKI 'the most diffident and undeveloped' workers who were to be educated gradually in administration so that eventually they could 'take upon themselves the burden of government'.[60]

This major reform, significantly, was not discussed by the IX Party Congress in March-April 1920 which concentrated on industrial organization, the role of the trade unions, and the system of one-man management. These issues brought the Politburo and the emergent Workers' Opposition into conflict. The congress rejected the 'syndicalist' demands that industry be transferred to the trade unions and resolved that 'the trade unions . . . must gradually transform themselves into auxiliary organs of the proletarian state'.[61]

In spite of strong reservations the III All-Russian Congress of Trade Unions in April 1920 endorsed party policy on state management of industry and approved NKRKI's establishment. It urged all trade unionists 'to adopt the most active and energetic participation in the work and organisational establishment of RKI'.[62] The trade union strategy was to colonise NKRKI and to take it from within.

NKRKI's leaders in February 1920 met representatives of the workers' inspectorates. They approved a plan for the reconstruction of control and resolved to delegate workers from industry into the central NKRKI apparatus. The presidium of VTsIK on 26 April 1920 issued a decree on the merger of the workers' inspectorates with NKRKI. VTsSPS the same month decided to liquidate the Workers' Food Supply Inspectorate.[63] The trade unions and departments, however, only reluctantly surrendered control of the workers' inspectorates as NKRKI in 1920 repeatedly complained.[64]

RABKRIN IN ACTION (FEBRUARY 1920 – MARCH 1921)

The new NKRKI was headed by politically reliable individuals representing the centrist party element. Stalin was appointed *narkom* of NKRKI, giving him oversight over the entire state administration from top to bottom.[65] But, despite what his later critics claimed, in 1920–1 Stalin was absorbed in work on the military front, in the People's Commissariat of Nationalities and in the Politburo, and exercised only nominal leadership over NKRKI. Effective control lay with his deputy V.A. Avanesov.[66]

Stalin's leadership linked NKRKI directly with the Politburo and Orgburo. The agency's main links, however, were the principal governmental bodies. NKRKI, as a commissariat, was represented within Sovnarkom, the lesser Sovnarkom and STO. As a governmental body it also came under the jurisdiction of the presidium of VTsIK. It received instructions and assignments from party, governmental and soviet organs.[67] This arrangement placed NKRKI at the centre of government work, in a position to influence policy-making through the supply of information, advice and recommendations, and supervising the implementation of policy, monitoring its effectiveness and providing feedback.

NKRKI's work was co-ordinated with that the the People's Commissariat of Justice (NKYust) and the Cheka. From 1920–4 V.A. Avanesov (deputy narkom of NKRKI) served also on the Cheka collegium.[68] The Cheka remained autonomous, accountable only to the Politburo, and was the one state institution not subject to NKRKI control.[69] With this exception NKRKI supervised all seventeen commissariats, including their central and local organs. Its position within the central state apparatus in 1920 is outlined in Figure 1.1.

NKRKI inherited NKGosKon's organisation and personnel. It was led by its six-man collegium. The management of affairs was assigned to its organisational-instruction administration. Investigatory work was carried out by seven inspectorates of 'general assignment': technical and industrial, agriculture and food supply, administration, finance, education and propaganda, labour safety and public health; and two 'special assignment' inspectorates: military–naval, communications and transport.[70]

NKRKI RSFSR assumed the leadership of NKRKI organs in the other republics. RKI organs were set up at all levels of administration – autonomous republic, autonomous oblast, guberniya and uezd. These

26

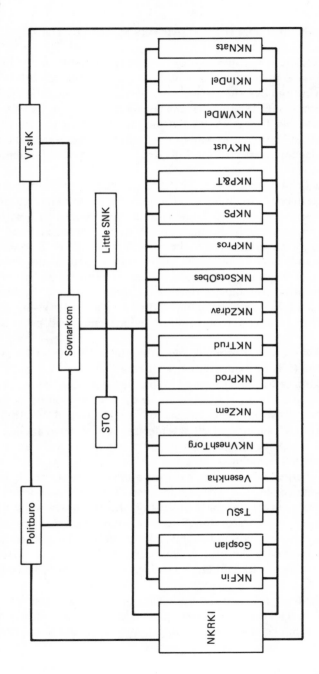

Figure 1.1 Central party–government apparatus RSFSR (1920)

bodies were established on the principle of dual subordination, accountable to NKRKI and to the local soviet. Local organs of NKRKI's communications–transport and military–naval inspectorates were accountable solely to NKRKI.[71] NKRKI acquired a huge staff of controllers and officials. The total staff of the tsarist GosKontrol in 1917 stood at 3,000, that of NKGosKon in 1920 at 10,000, whilst NKRKI's by 1922 had risen to 12,000 'erkaisty'. This fourfold increase in staff in five years reflected the expansion in the scope and detail of financial control. NKRKI's permanent staff was also augmented by volunteer controllers. Most of the senior staff were former tsarist officials. The proportion of Communist officials was small and drawn mainly from the least experienced party members. NKRKI officials were badly paid and the low quality of its personnel became a byword.[73]

VTsIK's decree of 7 February 1920, establishing NKRKI, proposed three main forms of popular control:

1. the delegation of workers into NKRKI's organs for periods up to four months through elections in enterprises, institutions, and in rural areas.
2. the election of RKI assistant cells (*yacheiki sodeistviya*) in enterprises, institutions and attached to local soviets
3. the involvement of workers in NKRKI mass investigations.

All workers and peasants enjoying the franchise under the RSFSR constitution were eligible for election to NKRKI. The unions could veto candidates and propose their own nominees. In addition NKRKI's special Complaints Bureau received and processed complaints, petitions, information and proposals from the public.

On 17 March 1920 NKRKI issued detailed instructions, signed by Stalin, on developing popular control.[73] The first election of workers to NKRKI took place in September 1920. NKRKI for the first time was able to organize directly in the enterprises and institutions which previously had been the preserve of the trade unions. Its task was to develop within a revolutionised work force the consciousness of producers and builders of Communism rather than that of factory hands or trade unionists. NKRKI was thus to occupy an intermediate position between the managers and the unions.

NKRKI's principal concern, like its predecessor, was with financial control and budget management. The People's Commissariat of Finance (NKFin), under Sovnarkom's direction, drafted the budget. NKRKI checked the budget and was responsible for enforcing budgetary discipline, and for auditing the financial material transactions of all commissariats and institutions.[74] NKGosKon's work of financial control expanded enormously with the huge growth of state activity under war communism. Three systems of control were employed: (i) preliminary checking of expenditure proposals to determine expediency and legality; (ii) factual investigation of financial and material reserves (*reviziya*) checking the work of management; (iii) post-audit accounting of the finances of institutions.[75] NKRKI's relations with the state institutions were strained by this over-elaborate system of financial control. The disruptive effect of preliminary financial control on the work of the institutions drew particular criticisms with managers and administrators insistently demanding its abolition.[76]

At the I All-Russian Conference of NKRKI Workers in Moscow, in October 1920, Stalin outlined the inspectorate's role. His general views on state administration exemplified a predominantly 'statist' conception of socialist construction:

> Comrades, a country is not governed by those who elect their delegates to parliament, under the bourgeois system, or to the Congress of Soviets under the Soviet system. No, a country is actually governed by those who have in fact mastered the executive apparatus of the state and direct it. If the working class really wants to master the state apparatus for governing the country it must have experienced agents not only in the centre, not only in the places where questions are discussed and decided but also in the places where those decisions are put into effect. Only then can it be said that the working class has really become the master of the state.[77]

The emphasis on strong, efficient government, staffed by 'proletarian' cadres, constituted a central and enduring element in Stalin's thought.

NKRKI, Stalin argued, was to perform two basic functions: firstly to improve administrative efficiency, particularly bookkeeping and accounting work; second, to proletarianize the apparatus, and provide a training ground for future administrators. It should not regard the institutions as 'alien bodies', and should avoid 'police methods'. NKRKI was to co-operate with the institutions and seriously study the defects in their organisation and work. Unfortunately, NKRKI's officials, he admitted, still incurred the 'hatred' of 'some arrant bureaucrats' and even of some Communists. The controllers, he urged, should persevere and should not 'spare' individuals whatever position they occupied. These individuals, as befitted NKRKI's status, were to be recruited from officials of 'irreproachable moral purity'.[78]

At the Moscow Guberniya Party Conference in November 1920, Lenin noted serious shortcomings in NKRKI's work and organisation:

RKI exists as an aspiration and it has proved impossible to put it in order because the best workers have been taken for the front and because the cultural level of the peasant mass does not enable them to advance workers in sufficient numbers.[79]

The refusal of local party organs to assist RKI compounded its difficulties. The inspectorate had still to prove itself. Lenin, nevertheless, continued to defend NKRKI both as an agency of state and popular control.

NKRKI in 1920 carried out extensive work in financial control, investigating the administrative and economic institutions, fighting corruption, checking procurement and military supplies, dealing with the fuel crisis, etc. Its work, however, was cursory and fragmentary and yielded few significant achievements.[80]

NKRKI's report for the year painted a grim picture of the agency's plight:

The first half of the current year was especially rich in conflicts. During this period the reorganisation of the former GosKontrol into RKI and its proletarianization had only just begun. The majority of RKI organs were still characterised by a failure to comprehend their tasks or an inability to perform them, by an excessively formal handling of issues, by the direction of their work towards excessively meticulous and formal control over financial and material questions only . . . This was facilitated also by the composition of the staff of the RKI organs – almost entirely non-party and to a significant degree of old bureaucrats [*chinovniki*] . . . Naturally such organs enjoyed no confidence amongst the soviet executive committees and their subordinate institutions, possessed no authority in their eyes, and were powerless [*bessil'nyi*].[81]

NKRKI continued to be dogged by the obstructiveness of the commissariats, local soviets and trade unions who were reluctant to assist the inspectorate in its work.[82]

Trotsky in an outspoken article in January 1921 castigated NKRKI. The attempt to develop the utopian notion of popular control through NKRKI, he argued, remained 'completely unresolved'. His criticisms struck at the very principles underlying NKRKI:

It is impossible to create a separate department which can concentrate in itself, so to speak, governmental wisdom and which is really able to check the remaining departments not only for their honesty and efficiency but also the the expediency and correctness of their work as a whole. Every department knows that in every case when it is necessary to change course and to carry out serious organisational reform it is useless to turn to the Workers' and Peasants' Inspectorate for advice. Moreover, the inspectorate itself is becoming the clearest victim of the lack of correspondence between decrees and the apparatus and is itself being transformed into the most powerful factor of bureaucratism and arbitrariness.[83]

The rationalisation of economic administration, Trotsky argued, necessitated a unified economic plan against which performance could be judged and improvements assessed. The departments themselves were to be responsible for improving their work. What was needed was greater co-ordination amongst the economic departments, through the plan, not a 'super-department', NKRKI, imposing its directives from above.[84]

Within NKRKI a bitter conflict arose concerning the agency's work. Young Communist officials pronounced NKRKI a success, but demanded compulsory powers over the commissariats to increase its effectiveness, and urged closer links with the Cheka and VTsSPS.[85] M.K. Vetoshkin (a member of NKRKI's collegium) in March 1921 denounced the 'infantile leftism' of the radicals. He pictured NKRKI, 'the forgotten commissariat', as an agency in complete disarray, starved of resources and qualified personnel. NKRKI had failed both as an agency of mass control and rationalization. It lacked authority, its proposals were ignored or obstructed and, even in Moscow, its functionaries were unceremoniously kicked out of the institutions they were investigating. However, he insisted that the voluntary principle underlying NKRKI's relations with the institutions be retained. A major effort was needed to raise its authority and competence and to win the co-operation of the institutions.[86]

THE X PARTY CONGRESS AND THE REDIRECTION OF CONTROL

In the second half of 1920 the regime was hit by a tidal wave of unrest in industry and in the countryside. Acute social distress fuelled political protest which erupted in the Kronstadt revolt. The ending of the civil war removed the justification for the system of state regulation of the economy developed under war communism. Demands for fundamental reform gathered pace. This culminated in the trade union controversy of 1920–1 which deeply split the party. The libertarian left of the party found its voice in A. Kollontai's pamphlet *The Workers' Opposition* which lauded the self-activity of the proletariat in socialist construction, denounced bureaucratisation in the party and soviet apparatus and demanded the transfer of industry into the hands of the trade unions.[87]

The X Party Congress endorsed Lenin's theses on the trade unions, which reaffirmed the state's control of industry but also asserted the unions' autonomy from the state. Trotsky's plan for the statisation of the unions was rejected. The congress was a milestone in the development of the Soviet regime with its resolution on 'Party Unity' which banned factions and its resolution on the 'Anarcho-Syndicalist Deviation' which ruled the views of the Workers' Opposition on trade union control of industry to be 'inconsistent with membership' of the party. The congress dramatically tightened internal party control by establishing a new party Central Control Commission (TsKK). Prominent oppositionists were purged from the trade unions and soviets, undermining further the ability of these bodies to check the growing power of the state administration. In 1921, the opposition parties were banned, firmly consolidating the Soviet one-party state.

NKRKI played little part in these momentous debates. The Workers' Opposition saw NKRKI as a barrier to trade union power. Kollontai in her famous article ignored the agency as an irrelevance. Many in the trade unions and soviets regarded NKRKI with suspicion and contempt. Significantly, the Kronstadt insurgents in March 1921 scrapped the local RKI organs and transferred their functions to an elected Council of Trade Unions.[88]

On the eve of the congress, the party fraction in NKRKI sent a memorandum to the Central Committee on the need to clarify its powers, functions and methods of work and to strengthen the local RKI organs. Trotsky in a telegram to all narkoms again denounced the incompetence of Stalin's NKRKI. In reply, NKRKI issued a small brochure to the congress delegates which attacked Trotsky's haughty disdain for the inspectorate, and demanded more resources and personnel as a matter of urgency.[89] The congress, however, in response to union pressure, ruled only that NKRKI should establish no permanent institutions in the enterprises but should work through the factory committees in order to avoid 'harmful parallelism'.[90]

Following the X Party Congress the central party–government apparatus was restructured. In 1921 the Politburo's links with Sovnarkom were strengthened with the former assuming a greater role in policy-making and directing the work of government.[91] The introduction of NEP with the deregulation of trade, the adoption of the tax in kind, and the leasing of certain enterprises to private entrepreneurs also saw the dismantlement of the bloated and highly centralised state administration developed under war communism.

The Bolshevik regime, nevertheless, still depended on the state for its survival. Lenin summarised the problem:

> Without the apparatus we would long since have been crushed. Without a systematic and tenacious struggle to improve the apparatus we would be overwhelmed before the foundations of socialism have been created.[92]

The party's task was to improve the efficiency of the state administration and to root the regime more firmly in society.

NKRKI assumed a central place in this strategy. In 1921 attempts were made to reorientate NKRKI's work away from the detailed financial control to a wider concern with the improvement of the state administration.[93] The introduction of NEP also placed before NKRKI quite new tasks and responsibilities. Already in April 1921 a meeting of NKRKI provincial representatives was held to discuss the inspectorates work under NEP.[94] Lenin strove to draw NKRKI closer into the work of improving the governmental apparatus, especially bookkeeping and accounting.[95]

In the spring of 1921 the party tried to strengthen NKRKI's popular control work. Lenin, addressing the mineworkers' trade union congress in January 1921, urged full participation of workers in NKRKI as a means of fighting bureaucratism.[96] In March 1921 NKRKI and VTsSPS approved an instruction regulating relations between them and in April 1921 they jointly appealed to the unions to assist the RKI organs and to adopt a less intransigent attitude.[97] The unions were to ensure a regular flow of workers into NKRKI, assist in selecting qualified workers for the inspectorate, and help it in its work. Attempts were made also to strengthen NKRKI's links with the party's youth wing, the Komsomol.[98]

In April 1921 NKRKI issued instructions to strengthen the assistant cells. The Central Committee ordered all party members to assist NKRKI's work of rationalizing the administration and developing mass control.[99] Early in 1921 the agency's work was extensively publicized through the holding of 'RKI weeks', aimed at drawing in party members, trade unionists, non-party workers and peasants. Mass participation in NKRKI was seen by Lenin as a means of overcoming the regime's social isolation and broadening its base of support after the crisis of the winter months.[100]

NKRKI continued to draw fire from all quarters. The situation came to a head in September 1921, prompted by an NKRKI report to Sovnarkom on the timber industry. Lenin, in a letter to Stalin, railed at the inspectorates' unconstructive approach to problems:

> The task of Rabkrin is not so much 'to catch', 'to expose' (this is the task of the courts, with which Rabkrin is closely involved, but is by no means identical) as much as to be able to correct. The ability to correct in time – this is the main task of Rabkrin. Has Rabkrin carried out its task and duty? Does it properly understand its task. This is the basic question. And to this question we must answer in the negative.[101]

Greater solidity needed to be introduced into the inspectorate's work.

Stalin brusquely warned against overhasty criticism of NKRKI. The existing shortcomings, he argued, stemmed from the novelty and difficulty of its work, and its lack of experienced party workers. Little could be expected from this 'impoverished inspectorate', this 'puny organism', other than its ability to act as a 'barometer' warning of problems in the apparatus.[102]

An NKRKI resolution of 2 September 1921 attributed all these defects to the lack of party workers.[103] The Central Committee, in response, transferred 250 Communists to NKRKI and attempted to strengthen the local RKI organs.[104]

Following the X Party Congress several legislative enactments were approved which defined NKRKI's new role under NEP. They attempted also to impress on the state institutions the importance of NKRKI's work and the need for greater co-operation in control. VTsIK on 18 August 1921 approved a decree 'Concerning the strengthening of the activity of RKI', underlining NKRKI's responsibilities in assisting Sovnarkom in enforcing new legislation concerning industry, agriculture, trade and taxation.[105]

NKRKI on 2 September 1921 adopted a thesis which underlined three basic tasks for the inspectorate under NEP – improving accounting work in the economic organs, defending the interests of the state in its dealings with the private sector, and strengthening factual investigations of financial and material reserves.[106]

In the first half of 1921 preliminary financial control by NKRKI over a broad range of expenditure was abrogated.[107] On 28 September 1921 Sovnarkom relieved NKRKI of responsibility for all preliminary financial control, so intensely disliked by the industrial, trading and administrative organs.[108] Its abolition complemented the introduction of commercial profit and loss accounting (*khozraschet*) and the attempt to devolve responsibility and stimulate initiative amongst managers and administrators. NKRKI retained its responsibility for current and post-audit accounting in all state and economic institutions.

VTsIK on 9 January 1922 approved a decree outlining in detail NKRKI's responsibilities under NEP. It defined its position thus:

> RKI is an unified organ of socialist control, through which the Soviet government with the direct participation of the workers and peasants, carries out supervision of the activities of all state institutions and enterprises and equally of the social organisations in the centre and localities.[109]

It confirmed NKRKI's responsibilities for financial control and popular control. The decree, on Lenin's insistence, also extended NKRKI's control to state enterprises leased to private entrepreneurs, which much to his indignation had been overlooked.[110] The main stress, however, was placed on NKRKI's role in improving the state administration and overseeing its work.

The decree of VTsIK of 16 March 1922 underlined the agency's role in adjusting the state apparatus to meet the requirements of NEP. It gave NKRKI various new powers: to prohibit or halt illegal decisions by institutions which threatened material loss to the state, to impose penalties on responsible officials in such cases, to propose to institutions the correction of deficiencies in their work; and to demand the removal of officials guilty of serious mismanagement.[111]

Attempts were made to draw NKRKI more directly into the work of managing the state administration.[112] On Lenin's initiative, NKRKI in June 1921 set up a special commission (Komsokhoor) to assist the economic organs adjust to NEP. The commission, headed by A.A. Korostelev, was staffed mainly with industrial workers, which Lenin believed would be more successful than a commission made up of 'Rabkrin bureaucrats'. The commission was to help the economic organs introduce khozraschet and other organisational reforms. The commission, nevertheless, was quickly scrapped with no major achievements to its name.[113]

NKRKI investigated the role of small industries in the Moscow region in promoting industrial recovery and also the newly established industrial trusts.[114] It investigated the organisation of foreign and internal trade and monitored the effect of NEP on the rural economy, implementing and explaining party policy. NKRKI's workers in the summer of 1921 helped NKProd collect the new tax in kind. In the winter of 1921 – 2 NKRKI supervised the shipment of food supplies into the famine-stricken areas of the Volga, Southern Urals, and Ukraine. NKRKI's work in improving the state administration was neglected. Only in February 1922, on Lenin's prompting, was a special department of 'normalization' set up within NKRKI to co-ordinate this work.[115] NKRKI's work in fighting official crime by contrast grew enormously. In 1921 and 1922 a total of 2,385 and 2,682 cases respectively were brought before the courts by NKRKI. These cases embraced a wide range of offences, including mismanagement, corruption, negligence, etc. Individual cases, involving major Soviet institutions, received extensive publicity.[116] NKRKI's preoccupation with 'police methods' of control soured relations with the institutions and even drew Lenin's censure. It also complicated NKRKI's relations with NKYust.

NKYust in the winter of 1921 – 2, on Lenin's instigation, brought a number of 'political cases' before the courts in Moscow.[117] These cases were to dramatize the problems of inefficiency, mismanagement and corruption in the apparatus. NKRKI initiated two of these 'show' trials – one involving the production of motor ploughs at the Moscow motor works, and another concerning disorganization in the planning of yards for the repair of barges on the Volga.[118] The use of the courts in fighting disorganization was strongly opposed by D.I. Kurskii, narkom of NKYust, and by V.V. Osinskii and P.A. Bogdanov, former and current chairmen of Vesenkha.[119]

RABKKRIN (1920 – 2): AN OVERVIEW

Already by 1921 Lenin was publicly rejecting as an utopian 'fairy tale' the notion that state functions could be taken over by ordinary citizens.[120] NKRKI's role was now more limited – to organize participation in state affairs, to train cadres for administrative work and also to anchor the regime more securely in the society.

The popular control movement developed slowly despite intense efforts in the summer of 1921 to publicize its aims. The numbers involved in NKRKI's work of popular control grew from 60,000 in 1920 to 124,000 in 1921. In the winter of 1921 – 2 the movement collapsed and in 1922 only 25,000 participated.[121] These figures were modest in comparison to the grandiose task set NKRKI in 1920.

The work was impeded by the hostility of managers, administrators and trade unionists to this rival agency. Within NKRKI criticisms were voiced that the agency itself had failed properly to organize and utilize the movement and as a result enthusiasm for popular control had waned.[122] In many regions the assistant cells maintained an existence only on paper, in others cells arrogated to themselves wide-ranging powers, even assuming in some instances the responsibilities of the Cheka.[123]

With the introduction of khozraschet in industry and the general financial stringency of this period managers refused to pay the wages of workers elected for control work. Reasons of economy provided a pretext for undermining what was seen as a meddlesome, disruptive and often vindictive system of control. Early in 1922 VTsIK adopted a decree to provide NKRKI with a constant supply of workers to be elected in the factories and to be paid by the enterprises.[124] This token commitment to the principle of popular control failed to halt the movement's collapse.

NKRKI's strained relations with the state and economic institutions exacerbated the problems of control. This issue was dramatized by a case brought before the Supreme Tribunal of VTsIK in March 1922. The case, initiated by Lenin, issued from the suicide of V.V. Oldenborger, a prominent non-party specialist and chief engineer in the Moscow Water Works. His death followed a sustained campaign by NKRKI, the Cheka and the trade unions who had slanderously accused him of sabotage. The campaign was motivated by personal malice and by a desire on the part of the conspirators to force the Politburo to reopen the debate on the employment of bourgeois specialists.[125]

The officials involved were severely reprimanded and the ringleader sentenced to imprisonment.[126] The case underlined NKRKI's unhealthy relations with the economic organs, and the problem of 'intrigue' in its work,[127] and was widely publicized in an attempt to reduce incidents of '*spets*-baiting', the harassing of specialists, which was still prevalent in industry.

In the first two years of its existence, NKRKI was preoccupied with financial control and paid little attention to rationalization work. V.V. Kuibyshev reviewing this period in 1924 declared with hindsight:

> The old RKI which sought to control everything in the end achieved in certain respects a diminution of the responsibility of departments and of department heads for the state of their apparatus. Since RKI participated in every aspect of work of the various departments, since every operation required the visa, the stamp of RKI's representative, the responsibility which should have been shown by the departmental heads was diminished.[128]

This situation exacerbated the disorder in the apparatus, intensified the process of centralisation which overloaded Sovnarkom and undermined its ability effectively to manage the state machine.

NKRKI's failure deepened dissension within its ranks. In January 1922 M.K. Vetoshkin, in an article entitled 'RKI at the Crossroads', demanded a major reappraisal of the agency's work. NKRKI's collegium, he argued, was paralyzed by indecision concerning the agency's future. The attempt to create an organ of 'unified socialist control' had been a dismal failure. NKRKI's roles as an agency of rationalization and mass control should be abandoned and it should concentrate on the task of financial control. Too many NKRKI officials still harboured utopian notions of the agency's mission. These 'dreamers' could not come to terms with the grey, humdrum realities of financial control which NEP required.[129] Vetoshkin's plan was supported by NKRKI's former tsarist officials but denounced as 'liquidationism' by the younger, radical Communists.[130]

NKRKI's enormous power remained a matter of concern. At the XI Party Congress in March 1922 Preobrazhenskii criticized the concentration of power in Stalin's hands. Lenin, however, was resolute in his defence:

> Now regarding the Workers' and Peasants' Inspectorate. This is a gigantic undertaking; but to be able to handle investigations we must have at the head of it a man who enjoys high prestige otherwise we shall become submerged in and overwhelmed by petty intrigue.[131]

NKRKI's shortcomings were not considered unique at this stage. At the congress Lenin noted that of the eighteen existing commissariats fifteen were quite useless.[132] In the following months NKRKI was to be singled out as the commissariat which exemplified the defects of the state in their most morbid form.

CONCLUSION

The experiment with NKRKI reflected a tension in the Bolshevik party between the leftist libertarian wing which stressed the importance of popular initiative and self-activity and the statists who stressed central direction and who distrusted 'spontaneity'. This division reflected a basic rift in attitude and philosophy which lay at the heart of Bolshevism as a political movement, a division exemplified in Lenin's own writings – the centralism of *What is to be Done?* against the neo-anarchism of *State and Revolution*. NKRKI was the instrument whereby Lenin tried to reconcile these different currents. In effect, this involved the application of an administrative solution to a political problem. As organized, independent opposition was eliminated, so he tried to broaden the scope for controlled participation in the work of socialist construction.[133]

NKRKI, under Stalin's leadership, provided part of the solution to the problem of organizing the proletarian dictatorship. NKRKI was to control and strengthen the state administration and to check the centrifugal forces in the commissariats, local soviets and trade unions. NKRKI was to provide a vehicle for popular control without the syndicalist dangers associated with workers' control. Thus the Bolshevik party consolidated its dominance, ruling in the proletariat's name through the state apparatus. However, by 1922 NKRKI was in disarray: the popular control movement had collapsed, its financial control work had been compromised by the introduction of NEP, and its work in rationalizing the state apparatus remained in its infancy.

2 Lenin's Plan for the Reorganization of Rabkrin (1922–3)

The stabilisation of NEP in 1922 allowed for a more considered examination of policy. Socially isolated, the regime constituted, in M. Lewin's phrase, 'a dictatorship in the void', its survival guaranteed only by the power of the party–state administration.[1] The effectiveness of that apparatus became a major preoccupation of an insecure leadership. In the final months of his active life Lenin initiated a major reappraisal of the regime's policies. A cornerstone of this legacy was his celebrated and ambitious plan to reorganize Rabkrin, an attempt fundamentally to rethink the organization of the proletarian dictatorship and to develop mechanisms to combat the tendencies towards authoritarianism and bureaucratic degeneration already manifest in the Soviet one-party state.

DILEMMAS OF STATE AND PARTY CONTROL

At the XI Party Congress, in March 1922, Lenin highlighted the problem of party–state organization. He acknowledged the party's dependence upon the state but asserted that it had failed to steer this alien machine, which was careering like a car out of control, 'driven by some mysterious, lawless hand'. The success of NEP and ultimately the regime's survival, he insisted, depended on the party's ability successfully to manage the economy. Party members had to acquire administrative and mangerial skills. Mastery of the state was inhibited by the lack of culture and inexperience of party members in administrative posts.[2]

Confusion and disorder reigned in the administration, heightened by the ignorance, inexperience and conceit (*komchvanstvo*) of party members in key positions. The commissariats manifested all the worst features of bureaucracy, irresponsibility, passivity, intrigue and sabotage. Sovnarkom was overwhelmed with petty administration, and its work complicated by a plethora of interdepartmental commissions. The chaos within the commissariats induced Sovnarkom to interfere excessively in their work, thus undermining their independence and exacerbating the problem. The insistence of departments on referring matters from Sovnarkom to the Politburo for final resolution obscured and complicated party–government relations.

To deal with these problems Lenin submitted a series of proposals to the congress to relieve the Politburo and Central Committee of 'minor matters', to increase the responsibilities of the commissariats, to raise the prestige of Sovnarkom and to concentrate its attention on 'executive control'.[3] In addition, measures were to be taken to improve the organisation, personnel and work practices of the commissariats.

The progressive fusion of party and state functions remained a cause of concern. Prominent leftists, such as V.V. Osinskii and Yu. Larin, argued strongly for this trend to be reversed. The XI Party Congress in its resolution reaffirmed the need clearly to demarcate the respective rights and responsibilities of party and soviet bodies.[4]

In 1922 Lenin repeatedly returned to the vexed question of party–state relations, and the problem of controlling this 'vast army of state employees'.[5] He was also concerned by the quality of leadership which party members in key posts were able to provide. In 1921 and 1922 he strove to reduce the influence of leftist activists in Gosplan and Vesenkha, replacing them with the party workers with greater practical experience.[6]

Since the summer of 1921 the influence of Sovnarkom and STO had declined, partly as a result of Lenin's indisposition through illness. To redress the balance, Lenin, early in 1922, worked out a plan to give his deputies in Sovnarkom, A.D. Tsyurupa and A.I. Rykov, special responsibility for overseeing the work and organization of the government, especially on policy implementation. NKRKI was to assist the deputies by providing specialist personnel.[7]

The scheme was developed by Lenin in a draft decree of 11 April 1922. Sovnarkom was to make the efficient running of the administration one of its central concerns. In performing these functions the decree noted 'the main apparatus of the deputies is to be the People's Commissariat of Workers' and Peasants' Inspection'.[8]

The plan was submitted to the Politburo. Trotsky baulked at the proposal to involve NKRKI in the work. In a note to his Politburo colleagues he argued that NKRKI was staffed mainly with officials who had 'come to grief' in other fields, and that the agency was riddled with intrigue. Therefore, 'the plan to pull up the Soviet state apparatus by using Rabkrin as a lever is plainly make-believe'. Trotsky scoffed at the idea of using NKRKI as an outside agency to restructure the administration, and he doubted the practicability of using it either as an agency of social control or as a training ground for future administrators. He still envisaged a limited role for NKRKI as a traditional control agency modelled on its tsarist predecessor, concentrating on accounting work and on financial and budgetary control.[9]

In a note to the Politburo, on 5 May 1922, Lenin reaffirmed his faith in the scheme. Trotsky was 'fundamentally mistaken'. NKRKI was essential if the party was ever to get on top of the 'awful departmentalism', 'intrigue' and mismanagement which was rife in the appratus. He urged major changes in NKRKI's work and proposed measures to cut its staff and improve pay. On the question of popular involvement in control work, he re-emphasised the need to involve hundreds of thousands of the most able and honest workers. Without NKRKI, he declared, 'it is impossible to teach the non-party workers and peasants the art of administration, and from this task it is impossible either in principle or practice to retreat at the present time'.[10]

Following this clash of views no regulatory order was issued, although Lenin's plan for his deputies was taken as the basis for determining their responsibilities. In April 1922 Lenin proposed to the Politburo that Trotsky should become one of his deputies in Sovnarkom, as part of his design to strengthen the government machine as a counterweight to the party apparatus.[11] On two subsequent occasions the same proposal was made and each time was rejected by Trotsky.

On 2 April the XI Party Congress elected Stalin as party General Secretary and appointed V.M. Molotov and V.V. Kuibyshev as his deputies. These moves to strengthen the Secretariat were designed to give effect to Lenin's demand, made at the congress, for improvements in the management of the party's cadres policy.[12] Stalin's appointment suggests that his unhappy experience at NKRKI had not unduly damaged his reputation as an able and tough administrator.

Stalin's transfer gave Lenin the opportunity to realise his scheme for the reorganization of the government. Stalin was relieved of his post as narkom of NKRKI on 25 April. Sovnarkom on 30 May appointed A.D. Tsyurupa as his successor.[13] Tsyurupa was a highly skilled administrator and enjoyed Lenin's confidence as his most capable deputy. This appointment established the bond between Sovnarkom and NKRKI which Lenin wished to forge in the fight against bureaucracy.

Adapting NKRKI to cope with its new tasks proved difficult. In a letter to NKRKI's leadership in August 1922, Lenin complained that the agency's work in improving administration was not 'entirely satisfactory'. Modern western science had to be harnessed to overhaul the antiquated state machine.[14] On his advice a special 'department of normalisation' was set up in NKRKI and an NKRKI commission was sent in the autumn of 1922 to the USA and Germany to study administrative and industrial rationalisation.[15] This reflected Lenin's keen interest in Taylorism and western techniques of scientific management.[16]

Inside NKRKI, a wide-ranging debate was inaugurated on its future with the establishment of commissions to reduce its staff and improve its organisation.[17] Lenin kept himself informed of developments, consulted with Stalin and remaining members of the NKRKI collegium.[18] Progress, however, was slow, inhibited in part by Tsyurupa's ill health.

From May to October 1922 Lenin was forced to retire from active work and Sovnarkom was entrusted to Rykov, Kamenev and Tsyurupa. However, on his return to work he found that his deputies had proved unequal to the task. In his speech to VTsIK on 31 October he repeated his call to the party to strengthen Sovnarkom and improve state administration.[19] In December he issued further instructions to develop the role of the deputies.[20]

Frustrated by the lack of progress, Lenin at the end of 1922 began to contemplate a more drastic solution. In conversation with Trotsky he proposed, through a 'special commission of the Central Committee', to involve the party itself directly in the fight against bureaucracy in the state apparatus. Trotsky argued that the problem was connected to the system of appointments run by the Orgburo and dominated by Stalin's Secretariat. Lenin, Trotsky avers, proposed the formation of 'a bloc' against bureaucracy in general and the Orgburo in particular'.[21] The cementing of the bloc, Trotsky argued, was prevented by Lenin's illness. Trotsky's refusal to accept the post as Lenin's deputy in Sovnarkom and continuing differences between the two over NKRKI were also major stumbling blocks to any alliance. In a letter, dated 13 December 1922, Trotsky reaffirmed his continuing hostility to NKRKI.[22]

The need for reform was emphasised by the widespread discontent in the state and economic institutions concerning NKRKI's work. Pressure mounted for a thorough overhaul of financial control, with NKFin pressing its own claims in this area. NKRKI's work in combating official crime also came under growing criticism from NKYust and the newly established Procuracy.[23]

The debate on the organization of state control coincided with mounting concern over the system of internal party control. In September 1920, at the height of dissension within its ranks, the party established its own Central Control Commission (TsKK). TsKK was elected by the party congress and its work was closely co-ordinated with the Politburo, Secretariat and Orgburo. It was responsible for enforcing discipline, purging the party ranks and generally supervising the changing social and ideological composition of the party. TsKK headed an extensive network of control commissions (KKs) attached to the local party organs.[24]

TsKK in 1921 was deployed by the Politburo against the Workers' Opposition and Democratic Centralist groups. This provoked fierce controversy in the party and in February 1922 members of the Workers' Opposition referred the matter to the Comintern. In the early months of 1922 *Pravda* carried several articles demanding TsKK's abolition.

The issue was brought to a head at the XI Party Congress in March 1922. An opposition motion to abolish TsKK, although strongly supported, was defeated. Lenin resolutely defended TsKK as a 'splendid institution' whose powers should be extended.[25] Nevertheless, the party congress reduced the membership of TsKK from seven members and three candidates to five members and two candiates.

TsKK's unpopularity deeply concerned the commission's leadership. A.A. Sol'ts, one of TsKK's leaders, in *Pravda* in December 1922 called for the XII Party Congress to resolve TsKK's position once and for all.[26]

LENIN'S PLAN FOR THE REORGANIZATION OF RABKRIN

After his second stroke, on 12 December 1922, Lenin, compelled to retire from active work, seriously reflected upon the regime's development and began urgently to formulate some guiding principles to shape its course. In the following weeks he considered a number of stubborn issues which beset the party – the nationalities problem, the future of NEP, the peasant question, the problem of economic development, the role of Gosplan, and finally the enduring problem of party–state administration and control. Inextricably bound up with these questions was the delicate matter of the 'succession'.

In the field of party–state organization three major issues dominated. First, the disorganization in the governmental apparatus – the overloading of Sovnarkom, the lack of leadership in government work, the disorder in the commissariats, lack of initiative at lower levels, weak organizational structures and inefficient work methods. Second, the question of demarcating responsibility between government and party bodies, specifically between Sovnarkom and the Politburo and Central Committee. Third, the problem of the party apparatus itself – the excessive concentration of power in the centre, the growth of secrecy and irresponsibility, the decline of inner-party democracy.

In December 1922 Lenin dictated his *Letter to the congress* outlining draft proposals for a total reorganization of the central party–state apparatus.[27] The plan, developing the ideas discussed with Trotsky, dealt simultaneously with these three problems. The Central Committee was to be enlarged from forty-seven to 100 members. The new members, mainly workers, were to be responsible solely for improving state administration.

The party was to be directly involved in improving the administrative apparatus. The new members of the Central Committee were to be assisted in this work by NKRKI which was to provide expert help and advice. NKRKI was to be transformed into a small, specialist agency for this task.[28] The plan aimed to restore the Central Committee's authority, revitalize internal party democracy and satisfy the demand of the party's proletarian activists for a greater say in policy-making. It reflected also Lenin's touching faith in the judgement and honour of the proletarian cadres.[29]

In the following weeks Lenin expended much of his failing energy on reworking this plan.[30] The revised scheme went through successive drafts and was presented in two articles – *How we should reorganize Rabkrin – a proposal to the XII Party Congress* and *Better fewer, but better*. The articles, published in *Pravda* on 25 January and 4 March 1923, provide Lenin's last word on the vexed question of state control.

'How we should reorganize Rabkrin'

In his first article Lenin presented an ambitious scheme for restructuring the central party–state apparatus. NKRKI posed a 'huge difficulty' that was still unresolved, nevertheless it remained an essential instrument if the party was to tackle the 'extremely urgent' task of improving the state administration.[31] The state institutions, he argued, had not undergone any serious changes, the tsarist institutions with all their defects had been merely repainted.

The problem of the state machine could not be isolated from the question of party–government relations and internal party organization. To deal with these three issues Lenin advanced a far-reaching plan to unite (*soedinit'*) the governmental control agency (NKRKI) with the party control agency (TsKK). TsKK–NKRKI, closely linked to the leading party and governmental bodies, was conceived as a regulating mechanism within the party–state apparatus.

Lenin aimed to transform TsKK. It was to be increased from ten to between seventy-five and 100 members, mainly workers, elected by the party congress from the most able activists. The commission was to be led by an elected presidium. TsKK was to become a leading party organ, alongside the Central Committee.

TsKK and NKRKI were to be joined together. TsKK members were to be seconded for work in NKRKI with the inspectorate retaining its separate identity.[32] TsKK and NKRKI joint work was to be co-ordinated through joint sessions of their leadership. TsKK, previously occupied exclusively with party control, was (via NKRKI) to establish its supervision over state control. NKRKI, which had been concerned mainly with financial control, was to be converted into a small, highly-specialized agency responsible for studying and rationalizing all facets of state administration.

NKRKI was to be drastically reduced in size, its central staff cut from 1,200 to 300–400 officials, comprising mostly technical specialists. NKRKI's expert staff were to be highly paid and selected for their honesty, and experience of administrative work, knowledge of the basics of 'the scientific organisation of labour', administration, bookkeeping, etc. The agency was to combine scientific study of the state with practical work in remedying its defects. NKRKI was also to direct the work of the scientific institutes concerned with the study of organization and rationalization.

This arrangement, Lenin argued, would benefit both TsKK and NKRKI. The expertise and technical competence of NKRKI would be balanced and complemented by the political reliability of the proletarian, class-conscious cadres of TsKK.

The TsKK-NKRKI reform was tied to a reorganization of the central party organs. Reviewing developments in the party, Lenin noted:

> The CC plenum of our party has already manifested a tendency to develop into a kind of *higher party conference*. It meets on average only once in two months and the day to day work, in the name of the CC, is carried out by our Politburo, Orgburo, Secretariat, etc. I think that we should follow the path on which we have set out to the end, and finally transform the CC plenum into a higher party conference, meeting once in two months *with the participation of TsKK* (emphasis added).[33]

The new 'higher party conference' was to comprise the existing members of the Central Committee and seventy-five to 100 TsKK members. The members of TsKK, drawn from 'the workers and peasants', were to be elected, like Central Committee members, by the party congress. TsKK members were to be of the highest calibre:

> Those elected must be subjected to the same party tests as ordinary members of the CC, for they must be able to exercise all the same rights as CC members.[34]

TsKK members (via NKRKI) would become experts in the theory and practice of state organization and specialists in different policy areas at the service of the central party organs:

> Without a doubt such a reorganization will benefit our own CC, no less than Rabkrin, in the sense of contact with the masses and in the sense of the regularity and solidity of its work. Then it will be possible (and essential) to bring in a more strict and responsible order in preparing the sessions of the Politburo, at which a set number of TsKK members must attend.[35]

TsKK was conceived in part as an assistant organization to the Politburo, providing an independent source of information and advice, reviewing policy, and overseeing the state administration. All documents referred to the Politburo were to be sent for preliminary examination to TsKK.

The plan was designed also to prevent the excessive concentration of power in the Politburo, to avoid the dangers of intrigue and factional splits. The higher party conference was to become an authoritative forum which would check the power of the central bodies, and monitor their work:

> The members of the CC and the members of TsKK through such a reform would be many times better acquainted, better prepared, for the sessions of the Politburo (all papers, referring to these sessions, must be received by all members of CC and TsKK no later than twenty-four hours before the Politburo session).[36]

TsKK's involvement in the higher party conference would ensure the expertise, competence and authority of that body. The conference, Lenin trusted, would check the Politburo, Secretariat and Orgburo, establish their accountability and assist them in decision-making.

TsKK was to supervise the leading party organs, and keep a watchful eye on Stalin's Secretariat:

> The members of TsKK, who are obliged to attend in a certain number all the sessions of the Politburo, must form a tightly knit group, which

'without respect for persons', must see to it that nobody's authority, *neither that of the Gensek nor any other member of the CC*, should serve as an obstacle to their putting interpellations, seeing all the documents, and in general to their keeping themselves informed of all things and of seeing to it that affairs are properly conducted (emphasis added).[37]

TsKK's was to become a watchdog, combating secretiveness, irresponsibility and degeneration in the central party organs.

The new higher party conference, representing the collective intelligence of the party, was to become an extended party council, a forum more representative of the party's proletarian base, more competent, stable and authoritative. Lenin thus hoped that 'the influence of purely personal and accidental factors in our Central Committee will be reduced and by this means also the danger of a split will be diminished'.[38] He wished to buttress the collective leadership with institutional support. Here, what Lenin could not foresee, the strained relations between Stalin and Trotsky was to prove crucial. The conference was to have wide responsibility – supervising party policy, identifying problems, preparing timely measures to avert dangers which threatened the regime and which might occasion a split.

'Better fewer, but better'

Lenin's second article concentrated on how the state administration should be improved, outlining the principles which informed his scheme to reorganize Rabkrin.[39] The problem of the state, Lenin argued, was primarily cultural, being rooted in the country's economic and social backwardness. This required of the party itself great political maturity, and a realistic appreciation of the problem and dangers which beset it. This assumed particular importance with the eclipse of the old westernized intellectual elite by the new breed of party officials.

In an evident swipe at the zealots of Proletkult, he warned against seeking glib solutions to the problems of the state apparatus in appeals to 'proletarian culture'.[40] The party had to break with its old attitudes and habits. It had to reject the notion that ignorance could be compensated for by political zeal. The watchwords were to be care, patience and perseverance. TsKK–NKRKI's role was to educate the party concerning the problems that confronted it.

NKRKI in its existing form did not enjoy a 'shadow of authority', being amongst the worst organized of the state institutions, and nothing could be expected of this 'hopeless affair'. It had to be fundamentally restructured, not as with its numerous past reorganizations, but transformed into 'something really exemplary, something that will win the respect of all and sundry for its merits and not only for its rank and title'.[41] 'Extraordinarily strict criteria' were to be applied in recruiting officials for TsKK–NKRKI both from amongst 'the advanced workers', and from 'the really enlightened elements'. Here was to be applied the rule 'better fewer, but better' in turning NKRKI into a prestigious, specialized body, with staff 'not inferior to the best West European standards'. Summarizing this approach he warned:

> If we do not arm ourselves with patience, if we do not devote several years to this task, we had better not tackle it at all.[42]

TsKK–NKRKI's task was to establish a state administration which would ensure the regime's survival, creating a finely-tuned instrument of socialist construction. The state machine was to be reorganized on scientific principles, stripped of the 'superfluities' of the tsarist state and reduced to 'the utmost degree of economy', an apparatus geared to the task of economic modernization through which also 'the workers will retain their leadership of the peasantry'.[43]

The proposed unification of party and state bodies (TsKK and NKRKI) breached established organizational principles and would, Lenin acknowledged, provoke strong condemnation. A precedent for such an arrangement, he argued, existed in the close links between the Politburo and the People's Commissariat of Foreign Affairs (NKInDel) which had proved so salutary in foreign policy. Opposition on this score arose only from the 'dustiest corners' of the state institutions and deserved only 'ridicule'.[44] The danger of TsKK–NKRKI officials disrupting the work of the civil service was similarly raised, only to be dismissed out of hand.

TsKK–NKRKI was conceived by Lenin as a self-regulating mechanism within the party–state apparatus. NKRKI was to assume various roles, the equivalent of a modern civil service commission, policy review staff and ombudsman. TsKK was to act as the keeper of the party's conscience and guardian of its unity. The party, threatened internally and externally and committed to a revolutionary programme of 'socialist construction', required such an agency to help it chart its course, eschewing the temptation of simple or extreme solutions:

> This is how I link up in my mind the general plan of our work, of our policy, of our tactics, or our strategy, with the functions of the

reorganised Rabkrin. This is what in my opinion justifies the exceptional care that we must devote to Rabkrin in raising it to an exceptionally high level in giving it a leadership with CC rights, etc . . . These are the lofty tasks that I dream of for our Rabkrin. That is why I am planning for it the amalgamation of the most authoritative party body with an 'ordinary' people's commissariat.[45]

DISCUSSION OF LENIN'S PLAN

The Politburo's Reaction

This revolutionary scheme left the party leadership aghast. Within the Politburo an extraordinary attempt was made to suppress the plan. Trotsky provides the only available account:

> How did the Politburo react to Lenin's project for the reorganisation of Rabkrin? Comrade Bukharin [editor of *Pravda*] hesitated to print Lenin's article, while Lenin on his side insisted upon its immediate publication. N.K. Krupskaya told me by telephone about this article, and asked me to take steps to get it printed as soon as possible. At the meeting of the Politburo, called immediately upon my demand, all those present, comrades Stalin, Molotov, Kuibyshev, Rykov, Kalinin, Bukharin, were not only against Lenin's plan, but against the very printing of the article. The members of the Secretariat were particularly harsh and categorical in their opposition. In view of the insistent demand of Lenin that the article should be shown to him in print, comrade Kuibyshev . . . proposed that one special number of Pravda should be printed with Lenin's article and shown to him, while the article itself should be concealed from the party.[46]

Only after heated discussion did Trotsky and Kamenev prevail on their colleagues to authorize publication.

The article concerned in this incident was *How we should reorganize Rabkrin* in which Lenin outlined his substantive proposals to reorganize the central party–state apparatus. It was against this aspect of the plan that the Politburo took such exception.[47]

The leadership remained uncertain how to react. Finally, a month after publication, Zinoviev in *Pravda* cautiously welcomed the plan which he argued:

> belongs to that number of great ideas of comrade Lenin which at first

seems unexpected and only later does its scope become clear for the whole party.[48]

Osinskii noted that the article had been a 'surprise' and 'not by any means only to the broad party periphery'.[49] A delegate to the XII Party Congress averred that Lenin's article had struck many Communists like a 'kind of bombshell'.[50]

Opposition in the Politburo, according to Trotsky, was spearheaded by Stalin and his Secretariat deputies, Kuibyshev and Molotov, who reacted with 'extreme hostility' to the scheme. Lenin's criticism of NKRKI, he argued, was a veiled attack on Stalin, its former head, and the TsKK–NKRKI reform a means of curbing the Secretariat's power:

> The conduct of Stalin upon this question first clearly proved to me that the proposal to reorganize TsKK and the Central Committee, was directed by Lenin solely and entirely against the bureaucratic power of Stalin, then already excessive, and against his disloyalty. Hence Stalin's stubborn opposition to Lenin's plan.[51]

Lenin's relations with Stalin at this time were at breaking-point. Disagreements over policies – the nationalities question and the Georgian affair, the foreign trade monopoly – and disquiet over Stalin's style of party management had embittered feelings. In a supplement to his secret testament, written on 4 January 1923, Lenin denounced Stalin's 'rudeness' and urged his dismissal as party General Secretary. In March 1923 Lenin threatened to sever relations with him.[52] According to Trotsky, Lenin was preparing a 'bomb' for Stalin at the party congress.[53]

At this critical juncture Stalin was shielded by his Politburo colleagues. In the version of Lenin's first article published in *Pravda* the damaging reference to 'the Gensek and other members of the Central Committee', who might impede TsKK-NKRKI's work, was deleted.[54]

The Politburo majority considered Lenin's plan half-baked and opposed it on political and practical grounds. The new body, they feared, would obstruct the Politburo and the central party bodies and weaken their authority. The new higher party conference would be unwieldy and inflexible, would slow down decision-making and complicate the task of co-ordinating the central party organs. Lenin's criticism of NKRKI and his veiled attack on Stalin were issues of secondary importance.

The proposed higher party conference also threatened the standing of the Central Committee and alarmed its members. The difficulty of finding sufficient party members of the right calibre to staff both the enlarged TsKK and the Central Committee became a major objection to the scheme. The publication of Lenin's plan forced the leadership's hand. Intense discussions were conducted behind the scenes as rival proposals were worked out for presentation to the Central Committee. Stalin's Secretariat prepared counter-proposals involving enlarging the Central Committee from twenty-seven to fifty members. The Central Committee was to be strengthened, with the convening of regular plenums, the presentation to it of detailed reports by higher party organs, and the referral to it of major issues for decision.[55] These measures were to make the Central Committee more representative of the party rank and file, and to satisfy demand for greater inner-party democracy. No provision was made for the unification of TsKK with NKRKI or for setting up Lenin's 'higher party conference'.

Trotsky condemned this proposed expansion of the Central Committee:

> The Central Committee must retain its strict form and its capacity for quick decisions. For this reason its further broadening makes no sense . . . More complicated relations between the Politburo and the plenum threaten to cause great harm to the accuracy and correctness of the Central Committee's work.[56]

He urged instead the creation of a 'special party council', comprising the Central Committee, TsKK (to be increased to seventy-five members) and twenty to thirty representatives from oblast and local party organs.[57] The council, elected by the congress, was to have broad supervisory functions – checking the work of the Central Committee and central party bodies, examining the work of the state institutions, combating 'thermodorian' and 'petty-bourgeois' tendencies in the party and state administration.

The Central Committee plenum, on 21 February, was a stormy affair. Trotsky's plan for a 'double centre arrangement' was attacked by other party leaders as an attempt to undermine the authority of the Central Committee and the central party bodies as part of a strategy to split the party.[58] Trotsky's antipathy to NKRKI, his refusal to become Lenin's deputy were cited against him. Trotsky insisted that in presenting his scheme he had defended 'the essential idea of the letter [Lenin's article] or, to put it more accurately, those of its ideas which seemed essential to me'.[59] In turn he pointed to the disparity between Lenin's plan and that of the Secretariat, noted Lenin's criticisms of Stalin, recalled the Politburo attempts to suppress Lenin's article, and threatened to expose the affair at the forthcoming party congress.[60]

A commission was set up to examine the schemes and reported to the

Central Committee on 24 February 1923.[61] Its recommendations were based largely on the Secretariat's plan. It proposed enlarging the Central Committee from twenty-seven to forty full members and included provisions to increase its authority. No mention was made of Lenin's proposed 'higher party conference'. The proposal, however, incorporated Lenin's plan to expand TsKK and unify it with NKRKI. The new TsKK–NKRKI, however, was to be subordinated to the higher party bodies.

The Central Committee condemned Trotsky's scheme and endorsed the commission's recommendations. The reform of the central party apparatus, including TsKK, was worked out in detail in a draft resolution for presentation to the XII Party Congress, 'The proposals of the Central Committee of the RKP(b) for the improvement of the central party and state institutions', and published in *Pravda*.[62] The Central Committee also approved in principle the unification of TsKK and NKRKI. The details were worked out by a commission, chaired by F.E. Dzerzhinskii.[63]

Trotsky, having been defeated in the Central Committee, was compelled to accept the new scheme. In a speech to the Ukrainian party conference in April 1923 he noted the party's need for an instrument to control the apparatus. At the same time he stressed that TsKK–NKRKI should not be regarded as a 'panacea' or 'means of salvation' and warned 'It would be absurd to think that we have created an organ which can solve everything'.[64]

The Party's Reaction

Lenin's articles initiated a major debate in the party on the organization of the state. The proposed reorganization of the control organs dominated the pre-congress discussion in *Pravda* in March–April 1923.[65] Opposition to the plan was vociferous, and came from both the party's right and left wing. This provided the first (and only) serious debate on state control in the 1920s, and raised fundamental questions concerning the nature of the regime, and the character of the state's relations with society. Significantly, most of the participants in this debate avoided the burning question of whether control was needed over the central party organs, and concentrated instead on the plan's implications for the administrative and economic institutions.

L.B. Krasin – a view from the right
The right wing's objections to the plan were voiced by L.B. Krasin

(narkom of NKVneshTorg). In an article entitled *Control or Production*, he elaborated a brilliant, cogent and vigorous attack on Lenin's plan. As a distinguished senior party member, an engineer and experienced administrator, a maverick on many policy issues, and a leading right-wing spokesman, Krasin articulated the views of a broad section of managers, administrators and specialists.

Krasin expressed incomprehension and alarm at Lenin's scheme to transform NKRKI into 'a super-Rabkrin', 'some kind of heart and brain of the whole soviet apparatus'. This was a long-standing issue of contention between the two. Whereas Lenin had always stood for the strengthening of NKRKI, he, Krasin, had 'long since struggled against the hypertrophy of control and the overevaluation of its significance'.[66]

Administration, Krasin argued, could be organized either according to the 'production' or the 'control' principle. These two principles were antithetical, with one always assuming dominance. This opposition had been confirmed by past experience with NKRKI. He warned against the attitude of party zealots who saw control as the solution to all problems. The party's obsession with control was a throwback to the workers' control movement of 1917–18 and the administrative practices of war communism. These early experiments in control, whilst politically necessary, Krasin argued, had been administratively disastrous, having a 'devastating' effect on production, and resulting in a 'colossal wastage' of materials and resources.

The strengthening of NKRKI would create a powerful control lobby with its own interests and outlook in opposition to the operative commissariats. The low quality of NKRKI's officials exacerbated tensions between controllers and managers:

> Our control and inspection organs are the main refuge of the 'know-alls' (*vseznaeki*), especially if they have good party service. Many excellent comrades who have distinguished themselves both in previous party work and in the military struggle consider themselves to be magnificent controllers and inspectors. In reality when they come into contact with matters concerning production they succeed only in introducing excessive bureaucratism and red tape, they create obstruction, they strike where it is not really necessary and sometimes they allow to pass without scrutiny cases of really scandalous neglect.[67]

Incompetent party members employed in administration, he argued, should be mercilessly expelled and sent to 'learn their lessons'.

The existing multiplicity of control organs was the 'main reason' for the 'insufferable bureaucratism' in the apparatus. Lenin's scheme, he argued, betrayed a primitive understanding of administration. The tightening of control would exacerbate bureaucratism. The plan would transform the parasitic NKRKI into a 'super-commissariat' of control akin to its despised tsarist predecessor.

It was essential, Krasin argued, to restructure state administration on the precept – 'maximum production and the minimum of control'. Control had to be 'located within production itself'. The state organs should become self-regulating units, modelled on the most advanced western state and corporate institutions. By the use of inducements and a more flexible approach, Krasin argued, the non-party specialists, whose co-operation was essential for the regime's survival, could be won to the party's side.

Effective management of the state administration and the development of realistic policies necessitated sweeping changes in the composition of the central party and government bodies by drawing in the technical specialists:

> The strict maintenance of the party's political line and of state power must not obstruct the restoration of production, and in order to prevent this, it is necessary that within the state and leading party apparatus the producers and managers, party members of necessity, be given at least as much influence as journalists, litterateurs and pure politicians.[68]

This, Krasin argued, would have a more salutary effect than a 'purely mechanical reform' intended to draw tens of inexperienced worker Communists into TsKK and giving them oversight of economic and administrative affairs.

Lenin's plan dismayed and frightened the managers and administrators. Krasin, reflecting this pervasive concern, issued an ominous warning:

> All we managers – in this I stress not specialists [*spetsy*], but party managers – await this reform literally with terror and we fear incredible devastation in the field of production and in our apparatus which even without this is already badly formed.[69]

Views from the left
Lenin's design came under a fusillade of fire from a section of the party's left wing, led by V.V. Osinskii, V.M. Smirnov and Yu. Larin. All three had worked in Vesenkha when under left-wing control in 1918. They

attempted to attract support from those party workers assigned to key managerial posts after 1917. Their main support, however, was still drawn from the trade unions and from the soviets.

Osinskii noted that the TsKK–NKRKI plan directly repudiated the XI Party Congress ruling on the separation of party and state functions. Unification of party and state bodies always led to the subordination of the latter to the former. The party substituted itself for the state organs and assumed administrative functions for which it lacked the necessary expertise. Within the state administration it fostered 'irresponsibility' and 'bureaucratic passivity'.[70]

This trend, Osinskii argued, had been set in train by Lenin in 1918 with the repudiation of workers' control and the decision to employ bourgeois specialists. The TsKK–NKRKI reform would complete the process. To avert these dangers, Osinskii outlined the Democratic Centralists' plan for reorganizing the government apparatus. Party and state responsibilities had to be clearly demarcated and the powers of soviet institutions restored. Sovnarkom was to be restructured on the model of a western-style 'Cabinet' accountable to a revitalized VTsIK, the Soviet parliament.

The restructuring of government on the basis of the executive–legislative division was intended to make government more accountable based on a revived soviet democracy. Decision-making was to be decentralized and party interference in government (a principal cause of bureaucracy) limited. He demanded also the revitalization of party democracy. TsKK, he proposed, should be abolished by the party congress. NKRKI was to be reduced in size and transformed into 'the central instruction staff of Sovnarkom'.

Lenin's plan, Osinskii argued, evinced a deep distrust of the competence of party members to manage the state machine. Party members were to be ousted from administrative posts and transferred to control work. The places vacated were to be filled by non-party specialists, surrendering the 'leading positions of the proletarian dictatorship in the economic field' to the bourgeois specialists.[71] Osinskii repudiated Lenin's plan to build socialism 'with alien hands'. He defended the policy of proletarianizing the apparatus, emphasizing the success of party members appointed to managerial and administrative posts. Only by practical involvement in administration, not control, could workers acquire administrative experience. To this end, administrative controls had to be relaxed and the initiative of party managers and administrators increased.

Smirnov warned that the party's reliance on TsKK–NKRKI would divert the attention of the leading organs from their primary function:

> If the Central Committee is linked with party work by means of a control organ, then this will be the best means of isolating the party from the government. The party in those circumstances will inevitably become an organ which does not lead but only controls soviet work.[72]

The Politburo and Central Committee would lose the capacity for political direction and, swamped by administrative detail, would stumble into short-term policy expedients.

In an article on industrial administration Larin deprecated the existing bureaucratic style of management and the lack of channels for mass participation. Noting the complete failure of NKRKI's efforts in this field and the progressive isolation of the state from society, he asserted:

> Control of the [workers' and peasants'] inspectorate is now the usual old state bureaucratic control . . . which in no way replaces and cannot replace the live social control of the workers' organisations.

To counterbalance Vesenkha's centralized administration, Larin proposed the establishment of elected workers' councils at enterprise and trust level. These councils were to replace NKRKI and provide channels for effective popular control.

A manifesto issued by the far left Workers' Group in February 1923 decried the NEP and the system of industrial administration inaugurated by the IX Party Congress. It denounced the system of one-man management in industry and the employment of bourgeois specialists. It demanded the restoration of workers' control in the factories and the replacement of the political soviets by 'production soviets' as organs of government. NKRKI, the instrument of government control in industry, was to be superseded by control exercised by the 'production trade unions'.[74]

The plan's defenders

The dominant centrist element in the party supported the party leadership. This view was expounded by the prominent ex-Menshevik A.S. Martynov. In a vigorous polemic he argued that Krasin continued to perpetuate the mistaken managerial view that the main faults of the apparatus arose from the activity of ignorant and conceited 'control dilettanti'. Control, he argued, could not be abandoned but neither should it 'assume an abnormal form which can disorganise production'.[75] A robust control agency was needed to fight the rampant departmentalism and localism in the apparatus.

The state institutions, staffed by politically unreliable elements, wavered under internal and external pressures. Many party officials feared that this alien apparatus would corrupt the party or slip out of its grasp. The party could not slacken its hold and had to maintain ideological vigilance and apply a class approach to the problem of state control.

Kamenev in a vigorous defence of party control over the state apparatus denounced Osinskii's views as a 'revision of Leninism'.[76] G.I. Safarov charged Krasin, Osinskii and Smirnov with forming a 'united front' of the right and left against the party leadership and promoting 'Menshevik revisionism'.[77] Critics of the plan were taken to task for their political naiveté and accused of unwittingly becoming the mouthpieces of those elements in the state administration who, for political motives, wished to see party control slackened or abandoned.

These fears were shared by party officials in the centre and the localities who were uncertain of their ability to control and manage the apparatus. The party's precarious position under NEP fostered caution. In the commissariats, the trade unions and the local soviets, opposition to central control remained strong. In the spring of 1923 demands were renewed by local soviets for the liquidation of the provincial (*guberniya*) RKI.[78]

The debate in *Pravda* was part of a wider discussion. Lenin anxiously canvassed the reactions of Tsyurupa and other NKRKI leaders to his plan. The proposed unification of NKRKI and TsKK was generally welcomed by its leading officials as a means of strengthening the inspectorate and increasing its effectiveness.[79]

In an important article E.F. Rozmirovich, an influential old Bolshevik and a senior NKRKI official, issued a pertinent warning. In the past, she argued, NKRKI's work had been bedevilled by the attempt to combine in one organization both a political, control–supervisory function and a scientific–rationalization function, to the detriment of the latter. The new NKRKI, she argued, should be exclusively a rationalization body, uncompromised by control work, working in co-operation with the administrative and economic institutions.[80]

THE XII PARTY CONGRESS

Lenin intended making the TsKK–NKRKI reform the centre-piece of the impending XII Party Congress to which his proposals had been specifically addressed. He attached great importance to the plan, and wished to present a report on his ideas to the congress.[81] Full discussion of the scheme was necessary to mobilize maximum support and to iron out any difficulties.

In March 1923 Lenin's condition worsened irretrievably. The emergent triumvirate of Zinoviev, Kamenev and Stalin was left a free hand to reshape the reform and excise its more contentious proposals.[82] The Central Committee, on 5 April, decided to refer the issue for discussion to a special organizational section of the XII Party Congress, thus regulating debate by taking the subject off the congress floor.[83]

The XII Party Congress opened on 17 April 1923 in Lenin's absence. The congress was tightly organized, with few oppositionists in attendance, and was characterized by a marked absence of open dissension.

Stalin provided the keynote to the leadership's reaction to Lenin's plan. In his report to the congress, he argued that it was 'in essence' directed at ensuring effective party control over the state. The plan, he argued, constituted:

> A well ordered system for the reorganization of TsKK and NKRKI in order that the reorganized control apparatus shall transform itself into a lever for the improvement of all the component parts of the machine, for the replacement of the old, unsuitable parts by the new.[84]

Lenin's proposal to reorganize and check the central party organs was passed over in silence.

The congress agenda made no provision to debate Lenin's proposals. The issue instead was referred to two specially-elected organizational sections.[85] One section, chaired by Molotov, examined the plan for the reorganization of the central party apparatus and TsKK. A second section, chaired by Dzerzhinskii, examined the unification of TsKK and NKRKI, and the organization and work of the state control agency.

A.D. Tsyurupa, narkom of NKRKI and Lenin's trusted subordinate, at one section meeting denounced these procedural tactics to steamroller the congress. Underlining the importance attached by Lenin to the TsKK-NKRKI reform he declared:

> This question is being handled by us with insufficient attention . . . if Vladimir Ilich were at the congress he would make this question the lynch-pin of the congress.[86]

He complained that no report on Lenin's plan was being presented to the congress. Instead it had been relegated for discussion in a section 'on a par with every other organizational question'. Yu.S. Myshkin, who at the XI Party Congress had moved the resolution for TsKK's abolition, demanded time to debate the reform.[87] E.I. Bumazhnyi also noted the unseemly haste and secrecy with which the issue was being handled.[88]

Although the plan was not formally debated on the congress floor, many delegates voiced their opinions. These contributions did not greatly advance the debate and can be dealt with briefly. Significantly they revealed grave disquiet at the party's relations with the industrial managers.

The senior members of the Politburo, excluding Trotsky, endorsed the plan. Zinoviev claimed that the proposal outlined by Stalin had been adopted 'silently' by the whole congress. He denounced Krasin's alarmist talk of the 'terror' felt by managers, emphasizing the need for closer party involvement in economic management. The good managers, he argued, had nothing to fear. The party would select only the best workers for TsKK–NKRKI.[89] Kamenev warned of the influence of the new bourgeoisie in the apparatus and the ideological tendencies associated with it. This stratum sought to free state administration from party control.[90] He insisted on the need for a clear class approach to the question and the assertion of party control over the administration. Bukharin criticized Krasin's neutral, managerial conception of production. Party control was essential to ensure that production was organized and developed along socialist not capitalist lines.[91]

Krasin's views were subject to a barrage of criticism. G.Ya. Belen'kii argued they would turn the party into an '*agitpunkt*' with no direct control over production.[92] G.E. Evdokimov accused Krasin of a managerial deviation which aimed to oust the party from production.[93] Preobrazhenskii emphasized caution, stressing that nothing should be done to deepen anti-party feeling amongst managers. Managers and specialists should be involved in decision-making through Central Committee commissions but political direction had to be retained in the party's hands.[94] From the left G.I. Safarov, L.S. Sosnovskii and Yu.Kh. Lutovinov also condemned Krasin's views.[95]

Krasin stuck to his guns, reiterating that the composition of the Central Committee should be changed to reflect the party's new responsibilities by drawing in managers and technical specialists. He emphasized that his concern was shared by many prominent party figures, including even some narkoms, who felt intimidated and unable to speak their minds.[96]

Trotsky stressed the need to develop NKRKI's work in rationalizing accounting in industry, but overlooked the general question of the TsKK–NKRKI reform.[97] The spokesman of the far left resisted from attacking the scheme on the congress floor although an 'anonymous

platform', attributed to Osinskii, was circulated which demanded the
removal of Zinoviev, Kamenev and Stalin from the Central Committee
and also urged changes in party policy.[98]

Not unexpectedly, the unification of TsKK–NKRKI was welcomed
by TsKK as a means of increasing its authority and influence.
Shkiryatov of TsKK urged close co-operation with the Central Committee:

> What kind of organ is TsKK? This is not an organ that stands over or
> under the Central Committee – it is an independent organ which
> works jointly with the Central Committee. All questions of a
> controversial nature, and perhaps also non-controversial, must be
> settled without fail by this organ in order thus to clear the way for the
> Central Committee, in order that the Central Committee become
> more authoritative, and that the Central Committee in this respect
> understands its task.[99]

On the final day of the congress a report on the unification of TsKK–
NKRKI, signed by Dzerzhinskii, was issued which endorsed the reform.
Noting Trotsky's demand for greater state intervention to boost the
economy, Dzerzhinskii argued that without TsKK–NKRKI the party
would have no practical means of leading or directing the apparatus.
The problem was not one of excessive party control, but rather of the
party's inability to provide real and substantial assistance to the
economic organs. However, NKRKI's style of work had to be improved
to allay the fears of managers.[100]

The XII Party Congress placed great stress on establishing effective
party control over the state administration, noting that:

> Those deviations which counterpose the Soviet state to the working
> class and the party to the Soviet state are especially dangerous and
> destructive to the historical mission of our party.[101]

New emphasis was laid on the party's role in economic management.[102]
The congress, in approving the unification of TsKK–NKRKI, acknowledged the abandonment of the old rigid demarcation line between
party and state functions.[103]

Two resolutions, detailing the reorganization, were presented to the
congress on its final day, and were adopted without discussion and with
no opposition.[104]

The principal resolution, 'On the Organizational Question', drafted
by the Molotov commission, followed in detail the thesis approved by
the Central Committee in April.[105] The congress was to elect fifty

members to TsKK, 'primarily workers and peasants' with long party service and suitable for control work. TsKK was to retain its responsibility for party discipline but was now to assume responsibility for enforcing the party line in the state administration. TsKK was to be headed by a nine-man presidium, the members of which were to be of the calibre of Central Committee members. The narkom of NKRKI was to be appointed by the Central Committee from amongst the TsKK presidium. The NKRKI collegium was to include several members of the TsKK presidium and TsKK members were to be seconded to work in NKRKI.[106] Directives regarding the joint work of the two agencies were to be drafted by the presidium TsKK and collegium NKRKI. Joint sessions of these two bodies were to be convened fortnightly.

The congress enlarged the Central Committee's size to forty members with fifteen–twenty candidate members. Central Committee plenums were to be convened at least once every two months with the power to decide 'all the most fundamental issues'. This was intended, it was said, to make the Central Committee more representative, and to increase its authority.

TsKK was closely linked with the principal party organs. The resolution gave 'three permanent representatives' from TsKK's presidium the right to attend Politburo sessions.[107] All Central Committee members and all TsKK presidium members were to be supplied with Politburo documents. Moreover, three TsKK representatives were to attend meetings of the Orgburo.

The Central Committee and TsKK, both elected by the congress, were to work in harness. Full members of the Central Committee were barred from membership of TsKK in order to avoid an excessive concentration of power. All TsKK presidium members were entitled to attend Central Committee plenums with consultative voting rights. The Central Committee was empowered to delegate an unspecified number of its representatives to attend the TsKK plenums which were to be convened every two months, 'immediately prior to the Central Committee plenum'. TsKK's work was to be closely co-ordinated with the leading party organs.[108]

The scheme differed markedly from Lenin's plan. No mention was made of joint sessions of the Central Committee and TsKK, the new 'higher party conference'. Only members of the presidium of the TsKK were to attend Central Committee plenums and only then with consultative not deliberative votes. The plan to give TsKK members 'all the rights' of Central Committee members was rejected. TsKK was placed in a position of *de facto* subordination to the Central Committee.

TsKK's role in supervising the work of the Politburo, Secretariat and Orgburo, so vital to Lenin's scheme, was discreetly ignored.

This scheme avoided what had been seen as a central difficulty in Lenin's plan. A Soviet historian notes:

> The XII Party Congress on the basis of Leninist proposals [*sic*] determined the interrelationship between the party Central Committee and TsKK which avoided the counterposing of TsKK to the party Central Committee.[109]

The radical essence of Lenin's scheme was emasculated. TsKK, although strengthened, remained the Central Committee's poor relation.

A second resolution, 'Concerning the tasks of RKI and TsKK', drafted by a commission chaired by Dzerzhinskii, outlined the organization and functions of the control agency.[110] This resolution adhered closely to Lenin's proposals. TsKK–NKRKI's principal responsibility lay in 'the struggle for the state apparatus'. NKRKI was to be transformed into a 'model institution', staffed with technical specialists, and was to concentrate on the scientific study of the state administration and its rationalization.[111] The Central Committee assigned the Secretariat the task of finding suitable candidates for election to TsKK.[112] The work was entrusted to V.V. Kuibyshev on behalf of the Secretariat.[113] At the congress Kuibyshev consulted local delegations on the choice of suitable candidates for work in TsKK. The congress elected fifty members and ten candidates to TsKK including five former Central Committee members (V.V. Kuibyshev, E.M. Yaroslavskii, A.S. Kiselev, S.I. Gusev and T.S. Krivov) and three former members of TsKK (A.A. Korostelev, A.A. Sol'ts and M.F. Shkiryatov).[114] These individuals were to provide the leading core in TsKK–NKRKI.

The expansion of the Central Committee and TsKK signalled the first step in the campaign to broaden the base of the party leadership and replenish the leading organs with new members, largely drawn from the working class. Stalin more than any other Politburo member associated himself with this policy on which he was later to capitalize to great effect.[115]

Kuibyshev, who had proposed the suppression of Lenin's plan in the Politburo, was appointed head of the new TsKK–NKRKI. He was elected chairman of TsKK by the first TsKK plenum on 26 April 1923 and confirmed by the Central Committee. A proposal, advanced by the plenum, that Kuibyshev should also head NKRKI (in place of the more experienced Tsyurupa) was also approved by the Central Committee and confirmed by VTsIK on 30 April 1923.[116]

Kuibyshev was only thirty-four years of age and one of the rising generation of new leaders. His appointment consolidated TsKK–NKRKI's link with Stalin's Secretariat. In 1922–3 Kuibyshev had chaired a Central Committee commission which examined the industrial trusts and the work of the managers. Both Zinoviev and Trotsky commended his work. The new TsKK–NKRKI was to take over on a permanent basis the work of this commission.[117]

The TsKK plenum elected a presidium of nine members and five candidates, nominated by the party leadership from the commission's most senior figures.[118] The appointment of Kuibyshev, Yaroslavskii and Kiselev (individuals with past leftist sympathies) to head TsKK–NKRKI helped to sell the reform. The TsKK party collegium which was responsible for party discipline was headed by Yaroslavskii who, like Kuibyshev, was a former party Secretary.

The Central Committee instructed Kuibyshev to compile a list of candidates for appointment to the NKRKI collegium. A list of nine members was approved by the Central Committee and Sovnarkom on 5 May 1923.[119] TsKK assumed the leadership of NKRKI. At the same time TsKK–NKRKI was subordinated to the leading party organs.

The unification of TsKK–NKRKI transformed the organization of the Soviet central party–state apparatus. It established an agency which concentrated all party and state control work in its hands, and placed that agency at the disposal of the congress. The party thus gained direct oversight over the whole state administrative apparatus (See Figure 2.1). The congress confirmed the party's commitment to a 'control-centered' model of administration.

CONCLUSION

TsKK–NKRKI was conceived by Lenin both as a body to assist the leading party organs and as a watchdog over those same organs. TsKK relations with the central party organs was envisaged as a process of organic interdependence, or symbiotic interaction, rather than in mechanistic terms of checks and balances. He wished to temper the powers of the central party organs, but not to weaken central leadership.[120] The scheme would have placed on TsKK–NKRKI an impossible burden of complex and contradictory tasks. The weakness of these organizational checks on the party leadership was highlighted in

64

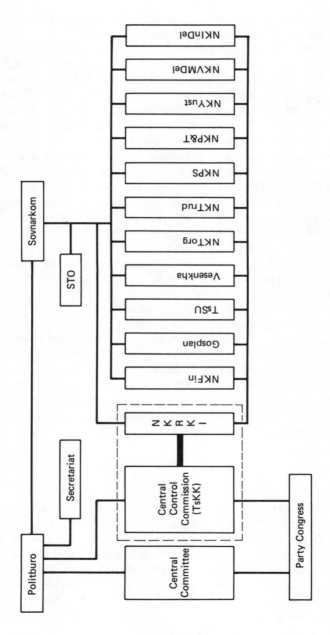

Figure 2.1   Central party–government apparatus (1924)

the ensuing succession struggle. The ability of determined individuals to circumvent checks was compounded by the enormous concentration of power at the apex of the party and the decline of inner-party democracy. The vagueness of Lenin's plan concerning TsKK's relations with the Central Committee blurred the lines of accountability and created an uncertainty which could later be exploited.[121]

The scheme was over-ambitious and underestimated the difficulties of implementation, and it remained stillborn. Lenin's demise prevented it being developed, and the Politburo and Central Committee recoiled from this novel, experimental scheme which threatened to introduce new uncertainties into party work. There was no strong lobby which could be mobilized behind the reform, and without consensus amongst the leaders as to the problems facing the regime no organizational arrangements could compensate. The leadership's plan, by contrast, had the virtue of simplicity, it was easier to put into effect and left the lines of command more clearly defined.

The question of who could control this powerful control agency became a matter of pressing concern. Stalin, as a Soviet historian notes, had a clear appreciation of the vital importance of control:

> Each step in the reorganisation of the newly created unified control organ, TsKK–RKI, passed under the direct leadership of the Central Committee and of comrade Stalin personally. Comrade Stalin even at this stage of activity did not cease to be deeply interested in TsKK–RKI and directed each step of the work of this organ.[122]

Stalin, NKRKI's former head, became the patron and mentor of the new TsKK–NKRKI.

66

Plate III   V.V. Kuibyshev (1888–1935) : Chairman of TsKK and narkom RKI
(May 1923–August 1926)

Novosti Press Agency
Plate IV   V.V. Kuibyshev (1888–1935) : Chairman of TsKK and narkom RKI
(May 1923–August 1926)

3 Rabkrin and the Organization of State Control (1923–30)

The unification of TsKK and NKRKI in 1923 established a powerful unified agency of party and state control. The despised and ineffective NKRKI was transformed into one of the central links in the party–state apparatus. By 1929–30 TsKK–NKRKI had become one of the most powerful institutions in the USSR, wielding enormous influence on policy-making. This was achieved through a long and complex process of adjustment, through which NKRKI developed its organization and function, and studiously cultivated its links with the Politburo and Sovnarkom. TsKK–NKRKI's rise to prominence was also shaped by the intense factional and policy disputes of the 1920s, in which it played a crucial part.

IMPLEMENTATION OF THE TsKK–NKRKI REORGANIZATION

The details of the reorganization of TsKK–NKRKI were worked out in the six months following the XII Party Congress. TsKK–NKRKI elaborated these details under the party's supervision. Care was taken to involve the representatives of other bodies in this work to ensure broad support for the plan.[1] The constitution of the USSR was approved by TsIK on 6 July 1923, establishing a new all-union tier of administration. Under Sovnarkom USSR twelve all-union commissariats were set up, including the new NKRKI USSR.

The XII Party Congress redefined NKRKI's responsibilities. NKRKI was relieved of 'full day to day, formal control over all financial and material operations of the state organs' which had caused so much conflict in the past.[2] On 6 September 1923, TsIK and Sovnarkom relieved NKRKI of its responsibilities for financial control which, together with many of the finance inspectors of NKRKI, were transferred to NKFin. This initiated a lasting feud between NKRKI and NKFin.[3] NKRKI retained the right of detailed examination of the quarterly and yearly budgets of the USSR, of the union and local republics, checking appropriations made by NKFin, and reviewing the production plans and their execution by the economic organs. In the field of economic planning NKRKI's work was co-ordinated with Gosplan and the Central Statistical Administration (TsSU).

TsIK on 12 November 1923 adopted a decree establishing NKRKI USSR. The task of the agency was 'to improve the state apparatus, to manage it properly, and to adjust it to the final ends of socialist construction'. NKRKI's duties included the practical and theoretical study of the state administration. NKRKI was to evaluate the work of departmental heads, assist those individuals in selecting officials for promotion, and oversee the training of officials. It was to examine the causes of official crimes and corruption, to investigate public complaints against officials, and make the machine more responsive and less officious. It was also to rationalize bookkeeping methods and office routine. More significantly, NKRKI's tasks included the 'carrying out of special orders and directions of the supreme organs of the USSR, as well as control and supervision over the prompt implementation of decrees and decisions of these organs'.[4]

NKRKI's inspectorates shadowed the work of the commissariats and government departments. It was empowered to investigate all central, regional and local, state and communal bodies, co-operatives, trade unions and joint-stock companies in receipt of state subsidies. It could request from these bodies information, demand reports from officials, and require their participation in investigative commissions. It could demand the removal of defects noted, advance measures to rationalize their structure, request the dismissal of officials, and propose disciplinary punishment. It had the right to participate, with advisory vote, in all commissions and meetings organized by TsIK and Sovnarkom in the centre or in the localities; in meetings of the collegia of the people's commissariats, executive committees and their presidia; as well as in all congresses, conferences, meetings and administrative sessions of state bodies, enterprises, trade unions, communal and co-operative organs.

The power of the new NKRKI was constrained by the strengthening of internal departmental control in the apparatus.[5] Sovnarkom underlined this ruling with a new decree 'concerning the responsibility of the leaders of institutions, departments and enterprises for the condition and work of the apparatus led by them'.[6] The decree instructed NKRKI and the institutions strictly to delimit their respective responsibilities. It empowered those institutions whose departmental control organs had been abolished in 1920, to set up new strengthened revision commissions and groups.

The unification of NKRKI and TsKK in 1923 placed the commissariat in a unique position, according it new authority and prestige and linking it directly with the leading party organs. From the outset the leadership of TsKK and NKRKI was entrusted to one man. The XII Party Congress ruled that all major questions were to be discussed at fortnightly joint meetings of the TsKK presidium and NKRKI collegium.[7] The TsKK presidium and secretariat closely scrutinized NKRKI's work,[8] and NKRKI's plan of work had to be approved by TsKK before submission to Sovnarkom. The joint session of TsKK and NKRKI reinforced the former's dominance. The collegium NKRKI came to meet less frequently and confined itself to minor issues.[9]

TsKK's size was increased by the congress from seven members to sixty (fifty full members and ten candidates). The membership was elected by the party congress, with the party Secretariat selecting the candidates. All members were to work full-time in TsKK. TsKK was led by a nine-man presidium, headed by its chairman V.V. Kuibyshev. From its origin, TsKK functioned as a highly centralized, hierarchical agency. The TsKK plenum was intended to serve the same function in respect of the presidium as the Central Committee in relation to the Politburo. From 1924 until 1928 it met on average every three to four months, between party congresses, thereafter less frequently. Formally it elected the presidium and laid down the guidelines for TsKK policy. In practice, the plenum was dominated by the presidium and provided only a restricted forum for debate.[10]

The TsKK plenum in June 1923 divided the sixty members of the commission into three groups, each with its own responsibilities. One group of fifteen to twenty members, working under the TsKK presidium, was to prepare materials for the Central Committee, participate in party commissions, investigate party organs under the Central Committee, and participate in the most important commissions given to NKRKI by the party. A second group of twenty-five–thirty members was delegated to work in NKRKI under the leadership of its collegium. These individuals, on TsKK resolution, could assist Politburo commissions and investigations. A third group of seven members, comprising the 'party collegium', were to examine breaches by Communists of party statutes, continuing the functions of internal party control originally assigned TsKK in 1921.[11]

From the outset NKRKI was directly subordinated to TsKK. The two bodies shared the same leadership. Kuibyshev in 1924 noted that 'the presidium TsKK in its personnel almost coincides with that of the collegium NKRKI'.[12] TsKK members headed the main NKRKI departments and inspectorates and also led the major investigations.

TsKK's report to the XIII Party Congress in 1924 declared:

> If NKRKI and TsKK are as a whole essentially organs of the party, then TsKK in its relations with the commissariat occupies the role of a fraction which leads and directs all the work of the commissariat and engages in direct practical participation in the work of RKI. In concrete terms this is achieved by the fact that the leading officials of the administrations, departments and inspections are mainly members of TsKK who are united in their turn by the TsKK presidium and secretariat.[13]

The TsKK presidium approved NKRKI's plan of work, heard its most important reports and took matters concerning NKRKI to the Central Committee.[14]

NKRKI's link with TsKK accorded the inspectorate new prestige and increased power, but at the expense of its own identity. E.F. Rozmirovich (a senior NKRKI official) at the TsKK plenum in March 1924 criticized excessive interference by the commission in the inspectorate's work, and argued that NKRKI should be allowed greater freedom to develop its scientific rationalization work.[15]

Lenin's hope of achieving a balance between the party and soviet organ was never realized. So close did relations between TsKK and NKRKI become that the two agencies were widely considered as one body.[16] From 1923 onwards the two agencies shared the same office block at 21 Ilinka (now Ulitsa Kuibysheva) in the centre of Moscow, near the Kremlin, and close by the party headquarters on Staraya Ploshchad.[17] NKRKI's monthly journal *Izvestiya RKI* was replaced by a joint journal of the two agencies *Byulleten' TsKK VKP (b) i NKRKI SSSR i RSFSR.*

TsKK was dominated by its presidium which in turn was tightly controlled by a handful of senior party figures. The XII Party Congress elected fifty members and ten candidates to TsKK. A presidium comprising nine members and five candidates was elected by the TsKK plenum. Of these fourteen members many were to play a conspicuous part in the agency's work, six being re-elected to the presidium in 1930 – E.M. Yaroslavskii, N.M. Yanson, A.A. Sol'ts, M.F. Shkiryatov, N.I. Il'in and T.S. Krivov. TsKK's membership was increased at subsequent party congresses and by 1928 stood at 195. The size of the TsKK presidium increased in the same period to thirty-two (See Appendixes E and F).

The XII Party Congress ruled that TsKK members should be chosen mainly from 'workers and peasants' who had long party service (*stazh*). The length of party membership for specific posts was laid down.

Political experience and loyalty rather than administrative and technical expertise became the hallmark of TsKK's members. The commission became a bastion of the party undergrounders. Of the sixty members elected in 1923, twenty-nine had been party members since 1905 or earlier, twenty-five since 1917, and only five since 1917.[18]

The XIII Party Congress in 1924 elected 150 members of TsKK following the unification of the local KK and RKI. Three categories of membership were outlined with their specific duties: (i) seventy members who were to work full-time in the central TsKK–NKRKI apparatus, including twenty workers and peasants from production work; (ii) thirty members who headed the most important local KK–RKI organs and were to remain at their posts in the localities; (iii) fifty members, workers and peasants who were to remain at their existing places of employment, providing the agency with its links with the grassroots. Strict criteria for party *stazh* were laid down for each category.[19]

At the XIV Party Congress Molotov noted with satisfaction the proletarianization of TsKK's ranks. In 1924 50 per cent of TsKK's members were categorized as workers, and in 1925 70 per cent.[20] A large proportion were metalworkers, who in the revolution had provided the backbone of Bolshevik support. The jump in the proportion of workers in 1925 was the result of recruiting local KK–RKI leaders into TsKK. This proletarian composition, whilst strengthening TsKK's links with the party rank and file, seriously limited the experience and competence of the membership and hindered the development of the agency's work.

TsKK's members were re-elected at each party congress. The turnover of members at the XIV, XV and XVI Congresses was high with less than half of the existing complement being re-elected.[21] This evidently was part of the Politburo's strategy to purge TsKK of waverers, although the commission produced few active oppositionists. It is significant that at the XV Party Congress it was the lowest category of member – the workers and peasants at their place of employment – who were least likely be re-elected.[22] A substantial core of members continued to be re-elected. Of the sixty members elected in 1923 nineteen were re-elected in 1930 (see Appendix F).

TsKK–NKRKI AND THE CENTRAL PARTY–GOVERNMENT APPARATUS

TsKK–NKRKI was placed at the centre of the party–government apparatus, straddling the two administrative hierarchies as an instrument of co-ordination. The shifting relationship between the Politburo and Sovnarkom was reflected in TsKK–NKRKI's changing role. NKRKI, through TsKK, was directly tied to the leading party organs and its work heavily politicized although it retained its status as a government agency (see Figure 3.1). NKRKI, like other commissariats, had its own party cell.

Lenin's death in January 1924 was followed by a reshuffle of government posts. In February A.I. Rykov was appointed chairman of Sovnarkom, L.B. Kamenev became a vice-chairman alongside the existing deputy A.D. Tsyurupa. Kamenev was simultaneously appointed chairman of STO thus providing the link between the two leading government bodies.[23]

Kuibyshev, unlike his predecessor Tsyurupa (a Sovnarkom deputy), held no leading government post, reflecting his junior status within the leadership. NKRKI like all other commissariats was represented in Sovnarkom but, significantly, was not represented in STO until 1926.[24] These anomalies were part of the carve-up of leading posts amongst the ruling triumvirate, and these measures were intended also to reassure the commissariats, where many viewed the new NKRKI with trepidation.

NKRKI's work for Sovnarkom and STO was co-ordinated through its plan of work which had to be approved by Sovnarkom.[25] It was assigned tasks by Sovnarkom, STO and TsIK and presented to these organs co-reports on various questions, examined issues jointly with other departments, made recommendations on legislative proposals, and prepared draft decrees.[26]

Zinoviev's and Kamenev's defeat at the XIV Party Congress brought changes in the organization of the government apparatus. Rykov became chairman of both Savnarkom and STO. Sovnarkom and STO shared the same vice-chairmen,[27] and the administrative staffs of the two bodies were merged in order to avert conflict. Kuibyshev in February 1926 was appointed vice-chairman of both Sovnarkom and STO.[28] This gave NKRKI a major voice in the leading government organs. Subsequent leaders of NKRKI–Ordzhonikidze, Andreev and Rudzutak – all served as vice-chairmen of Sovnarkom and STO during their terms of office.

TsKK was bound to the leading party organs by a system of interlocking personnel appointments (see Figure 3.1). From 1923 onwards, TsKK worked closely with the Politburo. The chairmen of TsKK were all Politburo members who surrendered their Politburo and Central Committee seats during their period in office. These individuals, however, attended Politburo meetings and were active participants in its

74

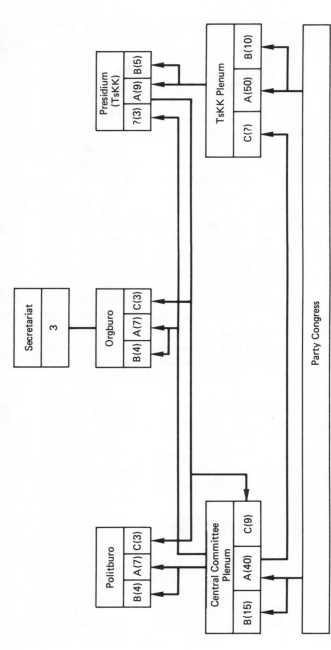

Key A Full members – full voting rights
B Candidate members – advisory voting rights
C Outside representatives – advisory voting rights

Note: TsKK was tied to the Politburo, Orgburo, Secretariat and Central Committee through a system of interlocking appointments. This diagram shows the membership of each of these bodies, including full and candidate members, but also shows the number of representatives which outside bodies could send to attend their meetings.

Figure 3.1 TsKK and the central party apparatus (1924)

deliberations. The Politburo, through TsKK–NKRKI, was connected directly with the entire party–state apparatus. TsKK became a major central party organ alongside the Secretariat and Orgburo.

The XII Party Congress in 1923 determined that three TsKK presidium members should attend Politburo sessions with advisory voting rights.[29] These members were to be chosen by TsKK and endorsed by the Central Committee. From 1923 onwards Kuibyshev, Yaroslavskii and Shkiryatov attended the Politburo in this capacity.[30] The Central Committee in April 1923 resolved that three of its members should attend sessions of the TsKK presidium;[31] these were to be chosen from Stalin, Molotov, Zinoviev, Zelenskii and Dzerzhinskii.[32]

The XV Party Congress in 1927 increased the number of TsKK representatives eligible to attend the Politburo to four full and four candidate presidium members.[33] In 1929 the TsKK representatives in the Politburo played a crucial role in the defeat of the Right. Following the XVI Party Congress in 1930, TsKK approved a list of nine presidium members who were eligible to represent it in the Politburo.[34]

The XII Party Congress empowered TsKK to delegate three members to attend the Orgburo's meetings.[35] TsKK and the Secretariat were closely linked from the outset through Kuibyshev and Yaroslavskii, both former officials of the Secretariat. The Secretariat co-ordinated TsKK-NKRKI's work with the Politburo and Central Committee. Stalin and Molotov supervised TsKK–NKRKI's work on behalf of the Central Committee.[36] The XIV Party Congress in 1925 empowered TsKK to delegate five members to attend Orgburo and Secretariat meetings.[37] Following the XVI Party Congress in 1930, TsKK approved a list of six presidium members to perform this function.[38]

The XII Party Congress ruled TsKK membership incompatible with membership of the Central Committee to prevent an excessive concentration of power.[39] All TsKK presidium members were to attend Central Committee plenums. The Central Committee was to send an unspecified number of its members to the TsKK plenums. Lenin's plan to turn TsKK into a watchdog supervizing the leading party organs on the Central Committee's behalf was never realized. TsKK from the outset was subordinated to the Central Committee and was conceived as an agency which assisted the leading party organs.

After 1923 joint Central Committee–TsKK plenums became an important forum for policy debate in the party. The number of joint plenums varied over time as indicated in Table 3.1.[40] After 1925 joint Central Committee–TsKK plenums became the major policy debating forum in the struggle with the united opposition of Zinoviev, Kamenev and Trotsky.

Table 3.1   Joint Central Committee – TsKK plenums

	XII–XIII Congress	XIII–XIV Congress	XIV–XV Congress	XV–XVI Congress	XVI–XVII Congress
CC plenums	18	18	9	8	6
Joint CC–TsKK Plenums	3	2	5	2	2

Joint Central Committee–TsKK plenums differed little from ordinary Central Committee plenums, but dealt principally with questions of internal party discipline and related policy issues. The sessions never assumed the function of scrutinizing and controlling the work of the higher party organs, part of the system of internal accountability and control which Lenin had envisaged for it in 1923.

The XIII Party Congress commended 'the regular fruitful work' of joint Central Committee–TsKK plenums.[41] Stalin at the XIV Party Congress described the Central Committee plenum as the 'supreme organ' of the party.[42] At the XV Party Congress he praised 'this leading centre of 200–250 comrades which meets regularly and decides the most vital questions of our economic construction', and claimed that the resolution of important questions was 'passing more and more from the hands of a narrow upper group into the hands of this broad centre'.[43]

The XII Party Congress gave all TsKK members the right to attend party conferences with a deliberative vote,[44] and from the XII Party Congress onwards, TsKK members made up a significant bloc. The new TsKK–NKRKI failed to halt the decline of the party Central Committee and congress; the agency itself accelerated the concentration of power in the Politburo and Secretariat.

TsKK, under Kuibyshev, became a centralized, hierarchical institution at the service of the Politburo. At the TsKK plenum in December 1925, an unsuccessful attempt was made to revitalize democracy within TsKK by strengthening the plenum's control over the presidium.[45] E.H. Carr rightly notes that democracy within TsKK had become a 'meaningless formality', and that the commission had become in essence a 'department of the central committee', assuming some of its most controversial and sensitive work.[46]

Within the new agency, policy was formulated in the joint sessions of the presidium TsKK and collegium NKRKI. TsKK–NKRKI worked in close consultation with the Politburo, co-ordinated by the Secretariat. Kuibyshev in 1924 noted the demise of the old Politburo commissions and their supersession by the new TsKK–NKRKI:

> At present there is noticeable a specific tendency that the largest and most important questions in the majority of cases are sent to TsKK preliminarily to be worked out and on the basis of the reports of TsKK and of those of the representatives of the departments and institutions concerned. The questions are resolved in the Politburo . . . there is a tendency to refer questions to TsKK which, utilising the RKI apparatus, is able to provide a more considered, more detailed, fuller examination of every question on the basis of material and social investigations which can be undertaken for every question.[47]

In 1923–4, NKRKI reports formed the basis of party directives – the investigations of the local soviet apparatus, the organization of trade, the administration of the Red Army.[48] Stressing TsKK–NKRKI's 'positive achievements', Kuibyshev declared 'we are more and more becoming an organ indispensable for the Central Committee in its work'.[49]

Under Kuibyshev, TsKK–NKRKI allied itself with the Politburo majority. In October 1924 Kuibyshev declared:

> TsKK is a party organ and does not have any other task beside those which the party places before itself. This organ was created to help the party to fulfill those functions which were placed on it. It is completely natural that all the work of both TsKK and NKRKI should be founded on the tasks and aims which our communist party places before itself . . . TsKK is not a leading organ and even less is it an administrative organ. TsKK and RKI are only organs of control for implementing by the party organs and government apparatus the resolutions of the party and highest soviet institutions.[50]

TsKK, under Kuibyshev, took a determined partisan stance against oppositionists in the party.

In December 1925, following NKRKI's investigation of TsSU (see pp. 123–7), Kuibyshev stressed TsKK–NKRKI's role in resolving major policy issues.[51] TsKK–NKRKI's work both at central and local level in assisting the party and government, he argued, had 'a great future'. Yaroslavskii welcomed this development of TsKK–NKRKI's work:

We are given the task of closely supervising all Politburo resolutions. All questions which require preliminary working out, preliminary checking, preliminary collection of materials are usually worked out by us in TsKK and RKI.[52]

Kuibyshev's report to the XIV Party Congress cited Lenin's proposal that TsKK–NKRKI should assist the Politburo and Central Committee, ensuring more effective direction and control. As a result of TsKK–NKRKI's work, he averred, the Central Committee had assumed close leadership of the state administration and economy.[53] To ensure the agency's success Kuibyshev urged the establishment of 'constant, close, organic contact between the Central Committee and TsKK, between the party committees and the KKs'.[54] The congress resolution stressed TsKK–NKRKI's role in working out policy proposals for the party.[55]

TsKK–NKRKI's links with the Politburo and Central Committee were strengthened and formalized after the XIV Party Congress. The Central Committee plenum in April 1926 approved a plan of work for the Politburo and Central Committee for the year. Forty topics were listed for discussion, with reports being presented by the responsible commissariats. For twenty-five topics, covering a wide range of subjects, co-reports were to be presented by TsKK–NKRKI.[56] The party Secretariat co-ordinated this work.[57] A similar plan of work was approved in 1928.[58]

Yaroslavskii in 1927 reaffirmed TsKK's subordination to the Politburo:

TsKK cannot regard itself as an organ standing above the party, above the Central Committee – it is an organ which helps the party, which helps the Central Committee. TsKK cannot have any political line separate from that of the Central Committee. Such a double centre, if it were formed, would bring only harm to the party, it would be disastrous for the party; then it would be necessary to create some kind of organ, a kind of party council, which would coordinate these centres.[59]

This, he argued, had nothing in common with Lenin's plan for TsKK–NKRKI.

RABKRIN'S ORGANIZATIONAL STRUCTURE AND STAFF

NKRKI's collegium worked under the close supervision of the TsKK presidium and was dominated by its officials. Its membership was appointed by Sovnarkom and TsIK, with the Politburo approving key appointments. After 1923, the collegium was enlarged in accordance with its growing responsibilities. In August 1923 the narkom was assisted by two deputies and six collegium members. By December 1932 the number of deputies had risen to four and the number of collegium members to thirteen (see Appendix B).

In the second half of 1924, NKRKI's collegium met weekly (usually on Thursday or Friday evenings from 7 o'clock until midnight). It was attended by up to a dozen NKRKI officials and a few representatives of the institutions whose work was under discussion. Kuibyshev was largely occupied by his work in TsKK and entrusted the running of NKRKI to his two deputies S.E. Chutskaev and N.M. Yanson. Out of twenty-three meetings of NKRKI's collegium in this period Kuibyshev attended only six, the meetings being chaired in his absence by one of his deputies.[60]

Increasingly, joint session of the TsKK presidium and NKRKI collegium took over the direction of the commissariat's work. From March to June 1930 these joint sessions were held every ten days (on the 3rd, 13th and 23rd of each month) in the evenings. As many as forty-five individuals, mainly from TsKK, attended these sessions. They were chaired by Ordzhonikidze, or in his absence by his deputies, Akulov, Pavlunovskii and Rozengol'ts. These sessions discussed major policy questions and examined officials on their activities (*opros*). They approved resolutions and policy recommendations which were referred to the Politburo and Sovnarkom.[61]

Rabkrin's Organizational Structure

The problem of structuring and co-ordinating the different facets of NKRKI's work posed immense difficulties, resulting in frequent reorganizations. The ineffectiveness of NKRKI in the early years and the bitter dispute within the agency concerning its role, further complicated the issue. In November 1923, TsIK approved a new structure for the central apparatus of NKRKI.[62]

According to this decree, four main administrations (*upravlenie*) were established under the NKRKI collegium. The General Administration managed the commissariat's internal affairs, organization, staff, and co-ordinated its work. The vital Operational Administration carried out investigations and comprised nine inspectorates – industry, trade, agriculture, military–naval, finance, transport–communications, administration, culture–education, labour–health–social insurance – each shadowing one or more commissariats. The Administration for

Improving the State Apparatus, headed by E.F. Rozmirovich, and the Administration for Accounting and Bookkeeping, led by P.N. Amosov, assumed responsibility for rationalization work which now constituted a major facet of NKRKI's work.

Other specialist departments were set up in NKRKI. The Legal Department, headed by A.A. Sol'ts, provided legal advice and assisted in the investigation of criminal activity. The Information Publishing Department published the agency's journals and reports and publicized its work in the press. The Central Bureau of Complaints and Declarations received, processed and investigated citizens' complaints against administrative shortcomings and abuses.

Attached to NKRKI were formed other more specialized bodies. The Council for the Scientific Organization of Labour (SovNOT) led the work of the scientific institutes which studied administrative and industrial rationalization. The State Institute of Bookkeeping Experts, headed by B.A. Bor'yan provided advice on accounting and bookkeeping methods[63] (see Appendix D).

In the next two years NKRKI's central apparatus was subject to numerous reorganizations, aimed at strengthening the collegium's control, improving co-ordination and raising the agency's effectiveness. In 1924 a new unified economic inspectorate was created. The Operational Administration was scrapped and the inspectorates made accountable directly to the collegium. A new inspectorate for unplanned assignments was set up which absorbed the Central Bureau of Complaints. In 1925 the Administration for Improving the State Apparatus and the Administration for Accounting and Bookkeeping were replaced by two smaller departments.[64]

Serious disorganization continued to vex the agency's leaders. The XIV Party Congress attempted to define more clearly NKRKI's role and to settle a bitter dispute amongst its officials on this question. Three basic tasks were assigned to NKRKI: (i) control and supervision of the administration, combating official crime, enforcing policy implementation; (ii) rationalization of the structure and procedures of the administrative and economic institutions; (iii) policy investigation, and the formulation of policy proposals for the leading party and government organs.[65]

In the summer of 1926, NKRKI's central apparatus was fundamentally reorganized with the aim of introducing greater functional specialization into the agency's work. Three new sectors were established – control, rationalization, policy investigation – and all existing departments, sectors and inspectorates were brought under their control. The scheme failed and was soon abandoned.

Only at the end of 1926 did NKRKI eventually find a satisfactory and lasting solution to the problem. Under the collegium a new Department of Administrative Affairs (*upravlenie delami*) assumed charge of the agency's internal affairs. Co-ordination between TsKK and NKRKI was improved through a unified Organization–Instruction Department, headed by M.F. Shkiryatov. The important Sector of Control set up in the summer was retained, headed from 1926 to 1928 by N.M. Yanson, and thereafter by B.A. Roizenman. The Legal Department remained. SovNOT and the State Institute of Bookkeeping Experts were also retained.

The most important aspect of the 1926 reform involved scrapping the Sector of Rationalization and the Sector of Policy Investigation. In their place were set up twenty-eight *ad hoc* groups, responsible for investigating specific issues, concerning economic, social and administrative questions. This replaced the system of permanent supervision of commissariats by individual inspectorates. However, the centralized naval–military, and transport–communications inspectorates survived. This allowed NKRKI to utilize its limited resources more effectively, to pinpoint key problems, and to respond more flexibly to shifting political priorities as defined by the Politburo and Sovnarkom[66] (see Appendix D).

Rabkrin's Staff

Lenin in 1923 outlined the 'extraordinarily strict' criteria which were to be applied in selecting NKRKI officials, transferring it into a small model commissariat. NKRKI in the following months set up two commissions to screen officials, examine new recruits and to evaluate the work of the officials.[67] The quality and calibre of NKRKI personnel remained a matter of continuing concern for its leaders.

In 1922, NKRKI's central apparatus numbered 1,300 officials, and its total staff 12,000. In 1923 its total staff was slashed to 3,000, partly through the shedding of its responsibilities for financial control. Its size grew to 4,300 in 1925 but during the regime of economy campaign was again pruned back. In October 1929 the total staff numbered 3,569, of whom 513 worked in NKRKI, 513 in the republican NKRKI, 941 in the oblast RKI, and 1,602 in the okrug and uezd RKI.[68] After 1928, in response to the crisis in agriculture, the staff of the okrug and uezd RKI were doubled through transfers from higher levels. NKRKI's small staff set it apart from the large operative commissariats, and placed it alongside other specialist agencies such as Gosplan and TsSU.

The 513 officials employed in NKRKI USSR in 1929 were sub-divided into eight categories – twenty-eight higher administrative officials, six general administrators, nineteen operative heads, eighteen scientific workers, 275 controllers and inspectors, five statisticians, four accountants and bookkeepers, and 158 secretarial, clerical and other personnel.[69]

The reorganization of 1923 brought substantial changes in the agency's staff. Within NKRKI USSR the percentage of Communists rose sharply from 10.6 per cent in January 1923 to 30.6 per cent in 1924 to 48 per cent in 1929. In the lower NKRKI organs the level of party saturation had increased substantially by 1929 – republican NKRKI 48 per cent; oblast RKI 53 per cent; okrug RKI 59 per cent. For NKRKI as a whole there were 254 Komsomol members. This gave NKRKI the distinction of having by far the highest level of party saturation of any commissariat.[70]

The social composition of NKRKI was also changed, and its staff after 1923 substantially proletarianized. In 1929 24 per cent of the officials of NKRKI USSR and 35.8 per cent of all its officials were classified as workers. Of its staff as a whole, 22 per cent had over five years' experience of work in production. This made NKRKI the most proletarian of the commissariats. Nevertheless, officials from official backgrounds still predominated, making up 68 per cent of the staff of NKRKI USSR and 48 per cent of its total staff. Since 1917 the staff of the agency had been largely renewed with only 8 per cent of NKRKI's NKRKI's officials having previously been employed in the tsarist state apparatus.[71]

Efforts were made to raise the educational qualifications of NKRKI officials. Courses were set up at Sverdlov university in Moscow to train officials, and in 1925, sixty-eight student probationers were attached to NKRKI which became a ladder of advancement for the able and ambitious. In 1929 43 per cent of officials of NKRKI USSR, and 21 per cent of all NKRKI officials had higher educational training.[72] This was somewhat lower than most of the operative commissariats, reflecting the higher proletarian composition of NKRKI.

The reorganization of 1923 dramatically improved the material conditions of NKRKI officials. The average monthly salary of all NKRKI staff rose from thirty-one roubles in 1923 to sixty-eight roubles in 1924. This was achieved by salary increases and the sacking of low-paid staff. This was intended to improve the wretched lot of the *erkaisty* which Lenin had noted, and to attract a high calibre of recruit. NKRKI officials appear to have been paid higher salaries than comparable grades in other commissariats. In 1929, 79 per cent of all NKRKI officials received over 150 roubles per month whilst for all commissariats only 60 per cent fell into this category.[73]

As a result of these policies NKRKI acquired a staff which had little sympathy or understanding of the problems or outlook of the officials of the operative commissariats, particularly the bourgeois specialists. The commissariat's small size and unique role fostered a distinct departmental outlook. This did not, however, preclude bitter conflict between factions within NKRKI, particularly between controllers and rationalizers, which reflected not only narrow sectional interests, but fundamentally different conceptions of the agency's purpose.

Lenin's objective of transforming NKRKI into a small specialist agency ran into immediate difficulties. Kuibyshev in October 1924 noted the acute shortage of suitable 'Communist-specialists'. His emphasis on the recruitment of Communist into NKRKI undoubtedly weakened the position of the specialists and was strongly criticized.[74] Under his leadership, specialists were assigned a subordinate role in NKRKI, and this exacerbated NKRKI's difficulties in recruiting and retaining specialist personnel.

At the XIV Party Congress Kuibyshev insisted that in recruiting officials he had not discriminated against non-party specialists and had chosen individuals on merit. Out of a total staff of 404 employees in NKRKI's central apparatus there were many specialists – twenty-one economists, thirty-two engineers, three agronomists, twenty-four jurists, twenty-nine bookkeepers and accountants, and fifteen former inspectors from the tsarist agency of State Control.[75] He continued to express satisfaction with NKRKI's complement of specialists.[76]

Under Ordzhonikidze, renewed efforts were made to strengthen NKRKI staff.[77] The joint Central Committee-TsKK plenum in August 1927 called on the Politburo and local party organs to ensure that NKRKI was staffed with the best party workers, economic executives and administrators. It proposed also to strengthen NKRKI with a group of foreign specialists to ensure the most speedy adoption of the technical achievements from abroad, especially from America.[78] In the succeeding years, foreign and Soviet specialists were drawn into NKRKI's work in large numbers as consultants assisting in its investigations.

The Republican and Local Control Agencies

With the establishment of the USSR in 1923 TsKK–NKRKI USSR assumed the leadership of the republican TsKK–NKRKI, although these bodies were still formally appointed by their respective republican party and state bodies. The republican NKRKI after 1924 were merged with the newly created republican TsKK in the Ukraine, Belorussia, Transcaucasia, Uzbekistan and Turkmenistan. The leadership of each republican TsKK–NKRKI was entrusted to one individual and the agencies were modelled on TsKK–NKRKI USSR. In the RSFSR, no republican TsKK was established and NKRKI RSFSR, like NKRKI USSR, worked under TsKK of the CPSU.[79]

The XII Party Congress delayed unifying the local KK and RKI organs but requested that TsKK–NKRKI submit a report to the Central Committee on its feasibility.[80] The XIII Party Congress in May 1924 authorized unification of the KK and RKI organs in the localities. The KK–RKI network was set up at the oblast and okrug and uezd levels and in the urban centres. TsKK's membership was increased from sixty to 150 to include the leaders of the main KK–RKI organs. The KKs quickly assumed dominance over the RKI organs.[81]

The republican and local control organs were subject to dual subordination – to the central TsKK–NKRKI organs and to the local party and soviet organs who elected and approved their appointments. This allowed for a significant decentralization of power within the agency, and a measure of accountability of control organs to local bodies.

In May 1924, Kuibyshev reported that there were 51 KK–RKI organs in existence. The XIII Party Congress instructed local party organs to ensure that only the best officials were chosen for work in the KK–RKI organs.[82] By 1924 there were 116 KK–RKI organs in existence.[83] The XIV Party Congress set strict criteria for members of the KKs with emphasis on long party service.[84] Shkiryatov and Ordzhonikidze at the XV Party Congress complained that the most qualified workers were assigned to economic work and that the KK–RKI's were starved of competent officials. The congress resolution demanded improvements in the selection of personnel.[85]

In September 1928 there were 180 KK–RKI organs throughout the country. The number of KK members was given as 3,619, an average of twenty per commission. The social composition was predominantly proletarian, with 70 per cent workers, with 26 per cent of the officials having party membership dating to 1917 or earlier.[86] The poor quality of local control officials, however, remained a matter of intense concern. Ordzhonikidze in September 1929 complained that the KK–RKI organs were assigned only 'antediluvian party members who cannot be placed anywhere, whom no one wants'.[87] At the XVI Party Congress local officials reiterated these complaints.[88]

After 1929, resources and manpower were increasingly switched to the local control agencies to strengthen policy enforcement. In 1930 the new *raion* KK–RKI units were established and the weakness of the control agencies in the localities became a subject of mounting concern to TsKK–NKRKI's leadership.

RABKRIN AND THE 'SCIENTIFIC ORGANIZATION OF LABOUR'

The XII Party Congress entrusted NKRKI with leadership of the movement for the scientific organization of labour (*nauchnaya organizatsiya truda*, or NOT) in administration and production, with preparing proposals for improving and simplifying the apparatus, and ensuring effective co-ordination between institutions.

NKRKI in August 1923 established a Council for the Scientific Organization of Labour (SovNOT) to lead the scientific institutions active in this field. It was empowered to convene conferences regarding NOT, to correspond with foreign institutions, to acquire materials and literature on this subject, and through its journals and publications to disseminate information, and generally to stimulate initiative and interest in this work. It was also to lead the work of rationalization departments in the administrative and economic institutions.[89]

The NOT movement, inspired by American and German experience, reflected the cosmopolitan atmosphere of the NEP era. In industry the introduction of mass production techniques, the scientific work of F.W. Taylor and Frank Gilbreth on labour organization, provided a model for Soviet industry to emulate. These innovations appealed to a strong technocratic and science-orientated current in Russian Marxism. The adoption of NOT was, however, impeded by the lack of experienced workers. The adaptation of methods developed in the capitalist west also raised serious ideological problems.[90]

The principal institution responsible for promoting NOT was the Central Labour Institute, subordinate to VTsSPS. In 1923, the institute came under the supervision of NKRKI. The institute was led by A.K. Gastev, the leading Soviet disciple of Taylorism, and became an organizing centre for industrial rationalization. The institute advocated time and motion studies, the use of wage differentials, piece rates and the development of techniques of scientific management. It also urged closer trade union involvement in promoting production and innovation. The institute wished to develop the consciousness of workers as producers with responsibilities and interests in production.

Gastev's views were opposed by the left in the trade unions and the party who condemned his plans as attempts to emasculate the unions and increase labour exploitation. A rival leftist group was set up by P.M. Kerzhentsev, a former Proletkult leader, and organized around the journal *Time (Vremya)*. In July 1923, Kerzhentsev established the 'League of Time', a labour efficiency movement, which established its own voluntary cells in industry and by 1924 claimed 20,000 members. The supporters of this tendency were strongly represented in SovNOT.[91]

In order to resolve this conflict, NKRKI convened an all-Russian conference of NOT in March 1924. In the weeks preceding the conference, the two sides published their rival platforms.[92]

In *Pravda* in February 1924 Kerzhentsev denounced the Central Labour Institute for its indiscriminate advocacy of Taylorism and its disregard for the interests of labour.[93] The development of this movement, Kerzhentsev argued, required the mobilization of workers' initiative. The use of incentives and piece rates was denounced as divisive and calculated to weaken the position of the workers.

Kerzhentsev's views, supported by the left in the party and the unions, raised anew the anarcho-syndicalist spectre, and were scathingly attacked by A.A. Troyanovskii of NKRKI.[94] Gastev was supported by Zinoviev and Bukharin, and by prominent trade unionists like Tomskii and Andreev, and by E.F. Rozmirovich of NKRKI.[95]

At the all-Russian conference of NOT in March 1924, chaired by Kuibyshev, both factions presented alternative platforms. The leadership of the institute stressed Lenin's support for Taylorism and argued that it was 'incorrect and unprofitable to put the teachings of NOT on the basis of a polemic against Taylor and others'. The institute's platform was attacked by the Kerzhentsev group as a bourgeois influence within NOT, as a move designed to create an aristocracy within the working class, which showed an inability to see NOT as a 'class problem'.

Kuibyshev blamed the dispute on excessive theorizing and the failure to relate principles to practicalities. NOT, he argued, was not 'a complete system for the organization of labour' but should be regarded more modestly as a number of different methods whereby labour efficiency could be raised. The two approaches were complementary and should be combined for maximum effect.[96]

A compromise platform was eventually approved by the leaders of the two factions. The resolution, drafted under Kuibyshev's direction, endorsed the policy of the Central Labour Institute but included concessions to the opposition on the question of popular involvement.[97] The composition of SovNOT was changed, and the influence of Gastev and his supporters increased. Kerzhentsev and his supporters continued to press for a thorough-going Marxist approach to NOT, and denounced the uncritical adoption of western rationalization theory and techniques. He continued to advocate mass involvement in the NOT movement.[98]

After 1924, this intense debate subsided. The more pragmatic current – represented by Rozmirovich and Gastev – dominated the field of rationalization until 1929 when the debate was dramatically reopened.

THE PROBLEM OF DEFINING RABKRIN'S ROLE

The XIII Party Congress forced a major reappraisal of NKRKI's work. As a result of bitter managerial criticism during the 'scissors' crisis in 1923–4, NKRKI shifted its attention increasingly to rationalization work.[99] This was strongly resisted by NKRKI's controllers. Kuibyshev at the congress noted the demand from managers for such a change of emphasis.[100] Earlier, at a meeting of NKRKI workers, he had stressed the need 'to protest resolutely against the attempts to direct RKI's work along a purely academic path'.[101] It was essential, he argued, that NKRKI did not lose sight of others aspects of its work – controlling the apparatus, enforcing policy implementation and fighting official crime.

Kuibyshev wished to turn NKRKI into an administrative arm of the Politburo. Within NKRKI, E.F. Rozmirovich and A.K. Gastev fought to make rationalization the agency's prime function.[102] They wished to strengthen NKRKI as an independent, scientific institution, a counterweight to the party activists of TsKK. NKRKI's authority was to be increased and its relations with the state institutions placed on a new basis of co-operation.

Rozmirovich, an old associate of Lenin, became the driving force behind the rationalization movement in NKRKI. SovNOT became a major centre of rationalization and saw itself quite consciously as part of an international movement, organizing scientific research. NKRKI ran its own library and had its own publishing house which issued a vast quantity of rationalization literature.[103]

NKRKI in January 1926, on Rozmirovich's initiative, established the State Institute for Scientific Management (*Institut tekhnika upravleniya* or ITU) to work out proposals to rationalize the state and economic apparatus. Rozmirovich became its director. The institute became the hub of the rationalization movement in the USSR, drawing in dozens of specialists from different fields, publishing and translating a vast volume of rationalization literature. Attached to the institute was formed the

State Bureau of Organizational Construction (*Orgstroi*), headed by Rozmirovich, as a self-financing consultative agency which advised institutions on rationalizing their structures.

In 1925, NKRKI began publishing two weighty monthly periodicals on administrative and industrial rationalization – *Tekhnika upravleniya (Administrative Technique)* edited by Rozmirovich, and *Khozyaistvo i upravleniya (Economy and Administration)* edited by A.I. Stetskii.[104] The movement was strongly technocratic and internationalist in outlook. It took up the ideas of Russian Marxists such as A.A. Bogdanov and E.O. Ermanskii as well as western ideas developed by F.W. Taylor, F. Gilbreth and particularly those of the French theorist on administration Henri Fayol, which were strongly antithetical to Marxism.

In outlining NKRKI's work in 1924–5 Kuibyshev emphasized the need to select carefully its areas of operation, concentrating on key economic policy issues to assist the leading party and government organs.[105]

In NKRKI's report to Sovnarkom in November 1925, Kuibyshev demanded balance between the three aspects of the agency's work. Whilst rationalization was 'undoubtedly' NKRKI's 'basic task', the inspectorate could not turn itself into a technical agency. Control work remained of vital importance to ensure political control over the 'soulless machine' of the state apparatus. Moreover, to neglect NKRKI's work in investigating key policy issues would be to commit 'suicide', and to isolate itself from the leading party and government bodies.[106]

Kuibyshev at the XIV Party Congress again criticized the excessive emphasis on rationalization work at the expense of control and policy investigation.[107] This view was endorsed by the congress resolution.[108]

At the TsKK plenum in April 1926, Kuibyshev demanded an end to this prolonged bickering. The XIV Party Congress had denoted all three facets of NKRKI's work as of equal importance. Kuibyshev emphasized the need to correct the imbalance in the agency's work, away from rationalization back to control. He rebuked those in NKRKI who supported rationalization work and shunned the more abrasive aspect of control. Every TsKK–NKRKI worker had to acquire a respect and understanding of the importance of control and checking work.[109]

At the TsKK plenum, P.N. Amosov (head of NKRKI's accounting department) complained that the agency's proposals to rationalize accounting procedures in the metallurgical and textile industry had been obstructed by Vesenkha. The industrial glavki and trusts after 1923 created their own rationalization departments and spurned NKRKI proposals. To deal with this problem of 'departmental patriotism', Amosov demanded that NKRKI in the field of rationalization be given powers of compulsion, because only when its orders were obligatory would NKRKI achieve any success.[110]

Amosov's demand reflected the deep frustration felt by NKRKI's rationalizers. The proposal directly contradicted the XIV Party Congress's call for relations with the institutions to be based on co-operation. A.A. Sol'ts (head of NKRKI's Legal Department) condemned the proposal. He argued that excessive attention had been paid to rationalization work and that control work and the investigation of policy issues should in future take precedence.[111] Kuibyshev also condemned the proposal and rebutted Rozmirovich's accusation that he had neglected NKRKI's rationalization work.[112] The plenum rejected the proposal.

In the summer of 1926, the NKRKI central apparatus was reorganized into three main sectors, each responsible for a specific aspect of the agency's work – control, rationalization and policy investigation. Kuibyshev took charge of the Sector of Control.[113] In his diary in May 1926 he voiced his concern at NKRKI's drift into academism and his frustration with the rationalizers whom he denounced as 'crazy maniacs' who could not be trusted with 'serious, practical state work'.[114]

The XV Party Conference in October 1926 placed the checking of implementation at the centre of TsKK–NKRKI's work.[115]

In the face of continuing intransigence by the state institutions (especially from Vesenkha) in this field, NKRKI proposed to the Politburo and Sovnarkom in the summer of 1926 that the inspectorate be given wide-ranging compulsory powers in the field of rationalization.[116] In the spring of 1927, NKRKI renewed this campaign. Ya.A. Yakovlev (deputy narkom of NKRKI) in May 1927 demanded powers to 'compel' state institutions to simplify and reduce their apparatus.[117]

On 4 May 1927, Sovnarkom approved the draft decree submitted by NKRKI. This gave the agency compulsory powers over the institutions and enterprises in important areas – the simplification of accounting and bookkeeping, reducing staffs, reducing administrative overheads, reorganizing the structure of institutions, imposing disciplinary measures.[118] The voluntary principle regulating NKRKI's work was abandoned.

NKRKI's rationalization work was increasingly subject to political control by TsKK, and subject to the dictates of political expediency. After 1929 the independence of NKRKI's rationalizers came under growing attack and the very principles underlying its work were openly questioned.

Rabkrin and the Development of Popular Control

One of the most contentious aspects of NKRKI's work remained that of mass control. Following the collapse of the NKRKI assistant cells (*yacheiki sodeistviya*) in 1922, no attempt was made to grasp this nettle. The problem was ignored in Lenin's final articles on NKRKI and by the XII Party Congress. In 1923/4 it became the subject of a bitter row between NKRKI, the trade unions and the industrial managers.

NKRKI on 14 August 1923 prepared a draft decree to re-establish the cells.[119] They were to be set up in all major institutions and enterprises, as instruments of mass popular control, elected by the work force but subordinated to NKRKI. The cells were to be organized in conjunction with the trade unions and the party cells. The TsIK decree of November 1923, establishing NKRKI, instructed the inspectorate to prepare a thesis on the subject.[120] Consultations were held with Vesenkha, VTsSPS and other interested bodies. VTsSPS's presidium approved a cautious resolution 'to consider it expedient to organise assistant cells as an experiment in the larger centres and in certain enterprises'.[121]

In the autumn of 1923, the scheme met fierce opposition. Kuibyshev later noted that although the draft resolution for Sovnarkom had been prepared within 'modest limits', the plan met 'unexpectedly violent opposition from the economic organs and the trade unions'.[122] A Politburo commission recommended establishing elected RKI assistant cells in enterprises with over 500 workers and granting them wide powers. On 5 December 1923 a joint session of the Politburo and TsKK's presidium unanimously approved the plan.[123] The XIII Party Conference in January 1924 endorsed the decision.[124]

The prospect of yet another organization being established in the enterprises drew strong fire from managers. A compromise proposal in February 1924 that NKRKI should use the new revision commissions of the trusts in its work instead of the cells was quickly scotched.[125]

The TsKK plenum in March 1924, attended by managers, Red directors and trade unionists, discussed the subject. Kuibyshev emphasized the 'colossal significance' of the plan. N.M. Shvernik, presenting the main NKRKI report, stressed the need to establish the cells in order to provide the agency with 'thousands of eyes' in the enterprises and institutions.[126] The cells were to lead the work of the volunteer rationalization organizations in the enterprises (NOT commissions, cells of the League of Time) and to organize mass involvement in the struggle with bureaucracy.

F.E. Dzerzhinskii, Vesenkha's new chairman, argued that the plan was bureaucratically conceived, unproven and inexpedient. It would reinstitute the discredited '*glavkist*' methods of the past, and deprive managers and trade unionists of their responsibilities for improving the apparatus.[127] TsKK–NKRKI, he argued, should concentrate on improving the work of the higher economic organs and leave the enterprises alone.

VTsSPS's party fraction adamantly opposed NKRKI's plan. Dogadov of VTsSPS argued that the scheme would strip the trade unions of their responsibilities for rationalization and for organizing mass involvement in economic construction. The unions would be confined to narrow economic functions. The cells would disrupt management, functioning as departments of NKRKI. NKRKI, he proposed, should work through the trade union factory committees and enterprise production conferences.[128]

Nevertheless, the TsKK plenum resolved to establish NKRKI cells in all enterprises of over 500 workers.[129]

The opposition remained implacable. In April 1924 *Ekonomicheskaya zhizn'* canvassed the views of the main parties involved. The published articles revealed alarm amongst managers, with N.V. Arkhangelskii of the Institute of Red Directors, and P.A. Bogdanov, of Vesenkha RSFSR, voicing opposition. Whilst some unions (such as the leather workers) supported the plan, spokesmen of the powerful metal-workers, miners and print workers condemned the scheme.[130]

NKRKI officials in the press tried desperately to reassure the managers and trade unionists. The cells, A.M. Kaktyn' argued, were not a reincarnation of workers' control as developed in 1917. They aimed to channel workers' initiative so that it was not dispelled in diffuse 'democratic' and 'anarchistic' directions.[131]

But the Politburo was forced to bend with the current. NKRKI's assistant cells plan was dropped. The Central Committee with TsKK approved in its place a scheme for 'mutual assistance' between NKRKI and the trade unions.

On 21 May 1924 a joint NKRKI–VTsSPS circular was published which ruled that the trade union factory committees should become the main instruments of control in the enterprises.[132] Attached to the committees were to be formed special commissions responsible for production, trade, housing, safety and living conditions. The commissions were to organize popular involvement in control work and lead all rationalization organizations in the enterprise. NKRKI's work in the enterprises and institutions was to be organized through the trade unions.

Kuibyshev at the XIII Party Congress admitted that NKRKI's plan 'encountered great opposition from trade unionists and managers', and had been abandoned. Concerning NKRKI's work of popular control he assured the managers that they had no intention of reviving workers' control as practised in 1917/18.[133] The congress approved the new scheme prepared by the Central Committee and TsKK.[134] NKRKI's weak links with the populace remained a problem.[135]

NKRKI was reluctant to surrender control over the voluntary rationalization bodies to the trade unions. In March 1925 TsKK, Vesenkha and VTsSPS jointly instructed local RKI organs to avoid excessive interference in the rationalization work of the factory committees. Only in December 1925 did NKRKI finally authorize the liquidation of the NOT cells in the enterprises.[136] These arrangements did not secure any significant extension of mass involvement in rationalization work and remained a source of resentment in NKRKI.

The period of NEP saw a drastic decline in mass control work which NKRKI proved powerless to reverse, reflecting the new-found power of the managers and the trade unions.[137] An abrupt change occurred in 1928. As part of the left turn (which overturned the NEP consensus) political controls over managers and trade unionists were sharply tightened, and mass control organized through NKRKI was revived on a large scale.

Rabkrin and Judicial Control

The reorganization of TsKK–NKRKI in 1923 was associated with moves to regulate the agency's relations with organs of judicial control – NKYust, the Procuracy and OGPU. The period of NEP was associated with a significant relaxation of judicial and police control over the apparatus.

The XII Party Congress, instructed NKRKI not to become preoccupied with the uncovering of individual cases of illegality. As a result of pressure from the legal organs TsIK on 10 July 1923 removed NKRKI from the list of organs of criminal investigation.[138] NKRKI in future was obliged to submit evidence of crime to the legal organs for investigation, but retained the right to initiate legal proceedings against officials.[139] NKRKI was empowered to suspend all illegal orders and acts of the inspected organs. In 1924, as part of the relaxation of judicial controls, official crime was removed from the competence of the ordinary criminal courts and referred to special administrative courts.

NKRKI's controllers (headed by A.A. Sol'ts and with the support of

Kuibyshev) argued for greater involvement by NKYust, the Procurator and the courts in combating defects in the apparatus and the application of the principle of 'revolutionary legality'. Sol'ts in 1926 urged closer links between TsKK–NKRKI and the Procurator. These demands were successfully resisted by the legal organs.[140] In 1928, on NKRKI's initiative, judicial control over the state and economic institutions was again dramatically tightened (see pp. 162–3).

After 1923, close links were maintained between TsKK–NKRKI and the security organs. V.N. Mantsev, elected to TsKK by the XII Party Congress, from 1923 until 1925 served on the NKRKI and OGPU collegia.[141] Ya.Kh. Peters, a veteran Chekist with a formidable reputation, was elected to TsKK by the XIII Party Congress and from 1925 onwards served on both OGPU and NKRKI collegia and retained this crucial role until the early 1930s.[142]

The XV Party Congress elected three senior OGPU officials to TsKK – I.P. Pavlunovskii, M.A. Trilisser and S.F. Redens.[143] Pavlunovskii was appointed deputy narkom of NKRKI in 1930. In 1928, in the wake of the Shakhty trial and the grain procurements crisis, TsKK–NKRKI was pushed by the party leadership into still closer co-operation with OGPU. Trilisser became deputy narkom of NKRKI RSFSR in February 1930. The crisis of collectivization and industrialization further strengthened these links. The XVI Party Congress elected another four senior OGPU officials to TsKK – S.A. Messing, E.G. Evdokimov, V.A. Balitskii and G.E. Prokof'ev.[144] These personnel connections did not preclude competition between the two institutions; through these rival agencies the Politburo endeavoured to control the controllers.[145]

CONCLUSION

Lenin's plan for the reorganization of TsKK–NKRKI was never realized. From the outset TsKK–NKRKI was transformed into the control arm of the Politburo over both the party and state apparatus. Instead of the guardian of party unity TsKK–NKRKI became the instrument of the emergent Stalin faction which ruthlessly consolidated its hold on the party. TsKK–NKRKI after 1926 was transformed into a major power within the party–state apparatus. Under Ordzhonikidze TsKK–NKRKI became a major force within the political system, a central prop of the Stalin bloc and a decisive influence in the realm of policy-making. Lenin's attempt to balance the political and technical side of NKRKI's work was quickly jettisoned. NKRKI's role as an independent, scientific centre for rationalization was compromised as it took up its stance in developing and enforcing official policies. NKRKI after 1928 was quick to seize the opportunities offered to a determined control agency, assisting the party leadership in carrying through its modernization drive.

S.N. Ikonnikov, Sozdanie i deyatel'nost' ob''edinennykh organov TsKK–RKI v 1923–1934gg. (Moscow, 1971)
Plate V Presidium TsKK elected by the TsKK plenum convened by the XII Party Congress (1923). Sitting (left to right): Zhukovskii, A.A. Koreostelev, N.I. Il'in, V.V. Kuibyshev, A.A. Sol'ts, E.M. Yaroslavakii, T.S. Krivov. Standing: S.E. Chutskaev, A.S. Kiselev, M.F. Shkiryatov.

S.N. Ikonnikov, Sozdanie i deyatel'nost' ob"edinennykh organov TsKK–RKI v 1923–1934gg. (Moscow, 1971)

Plate VI Presidium TsKK elected by the TsKK plenum convened by the XIII Party Congress (1924). Sitting (left to right): E.M. Yaroslavskii, S.I. Gusev (fifth from left), V.V. Kuibyshev, N.M. Yanson, M.F. Shkiryatov, N.K. Krupskaya, N.M. Shvernik. Standing: A.V. Shotman (second from right).

4 Rabkrin and the 'Scissors Crisis' (1923–4)

Immediately following its unification TsKK–NKRKI was thrust into the middle of the political stage. Lenin's demise created a fluid situation in the party. A power struggle ensued in which the triumvirate of Zinoviev, Kamenev and Stalin, with the assistance of TsKK–NKRKI, sought to capture the levers of power and to squeeze Trotsky out of the race. This coincided with the 'scissors crisis' which cast doubt on the viability of NEP. Against this background TsKK–NKRKI sought to define for itself its role within the political system.

The new leader of the TsKK–NKRKI, Valerian Vladimirovich Kuibyshev, represented the new breed of younger party leaders.[1] His background was provincial middle class. Joining the party at the age of sixteen he lacked the education and cosmopolitan grounding of the older generation. He worked in the Bolshevik underground and in 1917–18 led the party organization in Samara, a stronghold of the Left Communists. He was one of the leaders of the Left Communists in 1918 but in November of that year adhered to the party line.

During the civil war, he worked as a political commissar and assisted in consolidating Soviet power in Central Asia. He won a reputation as a staunch defender of party orthodoxy and was a stern critic of the Mensheviks and Left SRs. In the trade union controversy in 1920 he supported Lenin's position,[2] demanding the expulsion of dissidents from the Central Committee. After the X Party Congress he was sent back to Samara to break the Workers' Opposition's control over the local party organization.

After the civil war, his career blossomed. He worked briefly in VTsSPS and Vesenkha and in October 1921 was appointed head of Glavelektro. He was elected a candidate member of the Central Committee at the X Party Congress. The XI Party Congress elected him a full member of the Central Committee and a candidate member of the Politburo. In April 1922 Kuibyshev and Molotov were appointed as Stalin's deputies in the party Secretariat.

Kuibyshev took to TsKK–NKRKI a reputation as a political loyalist and as a tough and efficient administrator. He was no ideologist but a man of strong convictions. His early leftist sympathies persisted in his antipathy towards the non-party specialists. He sought to cultivate his expertise in the field of economic management, planning and scientific rationalization, but his grasp of technical matters was suspect. He was not averse to political scheming, and under his leadership, TsKK–NKRKI was transformed into a loyal instrument of the Politburo. Under Kuibyshev, the day-to-day running of NKRKI was entrusted to his two deputies, S.E. Chutskaev and N.M. Yanson.

TsKK-NKRKI AND THE 'SCISSORS CRISIS'

TsKK–NKRKI's first two years as an unified agency proved difficult. The new agency lacked support within the party, and it encountered immense problems in organizing its work.[2] Intense ideological argument raged over NKRKI's work in the field of NOT. Strong managerial and trade union opposition successfully thwarted plans to establish NKRKI's assistant cells in the institutions and enterprises.

The regime's economic policy in 1923–4 was jeopardized by the 'scissors crisis'. The sharp rise in industrial prices relative to the price of agricultural produce, which Trotsky highlighted at the XI Party Congress, threatened trading relations between town and countryside. The Politburo settled on a policy of concessions for the peasantry, aimed at boosting agricultural output and stimulating peasant demand for industrial goods. Trotsky advocated a radical policy which sought to correct the basic imbalance in the economy between industry and agriculture, and, through state planning, to give priority to the development of heavy industry.

The Central Committee in September 1923 established three party commissions to deal with different aspects of the crisis: (i) the scissors commission to deal with the disparity in agricultural and industrial prices, (ii) a wages commission to deal with discontent in industry; (iii) a commission to examine internal party matters. The direct involvement of the party in resolving the crisis was symptomatic of its growing involvement in economic management.

Trotsky, in a letter to the Politburo in October 1923, denounced the leadership's economic policy. The same month the 'Platform of the Forty Six' presented the left's demands for a radical change in economic policy.[3] The joint Central Committee–TsKK plenum in October 1923 instructed the Politburo to speed up the work of the three commissions and take resolute measures to resolve the crisis.[4] In 1923–4 TsKK–NKRKI was drawn directly into the management of the economy.

Budgetary and Monetary Policy

In 1923–4 the Politburo rejected Trotsky's expansionary policies and adopted instead the cautious policy of a balanced budget and a stable currency. In order to stimulate the economy the tax on the peasantry was cut, thus limiting the budgetary allocations for industry. NKFin, headed by G. Ya. Sokolnikov, was the architect of this policy of orthodox budgetary management. NKFin drafted the budget and supervised financial policy generally.

NKRKI in June 1923 reasserted its claim to check the drafting of the state budget.[5] In the decree of TsIK of 12 November 1923 the inspectorate was given responsibility for 'the detailed examination of the quarterly and yearly budget of the USSR, of the union and local republics'.[6] This work was carried out by NKRKI's finance section which was headed until 1930 by Z.G. Zangvil'. V.A. Avanesov (deputy narkom NKRKI) in February 1924 argued that NKRKI was less concerned with the technical details of the budget than ensuring that it conformed to party policy.[7] In 1923–4 NKFin's influence in shaping budget policy remained dominant.[8]

In the summer of 1923 the party cut taxes on the peasantry and endeavoured to drive up the price of grain in order to increase agricultural marketings. In September 1923, to finance the grain-purchasing campaign for 1923–4, Sovnarkom authorized an increase in the rouble issue which resulted in rapid inflation.[9]

Early in 1924, the currency was reformed with the establishment of the chervontsy rouble as the basic unit of currency. The rouble was linked to gold and future issues were tightly regulated by the treasury and Gosbank. Priority was set on the maintenance of a stable currency. The regime strove to create a balanced budget, pursued a cautious policy in the field of credit, and worked for a favourable balance in foreign trade. Strict financial orthodoxy was enforced by NKFin.[10]

All this severely constrained the Politburo's economic policy options. The left wing of the party was strongly critical and argued for a more active, interventionist role for the state.[11] Within the Politburo, the policy was viewed with concern, especially by Kamenev, who feared it would restrict expansion.

An NKRKI commission, headed by S.E. Chutskaev, supervised the currency reform's implementation.[12] In March 1924 TsKK–NKRKI instructed the local control agencies to assist the financial organs to: (i) ensure that budget deficits in the central and local state organs were reduced to a minimum; (ii) stimulate trade turnover in the economic organs; (iii) help attain active trading balances; (iv) establish strict financial discipline in state and economic organs.[13]

The reform successfully stabilized the currency and provided the framework within which the regime's economic policy was to be developed. Kuibyshev stressed the importance of the reform in combating inflation and providing a basis for increased planning in the economy.[14]

Economic Planning

Trotsky, in his letter to the Politburo in October 1923, condemned the failure to utilize Gosplan to deal with the 'scissors crisis'. Planning was essential to divert funds into the heavy industry sector, to correct the basic imbalance in the economy and ensure the most rapid expansion of the economy under state direction. Trotsky was supported by the left wing of the party and by the leftists in Gosplan and Vesenkha. At the Central Committee plenum in December 1923, Trotsky's position was defended by G.L. Pyatakov and E.A. Preobrazhenskii. These proposals were vigorously resisted by the Politburo and denounced by Rykov and Kamenev as adventurist and unrealistic.[15]

The XIII Party Conference in January 1923 rejected the opposition's demands for more economic planning, although its resolution noted the development of more favourable conditions for the extension of economic planning and the growing need for planning to correct imbalances in the economy.[16]

Following the conference, efforts were directed at strengthening Gosplan. In January 1924, A.D Tsyurupa was appointed its chairman, and party spokesmen adopted a more sympathetic approach to the cause of planning.[17]

In the spring of 1924 a high-powered TsKK–NKRKI commission carried out a detailed investigation of Gosplan. NKRKI spokesmen argued for the expansion of Gosplan's role and the strengthening of its links with the agency.[18] Kuibyshev at the TsKK plenum in March 1924 enthusiastically reviewed the commission's work.[19] The commission also enjoyed support in the party.[20] TsKK–NKRKI approved its recommendations which were widely published.[21]

Gosplan's principal task, it argued, should be 'to establish a general perspective plan for the economic activity of the USSR for a number of years (5–10)'. The report condemned the prevailing disorganization in NKFin's allocation of credits. Gosplan should draw up a financial plan for the allocation of finance and credit which was to be co-ordinated

with the state budget, thus enabling the state to play a more interventionist role in stimulating industrial recovery. Gosplan was to work out
measures for the plan's implementation, and thus ensure for STO the
means to regulate the economy. Gosplan's powers were to be extended
and 'the people's commissariats and not merely their planning commissions should be accountable to Gosplan'.[22]

A new organizational centre comprising Gosplan, TsSU and NKRKI
was to be established, and given responsibility for planning, co-ordinating and directing the economy. TsSU was to provide Gosplan with
statistical data on the state of the economy. NKRKI was to carry out
investigations on Gosplan's behalf and assist in enforcing planning
directives.[23] The commission envisaged a move from financial management towards a system of planning. TsKK–NKRKI's proposals
were supported by Tsyurupa in Gosplan.[24]

Sokolnikov's NKFin strongly opposed any scheme to plan credit
assignments or any proposals which threatened its supremacy in
economic policy.[25] In the party, the close affinity between TsKK–
NKRKI's commission's proposals and those of the left caused alarm.
The successful resolution of the 'scissors crisis' by traditional methods of
financial management in the spring of 1924 also served to re-established
NKFin's authority.

Confronted by this opposition, Kuibyshev was forced into a *volte face*
at the XIII Party Congress. The TsKK presidium, he claimed, having
heard the TsKK-NKRKI commission's report on Gosplan, was
'shocked' by its 'resolute and hasty conclusions'. After long deliberation
the presidium 'had the courage' to reject its proposals.[26] In place of this
radical reform, a series of modest measures were worked out with
Gosplan for generally improving the organization of its work.[27] The
affair irreparably damaged relations between Kuibyshev and Sokolnikov. The incident, however, revealed a powerful pro-planning lobby
(including TsKK–NKRKI) and a willingness by some party leaders to
flirt with the leftist planners.

RABKRIN AND INDUSTRIAL POLICY

Industrial policy in 1923–4 was dominated by the 'scissors crisis'. The
Politburo sought to reduce industrial prices in order to correct the
trading imbalance between town and countryside, and thus consolidate
the alliance (*smychka*) between the peasants and workers. NKRKI was
drawn into this work through its specialist competence in rationalizing
and accounting work.

Reduction of Industrial Costs and Prices

In the summer of 1923 the party approved a number of measures to cut industrial costs and prices. A credit squeeze was applied by Gosbank to compel industry to reduce its prices and boost sales. The Central Committee in September established its 'scissors commission' to cut costs and prices. Trotsky advocated measures to improve industrial efficiency and boost output in order to cut costs, but condemned the Politburo's policy of cutting profits which reduced available resources for investment. In his letter to the Central Committee in October 1923 he condemned the resort to administrative measures to cut industrial costs as arbitrary, and refused to participate in the commission's work. Vesenkha, under Rykov, only reluctantly in the autumn of 1923 abandoned its commitment to profit maximization. Within Vesenkha, official policy continued to be opposed by the left, headed by Pyatakov.[28]

In 1923–4, TsKK–NKRKI worked alonside the Central Committee's 'scissors commission'. The reduction of production costs became the main focus of NKRKI's work in industry.

Coal industry

In 1923–4, an NKRKI commission (headed by N.K. Goncharov of TsKK) investigated Donugol, the principal coal trust in the Donbass, to determine production costs in the industry and to ascertain the scope for price reduction.[29]

The basic monthly accounts of Donugol were compiled by UGKP (the Administration of the State Coal Industry). These accounts were used by Gosplan to set the production costs and selling price for the trust. In 1922 Gosplan calculated production costs at 17.21 tovarnykh kopeks (k) per pud, between 6 and 7 tovarnykh k below UGKP's estimate. NKRKI commission determined that the actual production cost of coal in 1922/3 was 16.55 tovarnykh k. This was broadly in line with Gosplan's estimate based on theoretical adjustments of UGKP's figures. The commission worked out new accounting procedures for the trust, which Kuibyshev claimed were approved by the leaders of the Donets industry.[30]

The cost of coal, calculated in prewar roubles, had increased from 10k per pud in 1913 to 14.37k per pud in 1923. This increase in cost the commission blamed mainly on the disorganization in Donugol's administration. A. Segal', the commission's engineer, argued that these defects could be corrected in the coming year. With the introduction of khozraschet into the mining trust, administrative efficiency would be

improved. The conclusion of a new collective agreement with the trade
unions should also aim to secure a great increase in labour productivity.[31]

Gosplan calculated production costs of coal for 1923/4 at 23
chernovykh k per pud, the NKRKI commission at 20.5.[32] The controversy over costs became embroiled in the debate over output. Already
in 1923 difficulties had been encountered in selling coal stocks.
NKRKI's efforts to reduce costs and prices was aimed at easing the sales
crisis. Gosplan approved an output target for 1923/4 of 500 million
puds, 323 million puds to be produced by Donugol. The trust lobbied
hard to have its output target raised further.[33]

In February 1924 a joint session of TsKK and Gosplan discussed coal
output for 1923/4. A Politburo commission (led by Tsyurupa and
Avanesov, and including Dzerzhinskii, Kuibyshev, Krzhizhanovskii,
Mezhlauk, Strumilin and Gubkin) examined the matter.[34] Donugol's
output target was raised from 415 million puds to 455–500 million
puds.[35]

Gosplan resolved that the production cost of coal for 1923/4 should
be set at 20.6k, in line with NKRKI's target. The selling price of coal was
set at 21 chernovykh k.[36] State subsidies covered the deficiency between
total costs (including credit repayments and trading costs) and price. On
NKRKI's advice, a special commission was established to deal with the
sales crisis. In the following year, the situation in the coal industry
considerably improved. In 1924/5 the production cost of coal stood at
16.05k per pud.[37]

Metallurgical industry

In the autumn of 1923 a TsKK–NKRKI commission, headed by the
engineer P.V. Grunwald, investigated the Yugostal metallurgical trust.
The commission examined the trust's oldest plant at Yuzovka, with the
aim of determining production costs and selling price of metal for the
whole trust.[38]

The commission reported that production costs per pud of pig iron
had risen from 46.8k in 1913 to 1r 24.5k in May 1923, an increase of 266
per cent. By November 1923 the production costs were estimated at
1r 33.21k. The commission proposed measures to reduce the price of
iron ore, manganese and coke supplied to the works and to concentrate
production in the most efficient works. It advocated that production
costs for 1923/4 should be set at 1r 8.5k per pud. To cover administrative
costs, tax, insurance, amortization and profits a further 15 per cent was
to be placed on the basic production costs giving a price of 1r 25k. These
cost and price levels were to be applied to the whole Yugostal trust.

The Convention of Metal Syndicates in October 1923 proposed that the price for pig iron in 1923/4 should be set at 1r 50k. Yugostal the same month proposed a price of 1r 80k. NKRKI's proposal to reduce the price to 1r 25k placed enormous pressure on the industry at a time when labour costs were rising. A.A. Troyanovskii, head of NKRKI's industrial inspectorate, argued that the selling price of pig iron should eventually be reduced to 75k per pud.[39]

In February 1924, TsKK–NKRKI discussed its proposals with representatives of Yugostal, Glavmetall, Gosplan, NKPS, NKFin and the unions. The scheme encountered strong opposition. Yugostal complained that the commission's provision for credit repayments at 6.6 per cent of production costs was inadequate. Glavmetall and Gosplan objected to the proposal that profit margins should be calculated at 2 per cent of production costs and proposed instead a level of 5 per cent. The matter was discussed by an interdepartmental commission attached to NKRKI's industrial inspectorate. NKRKI's price of 1r 25k was approved by the Convention of Metal Syndicates, Glavmetall and Gosplan's industrial sector. With an output of 32 million puds of pig iron this involved a saving of 8 million roubles. The target was accepted by the industry under protest. In April 1924 Troyanovskii expressed the hope that Glavmetall and Vesenkha would 'without delay and energetically stir themselves to put into effect all of RKI's proposals'.[40]

NKRKI in 1924 also investigated the Nadezhdinskii metallurgical works in the Urals. The commission's findings were discussed by an interdepartmental commission attached to NKRKI. As a result, the commission cut the selling price for pig iron from the trust from 1r 50k to 1r 25k per pud in 1923/4, to be subsequently reduced to 95k.[41]

The price of pig iron for 1923/4 for both Yugostal and the Urals industry was set at 1r 22k.[42] In the following twelve months the production costs for pig iron were dramatically cut. The actual level of production costs achieved in 1924/5 was 83k per pud.[43]

Cotton and light industry

In the winter of 1923–4 an NKRKI commission, headed by V.M. Kosarev, investigated the Turkestan cotton industry. The commission was attached to STO and included experts from NKFin and Vesenkha. On the basis of NKRKI's recommendations, the price of raw cotton was cut from 27r 79k to 21r 50k per pud.[44]

NKRKI also claimed 'significant results' in other industries (Bakhmut and Baskunchak trusts), paper (Tsentrobumtrest), printing (various printing works in Moscow) and textiles.[45] Kuibyshev noted that the price cuts would boost sales to the peasant market and stimulate production.[46] TsKK–NKRKI worked alongside the Central Committee's 'scissors commission'. Concerning its investigation of the printing industry Kuibyshev noted:

> All measures which were noted in connection with this were introduced by us for the approval of the Politburo and STO commission for reducing prices and were there adopted.[47]

Iron ore industry

In the summer of 1924 NKRKI and NKRKI UkSSR investigated the Southern Ore Trust which administered the giant Krivoi Rog complex. As the main supplier of iron ore the trust's work was of central importance for the country's metallurgical industry.

The trust recommended that production costs for 1924/5 should be 8.0k per pud. NKRKI recommended that costs should be set at 6.6k per pud.[48] NKRKI's commission was highly critical of the trust's work – the disorganization in production, the excessive spending on materials and fuel. Overstaffing and low labour productivity was also criticized and attributed to the collective agreement signed by the trust and the union in August 1924.

NKRKI's figures were contested by the trust, and were referred to an interdepartmental commission for resolution. The commission set production costs for iron ore for 1924/5 at 7.7k (a reduction of 3.7 per cent on the figure of the trust), as opposed to the 17.4 per cent cut demanded by NKRKI. The interdepartmental commission's figures were approved by Sovnarkom. The trust successfully attained the cost levels proposed. For 1924/5, the production costs for iron ore was 7.7k per pud.[49]

Oil industry

NKRKI, in the summer of 1924, investigated the main oil trust, Azneft, to determine production costs.[50] The commission, headed by A. Segal' but supervised by Novoselov of TsKK, carried out an extensive examination of the trust's expenditure, cost accounting, technical efficiency, labour productivity and administration.

Crude oil production had fallen from 570 million puds in 1913 to 230 million puds in 1921. Oil remained a basic fuel for industry and its price a major determinant of industry's production costs. NKRKI calculated production costs in Azneft at 25.6 k per pud. On this basis, Gosplan in the autumn of 1924 fixed the selling price for 1924/5 at 30 k per pud. Azneft estimated production costs at 32–3 k per pud.

NKRKI's calculations assumed a dramatic cut in amortization costs.

Segal' argued that the trust's basic capital should be valued at 110 million chernovykh roubles. Amortization costs were calculated at 17 per cent of basic capital. With an output of oil of 260–279 million puds in 1924/5, amortization costs were calculated at 7.5–7.7 k per pud. In addition, NKRKI proposed rescheduling the repayment of credits to reduce current costs.

Azneft vigorously contested NKRKI's figures. Segal' noted the bitter hostility of Azneft's managers to his calculation; they feared that the price for crude oil would be set at the level of production cost.

Segal' defended the price approved by Gosplan, arguing that it was competitive with other fuels and that, if proper measures were applied, production costs could be reduced sufficiently to allow the trust to accumulate a surplus for future investment.[51]

N. Solov'ev challenged NKRKI's calculations. The trust's basic capital was valued by Azneft at 220 million pre-war roubles. The replacement cost of capital was 250 million roubles rather than the 110 million roubles calculated by NKRKI. Amortization costs calculated by the trust for 1924/5 were 15 k per pud compared to NKRKI's figure of 7.5 k. NKRKI's calculations, Solov'ev argued, placed 'under threat the economic basis of one of the largest and most important of the state trust'.[52] A. Prityula denounced Segal's figures as bogus, and claimed that they had been given credence only because they coincided with the interests of the main industrial oil consumers.[53]

Unperturbed by these criticisms, Segal' attacked Azneft's technical backwardness and the disorder in its administration. NKRKI also advanced proposals for rationalizing the trust.[54] In February 1925 Vesenkha instructed Azneft to implement NKRKI's instructions.[55]

NKRKI in 1924 also investigated the smaller Grozneft oil trust. As a result of NKRKI's work, the proposed level of production costs for 1924/5 was cut from 25.18 k per pud to 15.79 k per pud.[56]

Although substantial reductions in the production costs of both trusts were secured in 1924/5, in neither case were NKRKI's targets reached, in spite of the pressure placed on Azneft and Grozneft. In 1924/5, the actual production costs in Azneft were 30.08 k per pud and in Grozneft 19.82 k per pud.[57]

Other industries

NKRKI also investigated a number of individual works. Its investigation of the Petrovskii metallurgical works in the summer of 1924 produced proposals for a drastic cut in production costs for pig iron, steel, roofing metal and shaped metal. On the basis of NKRKI's calculations Gosplan determined production costs for these items for 1924/5.[58] Similar investigations were carried out at the Makeevka metallurgical works and at the Krasnyi Aksai and Profintern agricultural implements works.[59]

In 1924, NKRKI investigated twelve works in the Moscow region which specialized in instrument manufacture and claimed large cost reductions. At the Elektrostal works production costs for high-quality instrument steel was cut by 10 per cent.[60] NKRKI's investigations at a number of electrical power stations also resulted in proposals for cuts in generating costs and in the tariff charged to industry.[61]

NKRKI in 1923/4 examined the state of accounting work in fifty-two enterprises and in 1924/5 in 132 enterprises.[62] This was used also as a a means of forcing down industrial costs, leading to serious altercations between NKRKI and the trusts and enterprises.

NKRKI's impact on industrial costs and prices in 1923/4 cannot be exactly quantified. NKRKI's investigations supplemented the immense pressure applied directly by Vesenkha, and by Gosbank through the credit squeeze. By the spring of 1924 substantial cuts in industrial prices had been secured and the worst of the 'scissors crisis' had passed before NKRKI's work came into full swing.[63] In the year ending in October 1924, the wholesale price of all industrial goods was reduced by 29 per cent.[64]

Wages Policy

Soviet industry in July 1923 was hit by a wave of labour unrest. This was caused by a sharp fall in real wages in individual sectors, exacerbated by lengthy delays in wage payment and the substitution of goods in place of money wages.[65] The introduction of the chernovykh rouble in 1923 created additional difficulties in calculating comparative wages in different sectors. Attempts by light industry in 1923 to maximize profits created problems of liquidity and resulted in delays in the settling of accounts between enterprises.

Mounting labour unrest coincided with growing oppositional activity within the party and Trotsky's breach with his colleagues over economic policy. The Politburo in August set up a special commission (including Dzerzhinskii, Kuibyshev, Avanesov and Rudzutak) to look into the problem.[66] The Central Committee in September approved the commission's proposals and authorized large increases in the wages of workers in heavy industry and on the railways where discontent was most acute. It also approved measures to ensure that wages were paid promptly and in cash. TsKK–NKRKI was given responsibility for enforcing these measures.[67]

The Central Committee on 24 September authorized the setting up of a special wages commission.[68] On 22 November (on the Politburo's orders) this was formed, comprising four representatives of TsKK, and individual representatives of the Central Committee, NKFin, NKTrud and VTsSPS. The commission, headed by Kuibyshev, had the status of a joint Central Committee–TsKK commission.[69]

The XIII Party Congress in January 1924 demanded urgent measures by industry and the trade unions to combat deficiencies in the payment of wages.[70] In January, a new TsKK–NKRKI wages commission was set up, chaired by N.M. Yanson and including representatives of the Central Committee, NKFin, NKTrud and VTsSPS.[71] This operated through its own commissioners in the main industrial centres and relied in its work on NKRKI's apparatus.[72] NKRKI instructed its local organs to assist in the commission's work.[73]

Following TsKK representations to the Politburo, STO in March 1924 was obliged to merge its own wages commission with the TsKK–NKRKI commission, transferring to the latter the right to report directly to STO.[74]

The TsKK–NKRKI wages commission was empowered to investigate enterprises of all-union significance. It was responsible for uncovering delays and deficiencies in the payment of wages.[75] Particular attention was paid to eradicating delays in wage payment and defects in food supply in key industries such as the Donbass coalfield.[76] Attention was also directed to the problem of low labour productivity in industry, and examination of how the wage system could be used more effectively to boost efficiency.[77] In July 1924, the commission adopted a resolution to establish uniformity in wages policy in the institutions and industries.

The commission was empowered to approve collective agreements between the unions and the institutions and to resolve disputes in the interpretation of wage regulations.[78] NKRKI also supervised the enforcement of party policy concerning the wages paid to specialists.[79] This was part of a strategy to take the sting out of worker discontent. The problem of delays in wage payment had been eased by the spring of 1924, but was not fully resolved until the end of the year.[80]

The Central Committee in August 1924 approved a resolution (based on a TsKK–NKRKI report) to improve labour productivity.[81] Kuibyshev in a speech to the Club of Red Directors in September 1924 noted that in 1923/4 industrial output had grown by 24 per cent and production costs by 30 per cent. Wages continued to rise faster than output, with consequent inflationary pressure on prices. Gosplan estimated labour productivity in industry at only 66 per cent of the pre-war level. The increased utilization of capacity had lowered costs, but had been negated by an average increase in wages of 90 per cent in eighteen months. The problem, Kuibyshev argued, could be solved in the long run by the modernization of industry: 'electrification, mechanisation, and the introduction of new technical processes and the more rational utilisation of the installations at our disposal'. The problem, however, required immediate attention – by the improved utilization of labour, by the intensification of the labour process and the maximum use of working time. Recalling his speech to the NOT conference earlier in the year, he noted 'even Lenin declared that the practical application of piecework and of everything which is scientific and progressive in the Taylor system is necessary'.[82]

RABKRIN AND AGRICULTURAL POLICY

Lenin in 1923 stressed the role of NKRKI in maintaining the worker–peasant alliance and informing the Politburo of rifts in relations between these two classes. A key part of NKRKI's work was in monitoring agricultural policy, especially the work of TsSU, Gosplan, NKTorg and NKZem in determining the size of the grain harvest. On these estimates, the state budget and general economic policy hinged.

In dealing with the 'scissors crisis' the Politburo endeavoured to raise the price of agricultural produce through the expansion of grain exports, taking advantage of the good harvest of 1922. This strategy was promoted by NKFin as a means of strengthening the peasant economy, building up the country's foreign currency reserves, and through increased consumer demand stimulating industrial recovery. This policy was criticized by the opposition, and was resisted by Gosplan; the scheme's critics favoured a cheap food policy.[83]

The export of grain was stoutly defended by the party leaders at the XII Party Congress. A limited liability company, Eksportkhleb, was set up by NKVneshTorg to organize the operation. An export target of 225 m puds of grain was approved by Sovnarkom.

A TsKK–NKRKI commission was established to assist the responsible agencies in this work. This reported to the Politburo and TsKK presidium on 5 June 1923 that the proposed target was fully attainable. On its recommendation, a special STO commission was established to monitor the operation. NKRKI supervised the purchasing operations,

and investigated transport and storage arrangements and the organization of railway and port facilities to handle the shipments.[84] The
successful realization of the plan helped ease the 'scissors crisis'.

The tax concessions granted to the peasantry constituted the most
controversial aspect of official policy in agriculture. At the XII Party
Congress the policy was strongly criticized by the left. Trotsky argued
the need to increase the tax burden on the peasants as a means of
financing new industrial investment. He was supported by prominent
leftist planners and executives such as Preobrazhenskii and Pyatakov.
The most extreme advocate of this strategy (Yu. Larin) proposed a 20
per cent increase in the tax on the peasantry.[85]

The Politburo emphasized instead the need to placate peasant
grievances and saw tax cuts as the best means of stimulating production
and promoting recovery. At the XII Party Congress Zinoviev and
Kamenev defended the policy. Kamenev noted the need to produce a
unified, monetary tax and to reduce the tax burden. Sokolnikov,
narkom of NKFin, envisaged a reduction in the tax burden on
individual households as agriculture recovered. The congress confirmed
official policy, stressing the primacy of agriculture in the economy and
the dependence of industry on this sector.

In May 1923 the new unified tax was approved, to be paid either in
kind or in currency. TsKK–NKRKI investigated the organization of the
tax system and its impact on the peasantry and submitted its report to
the Central Committee. Sovnarkom, on 24 August 1923, substantially
cut the tax.[86] Kuibyshev, in reviewing the Sovnarkom decree, stressed
NKRKI's part in developing this policy:

> Thanks to our proposal the general sum of tax was cut by 5% and thus
> 18% of tax payers – the poor peasants [bednyaks], the horseless
> households – were freed from paying tax.[87]

This reform was intended to stimulate production and to lessen the
impact of party policies on stratification in the countryside.

NKRKI in the autumn of 1923 supervised the collection of this tax by
NKFin.[88] The tax reductions were evenly applied to all households and
did little to redress the growing inequality in the countryside. More
seriously, the policy dashed the hopes of the left, who wished to channel
investment into heavy industry.

The reliance on economic incentives and market forces to stimulate
agricultural production accelerated social differentiation in the countryside, and strengthened the position of the kulaks. The precise impact
of NEP in the countryside remained unclear and this uncertainty

fostered doubt and speculation. At the XII Party Conference in January 1924, Zinoviev, Rykov and Krupskaya voiced disquiet at the effect which the party's policy had on the structure of peasant society and on the power of different strata.[89]

In 1924 TsSU published a major report on stratification amongst the peasantry. TsKK–NKRKI also investigated these processes. In 1923 a commission (headed by Kuibyshev) carried out a preliminary study of the problem.[90] Early in 1924 a report on this question was compiled by Ya. A. Yakovlev, head of NKRKI's agricultural section and head also of the Central Committee department for agriculture.[91]

At the XIII Party Congress in May 1924 Kamenev, in his economic report, drew on the work of both TsSU and NKRKI in assessing the effect of party policy on rural stratification. On this basis, he claimed that the poor and middle peasants remained the decisive force in the countryside.[92] The alliance with these strata in the countryside, it was argued, had not been compromised by party policy. The congress assigned TsKK–NKRKI special responsibility for monitoring the growth of the agricultural co-operatives.[93]

RABKRIN'S RELATIONS WITH THE ECONOMIC INSTITUTIONS

The unification of NKRKI and TsKK strengthened the party's hold over the state administration and eroded the power of Sovnarkom and STO. Increasingly TsKK–NKRKI came to be viewed as the arm of the Politburo within the government apparatus. TsKK control over NKRKI was firmly established. In enforcing official policy during the 'scissors crisis', TsKK officials closely directed NKRKI's work.

In October 1924 A.M. Kaktyn', head of NKRKI's economic inspectorate, reported a 'mass exodus' of specialists from his department. TsKK officials interfered excessively in the work of the specialists, regarded them with distrust and made them feel like 'pariahs'. Another official noted the reluctance of agronomists and engineers to work in NKRKI because they had to follow a 'class approach', 'a certain political line', which was not required elsewhere.[94] Criticisms were made of the unrealistic demands placed on industry and the damage done to NKRKI's reputation and its relations with the institutions.

NKRKI's department for accounting and bookkeeping, headed by P.N. Amosov (which had been active in the campaign to force down production costs) came in for particular criticism. A meeting of accountants from Vesenkha and the trusts in 1923 resolved to boycott this organization and to refuse future co-operation with NKRKI.[95] NKRKI's proposals to rationalize accounting work were also blocked by industry.

These problems were exacerbated by NKRKI's campaign against official crime. In 1923 and 1924 NKRKI's industrial inspectorate carried out 400 investigations of various industrial, trading and administrative agencies. As a result NKRKI instituted legal proceedings against 386 individuals, a third of whom were found guilty of various misdemeanours – mismanagement, corruption, bribery, misappropriation, abuse of power, etc.[96] In at least one case, the death penalty was applied.[97]

Early in 1924 a determined counter-attack against NKRKI was launched. Through the defeat of NKRKI's assistant cell scheme, the managerial interest recouped some of the ground lost by TsKK–NKRKI's establishment in 1923. NKRKI's plan for the extension of Gosplan's role was hastily withdrawn. Other NKRKI reports – on the construction of the Volkhovstroi power station and on the organization of internal trade – were also savagely criticized by industrial spokesmen.[98]

By the spring of 1924 NKRKI's relations with industry were tense. Attempts were made to lure key specialists from NKRKI to industry, which argued a prior claim to their expertise.[99] Industry resorted to concealment, obstruction and non-co-operation. This created a counter-reaction, and further attempts to impose NKRKI proposals on the unwilling institutions. The second all-Russian conference of NOT, convened by NKRKI in March 1924, stressed the need for hamonious relations with the institutions.[100]

At the TsKK plenum in March 1924, Kuibyshev noted difficulties in NKRKI's relations with the legislative bodies:

At the last plenum one of the deficiencies noted in the work of RKI was the excessively small quantity of realized material. The colossal investigative work which was carried out did not yield the results anticipated by way of the implementation of specific concrete proposals based on investigation results.[101]

This state of affairs damaged morale in NKRKI. Measures were needed to rectify NKRKI's work and ensure closer co-operation with the party and government organs. In a speech to future NKRKI workers at Sverdlov university in April 1924 Kuibyshev denounced departmentalism and localism, warned of the danger of excess control in alienating the institutions and undermining responsibility. The problem of NKRKI's ineffectualness had been only partially eased by its links with the party organs:

> In practice we experience great difficulty in realising the improvements which we propose because the departmental heads often refuse to implement any of our measures. In the majority of cases we are assisted by the party order. The unification of RKI and TsKK gives us the opportunity to find justice or to find such an organ which will help us implement these measures . . . In all cases this is not so easy because the leaders of the economic organs know this route as well and they oppose the proposals which we make to the party Central Committee. In the Central Committee we have to struggle with the commissariats on many questions.[102]

TsKK–NKRKI AND THE INTERNAL PARTY STRUGGLE

The establishment of TsKK–NKRKI did little to check the growing concentration of power in the party. Zinoviev's attempt in the summer of 1923 to depoliticize the Secretariat and bring it under Politburo control failed.[103] TsKK–NKRKI, which Lenin had intended as a mechanism to supervise the leading party organs became the instrument through which further power was concentrated in the Politburo and Secretariat.

In the autumn of 1923, the triumvirate was challenged by Trotsky. During the 'scissors crisis' TsKK and NKRKI, as party and government control agencies, were directly involved in the struggle with the Trotskyist opposition.

Trotsky in a letter to the Central Committee–TsKK plenum in October 1923 protested against distortions of Lenin's plan for TsKK–NKRKI and exposed the Politburo's efforts to suppress it. Summarizing the result of the reform he noted:

> Later on that article became a special weapon in the hands of those who had not wanted to print it, a weapon which they attempted to use against me. Comrade Kuibyshev, then a member of the Secretariat, was placed at the head of the TsKK. In place of a struggle against Lenin's plan, a policy of 'drawing its teeth' was adopted. Whether the Rabkrin acquired in this way the character of an independent, impartial institution, defending and confirming party justice against all kinds of administrative superfluities – it is hardly necessary to go into that question, since the answer is perfectly clear.[104]

According to Trotsky, Kuibyshev admitted that the 'Trotskyist' deviation had been fabricated to discredit him, declaring 'We find it necessary to conduct a struggle against you but cannot delcare you an enemy. That is why we have to resort to such methods'.[105] This campaign, Trotsky argued, took the form of a 'real conspiracy' in which Kuibyshev was implicated:

A secret political bureau of seven was formed; it comprised all the members of the official Politbureau except me, and included also Kuibyshev . . . All questions were decided in advance at that secret centre, where the members were bound by mutual vows. They undertook not to engage in polemics against one another and at the same time to seek opportunities to attack me. There were similar centres in local organisations and they were connected with the Moscow seven by 'strict' discipline.[106]

TsKK had become a 'tool of the Central Committee's Secretariat' with Kuibyshev and Yaroslavskii as agents of the Secretariat.[107]

Kuibyshev at the XIII Party Congress reported opposition attempts to neutralize the agency:

They told us that TsKK is a body like the Central Committee, they demanded some kind of independent line and neutrality from us, which would enable us to approach the on-going struggle 'from outside' and dispassionately and calmly evaluate all the contendents, praising and blaming each 'according to his work'. They flattered us, saying 'you are a body elected by the Congress, you are equal in rights with the Central Committee, you are responsible for your policy only to the Congress, and you ought therefore to have your own line, and be as independent of the Central Committee as possible.[108]

These proposals, whilst compatible with Lenin's original plan, ran counter to the rulings of the XII Party Congress.

Attempts to sway TsKK–NKRKI's loyalty from the ruling triumvirate were to no avail. Kuibyshev reported:

This position 'above the party', above the on-going struggle, in which the future of the party, its unity, its Bolshevik line would be resolved – this tempting position did not tempt TsKK. We resolutely rejected it.[109]

TsKK, Kuibyshev declared, followed a policy of 'unqualified, resolute support of the Central Committee and its Bolshevik line'. This policy was backed 'almost unanimously' by the members of TsKK.

In a private letter written at this time, Kuibyshev spoke of his unflinching commitment to the fight against the opposition.

> I am entirely a part of the struggle, without reserve. I accept it with all its crudity, harshness and mercilessness to everything that stands in the way. I accept it, and more than that, I am myself in it completely with all my being and with all my thoughts.[110]

Trotsky's letter of 8 October 1923 to the Central Committee and the 'Platform of the Forty Six' the same month drew a concerted counter-blast from the Politburo. The joint Central Committee–TsKK plenum on 27 October 1923 ruled that:

> The attack of comrade Trotsky, directed at the Politburo, objectively assumed the character of a factional declaration which threatened to strike a blow against the unity of the party and to create a crisis within the party.[111]

TsKK's subordination to the Central Committee became a cardinal principle of its work. The vagueness of TsKK's constitutional position allowed the Politburo to deploy it in the struggle with the opposition as it wished. Joint Central Committee–TsKK plenums or sessions were convened in October 1923 and on two other unspecified occasions, between the XII and XIII Party Congresses. The XIII Party Conference in January 1924 condemned the opposition's factional activity and repudiated its platform. TsKK's party collegium, headed by Yaroslav-skii, was responsible for enforcing the party's ruling and purging the opposition.[112] TsKK's work in the party was complemented by that of NKRKI in the state administration.

THE XIII PARTY CONGRESS

The XIII Party Congress in May 1924 provided an opportunity to take stock of TsKK–NKRKI, which remained widely unpopular in the party. (The agency's role in enforcing official policy during the 'scissors crisis' had deepened this antipathy.)

In his report, Kuibyshev raised 'the very complicated problem' of NKRKI's relations with the managers, dramatized by the row over the RKI assistance cells:

> An impression is created that in the form of RKI and TsKK the party created an organ which pounces left and right, occupies itself in

catching and investigating those guilty of deficiencies, attempting to compromise managers, aggravating unnecessarily relations with them and in the end bringing into the state apparatus nothing but demoralisation, disintegration and disorganisation.[113]

This impression, he declared, 'does not in any measure conform to reality', and the allegation remained 'unproved'. The agency whilst not abandoning its punitive role should respect managers and administrators and strive to eliminate 'mutual misunderstanding'.[114]

In contrast with his speech at Sverdlov university, Kuibyshev tried to minimize the hostility encountered by TsKK–NKRKI in its work:

A large number of the corrections to the state apparatus proposed by us are introduced simply by means of agreement, and with many comrades who lead the department and institutions we have the fullest contact. We work in co-operation with them and all our instructions, if they appear to be sound, if they really improve the situation, are implemented by mutual agreement without any reporting on the part of RKI and TsKK to the higher organs.[115]

As NKRKI's experience and expertise increased, he argued, so its relations with the institutions and enterprises would be improved and placed on a voluntary basis.

NKRKI's 'modest forces', Kuibyshev complained, were inadequate for handling the great tasks assigned it by Lenin. Morale in the agency was low. To overcome its difficulties NKRKI was forced to seek closer support from the party:

The link with the party, support from the side of the party, the interest of the party in all the work of RKI and TsKK is the primary condition for the success of the work of RKI and TsKK.[116]

Kuibyshev's report on TsKK–NKRKI's work was not discussed on the congress floor.[117] Instead a commission, chaired by Kuibyshev, was elected to review the agency's work. The problems associated with TsKK–NKRKI's work were thus neatly avoided. Kuibyshev's report was approved by the congress without debate.

One delegate complained that 'the party has still not, in all its layers, understood and mastered the tasks of the control commissions and reorganised RKI', and that many party members mistakenly saw TsKK–NKRKI as a department of criminal investigation, as 'a kind of party GPU'.[118]

The congress resolution included a firmly-worded injunction regard-

ing TsKK−NKRKI's future work and its relations with the managers
and administrators. This public reproof was administered in spite of
Kuibyshev's vehement protestations:

> The control commissions and the organs of RKI in studying the state
> administration and in carrying out investigations must not proceed
> from preconceived ideas regarding the unsuitability of the leaders of
> the organs, being studied and investigated, to lead the work entrusted
> to them. The work of the party in selecting the leaders of the
> institutions and the economic organs has already yielded great,
> positive results, placing at the head of the state and economic
> apparatus steadfast and experienced party members.[119]

It enjoined NKRKI not to impose its proposals on departments or try to
by-pass departmental heads. These methods undermined responsible
leadership and were counter-productive.

The congress approved the unification of the KK and RKI organs in
the localities. It urged TsKK−NKRKI and the party and government
bodies to establish closer links at all administrative levels. NKRKI was
instructed to concentrate on questions of primary importance and to
raise the quality of its work. The congress assigned TsKK−NKRKI
responsibility for co-ordinating all control work carried out by Gosplan,
TsSU, NKFin, OGPU and the trade unions in order to reduce the
number of investigations, to eliminate duplication and curb disruption.[120]

CONCLUSION

TsKK−NKRKI growth in this period produced important changes in
the way the party−government apparatus was organized. The unification of TsKK and NKRKI gave the Politburo a powerful instrument
with which to regulate the party and state apparatus. TsKK−NKRKI,
which had been conceived as a party watchdog, was transformed into
the Secretariat's handmaiden in the service of the ruling triumvirate. It
provided the Politburo with a bulwark of support within the central
party apparatus.

At the same time, the impact of NKRKI's work was severely
constrained, leading to disenchantment within the agency. Kuibyshev in
May 1924 noted:

> The work carried out by us cannot be compared in any way with the

huge tasks which were placed on TsKK both by the articles of Vladimir Ilich and by the XII Party Congress resolution.[121]

The limits placed on this agency stemmed from its own internal weaknesses and from its weak control over the government organs. A further important limitation on NKRKI was the ability of state institutions to exercise their own countervailing power. With the consolidation of NEP the power of managers and trade unions in industry was increasingly entrenched, providing a formidable obstacle to NKRKI's work. In 1923/34 TsKK–NKRKI assisted the party in surmounting the 'scissors crisis'. It also played a vital role in consolidating the position of the emergent triumvirate and in securing the defeat and isolation of Trotsky.

5 Rabkrin at the High Point of NEP (1925–6)

The years 1925 and 1926 marked the high point of NEP and were characterized by steady and sustained economic growth. The 'scissors crisis' was long past. Agriculture prospered and industry swiftly attained pre-war levels of production. In this period of relative calm, NKRKI faced serious difficulties in developing its work in economic management. However, economic problems persisted and within the party the question of future development roused heated controversy. The defeat of the Trotskyist opposition exposed serious rifts within the ruling triumvirate between Stalin and his erstwhile allies Zinoviev and Kamenev, ushering in a new phase in the struggle for the succession.

RABKRIN AND ECONOMIC POLICY (1925)

In 1925 the situation in industry steadily improved as existing capacity was increasingly brought back into operation and production rose rapidly. The cost-cutting drive of 1923 and 1924, associated with the 'scissors crisis', was relaxed. NKRKI's attention was switched from control to rationalization work.[1] Following the severe criticisms directed at NKRKI in 1924, its work in the field of control was sharply constrained. NKYust and the Procuracy assumed a more active role in fighting official corruption and crime. Official crimes from 1924 until 1928 were referred to special disciplinary courts rather than the ordinary courts. In the autumn of 1924 mass purges of local institutions by RKI organs were also prohibited.[2]

In the field of budgetary policy, the party's priority was to secure a stable, balanced budget without recourse to the inflationary financial and monetary policies of 1923. NKFin remained responsible for drafting the budget. Under Sokolnikov's influence it bcame the most powerful economic commissariat, a bastion of rightist influence, and staunch defender of orthodox financial management. NKRKI exercised 'strict' supervision over the budget on behalf of Sovnarkom and the Central Committee.[3]

The Central Committee in January 1925 approved the creation of an all-union budgetary commission attached to TsIK to examine the draft budget compiled by NKFin. The proposal was approved by TsIK in March 1925. The commission, comprising fifty-six members, was to review the draft budget after if had been approved by Sovnarkom, to formulate additional recommendations and to present a report to TsIK. V.V. Kuibyshev, who had earlier clashed with Sokolnikov over the proposed reorganization of Gosplan, became chairman of the commission.[4]

The 1924/5 budget greatly underestimated the revenue for the year. The increase in revenue made possible important changes in policy. In January 1925 the party increased investment in the metallurgical industry and in April 1925 approved a substantial reduction in the agricultural tax.

Kuibyshev in February 1925 presented the budgetary commission's report to TsIK. The budget was revised in accordance with the increased revenue, and expenditure targets were raised. Kuibyshev proposed also that in future the budget should be regarded not as a 'directive' but as 'firm' and binding on those who were to execute it.[5]

In this period, relations between NKFin and NKRKI were fraught. One of Kuibyshev's biographers writes of this period:

The discussion of every financial question proceeded in a fierce battle between the workers of RKI and the workers of NKFin who occupied a conservative and sometimes even a hostile position . . . Kuibyshev firmly and actively led such battles and, regardless of persons, mercilessly exposed existing defects in the work of NKFin.[6]

The 1925 income tax reform was one of the subjects of contention between NKRKI and NKFin. Through NKRKI the Secretarial faction tried to penetrate further into the decision-making centres, and to weaken the dominant hold of NKFin over economic policy.

Industrial Policy

With the resolution of the 'scissors crisis' industrial policy underwent an important change in 1925. In 1924–5 the buoyancy of the economy led to a substantial increase in state investment in the metallurgical and electrical power industry. Industry steadily recovered, as capacity was brought back into operation, and output approached pre-war levels. The recovery was largely self-financed, and Vesenkha assessed the prospects for future growth with mounting optimism.

NKRKI's main task in industry in 1924–5, Kuibyshev argued in October 1924, was not simply to reduce prices but to ensure the maximum expansion in the production of mass consumption goods for the peasant market.[7] He also viewed with optimism the prospects for heavy industry. The party could no longer content itself with the production of cheap consumer goods for the peasant market:

> Only the development of industry, only its maximum growth can place before us the true realisation of socialism. We now speak of the achievement of pre-war levels of production. This aim can in no way be posed by us as final. We dream, and we consider this dream practical, of stepping over to a significantly higher stage of technique and development of our productive forces.[8]

TsKK–NKRKI was to have this perspective 'constantly before their eyes'. A 'gigantic step forward' was needed in the metallurgical industry, which provided the true indicator of the economy's development.

NKRKI began seriously to turn its attention to the rationalization of industry and to supervising capital construction work. It closely monitored the recovery of the metallurgical industry.[9] In 1925 it intervened to resolve a bitter dispute between NKPS and Vesenkha concerning the production of railway locomotives and took an optimistic view of the future growth of rail traffic.[10] It also undertook a detailed examination of the textile industry.[11]

Kuibyshev played a modest part in developing NKRKI's work as a rationalization agency, in September 1925 taking over the chairmanship of the STO Committee on Standardisation.[12] In 1925 there was a great expansion of NKRKI's work in the rationalization field, particularly the publication of literature. In industry, however, it was overshadowed by Vesenkha. Kuibyshev at a meeting of industrial executives in November 1925 stressed the importance of NKRKI's rationalization work and the need for co-operation with Vesenkha and the *glavki*.[13] The low quality of much of the rationalization work remained a problem, and threatened to discredit the whole movement.

Within NKRKI there ensued a protracted and bitter dispute between the 'rationalizers' and the 'controllers' regarding its future work. Kuibyshev was highly critical of those rationalizers who wished to emphasize this aspect of the agency's work at the expense of control work. He also stressed the need for NKRKI to work closely with the Politburo and Sovnarkom to resolve policy difficulties.[14] Within NKRKI there were other voices demanding close co-operation with Gosplan and TsSU, to create a directing centre to develop and enforce these policies.[15]

NKRKI's role in monitoring wages policy also declined. NKRKI continued to occupy an intermediate position between management and the unions in resolving conflicts, but remained committed to incentives as a means of boosting production.[16] At the TsKK plenum in January 1925 I.I. Korotkov (head of NKRKI's labour section) reported a substantial reduction of the outstanding wages owed by the trusts in the second half of 1924.[17] TsKK–NKRKI's wages commission continued to monitor outstanding problems.[18] With the improvement in the situation, this commission was abolished in September 1925.[19]

NKRKI's ineffectiveness in 1925 intensified the bitter feud within the agency concerning its future. The agency's ineffectiveness in industry was reflected also in key republics like the Ukraine.[20]

Agricultural Policy and the TsSU Controversy

In agriculture NKRKI assumed an increasingly important role in policy-making. Its responsibilities encompassed all aspects of rural life.[21] The TsKK plenum in October 1924 charged NKRKI with the task of assisting the Central Committee in monitoring the situation in the countryside.[22] In the autumn of 1924 NKRKI participated in Sovnarkom's commission established to examine the effect of the harvest shortfall.[23] NKRKI's main concern, however, was the policy of tax concessions to the peasantry and its effect on social stratification.

The policy of tax concessions to the peasants split the party. Bukharin's celebrated exhortation to the peasants 'enrich yourselves' epitomized the attitude of the right; the left strongly criticized the policy's effect in accelerating social differentiation in the countryside and its impact on industrial development. In 1924 NKRKI's finance section, headed by S.E. Chutskaev, examined the operation of the unified agricultural tax in the localities and assessed its impact on rural social stratification.[24]

Sovnarkom in May 1925 approved a draft decree worked out by its own interdepartmental commission on the united agricultural tax. This decreee cut the tax by 100 million roubles, a 40 per cent cut.[25] This reduced the peasants' contribution to budgetary revenue and increased the regime's dependence on market forces in stimulating economic recovery. NKRKI participated in the commission's work and its proposals for easing the plight of the poor and middle peasants were incorporated in the decree. An NKRKI report for 1924/5 claimed that the tax cut was based on the agency's preliminary work.[26] In 1925, NKRKI supervised the implementation of these tax cuts, and reported on the favourable response of the peasants.

The issue of rural social differentiation remained extremely contentious. In 1924 a Sovnarkom commission, headed by Ya. A. Yakovlev, investigated the problem but its report, published in 1925, was inconclusive.[27] The tax reductions approved by Sovnarkom in May 1925 added fuel to the controversy. In the summer of 1925 Yu. Larin denounced the party's agricultural policy for its effect on social differentiation.[28]

In June 1925 TsSU, headed by P.I. Popov, published its grain–forage balances which cast new light on the problem. It sought to determine the economic power of each peasant stratum by estimating its relative contribution in producing marketable grain. The figures showed that 60 per cent of all surpluses of grain were in the hands of households with a sown area larger than 6 dessyatin, who constituted only 14 per cent of the agricultural population.[29] The middle peasants accounted for 39 per cent of marketable grain, whilst the poor peasants' contribution was negligible.

The figures created a sensation, and confirmed the worst fears of the critics of party policy. The party's class policy of alliance with the poor and middle peasants, which NKRKI supported, appeared to have no foundation in reality. The policy of tax concessions had benefited mainly the kulaks, who now controlled the supply of grain on to the market.

Kamenev at a Moscow party meeting in September 1925 noted the promising prospects for the harvest but stressed the need to take account of the 'social context of the harvest'. Zinoviev in the press warned of the kulak danger if NEP were not properly regulated. In October Kamenev, as chairman of STO, in his economic report to the Central Committee highlighted the problem of rural differentiation. Quoting the TsSU report, he repeated his warning at a meeting of the Moscow party organization the following week.[30]

These attacks placed the policy of concessions in question, leaving Bukharin, its main advocate, in an exposed position. Disagreement between the defenders of party policy and its critics turned into an open struggle for control of the Politburo.

The Central Committee in October 1925 again discussed the issue. A report by Molotov acknowledged the growing problem of differentiation in the countryside but claimed that 'the mass of grain is produced and thrown on the market by the mass of middle peasants'.[31] The plenum resolved that the two deviations – the leftists' exaggeration of the kulak danger, and rightist complacency regarding differentiation – should be treated as equally dangerous.[32] Kamenev's statements were criticized by Stalin and Molotov as exaggerated and alarmist.

NKRKI set up a commission to examine TsSU's work. Kuibyshev raised the issue with Rykov, chairman of Sovnarkom, who agreed that TsSU's report of its work should be discussed by the government. After the report was debated in Sovnarkom it was decided that all was not satisfactory and NKRKI was charged to investigate TsSU's activities.[34]

As a result of this discussion, Sovnarkom in November 1925 established an interdepartmental commission, headed by NKRKI, to examine TsSU's work. The commission, led by Yakovlev, comprised specialists from TsSU, Gosplan and NKZem, many of whom had previously clashed with TsSU over its work.[35]

The TsSU investigation became a political campaign against the Zinoviev–Kamenev bloc. Sovnarkom, led by Rykov, clashed with STO, headed by Kamenev. NKRKI rallied the critics of TsSU. Within the party the struggle between the two factions intensified in the run-up to the party congress.

TsKK–NKRKI in November 1925 approved the commission's report and sent it to Sovnarkom. The report, drawing heavily on the work of N.M. Vishnevskii, an agricultural expert from Gosplan, savaged TsSU's findings.[36] TsSU's calculation of the total grain–forage balance for 1925/6 was criticized as exaggerated, resulting in the raising of the grain-purchasing target for the year and the underestimation of the budget requirements to realize these targets.[37] The exaggeration of the harvest size produced serious economic difficulties in the autumn of 1925.

TsSU's figures were criticized also for misrepresenting the position and power of the different peasant strata. Its use of undifferentiated consumption norms for all households, it was noted, distorted the estimates of marketable grain produced by different strata.[38] NKRKI also disputed TsSU's categories for defining households which it argued exaggerated the size of the kulak stratum and underestimated that of the middle peasant (serednyak) stratum.

The conflicting views of NKRKI and TsSU regarding the percentage of marketable grain produced by different strata of the peasantry are outlined in Table 4.1. TsSU's figures, NKRKI alleged, concealed the

Table 4.10 Marketable grain produced by different households (%)

	TsSU	*NKRKI*
Rich (kulak) and well-to-do peasants	61	28.6
Middle peasants (serednyak)	39	48.6
Poor peasants (bednyak)	nil	22.9

economic significance of the serednyak, exaggerated the kulak's power, and ignored the contributions of the bednyak.[39]

Sovnarkom and the Politburo approved the commission's report in December 1925. The report discredited TsSU's work, undermined the position of the opposition and affirmed the accuracy of the party's analysis of the situation in the countryside. TsSU's estimates of the precentage of marketable grain produced by the kulaks were subsequently reduced from 61 to 52 and then to 42 but NKRKI's figures were still hotly contested.[40]

Kuibyshev at the TsKK plenum in December 1925 argued that the TsSU investigation demonstrated TsKK–NKRKI's invaluable role in solving major policy issues on behalf of the highest party and government organs.[41] NKRKI's report for 1925 stressed its growing role in determining the government's 'political line'.[42]

At the Moscow party conference the same month Kuibyshev, in a report on TsSU, outdid Bukharin in his view of the problems in agriculture. He attacked the 'leftist' deviation as the principal danger facing the party. 'Panic fear of the kulak' and the exaggeration of differentiation, he claimed, posed the main danger because it was 'dressed in leftist phrases' and thus likely to gain wider currency in the party than the right deviation.[43]

The investigation provided a prelude to the XIV Party Congress, at which Stalin welcomed NKRKI's findings and poured scorn on TsSU's work:

> We believe that TsSU must give objective data free from any prejudiced opinion because attempts to adjust figures to this or that prejudiced opinion is an offence of a criminal character. But what can we believe of the figures of TsSU after this if TsSU stops believing its own figures?[44]

NKRKI's assessment of the situation in the countryside was approved. Stalin, however, dissociated himself from Kuibyshev's view that the deviation in agriculture posed the greatest threat.[45] Rykov defended NKRKI's findings that the serednyak remained the dominant force in the countryside.

The opposition responded vigorously. Kamenev insisted on the importance of the problem of differentiation which, he argued, the Central Committee had ignored. The extent of the problem remained uncertain since 'figures become entangled in the political struggle'. He denounced Stalin for defending a policy of which Bukharin was the true author and with which he disagreed.[46]

Zinoviev condemned party policies in agriculture. Kuibyshev's views on the two deviations in agricultural policy, he rightly noted, contradicted the Central Committee's line.[47] TsKK–NKRKI's self-proclaimed role as the Central Committee's servant was compromised.

Kuibyshev tried to calm the furore and defend the report from its detractors. The investigation, he insisted, had not been tailored to suit political ends.[48] The impact on TsSU was immediate and profound. The agency was reorganized and its autonomy restricted. P.I. Popov was sacked as director of TsSU and replaced by V.V. Osinskii.[49]

The row continued to reverberate in the party. A letter by eight prominent oppositionists to the joint Central Committee-TsKK plenum in July 1926 castigated NKRKI's investigation of TsSU as an 'impermissible experiment in juggling statistics' which concealed the extent of rural stratification and minimized the growing power of the kulak. They warned of the serious danger of attempts to 'bend statistics to fit preconceived political notions'.[50] The growth of capitalist farming under NEP pointed to a serious ideological dilemma for the party.

TsKK–NKRKI's intervention in this affair provided a foretaste of the future, raising also serious doubts regarding the management of policy-making. TsKK–NKRKI's status as an independent, rationalization agency was compromised by its own leadership which saw it as the administrative arm of the Politburo. The TsSU investigation helped cement together the new Stalin–Bukharin alliance. The investigation was used by TsKK–NKRKI's leadership to stress the need for the party to have its own independent, disinterested body to check the work of the economic commissariats.[51]

TsKK–NKRKI AND THE INTERNAL PARTY STRUGGLE (1925)

In 1924–5 TsKK continued its campaign to eradicate Trotskyist influences in the party.[52] *Sotsialisticheskii vestnik*, the Menshevik emigré journal, in May 1924 published the text of Trotsky's letter to the Central Committee of October 1923 which recounted the Politburo's attempt to suppress Lenin's plan. In 1925 Max Eastman, an American sympathizer of Trotsky, in his book *Since Lenin Died* also chronicled this episode.[53]

The Politburo in July 1925 required Trotsky to issue a letter confuting Eastman's account and denying the assertion that 'comrade Kuibyshev was placed at the head of RKI as an "opponent" of Lenin's plan of organisation'.[54] The letter was later disowned by Trotsky. The incident, however, pointed up the touchiness of the Politburo on this delicate question. In the centre and in the localities the row over Lenin's plan for the reorganization of Rabkrin continued to reverberate.[55]

Trotsky's defeat exposed divisions within the ruling triumvirate. In the autumn of 1925 these latent tensions erupted in an open split. Within the Politburo Zinoviev and Kamenev, the senior triumvirs, confronted Stalin, Bukharin, Rykov and Tomskii. The Zinoviev–Kamenev bloc, although a minority in the Politburo, was supported by influential figures including Sokolnikov, Krupskaya and, briefly, also Dzerzhinskii.[56] It controlled the Leningrad and Moscow party organization and was also strongly represented in the governmental apparatus. It constituted an alliance of disparate forces, which adopted a leftist view of economic policy, although Sokolnikov of NKFin was a noted right winger.

The opposition were united by their antipathy for Stalin and alarm at his efforts to turn the Secretariat (linked with TsKK–NKRKI) into the real centre of power within the party. Kuibyshev in NKRKI had endeavoured to limit Sokolnikov's power in NKFin. The expansion of NKRKI's role also threatened Kamenev's position in STO.

The opposition's birth was heralded by the publication of the 'Platform of the Four' early in September 1925. At the Central Committee plenum in October 1925 a temporary truce was concluded.[57] At this plenum a proposal was advanced that Stalin and Kuibyshev be appointed to STO. Kamenev indignantly condemned this attempt to subject his work to the control of 'political commissars' and the scheme was dropped.[58]

NKRKI's investigation of TsSU pulled the rug from under the opposition. In the weeks preceding the party congress TsKK–NKRKI capitalized on this advantage and forced the issue to a conclusion. The investigation provided the pretext for an open asault on the institutional bastions of the Zinoviev–Kamenev bloc. The initiative in this struggle was taken by TsKK–NKRKI with the support of Rykov, and with the connivance of Stalin and Bukharin.

TsKK's activities in this field were directed by Kuibyshev and by Yaroslavskii, head of the party collegium. In the autumn of 1925 TsKK took measures to discipline or dismiss some of the opposition's most outspoken supporters.[59] Dzerzhinskii was persuaded to distance himself from the opposition. Kuibyshev at the TsKK plenum in December 1925 eulogized Dzerzhinskii as a 'poet of rationalization' who was 'universally loved and respected' and 'all the speeches of whom in recent times promote enthusiasm [*pafos*] of rationalization'.[60]

The uneasy truce persisted until December 1925. At the Moscow and Leningrad party conferences, prior to the congress, the truce broke down. On 15 December the party majority presented proposals to the Leningrad party organization requiring it to submit itself to the central party organs. Zinoviev rejected the demand and resolved to continue the fight at the congress.

The TsKK plenum on 18 December overwhelmingly endorsed the Central Committee's policy and approved any measures necessary to maintain unity.[61] Krupskaya, who had been elected to TsKK's presidium by the XIII Party Congress, was pressurized unsuccessfully to renounce her support for Zinoviev and Kamenev. E.F. Rozmirovich, leader of NKRKI's rationalizers, was also notably reluctant to condemn her old acquaintances Zinoviev and Kamenev.[62] Support for the opposition in TsKK, however, appears to have been small.

In December 1925 an article by Vardin, a supporter of Zinoviev, in *Leningradskaya pravda* denounced Kuibyshev's view on the two deviations in agriculture as reflecting the outlook of a much broader ideological tendency then in ascendancy in the party:

> The old 'Left Communism' which was akin to the Left SRs has in fact survived in the ranks of our party; it has at its head the old leaders and against them the old Leninist–Bolshevik struggle is imperative.[63]

Vardin called for measures 'to eradicate the current phenomena of a Right deviation armed with Left SR phrases'. This blow was aimed directly at Bukharin and other prominent Left Communists of 1918 including Kuibyshev and Yaroslavskii from TsKK–NKRKI.

THE XIV PARTY CONGRESS

The XIV Party Congress, convened in Moscow in December 1925, formalized the defeat of the Zinoviev–Kamenev opposition, and confirmed the supremacy of the new Stalin–Bukharin leadership. Stalin's control of the Secretariat was allied to Bukharin's supremacy in the ideological realm, Rykov's control of Sovnarkom and Tomskii's control over VTsSPS. Central to this power structure was the Secretariat–TsKK–NKRKI axis.[64]

Kuibyshev's lengthy report to the congress on the work of TsKK–NKRKI dealt mainly with the commission's role in fighting the opposition. This report, unlike those delivered to the XII and XIII Party Congresses, was discussed by the congress, underlining TsKK–NKRKI's new-found legitimacy and growing presence.[65]

NKRKI's investigation of TsSU was widely taken to have been masterminded by the Secretariat. The opposition launched a concerted attack on the Secretariat's growing power and on Stalin's influence.

Kamenev warned of the serious implications of the TsSU investigation. Contentious and difficult issues could be resolved only by open debate and not by 'organizational struggle'.[66] This development endangered the rational resolution of policy disputes and threatened party unity. He attacked Stalin's methods of operation:

> We are against creating the theory of a 'leader'; we are against making a leader. We are against having the Secretariat combine in practice both politics and organization and placing itself above the political organ. We cannot regard it as normal; and we think it harmful to the party, to prolong a situation in which the Secretariat combines politics and organisation, and in fact decides policies in advance.[67]

Kamenev openly questioned Stalin's capacity to unite the 'Bolshevik general staff'.

Sokolnikov similarly denounced the concentration of power in the Secretariat.[68] Zinoviev complained that the Secretariat 'has now incomparably greater powers that it had under Vladimir Ilich', proposing measures to reorganize the Central Committee 'from the angle of a Politburo with full powers, and a Secretariat of functionaries subordinate to it'.[69]

Molotov dismissed these criticisms and insisted that the Secretariat and Orgburo remained subordinate to the Politburo and Central Committee.[70] S.I. Gusev (of TsKK) argued that charges concerning the 'boundless' power of the Secretariat and General Secretary were unfounded. TsKK's representatives who attended the Politburo's sessions and closely observed its work, and that of the Secretariat, saw no abuse of power.[71]

How far TsKK had acted as an autonomous agency remained uncertain. With the Politburo split, TsKK had been placed in a quandary, uncertain how to act. Whilst Kuibyshev had favoured decisive action, Stalin asserted that he had dissuaded his impetuous colleague from attending the Leningrad party conference 'because there was a hope that things would not go so far'.[72]

TsKK's relations with the leading party organs remained a contentious issued. Krupskaya denounced TsKK's contribution to 'the defence of party unity', and demanded that in party affairs it should show greater 'objectivity and independence of thought', especially 'Independence from any individual party member who is able to exert his opinion on it'.[73] TsKK, however, should not become a rival of the Central Committee but should work with it. Other oppositionists also argued for a return to Lenin's original plan for TsKK–NKRKI.[74]

TsKK spokesmen vigorously defended the commission's work. B.A. Roizenman questioned whether Krupskaya wished the members of TsKK attending the meetings of the Politburo to function as political commissars and declared 'The Poltiburo does not need commissars'.[75] S.I. Gusev accused the opposition of trying to set TsKK against the Central Committee, and thus to split the party. He complained that TsKK still lacked authority and was isolated from the Politburo and Central Committee. Gusev argued that party members should be obliged to inform on oppositionist activity to TsKK.[76] N.M. Yanson noted that 'Each time any group of party members begins to attack the Central Committee, it looks to TsKK for some kind of special impartiality'.[77] Kuibyshev and Yaroslavskii stressed that TsKK could not stand aside in this struggle.[78]

The opposition was routed at the congress. The old triumvirate was displaced by the new Stalin–Bukharin leadership, with Stalin staunchly defending Bukharin from opposition attacks. Kuibyshev as one of Stalin's most loyal lieutenants delivered an extravagant eulogy:

In the name of the whole TsKK I declare that comrade Stalin, as General Secretary of our party, is precisely the person who has been able, together with the majority of the Central Committee and with its support to gather around him all the best forces in the party and to put them to work. It is incontestable that the present leadership of the Central Committee between the thirteenth and fourteenth congresses has been the best of any of the hitherto existing Central Committee by way of improvement of leadership and in contact with local organisations . . . On the basis of real experience, of real knowledge of our leadership I declare in the name of the TsKK that this leadership and this general secretary are what is needed for the party in order to go on from victory to victory.[79]

Kuibyshev noted that TsKK's membership was still not entirely fitted for its work of purging the party and preserving its unity.[80] The XIV Party Congress saw a significant turnover in its membership aimed at eliminating these wavering elements.

Kuibyshev's speech paid little attention to NKRKI.[81] The new phase of economic reconstruction, inaugurated by the congress, required the development of NKRKI's rationalization work. In emphasizing the agency's responsibilities in this field the congress warned against any abuse of its role:

> Practical rationalisation measures will be successful and will really regenerate our techniques and organisation of our economy and administration only if it is introduced by the leaders of the corresponding state institutions with the active assistance of the broad working masses.[82]

The dangers of abandoning the principle of co-operation between NKRKI and the state institutions was clearly spelled out. TsKK–NKRKI should not assume a 'bureaucratic–centralist' leadership of the rationalization movement.[83] This reiterated the strictures issued by the previous congress and were intended to allay the fears of the managers and administrators.

The congress instructed NKRKI to revitalize mass control work and strengthen its links with the mass organizations and extend its work in the selection of personnel for the state and economic institutions. On Kuibyshev's urging, the congress affirmed that TsKK–NKRKI and the local KK–RKI should work more closely with the party organs.[84]

TsKK–NKRKI emerged from the XIV Party Congress a much stronger organization. TsKK became a bulwark of the new leadership.[85] The congress instructed it to delegate three members and three deputies to attend Politburo meetings, and five members and five deputies to attend the meetings of the Orgburo and Secretariat, with advisory votes.[86] TsKK–NKRKI's links with the Politburo and Central Committee were strengthened and formalized. Joint Central Committee–TsKK plenums became an important forum for policy debate.

The TsSU controversy in the autumn of 1925 demonstrated the difficulties of co-ordination between Sovnarkom and STO. In January 1926 Kamenev was dismissed as chairman of STO and as vice-chairman of Sovnarkom. A.I. Rykov, chairman of Sovnarkom, was appointed also chairman of STO, strengthening his hold on the economic apparatus.[87] A.D. Tsyurupa already held the post of vice-chairman of both Sovnarkom and STO. In January 1926 V.V. Kuibyshev, narkom of NKRKI, and Ya. E. Rudzutak, narkom of NKPS, were appointed vice-chairmen of both Sovnarkom and STO.[88] Through the new vice-chairman of Sovnarkom–STO, especially through TsKK–NKRKI, the Politburo's links with the government were greatly strengthened.

With the defeat of the opposition, Sokolnikov was replaced as narkom of NKFin by N.P. Bryukhanov in January 1926.[89] In April 1926 S.E. Chutskaev, deputy narkom of NKRKI, replaced Kuibyshev as chairman of the TsIK budgetary commission and was relieved of his duties in NKRKI in 1927.[90] NKFin's demise was underlined by the increased prominence of Gosplan and Vesenkha in planning the economy.[91]

RABKRIN AND ECONOMIC POLICY (1926)

In industry by 1926 85–90 per cent of basic capital had been brought into operation and was utilized at 75–80 per cent of capacity. The XIV Party Congress noted as a priority the need 'to pursue a policy aimed at the industrialisation of the country, the development of the production of the means of production and the formation of reserves for economic manoeuvre'. The aim was to turn the USSR from an importer to a producer of machines, to create economic self-sufficiency, and transform the economy on socialist lines. The congress instructed the Central Committee 'to utilise all resources, to observe the strictest economy in the expenditure of state resources'.[92]

The problem of capital accumulation was especially acute. Attempts to hold down wages met strong opposition. The collective agreement concluded in the textile industry in 1925 provoked unrest, with workers in the Ivanovo–Voznesensk region leaving the party in a mass exodus. A TsKK commission, sent to the region in February 1926, alleged that only a minority had left the party because of disagreement over policy.[93] Nevertheless, TsKK–NKRKI instructed its local agencies strictly to supervise delays in wage payment by state and economy organs to defuse potential unrest.[94]

The 'Regime of Economy' Campaign

To circumvent this problem a new strategy of accumulation was adopted. Vesenkha on 23 February 1926 issued an order 'The Regime of Economy', signed by Dzerzhinskii, which demanded strict economy in the state administration and the economy to finance the new phase of 'new industrial construction and radical reequipment of industry'.[95] Economies were to be secured by rationalizing production and administration and by ruthlessly cutting waste. Vesenkha assumed the leadership of this campaign, much to NKRKI's chagrin.

At the Central Committee plenum in April 1926 Trotsky denounced the Politburo's excessive caution in promoting industrial expansion. He proposed an ambitious expansion programme to be financed from three principal sources: (i) increased taxation of the peasantry with the shifting of the tax burden on to the kulaks; (ii) high industrial profits through increased retail prices; (iii) increased budget allocations to be released by 'holding down non-productive expenses'.[96]

This was seen by the Politburo as a threat to the alliance (smychka) with the peasantry. The plenum approved Rykov's report for cautious industrial expansion within the confines of NEP to be funded from three sources: (i) from the budget through reduced expenditure on the state administration; (ii) from the resources of industry itself through improved efficiency; (iii) from the savings of the populace.[97]

Kuibyshev at the TsKK plenum in April 1926 strongly defended official economic policy and categorically denounced the opposition's strategy of 'super profits' for industry and high taxation for the peasantry. The maintenance of the smychka necessitated a cautious taxation policy combined with a policy of cheap industrial goods for the peasant market. Within industry and the state administration, he asserted, lay 'huge reserves, huge possibilities for accumulation' which could be released by applying a 'severe regime of economy on all expenditure'.[98] All managers and administrators should have impressed on them the need for strict economy.

On 25 April 1926 a joint Central Committee–TsKK address, signed by Stalin and Kuibyshev, launched the campaign and underlined its political significance. It called on TsKK–NKRKI and their local organs to pay strict attention to the campaign – eliminating waste, mismanagement, reducing staffs, curbing abuses in wage payment, boosting efficiency, and raising labour productivity.[99]

In its early stages, the campaign was primarily directed towards industry where Vesenkha, under Dzerzhinskii, sought to secure maximum savings. STO on 18 May issued a decree for a 10 per cent increase in labour productivity in industry and transport for the rest of 1925–6 and strenuous efforts were made to reduce administrative overheads.[100]

Sovnarkom on 11 June 1926 adopted a decree 'Concerning the Regime of Economy', drafted by Dzerzhinskii and Kuibyshev, which signalled a great tightening of control and discipline in the state administration.[101] Institution and enterprise heads were instructed to adhere strictly to the campaign. The revision commissions of the industrial trusts were to be strengthened; NKFin was to enforce budgetary discipline and NKRKI was to check the administrative and economic institutions.

NKRKI threw itself into the campaign in the summer months. In May 1926 it issued instructions to local RKI organs to involve themselves in the campaign in co-operation with the trade unions and Komsomol to secure mass participation.[102] NKRKI endeavoured to strengthen the involvement of the press. A circular letter to the republican NKRKI in July sought to tighten control over the campaign.[103]

Intense pressure was placed on industry. In individual cases, NKRKI had to mount rescue operations to save trusts in difficulty.[104] Pressure from Vesenkha and NKRKI drew anguished protests from managers and reports in *Pravda* in July 1926 highlighted managerial opposition to the campaign. The Orgburo criticized attempts by managers to effect economies at the expense of working conditions, by cutting expenditure on housing and welfare.[105]

The campaign roused the ire of workers and the trade unions. The opposition seized upon this opportunity. The 'Declaration of the Thirteen' submitted to the joint Central Committee–TsKK plenum in July 1926 condemned the 'incorrect' application of 'mechanical pressure tactics from the top down'. Trotsky condemned the pressure applied on workers by 'a considerable proportion of managers' and demanded a party commission to investigate the conduct of the campaign.[106]

A pamphlet issued by the Democratic Centralist group, entitled *The Labour Question*, argued that the campaign had been used as a 'means of pressure' on the work force and that 'a complete autocracy of the administration' reigned in the factories.[107]

The TsKK plenum early in August 1926 discussed the difficulties and mistakes associated with the campaign and its resolution signalled the beginning of a retreat on this front.[108] NKRKI, which affected an even-handed approach to disputes between management and the unions, escaped the odium directed at Vesenkha, and played a part in redirecting the frustration of labour against management. In August 1926 NKRKI censured NKTrud and Vesenkha for ignoring breaches of laws on labour safety, conditions of work and overtime working.[109]

The Central Committee and Sovnarkom on 16 August 1926 adopted a joint address, 'Concerning the successes and deficiencies of the campaign for the regime of economy', signed by Stalin (for the Central Committee), Rykov (for Sovnarkom) and Kuibyshev (for TsKK–NKRKI).[110] Although successes had been achieved, the address conceded that mistakes had been committed. In some instances wages had been forcibly cut, in others living and working conditions had been attacked. These faults were blamed on managers and administrators who had misunderstood or wilfully misinterpreted the campaign.

The leadership resorted to crude demagogy in its search for scapegoats, adopting the rhetoric of the opposition:

Excessive bureaucratic staffs have been retained in administrative bodies while there has been inadmissible protection of the 'higher ranks' . . . while transport and motor cars have been impermissibly used by the 'higher ranks', while bonuses have been paid to the same 'higher ranks', while there have been marked increases in the pay of 'higher officials' in the form of endless official journeys and the issue of non-repayable advances.[111]

The failure of the trade unions to assist in enforcing the campaign and correcting defects was also censured. In a dramatic shift of policy it was decided to concentrate the campaign's fire on administrative expenditure in the state and economic apparatus. The joint address proposed a target saving of 300–400 million roubles, but set no time scale for its realization.

At the XIV Party Congress Kuibyshev had repudiated opposition charges that the cost of maintaining the apparatus was excessive or that the growth of the apparatus was at all abnormal.[112] This abrupt about turn was a calculated attempt to rescue the Politburo's economic policy and to demonstrate that a strategy of accumulation was feasible without recourse to increased taxation of the peasantry.

Sovnarkom on 17 August 1926 set up a commission (including representatives of NKTrud, Vesenkha, VTsSPS and TsKK–NKRKI) to review the wages of industrial workers.[113] In September Sovnarkom, on the commission's recommendation, approved large wage increases for the main industries.[114] The crisis underlined the fragility of NEP and the problem of reconciling industrial and agrarian interests in financing new expansion. NKRKI together with NKFin and NKTrud continued to monitor wages and salaries.[115]

The enforcement of the campaign constituted NKRKI's chief function after the XIV Party Congress.[116] The scope and intensity of the campaign soured relations between NKRKI and the industrial managers. In September 1926 in a series of articles in *Pravda* on the problem of bureaucracy D.Z. Lebed' reiterated the leadership's determination to eradicate this phenomenon from the apparatus scornfully dismissing the pessimism and defeatism of the opposition.[117]

The débâcle of the summer months left the campaign for economy temporarily marooned. At the TsKK plenum in October 1926 NKRKI spokesmen admitted that the campaign's effect could not be measured because of poor accounting work.[118] The problem of enforcing the campaign remained unresolved, admitted N.I. Il'in (narkom of NKRKI RSFSR), on account of managerial intransigence and poor control work.[119]

Rabkrin's Relations with Vesenkha

NKRKI's relations with Vesenkha in this period were further complicated by other developments. In the spring of 1926 Dzerzhinskii assumed effective leadership of the campaign for the regime of economy. He also initiated a discussion in Vesenkha for a fundamental reorganization of industrial administration.[120] He demanded a major overhaul of industrial management in an outspoken attack on control-centred administration.

In a remarkable letter, 'evidently addressed by him to Sovnarkom', Kuibyshev offered his resignation as narkom NKRKI and suggested that Dzerzhinskii should combine the leadership of both Vesenkha and NKRKI. Dzerzhinskii was already involving himself with the problems of industrial administration. He had also been made 'dictator' of the 'regime of economy' campaign and might be able to do something with the 'madhouse' of NKRKI.[121] This letter underlined Kuibyshev's exasperation with NKRKI's ineffectiveness and the acute infighting within the agency.

Dzerzhinskii's sudden death in July 1926 removed from the Politburo one of the last individuals with the power and authority to stand up to Stalin. V.V. Kuibyshev, Stalin's loyal lieutenant, was on 5 August 1926 appointed chairman of Vesenkha and relieved of his post as head of TsKK–NKRKI, but remained nominally a member of the TsKK presidium until the XV Party Congress.[122] Kuibyshev's promotion to Vesenkha clearly indicated the relative status of these two agencies.

Kuibyshev's appointment to Vesenkha placed industry within the ambit of the Stalin bloc. Kuibyshev brought to Vesenkha a more abrasive style of leadership than that of Dzerzhinskii, a greater faith in the salutariness of control work, and a less tolerant attitude to the non-party specialists. Valentinov, one of his subordinates in Vesenkha, later wrote:

With the transfer of Kuibyshev to his [Dzerzhinskii's] post the whole situation in Vesenkha changed. Kuibyshev came with directives from Stalin to strike down the intelligentsia who were raising their heads too high, who felt their power and significance in the economy. With the arrival of Kuibyshev there could be no talk either of complimenting the addresses of ex-Mensheviks, nor of 'second signatures', nor of any 'constitution for technical personnel' in factories and works. Such nonsenses had to stop. Former Mensheviks, who occupied important posts under Dzerzhinskii, had to be restrained, suppressed, demoted.[123]

Another specialist, the chemist Ipatieff, who also worked under Kuibyshev in Vesenkha, contrasted him unfavourably with other party executives and cuttingly remarked:

> I know of no more narrow minded, stupid man than he. His knowledge of industry was nil, and since he had no opinions of his own his superiors could easily persuade him to accept theirs. I did not like him nor he me.[124]

At the height of the conflict between the two agencies in the summer of 1926, NKRKI proposed that Vesenkha (the Supreme Council of the National Economy) should be renamed the People's Commissariat of Industry in conformity with its real function and responsibilities. This obvious snub to Dzerzhinskii and Vesenkha was withdrawn on Kuibyshev's appointment to the chairmanship of Vesenkha.[125]

Co-operation betwen NKRKI and the revision commissions of the trusts posed another major difficulty. In July 1926 M. Bronshtein, an NKRKI official, criticized the poor organization and ineffectiveness of the commission, proposing that NKRKI become an 'unifying centre' for all control work, with the power to direct the departmental control agencies, including the revision commissions.[126] At the TsKK plenum in October 1926 Samsonov, head of Vesenkha's control-revision administration, expressed admiration for NKRKI's ability to instil fear in officials and compel them to co-operate.[127]

At Vesenkha Kuibyshev immediately set about reorganizing control in industry. He abolished the revision commissions of the trusts and set up a special Vesenkha chief inspectorate headed by V.A. Avanesov presidium member of Vesenkha and Stalin's deputy in NKRKI from 1920 to 1923.[128] The Stalinist controllers tightened their grip on Vesenkha.

Kuibyshev in Vesenkha introduced immediate policy changes. In 1926 industrial sectors and leftist planners in Vesenkha demanded ambitious plan targets for 1926/7. Dzerzhinskii, in the face of intense opposition, had succeeded in reducing these targets. Kuibyshev on assuming his post in Vesenkha immediately adopted the targets of the rapid industrializers.[129] This decision was one of the first fruits of collaboration between the Stalinist controllers and the leftist planners and set the scene for a sharp acceleration of the industrialization drive NKRKI emerged as an enthusiastic supporter of industrial expansion promoted by Vesenkha and Gosplan.

TsKK–NKRKI AND THE INTERNAL PARTY STRUGGLE (1926)

The period between the XIV and XV Party Congress coincided with a new phase in the internal party struggle. In the spring of 1926 the united opposition, headed by Trotsky, Zinoviev and Kamenev was formed. From April to October 1926 the new opposition fiercely criticized official policies. The slow pace of industrial expansion became a key focus of this attack. The opposition continued to denounce the internal regime within the party, attempting to take the debate to the rank and file and to mobilize opinion amongst workers outside the party.

Following the XIV Party Congress, TsKK's work of party control was sharply tightened. Kuibyshev at the TsKK plenum in April 1926 complained that lack of clear Politburo directives in 1925 had inhibited the commission's work in curbing the Zinoviev–Kamenev opposition. He urged strengthening TsKK and the local KKs in the face of the new threat, and insisted on maintenance of an 'united centre' of TsKK and the Central Committee.[130]

TsKK's party collegium, headed by Yaroslavskii, played a leading part in enforcing party discipline and exposing oppositional activity in the summer of 1926.[131] The opposition's 'Declaration of the Thirteen' in July 1926 accused TsKK–NKRKI of betraying the party's trust, of becoming 'a purely administrative organ', which persecuted all independent and critical thought in the party:

> During the two years before the XIV Party Congress there existed a faction 'septemvirate', consisting of the six members of the Politburo and the chairman of TsKK, comrade Kuibyshev. This factional clique at the top decided in advance without the knowledge of the party, every question on the agenda of the Politburo and Central Committee, and unilaterally decided a number of questions that were never brought before the Politburo at all. It made party assignments in a factional manner, and its members were bound by internal factional discipline. Taking part in the work of the septemvirate, along with Kuibyshev, were those very leaders of TsKK, such as Yaroslavskii, Yanson, etc. who were conducting a ruthless struggle against 'factions' and 'groupings'.[132]

The opposition launched a concerted attack on official policy at the Central Committee plenum in July 1926. Stalin and Kuibyshev condemned the opposition.[133] The opposition was defeated and its leaders were ousted from their party and government posts. TsKK's role in safeguarding party unity was vigorously defended by official spokesmen.[134]

TsKK in the autumn of 1926 continued to closely monitor oppositional activity.[135] In October, the opposition accepted the Politburo's terms regulating their future conduct and temporarily capitulated.

CONCLUSION

The high point of NEP in 1925/26 marked a trough in NKRKI's fortunes following the reorganisation of 1923. Following the resolution of the 'scissors crisis' its fortunes went into temporary eclipse. The agency's impotence became a matter of deep concern to its leadership, and resulted in bitter infighting between the agency's 'rationalisers' and 'controllers'. The steady recovery of the economy after 1924, and the defeat of Trotsky temporarily left TsKK–NKRKI without an obvious role. This crisis was shortlived. In the autumn of 1925 conflict over agricultural policy split the Politburo and initiated a major struggle for power between Stalin and his erstwhile allies Zinoviev and Kamenev. TsKK's role in defeating the Zinoviev–Kamenev opposition was facilitated by NKRKI investigation in discrediting TsSU's work.

TsKK–NKRKI's role in this crisis allowed it to strengthen its position in the central party-government apparatus. These years also marked a watershed in economic policy, as the party turned toward promoting industrial growth. In 1926 the new united opposition of Trotsky, Zinoviev and Kamenev was formed challenging the leadership's strategy for capital accumulation to finance this new investment. TsKK–NKRKI acquired a new significance in defending party unity in this period of intensified conflict and in developing the Politburo's economic strategy. Kuibyshev's departure to Vesenkha closed an important chapter in TsKK–NKRKI's history. His successor inherited the task of defining the agency's role in these increasingly difficult circumstances.

Plate VII   G.K. Ordzhonikidze (1886–1937): Chairman of TsKK and narkom RKI (November 1926–November 1930).

G.K. Ordzhonikidze, Stat'i i rechi, *vol. 2 (Moscow, 1957)*
Plate VIII   G.K. Ordzhonikidze (1886–1937): Chairman of TsKK and narkom RKI (November 1926–November 1930).

6 Rabkrin and the 'Left Turn' (1927–9)

The years 1927 and 1928 were a watershed in Soviet history. Under Stalin's leadership the Communist Party effected a dramatic change of course, 'the left turn', which repudiated NEP and carried with it momentous implications for the economic and social life of the country. These changes were hotly debated. The struggle against the united opposition in 1926/27 was succeeded by a new struggle for power in the Politburo in 1928/9 between Stalin and the 'Right' opposition. The problem of controlling the party–state apparatus and managing policy formation in these rapidly changing circumstances was posed with new urgency. TsKK–NKRKI, under its new leader, was presented with new responsibilities and enormous possibilities for influencing the outcome.

Grigorii Konstantinovich Ordzhonikidze became head of TsKK–NKRKI in November 1926. Simultaneously he was appointed vice-chairman of Sovnarkom and STO but surrendered his candidate membership of the Politburo gained in July 1926.[1] He was a Georgian, born in 1886 into an impoverished noble family. He trained as a medical auxiliary (*feldsher*) but took up revolutionary politics in his teens. Thereafter he played a distinguished part in the underground movement in Russia and abroad, and served as a political commissar during the civil war in the Ukraine and Caucasus. In 1921 he took charge of party work in the Caucasus and was elected to the Central Committee. His blunt handling of the scheme to set up a Transcaucasian Federation in 1922 incited Lenin's wrath, who suggested that he be temporarily suspended from the party. Despite this, his career continued to flourish.[2]

Ordzhonikidze's friendship with his compatriot Stalin dated back to 1905. His transfer to TsKK–NKRKI was an astute move. Known universally as Sergo, he was popular and widely respected as an old Bolshevik undergrounder and party loyalist.[3] Fiery and strong-willed, he brought to NKRKI great energy and considerable administrative and political skills but could be dangerously impetuous and high-handed. Like Kuibyshev he was a political administrator with no technical training and with few pretensions as a theorist. In NKRKI in 1927 he had three deputy narkoms, N.M. Yanson, D.Z. Lebed' and Ya.

A. Yakovlev. He was assisted by his own personal secretariat, headed by S.F. Redens.

THE 'REGIME OF ECONOMY' CAMPAIGN

The central difficulty facing the Politburo after 1926 was the problem of capital accumulation and the financing of the new industrialization drive. The regime of economy campaign stood at the centre of the Politburo's strategy, with Stalin and Bukharin advocating stringent belt-tightening. The campaign was seen as a way of avoiding the unpleasant options of squeezing either the workers or the peasants.[4] In 1927 NKRKI assumed the leadership of the campaign for the 'regime of economy'. Trotsky, Zinoviev and Kamenev, the leaders of the united opposition, continued to press for a more rapid programme of industrial expansion.

On assuming the leadership of NKRKI, Ordzhonikidze faced the delicate problem of fence-mending with both trade unionists and managers after the débâcle of the regime of economy campaign in the summer of 1926. At the VTsSPS congress in December 1926 he defended, before an audience of sceptical trade unionists, the conduct of the campaign. Not having been involved himself, he could afford to speak frankly. He acknowledged that there had been serious errors, leading to deterioration in workers' conditions. The party, he insisted, had acted swiftly to correct these 'distortions' of the campaign, which stemmed either from error or wilful subversion of its intention.[5]

At the same time, overtures were made to the industrial managers. In December 1926 NKRKI convened a meeting of industrial managers to discuss their grievances. Managers complained of excessive investigations, harassment by inspectors intent on uncovering faults and acts of illegality. This undermined respect and confidence in NKRKI and fostered open hostility towards the controllers.[6] Ordzhonikidze insisted that NKRKI was not a 'punitive organ' and that it desired only to assist managers in correcting defects, bringing to this task the objective understanding of the disinterested observer. In the following months, efforts were also made to curb excessive investigation in industry.[7]

The raising of investment targets for industry in 1926/7 further strained the state budget. The party decree of August 1926 proposed savings from the state administration of 300–400 million roubles but left the time scale open. Sovnarkom in July approved a 10 per cent cut in administrative estimates for 1926/7.[8] The XV Party Conference in

October approved Rykov's report on the campaign.[9] The Central Committee in November demanded 'strict economy' in the expenditure of state funds.[10]

Sovnarkom on 7 February 1927 decreed a 15 per cent cut in administrative expenditure in all economic organs of all-union significance operating on khozraschet and all joint-stock companies with state capital. Vesenkha and NKRKI were to report to Sovnarkom by 1 April 1927 on its attainment.[11] In 1926/7 NKRKI investigated the organization of individual commissariats, industrial institutions, trading organizations and local soviets.[12] As a result, drastic reductions in staffs were approved. D.Z. Lebed', deputy narkom of NKRKI, in April 1927 noted a significant improvement in NKRKI's work, which had secured 'much more appreciable results' than in the first six months of the campaign.[13]

Individual investigations, however, were time-consuming and yielded only minor economies. In May 1927 Yakovlev, deputy narkom NKRKI, estimated economies in the state administration for 1926/7 at 40 million roubles. By the enforcement of strict saving norms, determined by NKRKI, he argued that at least 200 million roubles could be reduced from the budget by the beginning of the financial year 1927/8 if only the 'inertia' of the apparatus was overcome.[14]

Sovnarkom in May 1927 gave NKRKI powers to compel administrative and economic institutions to implement its proposals for a range of rationalization measures.[15]

The campaign was venomously criticised by the united opposition. The 'Declaration of the Eighty Four' in May 1927 condemned 'this bureaucratically distorted struggle to economise' which had damaged the position of the workers without yielding any tangible results.[16]

On 4 July 1927 Yakovlev, presenting NKRKI's report to Sovnarkom, proposed specific norms for economies. NKRKI's investigations in 1927, he argued, demonstrated that a 20 per cent cut in administrative costs was feasible without any ill effects.[17] Cuts of this order, he argued, required staff reductions of between 30–40 per cent, as achieved by NKRKI in various commissariats and institutions.

Ordzhonikidze in the summer of 1927 repeatedly raised the same demand.[18] The joint Central Committee–TsKK plenum in August 1927 endorsed NKRKI's scheme, noting that 300–400 million roubles should be saved in the coming year and approved measures to strengthen TsKK–NKRKI's role in improving administration.[19] Sovnarkom on 30 August 1927 approved a decree, prepared by NKRKI, for a 20 per cent cut in the 1927/8 estimates for state, economic and trading institutions. NKFin, Vesenkha and NKRKI were given responsibility for the decree's implementation.[20]

Official policy was scathingly attacked by the united opposition. The 'Platform of the Opposition' in September 1927 argued that Stalin and Rykov's regime of economy campaign had produced negligible results and it unreservedly condemned past efforts to effect economies at the expense of the workers. The campaign was bureaucratically conceived and produced unacceptable side effects. A target of savings of 400 million roubles of non-productive expenditure in one year, it claimed, was perfectly feasible. What was needed to attain this target was mass mobilization, the exercise of the 'class activity of the workers' to pressurise the bureaucracy.[21]

Yakovlev's speech to the X Ukrainian Party Congress in November 1927 outlined a new, more militant policy to deal with the defects in the apparatus, to break resistance to official policies, as part of a general assault on 'bureaucratism'.[22]

In supervising these cuts, NKRKI encountered intense opposition.[23] A meeting of managers, convened by the Council of the congress of trade and industry in November 1927, denounced the indiscriminate imposition of the 20 per cent cut on the trusts and enterprises. Managers from the major trusts condemned NKRKI's 'formalistic' and 'bureaucratic' stance, and accused it of applying 'desperate pressure'. Managers blankly refused co-operation or absolved themselves of the consequences.[24] This incensed the inspectors who retaliated by further tightening control.

Ordzhonikidze at the XV Party Congress in December 1927, claimed that in 1926/7 economies of between 80–100 million roubles had been made and that a 20 per cent cut in 1927/8 would yield a further 200–220 million roubles. Moreover, he declared that if managers 'ransacked' their expenses, this target could be exceeded.[25] Other NKRKI spokesmen argued that the target greatly underestimated the real potential for administrative economies.[26]

Yanson, deputy narkom of NKRKI, sternly warned officials who failed to comply with the directive that they would be disciplined and where necessary brought before the courts.[27] The congress instructed TsKK–NKRKI strictly to enforce the 20 per cent reduction in administrative–management costs in 1927/8.[28]

In February 1928 Ordzhonikidze reported to Sovnarkom that the campaign within the institutions operating on the state all-union budget was being successfully realized but indicated problems in the republican apparatus.[29] Sovnarkom instructed NKRKI to maintain strict control through its republican and local organs.[30] In April and July 1928 Vesenkha instructed the heads of the glavki to secure the 20 per cent cuts. Only pressure from NKRKI made some of the main glavki comply.[31] Evasion was widespread and took covert and ingenious forms.[32]

Ordzhonikidze in December 1928 reported that in 1926/7 and 1927/8 the campaign had successfully realized its target of 300 million roubles set in 1926. This figure (corrected for errors) excluded economies achieved in the union republics, including the Ukraine.[33]

A detailed breakdown of the figures in NKRKI's report, *Za udeshevlenie gosapparata* by A. Samarin, presented a less sanguine picture. Samarin's report revealed that in 1927/8 the economies achieved amounted to 230 million roubles instead of 325 million roubles – i.e., a 14 per cent cut in administrative expenditure overall compared to the 20 per cent cut the party had adopted. In the all-union industries, the shortfall was serious – a saving of 60 million roubles instead of 133 million roubles.[34] The main reason for this, he argued, was the indecisiveness of the heads of the economic organs. Nevertheless, the campaign's success, he argued, disproved managerial fears that it would destroy the apparatus.

The concealed costs incurred by the campaign – through delays, loss of efficiency, damage to morale, etc. – remained unexamined. NKRKI's resort to campaign methods further compromised its works as a scientific rationalization agency. NKRKI's own findings showed that the Soviet state administration in 1926 was significantly smaller than that of the capitalist countries.[35]

The severe economies imposed in 1927/8 could not be continued indefinitely. Sovnarkom on 17 May 1928 decreed that the budget estimates of administrative expenditure for the state institutions for 1928/9 was to be held within the limits of the previous year.[36] No target was set for industry. Ordzhonikidze in December 1928 acknowledged the need to reorientate the campaign.[37]

The XVI Party Conference in April 1929 pronounced the campaign a success and claimed that administrative–management expenditure had been cut by at least 300 million roubles and the apparatus cut by 100,000 individuals.[38] But the economies secured were quite inadequate to meet the growing demands for investment; the burden of financing new industrial investment fell increasingly on industry itself. The resultant pressure to cut labour costs and boost efficiency placed Tomskii (VTsSPS's chairman) in an invidious position.

RABKRIN AND INDUSTRIAL POLICY

In 1927 Kuibyshev's Vesenkha pushed the industrialization drive into a higher gear.[39] An increasingly confident industrial lobby pressed for a programme of rapid expansion. The war scare of 1927 and continued pressure from the united opposition pressed the Politburo in the same direction. NKRKI assumed responsibility for overseeing this policy of expansion.

Industrial Policy (September 1926–September 1928)

The control figures for 1927/8, approved by the Central Committee, proposed an investment of 1,183 million roubles in industry. The target was accepted with reservations by Gosplan, but NKFin and NKZem opposed it, fearing its effect on agriculture. In 1928 the target was raised to 1,304 million roubles, and the problem of financing this programme became the main issue of industrial policy. The party's support for industrial expansion increasingly cut the ground from under the united opposition.

Whilst NKFin's star waned, Gosplan's fortunes prospered. In April 1926 Gosplan set up a 'central commission for perspective plans' (chaired by Strumilin), in which NKRKI and TsSU were permanently represented.[40] Gosplan and Vesenkha drew up successive draft plans for the economy and outdid each other in their proposals to expand industry, provoking intense controversy, with strong opposition being voiced by representatives of agricultural interests, republican NKZems, NKFin and TsSU. NKRKI continued to press for closer links with Gosplan and TsSU.[41]

In March 1927 NKRKI proposed 'strengthening the leadership role of Gosplan', empowering it to direct the planning departments of the economic commissariats.[42] Sovnarkom on 8 June 1927 approved these proposals.[43] This attempt to strengthen Gosplan's control over Vesenkha and the other commissariats was short-lived and was abandoned in June 1928, when the rights of the commissariats, including Vesenkha, in planning were reaffirmed.[44]

The rationalization of industry

In December 1926 the Central Committee called for substantial cuts in industrial costs and prices to stimulate trade and boost industrial output. Vesenkha had earlier proposed a maximum cut of production costs of 1 per cent for the year. The Central Committee in February 1927 endorsed Gosplan's plan for a 5 per cent cut in production costs. It approved also a 10 per cent cut in the retail price of industrial goods to be attained by June 1927. TsKK–NKRKI was instructed strictly to discipline those officials who failed to comply with the resolution.[45] Ordzhonikidze in February 1927 warned that high industrial prices threatened urban–rural trade.[46] The Central Committee in March 1927 inaugurated a new campaign for industrial rationalization.[47]

On NKRKI's initiative STO set up a commission to supervise the campaign.[48] The campaign in 1926/7 secured only modest cuts – production costs fell 1.8 per cent. In October 1927 A.Z. Gol'tsman, a leading NKRKI official, criticized Vesenkha's failure to secure the necessary cuts.[49] Sovnarkom approved the commission's report and criticized disorganization in the administration of industrial rationalization.[50]

The 1927/8 control figures, prepared by Gosplan and approved by Sovnarkom, envisaged a 6 per cent cut in production costs to release resources for investment in industry and to reduce the prices of industrial goods.[51]

Ordzhonikidze at the XV Party Congress emphasized the great scope within industry for cost reduction through simple rationalization methods.[52] The congress in a major resolution on industrial rationalization noted that 'the reduction of costs is the central problem of industry and the resolution of this task must override all other tasks'.[53] NKRKI was to enforce the cuts.

At a meeting of managers in Moscow early in 1928, Ordzhonikidze condemned industry's failure to promote rationalization, and censured NKRKI's past work in this field.[54] In February 1928 NKRKI approved a thesis on its leading role in the rationalization drive. A new NKRKI bureau of rationalization was set up, headed by M.M. Kaganovich and staffed with Russian and foreign specialists.[55] In 1928 NKRKI's journal *Khozyaistvo i upravlenie* was superseded by *Za ratsionalizatsiyu* (*For Rationalisation*) which was less theoretical and more concerned with practical problems of rationalization.[56] In 1928 NKRKI and VTsSPS jointly began publication of a new journal, *Proizvodstvennyi zhurnal* (*Production Journal*) to promote efficiency.

Ordzhonikidze in March 1928 optimistically assessed the prospects for rationalizing Soviet industry. If the USSR was to catch up and overtake the USA it was essential to adopt western techniques, conclude technical agreements with western countries, invite foreign technical specialists and send thousands of young Soviet engineers to study in the west.[57] The 'Americanization' of Soviety industry – already enthusiastically advocated by economic executives – was adopted by NKRKI, which set itself a key role in organizing the incorporation of advanced technology into Soviet industry as part of the socialist restructuring of the economy.

The Politburo plan of work for 1928 made provision for a report by Vesenkha and co-report by NKRKI in July 1928 on the rationalization campaign.[58] At the TsKK plenum in August 1928 Kuibyshev (for Vesenkha) outlining the achievements already secured in this area.[59] M.M. Kaganovich (for NKRKI) criticized Vesenkha's neglect of rationalization and its failure to provide proper 'technical–organisation leadership' as distinct from 'statistical–economic leadership' of industry.[60] The TsKK plenum condemned Vesenkha's work as 'completely insufficient' for the needs of socialist construction.[61] The passive attitude of the party and trade union organs was also condemned.

Kuibyshev's role in promoting Vesenkha's rationalization campaign was supported by Stalin. The pressure which the campaign placed on the labour force was already antagonizing the unions and straining relations between Kuibyshev and Tomskii.[62]

NKRKI in 1928 proposed improvements in the organization of scientific research in industry.[63] Increasingly it directed its attention to reorganizing the administrative structure of industry, to ensure greater technical leadership by Vesenkha, the glavki and trusts.[64] This was an early shot in a sustained campaign waged by NKRKI for a thoroughgoing reorganisation of Vesenkha which came to fruition only in December 1929.[65]

In October 1928, Vesenkha reported a 6.2 per cent cut in production costs for 1927/8, a result described as 'completely satisfactory'.[66] Later a revised figure of 5 per cent was advanced by Vesenkha, a figure confirmed by Ordzhonikidze for NKRKI.[67] This success fuelled demands for further cuts in 1928/9.

Capital construction in industry
In this period a major new area of work was opened up for NKRKI in supervising capital construction work in industry. Investment in state industry rose from 916 million roubles in 1925 to 1,242 million roubles in 1926/7, concentrated in the electrical power and metallurgical industries.[68] Kuibyshev, whilst at NKRKI, in April 1926 noted widespread disorder in construction work and the lack of planning discipline.[69] In 1926, NKRKI reported on construction in the electrical power industry.[70]

NKRKI in 1927 expanded its work and investigated new construction in the metallurgical industry administered by Glavmetall, headed by V.I. Mezhlauk; NKRKI's report by G.V. Gvakhariya was highly critical. For individual projects, estimated costs in 1926/7 were between 160–300 per cent of the original estimates agreed by STO. The work of the planning agencies (Gipromez and Orgametall) was severely criticized.[71] Glavmetall fiercely contested the report's findings.

The Politburo on 12 May 1927 approved a resolution on capital construction work in the metallurgical industry which instructed Vesenkha to strengthen its supervision over this work. Its main recommendation, following NKRKI's proposal, was the establishment within Glavmetall of a special construction department '*stroi*'.[73] NKRKI's criticisms irked and incensed the industrial managers but a major confrontation between NKRKI and Vesenkha was averted.[74]

NKRKI in the summer of 1927 investigated over thirty metallurgical works undergoing reconstruction. Gvakhariya's report strongly criticized Vesenkha and Glavmetall's policy of concentrating investment in the older, existing works. In two years (1925/6 and 1926/7) Vesenkha had invested 344 million roubles in reconstruction of existing works and only 50 million roubles in new construction projects.[75] This policy, NKRKI argued, had been developed to secure the speedy expansion of output, and had been dictated at the behest of the most powerful trusts and enterprises. As a result new projects had been wilfully neglected and resources misallocated.[76]

STO on 16 November 1927 adopted a resolution on the reconstruction of the metallurgical industry.[77] This instructed Vesenkha to compile a detailed five-year plan for the industry together with a longer ten–fifteen–year plan. On this basis of this plan, individual projects were to be decided. The resolution gave no guidance on the relative weight to be given to new projects as opposed to reconstruction work. Glavmetall was instructed to draw up a list of works for reconstruction.

The Central Committee in August 1927 approved the 1927/8 control figures which included an investment target for industry of 2 milliard roubles. It proposed a 15 per cent cut in construction costs as 'a priority task'.[78] NKRKI's work in supervising construction work assumed growing importance.

In November 1927 STO approved a resolution, prepared by NKRKI, to improve capital construction work in the textile industry.[79] STO in January 1928 also approved a resolution, prepared by NKRKI, which censured construction work in the paper industry and reprimanded senior Vesenkha officials for negligence.[80]

To cope with the rapid expansion of NKRKI's work in supervising this new NKRKI department for capital construction work, headed by A.P. Rozengol'ts and A.I. Gurevich, was established in February 1928.[81] NKRKI began publishing detailed reports on capital construction in different industries.

In 1927/8 NKRKI investigated construction work in the electricity generating industry. NKRKI in May 1928 reported that the Goelro project, initiated in 1921, was on schedule for completion in 1931–2, but noted serious defects in individual stations under construction.[82] Power stations in the USSR took twice or three times as long to build as those in the USA, and actual costs were usually more than double the original estimates.[83] The Politburo on 31 May discussed NKRKI's report and adopted a resolution to correct the defects noted. STO on 6 July resolved to correct the work of Glavelektro.[84]

In this period, STO also adopted resolutions to correct defects in construction work, uncovered by NKRKI, in the chemical, rubber and glass industries.[85]

With the expansion of the construction programme there was a huge increase in the importation of industrial machinery. NKRKI early in 1928 investigated the use of imported equipment by the Yugostal trust, reporting serious disorganization in the trust's work, with equipment worth 20 million roubles lying unutilized. The long-standing abuses, it was alleged, were indicative of sabotage. On NKRKI's initiative the technical director of Yugostal, Svitsyn (who in the tsarist period had been the trust's director), was arrested by the OGPU. NKRKI's increasingly abrasive style seriously compromised its relations with Glavmetall and Yugostal.[86] This was intended as a warning to the industrial managers, and predated the notorious Shakhty trial of March 1928.

The Politburo, on NKRKI's advice, instructed Vesenkha on 23 February to ensure more efficient utilization of imported equipment and closer supervision of the procedures for ordering.[87] Sovnarkom on 24 April 1928 approved an NKRKI draft decree instructing Vesenkha and NKTorg on their work in this field.[88] In 1928, NKRKI also reported critically on the use of imported equipment on the railways and in the oil industry.[89]

NKRKI on 27 February 1928 convened a meeting of representatives of Vesenkha, Gosplan, the planning agencies, research institutes and individual managers to discuss the administration of construction work. Leading NKRKI officials Gvakhariya and Visochanskii argued that Vesenkha and the glavki should assume tighter control over projecting–planning and construction work through special construction departments, 'stroi'.[90] Vesenkha's spokesmen opposed this, arguing against excessive centralization of decision-making.

Sovnarkom on 1 June 1928 approved a decree for putting in order capital construction in industry and electrical construction, based on NKRKI's report. It instructed Gosplan to develop long-term plans for construction work and prospecting and approved the establishment of 'stroi' in the industrial glavki.[91]

In October 1928 Vesenkha claimed that in 1927/8 construction costs had been cut by 5 per cent, only a third of the target set. Even this figure was widely questioned.[92] Ordzhonikidze in December complained that the Sovnarkom resolution of June was being flouted by leading glavki, and was responsible for the very high costs and delays in completing projects.[39]

Industrial policy (October 1928 – April 1929)

The defeat of the united opposition in 1928 left the Politburo free to pursue its own policy of industrial expansion. The rapid pace of industrial growth advanced by Stalin, with the backing of the industrial lobby, split the Politburo. Bukharin's famous article *Notes of an Economist*, published in *Pravda* on 30 September 1928, became in effect the 'manifesto' of the new right opposition.[94] He warned of the intolerable strain placed on the budget by high industrial investment and warned that this would upset the delicate NEP equilibrium between industry and agriculture.

Vesenkha's presidium in September 1928 proposed an investment in industry in 1928/9 of 1,680 million roubles. This high target reflected the growing confidence of the industrial lobby. Vesenkha intended that most of this finance would be provided from the state budget. Gosplan, in spite of strong reservations, agreed to an investment target of 1,652 million roubles but insisted that industry itself should provide the bulk of the new investment. Rykov as chairman of Sovnarkom sought to moderate Vesenkha's demands, but met strong resistance from Kuibyshev. Sovnarkom's draft control figures, presented by Rykov, were rejected by the Politburo. The Central Committee plenum in November approved investment in industry in 1928/9 of 1,650 million roubles.[95]

NKRKI's leadership supported this ambitious programme for new investment.[96] NKRKI's main involvement, however, was in determining how that investment programme could be financed without precipitating a major crisis.

In September 1928 Vesenkha (in spite of opposition from its own specialists) proposed a cut of 5.9 per cent in production costs in 1928/9. Gosplan demanded a cut of between 8–10 per cent as the only means whereby the investment programme could be financed without placing an intolerable strain on the budget.[97] A.Z. Gol'tsman of NKRKI criticized Vesenkha's slackness in reducing costs, and claimed that there was scope for cost reduction far in excess of the 5.9 per cent proposed.[98] Yakovlev urged on NKRKI's behalf a target of 'not less' than 7 per cent.[99] Gosplan supported NKRKI's target.

The Central Committee in November 1928 endorsed a 7 per cent cut in production costs in industry for 1928/9.[100] The party approved a budgetary subsidy for industry of 803 million roubles for 1928/9.[101] Kuibyshev, in a private letter in October 1928, complained that he was unable to reduce the planned targets for capital construction and was obliged to take upon himself 'an almost unimaginable task in the realm of lowering costs'.[102] NKRKI encountered great managerial resistance in enforcing these cuts, and in the first half of 1928/9 production costs were cut by only 2–3 per cent.[103]

In October 1928 Z.M. Belen'kii presented a critical report to NKRKI on construction work carried out by Vesenkha.[104] NKRKI demanded a 15 per cent cut in industrial construction costs and a 11 per cent cut in house construction costs in 1928/9. The Central Committee in November approved NKRKI's figures, and STO on 21 December adopted NKRKI's draft resolution on how these cuts were to be attained. Vesenkha in January 1929 instructed industry to adhere to NKRKI's resolution on the organization of construction work.[105] Ordzhonikidze claimed that the 15 per cent cut in Vesenkha's costs alone would yield economies of 60–70 million roubles.[106] NKRKI supervised the preparations for the 1929 construction season.[107]

In *Notes of an Economist*, Bukharin argued that the industrial targets for 1928/9 ignored the shortage of raw material supplies. The plans were based on 'future' bricks with serious deficits in construction materials for 1928/9 anticipated.[108] In October 1928 NKRKI investigated the construction materials industry, and as a result output targets for bricks, cement and timber for 1928/9 were sharply increased. The investigation extricated the Stalin leadership from a difficult situation; it served to discredit Bukharin and the 'Right' whom Ordzhonikidze chided for their faint-heartedness.[109]

The forced development of agriculture required rapid expansion of related industries. In April 1928 Gvakhariya of NKRKI proposed an extremely ambitious programme for the development of the planned Stalingrad tractor works, aimed at facilitating the rapid mechanisation of Soviet agriculture. NKRKI's plan was ahead of its time and STO approved Glavmetall's more modest plan for a new works with a capacity of 10,000 units per annum.[110] Sovnarkom in June 1928 approved NKRKI's proposals for the development of the agricultural implements and machinery industry.[111] NKRKI in the autumn of 1928 raised the targets for tractor production in the Putilov works in Leningrad.[112]

TOWARDS THE 'REVOLUTIONARY RECONSTRUCTION' OF AGRICULTURE

From the autumn of 1927 onwards agricultural policy became a major area of concern for NKRKI.[113] The Politburo in 1926/7 stood out against the policy of the united opposition to tax the peasantry to finance industrialisation but increasingly was forced to examine the contribution which agriculture could make to facilitate rapid industrial growth. Even in the autumn of 1926 Yakovlev (NKRKI's chief spokesman on agriculture) had viewed the prospects for future development with caution.[114] The shortfall in the 1927 harvest and the mounting pressure from the industrial lobby for an agricultural policy which would facilitate rapid industrialization brought a dramatic change of stance.

The main area of contention concerned the future prospects for the expansion of grain production. In November 1927 F.A. Tsil'ko (NKRKI's expert on agriculture) proposed that the expansion of grain production should be based on a doubling of yields in ten years, an increase of 50 per cent in five years if growth was linear, and 30–35 per cent if exponential.[115] This would solve the grain problem and satisfy the needs of the industrialization drive. At the time this was regarded as little more than a reckless kite-flying exercise.

NKRKI's plan far exceeded anything previously countenanced. Vesenkha in 1926 had envisaged a growth in yields of only 8 per cent over five years. Gosplan in 1927 proposed a target of 6 per cent. A.L. Vainshtein (NKZem's agricultural expert) also supported this figure. In the summer of 1927 N.P. Oganovskii (an expert employed by Vesenkha and NKTorg) had proposed a target of 11.4 per cent.

NKRKI's plan went considerably further than even Oganovskii's projections. Technically, NKRKI argued, its plan was feasible, and would simply raise Soviet agriculture to the level of technical efficiency of west European agriculture. Economically it was practical, it would require no substantial state investment neither would it necessitate an increase in grain prices as an incentive. The simple technical improvements needed could be achieved largely by persuasion and the education of the peasant farmers concerning their benefits. Oganovskii rejected NKRKI's plan as reckless and unrealistic.[116]

At the XV Party Congress Yakovlev scathingly dismissed Gosplan and Vesenkha's plans for agriculture, as 'calculations of a reactionary nature'.[117] NKRKI's target of a 30–40 per cent increase in yields over five years, he argued, was realistic and attainable. Most of the investment for agricultural modernisation, he anticipated, would come from the peasants themselves. Stalin's speech dwelt on the backwardness of Soviet agriculture and the difficulty of ensuring grain, supplies, a problem in part the heritage of sub-division of peasant holdings after 1917. He proposed a gradual extension of the socialized sector to overcome this.[188]

The XV Party Congress indicated a major shift of policy, noting that 'uniting and transforming the small individual peasant farms into large collective farms [kolkhozy] must be made the party's principal task in the countryside'.[119] It instructed the party also to wage a more resolute struggle against the kulak. Bukharin endorsed this new policy.[120] In January 1928, Stalin declared that the party had rejected the capitalist path of agricultural development in favour of 'the socialist way of creating large farms in agriculture'.[121]

Kuibyshev in January 1928 was already speaking of 'a slogan or semi-slogan or half whisper' concerning the need to abandon the *smychka* in order to further industrialization.[122]

The defeat of the united opposition brought a reorientation in the party's agricultural policy. With the shortfall of the 1927 harvest the Politburo, under Stalin, decided to persist with the expansion of industry and to extract grain from the countryside, at government fixed prices, by administrative methods. In January–February 1928 party leaders were dispatched to the regions to act as plenipotentiaries. As Stalin increasingly embraced a leftist stance on agricultural policy relations with his Politburo colleagues, Bukharin, Rykov and Tomskii, were severely strained. Mounting peasant unrest also generated alarm in the rural party and soviet organs.

The procurement crisis strengthened NKRKI's grip over agriculture. In March 1928 the director of TsSU V.V. Osinskii was replaced by V.P. Milyutin, a member of the NKRKI collegium.[123] In March 1928 Ordzhonikidze (from NKRKI) and N.A. Kubyak (narkom of NKZem RSFSR) were appointed Sovnarkom plenipotentiaries in charge of the spring sowing campaign. [124] In June 1928 Yakovlev was appointed Ordzhonikidze's deputy in supervising the winter sowing campaign.[125]

In 1927 NKRKI investigated the state of agriculture – rural differentiation, organization and technique of peasant farms, the cooperatives, the state farms (sovkhozy), trade and migration. In his foreword to the report Yakovlev noted the party's resolve to restructure agriculture on a co-operative basis and through the creation of large production units, and its rejection of the rightist course of strengthening kulak agriculture.[126]

Stalin's speech on 28 May 1928, 'On the grain front', indicated support for NKRKI's plans. He denied that the procurement target for 1927/8 had been excessive and blamed the grain crisis on 'faulty planning and mistakes in economic co-ordination.' The crisis, he argued, stemmed firstly from the small peasant holding with their low percentage production of grain for the market (*tovarnost*) and secondly 'the anti-soviet action of the kulaks' in hoarding grain and holding the regime to ransom. Stalin advanced three proposals: (i) extending collective farming and co-operative agriculture; (ii) expanding and strengthening the sovkhozy; (iii) raising yields on small and medium-size peasant farms by 15–20 per cent in 'a few years'. By these methods, Stalin argued, an additional 200–300 million puds of marketable grain would be made available to the state within three or four years – 'a supply more or less sufficient to enable us to manoeuvre both within the country and abroad'.[127]

Yakovlev intensified NKRKI's offensive and launched a campaign to raise grain yields through the two newspapers under his editorship, *Krest'yanskaya gazeta* and *Bednota*. In June 1928 he organised a discussion of NKRKI's scheme amongst agricultural experts in Moscow. At this meeting L. Finkovskii of NKZem, a supporter of NKRKI's plan, denounced the professors of the Timyraezev Agricultural Academy for their restricted class perception of the question.[128] A heated debate was continued in the press.[129]

NKRKI vigorously promoted the socialization of agriculture, as a means of boosting grain production and restraining the kulaks. However, Yakovlev still insisted that collective farms would remain for a 'long time' as 'islets in the sea of peasant economy'.[130] NKRKI RSFSR reported to Sovnarkom RSFSR in April 1928 'On Ways of Developing Collective Farms'.[131] In May an NKRKI report on the new sovkhozy claimed that the socialized sector was more efficient than the private one. The most developed forms of socialist farming were alleged to be technically the most advanced.[132] Yakovlev's report to the All-Union

Kolkhoz Congress in June placed collectivization and the raising of yields on peasant holdings, through mechanization, at the forefront of the campaign to reorganize agriculture.[133] NKRKI's report on the development of giant grain sovkhozy was approved by Sovnarkom on 19 June 1928.

Gosplan, under growing pressure, in May 1928 increased its target for grain yields from 11.5 to 14.5 per cent.[134] In July NKZem published its five-year plan for agriculture in the RSFSR which envisaged an increase in grain yields of only 10.5 per cent. NKZem demanded massive state investment in agriculture to meet its targets.[135] However, under pressure from radical specialists like Kviring, Chayanov and Finkovskii, NKZem raised the output target for grain to 34 per cent, to be secured through a 21.8 per cent increase in sown area and only a 12 per cent increase in yields.[136]

Yakovlev in *Ekonomicheskaya zhizn'* in July outlined NKRKI's manifesto for agriculture. He demanded a radical reorganization and a 'technical revolution' to double yields in ten years. NKRKI's plan was neither 'utopian' nor 'fantastic' but, he insisted, development under socialism could not be measured by the yardstick of tsarist Russia. He attacked Oganovskii and Vainshtein and other experts 'with pretensions to learning' and denounced 'bourgeois hairsplitting'. The task of raising yields, which Sovnarkom had entrusted to NKRKI, could not be solved in the 'chancelleries of the commissariats' but instead was being thrashed out in the press. To realize this task NKRKI needed the support of experts fired with 'revolutionary enthusiasm'. Yakovlev declared '*we need a plan for the revolutionary reconstruction of agriculture*'.[137]

At the Central Committee plenum in July 1928 Stalin argued that a 'tribute' or super-tax be extracted from the peasantry to finance industrialization. Moreover, the textile link between the peasant economy and industry should be supplemented by a metal link to facilitate the modernization of agriculture along collectivist lines. The regime had to strengthen its links with the poor peasanty to deal with intensified class struggle. Strong criticism from the right forced Stalin to moderate his earlier proposals for developing agriculture[138] and the plenum criticised the excesses of the procurement campaign.

Nevertheless, the Central Committee, following NKRKI's initiative, approved the creation of new grain sovkhozy.[139] Sovnarkom and TsIK on 1 August 1928 adopted a decree making the expansion of the socialized sector a central part of the party's agricultural policy.[140] A new body (Zernotrest) was established, attached to STO, to manage these giant concerns. M.I. Kalmanovich was transferred from NKRKI to head this agency.[141]

In August 1928 Sovnarkom and Ekoso RSFSR discussed agricultural policy. At this meeting Chayanov of NKZem urged an 18 per cent increase of yields over five years. The socialized sector was to be extended and investment greatly increased. A special commission, headed by N.I. Il'in (narkom of NKRKI RSFSR) was to prepare a decree on the subject.[142]

Oganovskii in August 1928 denounced NKRKI's plan as irresponsible and a threat to the entire economy. NKZem's target of 13 per cent growth of grain yields instead should be regarded as optimal.[143]

The new Gosplan plan for agriculture envisaged an increase in grain yields of 11.4 per cent basic and 15.1 per cent optimum, aimed at doubling grain output in ten years in line with NKRKI's proposals. M. Golendo (head of Gosplan's agricultural section) rejected NKRKI's plan to increase grain yields by 30–35 per cent as unrealistic, although a few specialists supported this target.[144] Krzhizhanovskii even conceded that it might be technically feasible to raise yields by 20 per cent in five years if 'sufficient materials' were supplied.[145]

Rykov in Sovnarkom adamantly opposed NKRKI's plan. In September Sovnarkom approved Gosplan's new plan for agriculture based on a doubling of production in ten years with a 20 per cent increase in sown area and a 15.1 per cent increase in yields over five years.

Stalin at the Central Committee plenum in November 1928 highlighted the 'grain problem' as the main brake on rapid industrialization and attacked rightist spokesmen who feared a rupture in urban-rural relations.[146] The plenum, with Stalin's assent, approved the 1928/9 control figures based on Gosplan's recommendations for a 7 per cent increase in sown area and 3 per cent increased yields.[147]

At a TsIK session in November 1928 Tsil'ko denounced NKZem and Gosplan's 14 per cent target for grain yields as inadequate. Kubyak condemned NKRKI's plan as 'utopian' and 'impossible'.[148] Gosplan's plan began to disintegrate, as the winter sowing campaign failed to meet its targets, bad weather throwing into doubt the long-term plan.[149] The Politburo could either reduce industrial investment and direct more resources into agriculture or take up NKRKI's option of increasing output through higher yields.

The Stalin bloc seized on NKRKI's plan. Sovnarkom in December adopted a decree to raise grain yields by 30–35 per cent in five years. The decree, apparently drafted by the Il'in commission, was approved in spite of opposition from Rykov and his deputies in Sovnarkom RSFSR.

A press campaign was orchestrated by Yakovlev to secure support for NKRKI's plan. In an almost unprecedented move the decree was presented to TsIK for approval and was given legal force.[150]

Kubyak and the experts of NKZem RSFSR were forced humiliatingly to capitulate, although opposition within Gosplan persisted for some months.[151] The opposition from the agricultural lobby, including the agricultural sector of the Communist Academy, was brushed aside.[152] Ordzhonikidze praised Yakovlev's work in creating this daring new plan for the reconstruction of agriculture which would solve the problem of grain supply, strengthen the party's 'class position' in the countryside, and provide a firm economic foundation for the continued expansion of industry.[153]

RABKRIN'S RELATIONS WITH THE ECONOMIC INSTITUTIONS

The joint Central Committee–TsKK plenum in August 1927 stressed TsKK–NKRKI's role in enforcing policy implementation – the 'weakest link in the work of the state machine'. Vigilance was needed to combat the influence of hostile class elements in the administration. The resolution stressed the need to involve the courts in improving administration, to develop among the masses an attitude of 'intolerance' to mismanagement, waste, corruption and high-handedness and proposed mass mobilization as part of a general 'cultural revolution'. NKRKI had to be strengthened with the best workers and specialists, including foreign specialists, and was also to organise visits of Soviet specialists abroad to study the latest techniques and administrative methods.[154]

XV Party Congress

At the XV Party Congress in December 1927 the united opposition was routed. The congress coincided with mounting apparatus resistance to the Politburo's policies – the regime of economy, the grain procurement crisis, difficulties in industry. Against this background the Politburo's approach to the state apparatus shifted sharply to the left. This became part of a wider struggle between Stalin and the 'Right' opposition over the general strategy of economic development and for control over the party.

In his report to the congress Ordzhonikidze continued to stress the need for 'comradely' co-operation between NKRKI and the economic organs, and to get away from a situation where the two sides saw each other as 'hostile camps'.[155] The great majority of managers, he argued, recognized NKRKI's authority and assisted it in its work. At the same time, he warned, disputes between the controllers and managers should not be resolved by 'family circles' (*po semeinomu, po bratskomu*). Excessive investigations, however, remained a problem. There was also a much greater willingness by party cells and trade unions to assist NKRKI in its work. Criticisms of the incompetence and high-handed methods of NKRKI inspectors continued to be voiced.[156]

Apparatus resistance to official policies incensed TsKK–NKRKI's leadership. Ordzhonikidze quoted Lenin's injunction in 1922 for strict enforcement of party and government directives. He again emphasized the need to revive mass participation in NKRKI's work in order to strengthen control and broaden the regime's links with the people.[157] N.I. Il'in (narkom of NKRKI RSFSR) also urged the development of social control. Yakovlev proposed assigning a quarter of NKRKI's staff to the task of enforcing party and government decrees.[158]

At the congress NKRKI spokesmen launched a concerted attack on the legal organs. Ordzhonikidze outlined grave deficiencies uncovered by NKRKI in the work of NKYust in 1927. He insisted that NKYust should spearhead the campaign against resistance to party policies, against defects in the apparatus and quoted Lenin's letter to D.I. Kurskii in 1922 which denounced NKYust's formalistic approach to its work and urged the use of 'show trials' in the fight against bureaucracy.[159]

N.M. Yanson (deputy narkom NKRKI) demanded a 'minor revolution' in the legal organs. NKYust's work, he argued, suffered from a 'professional juristic deviation' reflecting the absence of proletarian cadres in the legal organs. In initiating prosecutions, he asserted, it adhered too literally to the letter of the law. The need to apply greater political judgement in NKYust's work and to proletarianize the legal organs was endorsed by A.A. Sol'ts and M.F. Shkiryatov of NKRKI.[160]

Yakovlev, backed by Ordzhonikidze, argued that the special disciplinary courts set up in 1923 to deal with official crimes were too lenient. He proposed that they be disbanded and that official crimes should again be subject to prosecution in the ordinary criminal courts.[161]

N. Krylenko (the Procurator) argued that the legal organs were responsible for judging the legality of offical actions and not their political expediency. NKYust's task was to ensure uniformity in the administration of justice and to prevent abuses by inexperienced officials, many former workers. The abolition of the special disciplinary courts, he argued, would overburden the ordinary courts and adversely affect the apparatus.[162]

The XV Party Congress approved NKRKI's proposals to strengthen legal control and to abolish the disciplinary courts. In January 1928, Kurskii was replaced as narkom of NKYust RSFSR by Yanson, who retained his membership of TsKK.[163] It provided an ominous foretaste of the future development of state administration in which legal niceties were not allowed to stand in the way of political necessities.

The XV Party Congress also approved a detailed resolution on the work of TsKK–NKRKI, based on the Central Committee resolution of August 1924.[164] The resolution dramatically tightened control over the apparatus and (unlike the two previous congresses) was silent on the need for good relations between NKRKI and the managers.

TsKK–NKRKI was greatly strengthened. The party congress elected several OGPU officials to TsKK. In February 1928 the NKRKI collegium was reinforced with seven new members.[165]

The Tightening of Control (1928)

After six years of peaceful development under NEP, during which the managerial lobby and the trade unions had acquired considerable power, the Politburo executed a dramatic change of course. The 'left turn' of 1928 brought a tightening of control over the apparatus, and a determined attempt to break the entrenched power of both the managers and the trade unions.

The Shakhty trial in March 1928, organized on Stalin's initiative, heralded this abrupt policy change. The trial of fifty engineers in the coal industry accused of sabotage and collaboration with former owners was the pretext for tightening control in industry. It highlighted the position of the bourgeois specialist in industry and the inability of communist managers effectively to supervise their subordinates.[166]

Neither the leadership of OGPU nor NKRKI assisted in preparing the trial. V.R. Menzhinskii, (chairman of OGPU) appears to have resisted this witchhunt. A *Pravda* editorial on 10 March 1928 censured NKRKI and OGPU for their laxity.[167] NKRKI on 23 March directed its local control agencies to co-operate closer with OGPU.[168] The joint Central Committee–TsKK plenum in April approved the conduct of the trial, and warned of the growing danger posed by counter-revolutionary forces.[169] Ordzhonikidze in May repeated the warning.[170] NKRKI,

OGPU and the courts were increasingly drawn into the campaign against saboteurs, wreckers and class enemies.[171]

In 1928, in the face of growing peasant and labour unrest, NKRKI's mass control work was dramatically revived. In January NKRKI and NKRKI RSFSR set up a joint 'complaints bureau' to hear public criticisms of maladministration.[172] Attempts were made to strengthen the local KK–RKI organs, and the RKI sections attached to local soviets.[173] In March *Pravda* and other newspapers, with Stalin's approval, began publishing a regular RKI bulletin, titled 'Under the control of the masses', aimed at mobilizing popular initiative.[174] The Komsomol congress, under Stalinist control, urged young communists to assist NKRKI through the Komsomol's 'light cavalry' detachments.[175] The party cells in industry were also strengthened.

The Central Committee–TsKK joint plenum in April inaugurated a 'self-criticism' campaign against bureaucracy in the apparatus with Stalin's full backing.[176] The slogan, stolen from the opposition, was intended to strengthen discipline and enforce a class approach to questions of policy. *Pravda* welcomed the campaign as a means of bolstering party and trade union democracy and strengthening 'mass control'.[177] In practice, it became a means of isolating the Right in industry and the trade unions and mobilizing support behind official policies.

Stalin's speech to the Komsomol congress assailed the degeneration of the apparatus. In a period of intensified class struggle the regime could no longer rely on the peaceful development to socialism. The apparatus had to be restructured and subjected to 'two-fold pressure' – from above by the Central Committee and NKRKI, and from below through social control. He advocated 'a broad tide of criticism from below against bureaucratism' aimed at 'rousing the fury of the masses o the working people against the bureaucratic distortions in ou: apparatus'.[178] The Central Committee on 3 June 1928 called on all party members and workers to assist in the campaign.[179] This sharp leftware turn in policy aroused the indignation of industrial managers, and at the end of June Stalin was forced to criticise distortion of the campaign.[18]

At the TsKK plenum in August 1928 D.Z. Lebed' reported on th campaign's success. The TsKK plenum's resolution, echoing Stalin' view, condemned 'the search for sensation, the irresponsible smearing o managers and administrators' but warned also against 'direct or cover persecution for inconvenient criticism.[181]

In the summer of 1928 many managers protested to the press of th campaign's adverse effect on labour discipline. *Pravda* condemne attempts 'to discredit the slogan of self-criticism itself in the guise of a struggle against distortions of it'.[182] At the VIII Trade Union Congress the vice-chairman of the metal workers union compared the self-criticism campaign with tsarist pogroms, managers rather than Jews serving as scapegoats for failures in government policy.[183]

Ordzhonikidze in March 1928 condemned the excesses of '*spets* baiting' in industry, emphasizing the loyalty of most specialists. The Shakhty trial, he argued, was part of a concerted ideological offensive against the regime aimed at a capitalist restoration. This, he declared, underlined the necessity for the regime to create its own proletarian technical intelligentsia:

> Certain clashes between the new red specialists and the old specialists will inevitably occur but the party and government are fully resolved to open wide the door to the young specialists.[184]

The Central Committee in July 1928 approved a resolution on the preparation of new specialists.[185] The new cadres policy emphasized the promotion of trade unionists and party activists into administrative work.[186] Rykov strongly resisted this policy, and cited Lenin on the need to secure the co-operation of bourgeois specialists.[187]

Ordzhonikidze at the XV Party Congress had insisted, counter to opposition claims, that the apparatus was loyal and under party control.[188] In 1928, in the wake of the Shakhty and Smolensk affairs, NKRKI began to purge the state and economic organs. Ordzhonikidze at the VIII Trade Union Congress in December 1928 cautiously welcomed the purge, and warned that officials who failed to implement government policy should be expelled.[189] However, NKRKI RSFSR in January 1929 halted the purge until the matter had been resolved by the XVI Party Conference.[190]

The intensification of control and the problem of control duplication compounded the difficulties of the apparatus. TsIK and Sovnarkom in April 1928 approved a decree, prepared by NKRKI, which required all control agencies, institutions, commissariats and trade unions to compile annual plans of their investigations. NKRKI was to approve these plans, eliminate duplication and prevent unauthorized investigations.[191] The problem, however, remained unresolved.[192]

NKRKI, in order to overcome apparatus resistance, sought closer support from the trade unions and party cells.[193] Ordzhonikidze in a speech to NKRKI workers in 1928 noted that the very best NKRKI inspectors were meeting 'fierce' opposition from officials, even from party members, who were being transformed into 'incorrigible depart-

mentalists'. Compelling these officials to give account before th
workers provided a most salutary lesson.[194] The fact that departmental
ism was being fostered by the intense pressure placed on the apparatu
was of little account.

TsKK–NKRKI AND THE INTERNAL PARTY STRUGGLE

Ordzhonikidze saw TsKK as a guardian of party unity and a bulwark o
ideological orthodoxy. He made some attempt to restore to TsKK it
orginal functions, assigned it by Lenin, as a supra-party body abov
factions.[195] Tactically TsKK–NKRKI in 1927 presented a more con
ciliatory stance to the opposition but in practice firmly supported th
Stalin–Bukharin bloc.

Following the publication of the 'Declaration of the Eighty Four' i
May 1927 TsKK again investigated the united opposition. Its leaders
Trotsky, Zinoviev and Kamenev were compelled to report to TsKK o
their activities. TsKK's party collegium, chaired by Yaroslavkskii, wa
unrelenting in this work. Yaroslavskii in *Pravda* in July repeatedl
denounced oppositional activity as a breach of the undertaking given i
October 1926.[196]

TsKK threw itself behind the new campaign. Ordzhonikidze presen
ted a report to the joint Central Committee–TsKK plenum in Augus
1927 on the expulsion of the opposition from the party. A joint session o
the Politburo–TsKK presidium in September formulated the main line
of the policy.

The 'Platform of the Opposition' in September 1927 demanded tha
TsKK be reconstructed:

> It is necessary to construct TsKK in the real spirit of Lenin's advice
> Members of TsKK must be (a) closely associated with the masses, (b
> independent of the apparatus, (c) possessed of authority in th
> party.[197]

Only in this way, it argued, could TsKK's authority be restored and th
ruling faction be made accountable to the party.

At a stormy joint Central Committee–TsKK plenum in October 192
Yaroslavskii and other Stalinists jostled, threatened and abused mem
bers of the opposition.[198] Another joint session in November 192
approved Stalin's proposal to expel five oppositionists from the Centra
Committee and six from TsKK, and to expel Trotsky and Zinoviev fron

the party. At the pre-congress conferences the struggle against the opposition featured prominently.[199]

The opposition persisted in trying to neutralise TsKK–NKRKI. Ordzhonikidze reported:

> The opposition demanded that TsKK should stand above the Central Committee, above the opposition and better still if it would stand with the opposition. The opposition considered that TsKK should lack any political physiognomy and like a poor matchmaker should run from one to another to achieve some kind of reconciliation. We consider that firstly one must be a Bolshevik, a Leninist and only then a member of TsKK.[200]

The opposition mistakenly believed that Ordzhonikidze had no stomach for the fight.

Amongst the opposition, Ordzhonikidze commanded respect. The Trotskyist Victor Serge described him as 'an honest and scrupulous man tormented by recurrent crisis of conscience' and a 'harsh but scrupulous character'.[201] Opposition scorn was reserved for the Stalinist hardliners in TsKK, particularly Yaroslavkii, Shkiryatov, Yanson and Peters.[202]

At the XV Party Congress, TsKK spokesmen – Ordzhonikidze, Yaroslavskii, Yanson and Shkiryatov – fulminated against the opposition.[203] A commission, chaired by Ordzhonikidze, drafted the resolution on this question.[204] The congress expelled Trotsky, Zinoviev and Kamenev from the party, bringing the most intense phase of the internal party struggle to a close.

In 1927 TsKK and OGPU co-operated closely in the drive against the opposition.[205] At the XV Party Congress TsKK members were denounced as 'Chekists' by the opposition. Yaroslavskii for TsKK praised OGPU's work.[206] Through TsKK and the Secretariat party discipline was tightened.

TsKK in 1928 was active in enforcing party discipline, monitoring oppositional activity, and ruling on the readmission of expelled members. Ordzhonikidze successfully persuaded many former oppositionists back into the party fold behind the policies of the 'left turn'. This conciliatory line was strongly criticized inside the party.[207] Nevertheless, he continued to lend his protection to ex-oppositionists in key positions.

The Stalin bloc appropriated the opposition's policy of all-out industrialization. In the spring of 1928, following the grain procurement crisis, a new grouping headed by Bukharin, Rykov and Tomskii crystallized. At the Central Committee plenum in July 1928 the two factions clashed bitterly over agricultural policy. In the early summer of 1928 Bukharin controlled a majority within the Politburo. Stalin, however, succeeded in rallying the waverers to his side. As head of TsKK–NKRKI, Ordzhonikidze attempted initially to play a mediating role, as the guardian of party unity. Bukharin claimed that in the summer of 1928 Ordzhonikidze 'came to see me and swore loudly at Stalin but at the decisive moment turned tail'.[208]

In the autumn of 1928 the struggle intensified, although both sides sought to avoid open discord. In October Bukharin submitted a series of economic demands to the Politburo. These were referred to a commission, including Stalin, Molotov, Rykov, Bukharin and Ordzhonikidze. Various compromises were advanced. The Central Committee plenum in November, however, condemned the rightist elements in the party. The TsKK plenum conflated the struggle with the Right with the struggle against bureaucracy.[209]

In the manoeuvres against the Right in the winter of 1928/9 TsKK–NKRKI worked closely with the Stalin bloc.[210] The TsKK party collegium, headed by Yaroslvskii, assisted the Secretariat in this work. Rightist support within TsKK appears to have been small.[211] TsKK–NKRKI was also used to limit rightist influence which was strongly entrenched, under Rykov's patronage, in Sovnarkom and STO and also against the Right in the trade unions. At the trade union congress in December 1928 the Stalin bloc captured control of VTsSPS, but many delegates expressed alarm with NKRKI's efforts to reorientate the trade unions' work towards production.[212]

Stalin in January 1929 moved to finish the job with the help of TsKK. A meeting of the Politburo, attended by Ordzhonikidze, Yaroslavskii, Shkiryatov and Sol'ts for TsKK, discussed the activities of the Right. At this meeting the TsKK members, it appears, exercised voting rights. This 'organizational encirclement' took Bukharin by surprise and ensured a safe majority for Stalin.[213] Bukharin's past communications with Kamenev provided the pretext for a resolution condemning the Right. On 9 February 1929 the Politburo and TsKK presidium approved a resolution criticizing Bukharin's contacts with Kamenev and censuring Rykov and Tomskii.

At the Moscow party conference in February–March 1929 the rightists were denounced by Molotov and Yaroslavskii. The joint Central Committee–TsKK plenum in April 1929 condemned the Right, sacked Bukhharin as editor of *Pravda* and ousted Tomskii from the chairmanship of VTsSPS.[214] The XVI Party Conference In April 1929 confirmed the rout of the Bukharin bloc with its resolution condemning the Right 'deviation' in the party.

CONCLUSION

The grain crisis and the Shakhty trial were the two hinges on which party policy in agriculture and industry turned in the spring of 1928. The 'left turn' momentously affected the whole direction and tenor of the party's work. The Stalin bloc appropriated the policies of the vanquished united opposition and, mobilizing powerful institutional support, embarked on an uncertain course, which clearly rejected NEP in favour of all-out industrialization and the modernization of agriculture on collectivist lines. This involved the creation of a control-dominated administrative system unseen since the civil war.

TsKK–NKRKI from the spring of 1928 onwards stood at the centre of the party's work. Its organization and personnel were strengthened to cope with its new tasks. New links were forged between TsKK–NKRKI and OGPU and NKYust. TsKK–NKRKI assumed growing influence in economic policy formation, in support of the radical industrializers in Vesenkha and Gosplan. TsKK–NKRKI in this process switched its fire from the left to the right. TsKK–NKRKI, at the head of a powerful control lobby, became the instrument for forcing through the new-found strategy of the emergent Stalinist bloc. In industry and agriculture NKRKI emerged as a major policy initiator in its own right in opposition to the operative commissariats.

7 Rabkrin and the 'Revolution from Above' (1929–30)

The nascent Right opposition was resoundingly defeated in the spring of 1929, thereafter remaining a powerful but leaderless tendency. The regime finally turned its back on NEP and in the following months the direction of economic policy was dramatically changed – the five-year plan was approved, the collectivization of agriculture was set in train. The 'year of great change' of 1929 gave way to the all-out 'socialist offensive' of 1930. The momentous 'revolution from above' unleashed in this period saw a fundamental reorientation of the party–government apparatus. The Politburo itself took a firm grip on economic policy. In this critical period TsKK–NKRKI, under Ordzhonikidze's forceful leadership, reached the apogee of its power and influence.

TsKK-NKRKI AND THE CENTRAL PARTY–GOVERNMENT APPARATUS

The dominance of the Stalin bloc within the leading party organs was firmly established; the leaders of the Right isolated.[1] The Politburo itself from 1929 onwards assumed a major role in directing economic policy, hearing reports from the main economic fronts, both from the main economic commissariats and TsKK–NKRKI. Politburo and Central Committee commissions, including representatives of key institutions and leading specialists, were widely employed in resolving problems.[2]

TsKK–NKRKI in 1929–30 acquired great influence over economic policy. The joint sessions of the TsKK presidium and NKRKI collegium, meeting every ten days and dominated by its Stalinist leadership, became a major forum of debate. Detailed reports on the state of individual branches of the economy were prepared by NKRKI's specialist groups, TsKK–NKRKI interrogated economic executives and specialists. Detailed resolutions were adopted by TsKK–NKRKI and submitted to STO, Sovnarkom and the Politburo. TsKK–NKRKI emerged as a major policy directorate and powerful trouble-shooting organization on the economic front.[3]

NKRKI was brought under still tighter direction of TsKK. It was reinforced with foreign consultants and specialists. The study and adaptation of western patterns of development, western technology and rationalization became its overriding concern. NKRKI supervised the employment of foreign specialists in Soviet industry.[4] In April 1929 a group of independent Soviet specialists was formed to assist NKRKI, which by August numbered some 300.[5]

The Politburo, supported by TsKK–NKRKI, usurped the role of Sovnarkom and STO in economic policy-making. Rykov retained his post as chairman of Sovnarkom and STO until December 1930, but his power had been eroded. Increasingly important in economic policy were his two deputies – Kuibyshev and Ordzhonikidze – the foremost advocates of rapid industrialization in the Politburo.[6] In May 1929 Rykov was replaced by S.I. Syrtsov as chairman of Sovnarkom RSFSR.[7] The republican NKRKI, especially in the RSFSR and the Ukraine, strongly supported the Stalinist leadership in forcing through its policies against Rightist opposition.[8]

These organizational changes and shifts in alliances corresponded with the new stage in economic policy, requiring a thorough overhaul of the party–state apparatus. The attack on the Right was coupled with an attack on 'bureaucracy'. The regime returned to the methods of mass mobilization of 'war communism'. Campaign techniques allied to administrative measures were deployed to break resistance to the 'general line'. The initiative in policy-making passed from the economic executives to the political controllers and the guardians of public order; new prominence was assumed by TsKK–NKRKI and OGPU.

Stalin at the Central Committee–TsKK plenum in April 1929, which confirmed the defeat of the Right, signalled the new change of policy.[9] It was imperative to link the state more closely with its mass base. The new class offensive against the regime by the 'wreckers' and kulaks demanded a resolute rebuff. To deal with the threat the party–state apparatus and the mass organizations had to be fundamentally overhauled:

> If we are to break the resistance of the class enemies and clear the way for the advance of socialism, we must, besides everything else, give a sharp edge to all our organisations, purge them of bureaucracy, improve their cadres and mobilise the vast mass of the working class and the labouring strata of the countryside against the capitalist elements of town and countryside.[10]

The main danger now came from the right, thus justifying this precipitate lurch to the left.

Ya.A. Yakovlev (deputy narkom of NKRKI) in a major report to the XVI Party Conference in April 1929 on the theme 'Bureaucracy' elaborated Stalin's ideas:

> We live in circumstances in which the socialist offensive which we are leading is meeting furious opposition from the kulak who fears that he will lose his position. The kulak, and in many cases, the nepman and the bourgeois intelligentsia, who are placed in our bureaucratic apparatus, attempt in the developing class struggle to swing some parts of our state machine to their side, to place it at their service. *Therefore, the question of checking implementation becomes the central question to which we must pay particular attention even greater than that which it was necessary to pay to this question a few years ago* (emphasis in the original).[11]

This crusade against bureaucracy was part of the struggle against the 'Right deviation', and against all opponents of industrialization and collectivization.

It was necessary, Yakovlev argued, to restructure and restaff the administration, inspiring it with a new class-conscious militancy. What was needed, he argued, was an 'improvement of the state apparatus which would make it capable of fighting against the kulak and the nepman'.[12] This sharp change of course struck directly at the rationalizers in NKRKI whose commitment to scientific research was to be submerged under the pressures for political conformity. The central priority was to reorientate the apparatus, to realize the new tasks set before it.[13]

The XVI Party Conference was a watershed. The conference authorized a full-scale purge of the state and economic institutions.[14] TsIK and Sovnarkom in June 1929 entrusted NKRKI with the conduct of the purge.[15] NKRKI established a Central Commission for the Purge, headed by the formidable Ya.Kh. Peters, a member of both the NKRKI and OGPU collegia.[16] Local purge commissions were established in the localities. From 1929 until 1932 the entire apparatus was systematically purged.[17] At the XVI Party Congress in 1930 Ordzhonikidze reported that 454,000 officials out of 2 million had been investigated, of whom 11 per cent had been purged.[18]

This period saw also an intensification of the 'self-criticism' campaign. Mass participation in control work in 1929–30 was also revived on a scale unseen since the early 1920s, organized through NKRKI, trade union temporary control commissions (VKK), Komsomol 'light cavalry', and through the press.[19] In 1929 the RKI assistant cells, which had been abolished in 1923 in the face of managerial and trade union pressures, were re-established, giving NKRKI a vital foothold in the institutions and enterprises.[20] The NKRKI purge commissions also became vehicles of popular control. The Central Committee and TsKK in March 1929 approved a resolution on the promotion of workers into administrative posts and approved the development of a system of 'patronage' (*sheftsvo*) of enterprises over institutions.[21]

Mass mobilization, and the heightened ideological offensive associated with it, was intended to strengthen the regime's base of support, to rouse popular enthusiasm behind official policies, and serve as a safety valve for defusing labour unrest. It was also used to pressurise the administrative apparatus and to break traditional trade union structures and attitudes.[22] In July 1929 N.M. Shvernik, a former TsKK–NKRKI official, replaced Tomskii as chairman of VTsSPS. Stalin at the XVI Party Congress noted that through the campaign for mass control VTsSPS had 'got rid of the old opportunist leadership'.[23]

The defeat of the Right, confirmed by the XVI Party Conference in April 1929, provided the background for this dramatic change in policy towards the apparatus. Ordzhonikidze in TsKK–NKRKI continued vigorously to press the campaign against the Right.[24] At the Central Committee plenum in November 1929 Ordzhonikidze, Yakovlev and Yaroslavskii from TsKK–NKRKI denounced the opposition.[25] The plenum removed Bukharin and Tomskii from their leading posts in the party. Ordzhonikidze in 1930 stressed the leadership's generosity towards the Right, claiming that 'we did everything possible to keep comrades Rykov, Bukharin, Tomskii and Uglanov at leading posts in the party'.[26]

At the XVI Party Congress in August 1930 Ordzhonikidze declared that the Right 'demanded from us, from TsKK, that we should occupy a position of some kind of Philistine justice', claiming that TsKK was 'higher than everyone and everything'.[27] This attempt to neutralize TsKK was brusquely dismissed by Ordzhonikidze who claimed 'TsKK was created by the party for the party and not for people who become confused, lose their heads and raise panic in the party'.[28]

RABKRIN AND INDUSTRIAL POLICY

The Stalin bloc had by the autumn of 1928 resolved on a major change in economic policy which went far beyond the confines of NEP.[29] The basic imbalance between industry and agriculture was to be resolved by the forced development of the former. Vesenkha seized the initiative from Gosplan in preparing the five-year plan, placing central priority on heavy industry. In the autumn of 1928 the more cautious planners and specialists in Vesenkha and Gosplan were ousted from their posts. NKRKI supported Vesenkha's ambitious programme for industrialization but also backed Gosplan's insistence that industry itself play a major role in financing this expansion.[30]

The fifth Gosplan planning congress in March 1929 hotly debated Gosplan and Vesenkha's variants of the plan. At the joint Sovnarkom-STO sessions in March 1929 the Vesenkha variant was supported by A.I. Mikoyan for NKTorg, and by Yakovlev for NKRKI.[31] Rapid industrial expansion, Yakovlev argued, was essential if the modernization of agriculture was to be realized, and the necessary increase in grain yields secured. The targets for tractors, agricultural implements and fertilizer were to be considered minimal. Everything should be done to bring the new works rapidly into operation.[32]

Rykov's attempts to moderate the plan were rejected by the Politburo. Stalin at the joint Central Committee-TsKK plenum in April 1929 outlined an economic strategy identical to that advocated by NKRKI. He urged the utmost development of industry, particularly the production of tractors, agricultural implements and fertilizer, in order to reconstruct agriculture, declaring 'rapid development of our industry is the key to the reconstruction of agriculture on the basis of collectivism'.[33]

The five-year plan was endorsed by the Central Committee. Sovnarkom on 23 April 1929 adopted the plan and the optimal variant was endorsed by the XVI Party Conference. The V Congress of Soviets on 29 May 1929 voted its approval. The plan envisaged an investment in industry during the plan period of 16.4 milliard roubles. Industrial output was to increase by 180 per cent, concentrated mainly on heavy industry. Expansion was to be financed mainly by industry itself through increased efficiency. The basic and optimal variants envisaged a huge increase in labour productivity (85–110 per cent) and a massive cut in industrial costs (30–35 per cent) to ease the strain on the state budget and slacken the pressure on agriculture. In the following months, on Vesenkha's initiative, the targets for some of the main industries were further increased.[34]

In the spring of 1929 NKRKI emerged as a powerful force in the field of industrial policy, which brought it into confrontation with Vesenkha. The dispute centered on conflicting assessments of the state of industry and the prospects for development. NKRKI (through its investigations of industrial rationalization and capital construction work in the preceeding two years) had arrived at a radically new conception of the state of industry. Within industry, it believed, huge reserves of materials lay unutilized which could be mobilized for raising still higher the targets set in the five-year plan; all that was needed was the political will and administrative muscle to release those reserves.

Ordzhonikidze in December 1928 claimed that there were vast reserves in industry which could be mobilized. In the following months, NKRKI issued orders to its local organs to tighten control in this area.[35] A.Z. Gol'tsman in a review of reserves in industry estimated excess stocks at 800–830 million roubles.[36] This pressure prompted STO on 8 March to order Vesenkha and NKPS to release reserves worth 250 million roubles.[37] In the field of capital construction NKRKI had already seriously clashed with Vesenkha; a major NKRKI report had outlined the deficiencies in Vesenkha's work over the past two years.[38] Z.M. Belen'kii in a report to the Higher Course on Capital Construction in Soviet Industry in March 1929 was scathing in his criticism of Vesenkha and alleged that wrecking was rife.[39]

Reconstruction of the Metallurgical Industry

Against this background, NKRKI began a systematic campaign fundamentally to rewrite the five-year plan for industry, beginning with the metallurgical industry.[40] In 1927/8 3.3 million tons of pig iron were produced. In the autumn of 1928 Vesenkha approved a target of 10 million tons for 1932/3. The target was strongly opposed by Gosplan's specialists, but was approved by Gosplan's presidium in December 1928. Vesenkha assigned Yugostal, headed by S.P. Birman, a key role in realizing this target. The trust produced two-thirds of pig iron output in 1927/8, and was set an output target of 5.2 million tons for 1932/3. No overall plan existed for the trust's reconstruction, and urgent discussions began in Glavchermet and Yugostal to determine how this increase in output could be attained. Vesenkha specialists envisaged a huge, costly programme of reconstruction to realize this target.[41]

From October 1928 to March 1929 an NKRKI commission (led by A.I. Gurevich) investigated the Yugostal trust. The commission included the consultant A. Karner, the director of a small German steelworks.

In the final months of 1928 NKRKI investigated the Stalin works at Stalino (formerly Yuzovka). Vesenkha's plan for the works had been drafted by its technical director (Svistyn), the former director of the Yuzovka works, who had been arrested on NKRKI's initiative in 1928.

The plan envisaged the investment of 65 million roubles, with the building of two large blast furnaces, the installation of two blast engines and the building of a Bessemer shop. Much of the existing plant at the Stalin works, including three blast furnaces, was to be dismantled and replaced. NKRKI, alarmed by the cost of the project and the precipitate action of Vesenkha in authorizing construction work, protested to STO and STO on 28 December 1928 halted all construction work at the Stalin plant.[42] The issue threw NKRKI's already strained relations with Yugostal into crisis.

In January 1929 NKRKI criticized Vesenkha's work of planning and projecting in the metallurgical industry.[43] A.P. Rozengol'ts (head of NKRKI's capital construction section) expressed alarm at the scale of construction work envisaged by Vesenkha for the metal industry. He proposed that the plan should be based on the raising of the productivity of existing plant by 35 per cent, through the adoption of rationalization methods developed in Germany and the USA.[44]

The fate of the Stalin works became the crux of the debate between NKRKI and Vesenkha. Rykov (chairman of STO) in early March summoned an interdepartmental meeting of representatives of NKRKI, Vesenkha, Yugostal, Glavchermet, the Stalin works, NKFin, Gosplan and various specialists to examine the issue. Two meetings were held under the chairmanship of G.M. Krzhizhanovskii. Whilst Vesenkha argued for a massive programme of new construction, NKRKI urged its programme of rationalization. Birman strongly defended the Stalin works project. Krzhizhanovskii's report to Rykov expressed alarm at the scale and cost of the project, and cited with approval the rationalization experience of the German metal industry. A final decision, he advised, should be deferred until Vesenkha and Yugostal had completed their plan for the reconstruction of the entire trust.[45]

In March 1929 Z.M. Belen'kii, a leading NKRKI official, castigated Vesenkha's work in this field. The Stalin works project, he argued, typified how enterprises extracted funds from the state. Already 800,000 roubles had been invested in this works and on this basis further investment was demanded. Incomplete and inadequate projects were approved and once adopted replaced by more realistic, more costly plans.[46]

In April 1929 *Torg. Prom. Gazeta*, Vesenkha's newspaper, published a letter which the editor of *Diktatura truda* in the town of Stalino had sent to Gosplan. This pleaded the cause of the works which, it argued, was undercapitalized and in urgent need of new investment. The scheme enjoyed powerful support, especially from the Ukrainian organizations.[47]

At a Vesenkha plenum early in April Birman bitterly attacked NKRKI interference in the trust's work; the high turnover of senior officials, some purged by NKRKI, had disrupted its work; the multiplicity of investigations the trust was subjected to by NKRKI and others created disorganization and poisoned the atmosphere.[48]

In April 1929 the optimal variant of the five-year plan was adopted with a target of 10 million tons of pig iron in 1932/3. The plan for the reconstruction of the Yugostal trust remained unresolved. At the XVI Party Conference in April Kuibyshev conceded that Vesenkha's plan was somewhat grandiose and underestimated the scope for rationalization. Nevertheless, he argued, the resources allocated to this vital sector should not be cut.[49]

Ya.A. Yakovlev, in his speech to the conference, sharply criticized Birman's article. Shortcomings within Yugostal, he argued, reflected the continued influence of 'wreckers' and 'pseudo-specialists' whose proposals were simply 'rubber-stamped' by ineffectual party administrators. The sabotage which NKRKI had exposed in 1928 persisted. The exaggerated reconstruction plan for the Stalin works illustrated a general problem in industry.[50]

This attack on Yugostal caused a furore. S.V. Kosior, first secretary of the Ukrainian party organization, repudiated Yakovlev's allegations. Yakovlev noted the anger of the Ukrainian delegates who wished 'to defend their comrade Birman'.[51]

Birman renewed his attack on NKRKI, denouncing the disruptive effect of excess control on the trust's work. He reaffirmed his support for the Stalin works project and condemned NKRKI's part in halting the scheme. He queried the competence of the German consultant employed by NKRKI. (Vesenkha's own German consultant, Puppe, had backed the plan.) Birman continued to defend the arrested Svitsyn, the architect of the reconstruction scheme.[52]

Gurevich, who had led NKRKI's investigation of the trust, repeated Yakovlev's charge that wreckers were at work in Yugostal. Yugostal and Glavchermet had failed critically to examine the Stalin works project and had no plan for the reconstruction of the trust as a basis on which to judge the expediency of the scheme. Rozengol'ts argued that wrecking influence was reflected in the trust's preoccupation with new construction projects, and its resistance to proposals to increase the utilization of existing plant.[53]

Vesenkha on 8 April presented its plan for the reconstruction of Yugostal to STO. NKRKI in May presented its own counter-plan (compiled by Gurevich and the metallurgical group) to STO.[54]

The Vesenkha plan, NKRKI alleged, was simply an amalgamation of the different plans submitted by individual works and lacked any strategy for restructuring and modernizing the trust. In seventeen of the existing furnaces retained, the coefficient of utilization was to be increased by only 1 per cent. For all furnaces the coefficient was to be increased by 6 per cent by 1932/3. In twenty-eight existing works NKRKI proposed that the coefficient should be increased by 35 per cent, in line with German industry.

These rationalization measures, NKRKI argued, made it possible to slash the reconstruction programme and reduce costs dramatically. Vesenkha proposed that ten existing furnaces be dismantled, twenty retained and another twenty new furnaces built. NKRKI argued that all thirty furnaces be retained and only eight new furnaces built. Whereas Vesenkha envisaged that the new furnaces would in 1932/3 produce 60 per cent of planned output NKRKI set a target of 30 per cent. Vesenkha's investment programme was to be spread, with twelve works being reconstructed simultaneously. NKRKI argued for the concentration of investment in the five most efficient works – Rykov, Tomskii, Dzerzhinskii, Voroshilov and Mariupol. Concentration of investment was advocated on technical, economic and organizational grounds. This would allow modernization of production in a limited number of giant new works.

NKRKI's plan excluded the Stalin works from the list of works for reconstruction. Birman in the summer of 1929 fought desperately to save the plan.[55] In July 1929 he took a group of experts and foreign consultants to Stalino. *Torg. Prom. Gazeta* reported the support of these experts for the Yugostal plan and their disagreement with NKRKI.[56]

STO failed to resolve the differences between NKRKI and Vesenkha. The matter was referred to the Politburo and examined by its commission.[57] The Central Committee on 8 August 1929 adopted its resolution 'Concerning the work of Yugostal'. Vesenkha's plan, it alleged, had been inspired by wreckers and failed to present a comprehensive scheme for the modernization and rationalization of Yugostal. It raised the output target for the trust from 5.2 million to 6.6 million of pig iron in 1932/3. The resolution proposed expanding only three works – Tomskii, Dzerzhinskii and Mariupol – which were to produce 3.5 million tons in 1932/3.[58] In an unpublished passage, which Ordzhonikidze blurted out at the XVI Party Congress, the resolution specifically rejected major reconstruction of the Stalin works.[59]

At the XI Ukrainian Party Congress, in June 1930 the reconstruction of the metallurgical industry, of Yugostal and Stalino, continued to be hotly debated and NKRKI's role in the affair was strongly condemned.[60]

At the XVI Party Congress in July 1930 Ordzhonikidze assailed the work of Vesenkha, Yugostal and Glavchermet. Vesenkha, he argued, lacked a 'seriously thought out and prepared five-year plan for the metallurgical industry'. He stressed NKRKI's role in redrafting the five-year plan for Yugostal and optimistically assessed the prospects for attaining the new output target and for realizing the utilization coefficients of existing plant which NKRKI had advanced.[61]

NKRKI in the summer of 1929, flushed with its success, embarked on a detailed study of the Uralmet trust. The investigating commission was headed by Gurevich and included several American consultants.[62] NKRKI reported that the Urals metallurgical industry administered by the trust was still extremely backward. Although 147 million roubles had been invested in the industry, output in 1928/9 was still below pre-war levels. The misuse of investment funds was severely criticized.

NKRKI reported that the industry was highly fragmented and localized. Uralmet administered a total of thirty-six works which were generally small, with low average output, and closely tied to their raw material sources. Transportation was underdeveloped. Little attention had been paid to the substitution of coke and coal for timber fuel. Concentration, specialization and mechanization of production as part of the long-term development of the industry had been neglected.

Vesenkha was upbraided by NKRKI for neglecting Uralmet. Ordzhonikidze argued that Uralmet suffered from greater disorder even than Yugostal. The trust administration repudiated these accusations.[63] Vesenkha and NKRKI both accepted the need to expand the industry. The industrial organs prepared a plan for the reconstruction of the Urals industry. Output was to be greatly expanded and concentrated in a few giant enterprises and the region transformed into a producer of special steels.

The Politburo, with representatives of TsKK-NKRKI, discussed the development of the Urals industry in May 1930. A report was presented by Gurevich for NKRKI. On 15 May the Central Committee adopted a resolution, 'Concerning the work of Uralmet' approving the transformation of the Urals into the country's second metallurgical base. It authorised the construction of two new giant metal works (Tagil and Bakal) in addition to the Magnitogorsk and Kuznetsk works and the Zaporozh'e works in the Ukraine. Concerning the existing works 'it proposed the concentration of production in six selected plants. It approved the concentration of production on high-quality steel.[64] Vesenkha played a large part in drafting this resolution but NKRKI also claimed credit for the plan.[65]

In 1929/30, NKRKI closely supervised construction work of the expanded plants of the Yugostal trust. In the summer of 1930, Vesenkha proposed to raise output targets for the Yugostal trust by speeding up the completion of the new works and expanding their capacity. It proposed that the target for the three principal works (Tomskii, Dzerzhinskii and Mariupol) should be increased from 3.5 million tons to 6.9 million tons of pig iron in 1932/3.[66] NKRKI strongly supported the proposal.

The revision of plans for Yugostal and Uralmet prepared the way for raising the overall targets for the metallurgical industry.[67] In June 1930 the Politburo raised the target for pig iron for 1932/3 from 10 million tons to 17 million tons. Stalin at the XVI Party Congress enthusiastically hailed the new target, urged the further 'forced development' of the industry to catch up with the west and warmly welcomed the plan for a second metal base.[68] Ordzhonikidze credited NKRKI, Vesenkha and the local party organs with raising the plan target.[69] The congress endorsed the new figure.[70] Within months Kuibyshev in Vesenkha became convinced of its impracticality and sought behind the scenes to adjust the plans accordingly,[71] but Ordzhonikidze in NKRKI remained firmly committed to the target.

Revision of Planned Targets for Industry

The rout of Yugostal, the most powerful industrial trust, opened the floodgates for the revision of targets in all major industries. NKRKI's conception of the state of industry received the Politburo's blessing. Together with the radical planners of Vesenkha and Gosplan the inspectorate embarked on a campaign fundamentally to rewrite the optimal variant of the five-year plan.

Raw cotton production
The five-year plan proposed a dramatic expansion in the textile industry, and associated with this an increase in raw cotton production from 215,000 tons in 1927/8 to 606,000 tons in 1932/3.[72] In 1927/8 37 per cent of total cotton consumption was supplied from imports. The plan envisaged self-sufficiency in raw cotton by 1932/3, and the target was approved on the promptings of the textile industry. On 3 May 1929 the Central Committee approved a resolution on the textile industry stressing the need to take up the slack in the industry and to boost raw cotton production to avoid production discontinuities.[73] These decisions were taken against the advice of the cotton glavk (Glavkhlopkom).

In July 1929 Glavkhlopkom reported that 700,000 tons of raw cotton would be needed in 1932/3. The glavk insisted that the target could not be attained without substantial imports. NKRKI promptly investigated the industry. Its report savagely criticized Glavkhlopkom's failure to expand production, and hinted directly at sabotage.[74]

The Politburo heard reports from Glavkhlopkom and NKRKI. Glavkhlopkom insisted that the output target should not be increased. NKRKI proposed an output target for 1932/3 of 916,000 tons, sufficient to satisfy demand and to build up reserves. The Central Committee on Committee on 18 July 1929 approved its resolution, 'Concerning the work of Glavkhlopkom', which outlined the new plan for the cotton industry, settling for a revised target of 800,000 tons.[75]

The Central Committee censured Glavkhlopkom and developed further NKRKI's plan for industry. It proposed a massive extension of the area under cotton cultivation, the raising of yields by 15 per cent in the period of the plan, and a large extension of the socialized sector. Measures were advanced for the mechanization of the industry and for increased use of fertilizer. An irrigation policy, advanced by NKRKI, based on small-scale low-budget projects was approved.[76]

Vesenkha's leadership endorsed the new targets, and Kuibyshev in July 1929 voiced approval of NKRKI's work.[77]

The Central Committee resolution provided a prelude to the collectivization of cotton cultivation in the winter of 1929/30 which NKRKI was closely involved in developing.[78] Within NKRKI in the summer of 1930 prospects were still optimistically assessed; Glavkhlopkom's pessimism, NKRKI argued, had been confounded.[79]

At the XVI Party Congress Ordzhonikidze confidently predicted that the output target set for the industry would be attained.[80] Kuibyshev supported official policy and stressed the need to boost production to satisfy the demand of the textile industry.[81]

The timber industry

The five-year plan envisaged that timber procurement would rise from 41 million cubic metres in 1927/8 to 125 million cubic metres in 1932/3 to meet domestic demand, and boost timber exports.[82] A powerful NKRKI commission began a lengthy investigation of the timber industry in December 1928.[83]

In April 1929 a major NKRKI RSFSR report criticized the tardiness of the industry in exploiting the country's huge timber reserves. It condemned the fragmentation of procurement work between Vesenkha, NKPS and NKZem, and the damaging effect which competition between different trusts was having on the industry. The report proposed an ambitious programme to mechanize the industry, extend the felling season, advance forest management, and improve the supply of labour as part of a programme to colonize the forest zone. Sovnarkom RSFSR approved the basic plan in June 1929.[84]

In the summer, demand for construction material, pit props, and fuel rose sharply. On 20 June 1929 the Politburo demanded an immediate increase in the targets for the timber industry, and an increase in timber exports to relieve pressure on the country's trading balance.[85] An NKRKI resolution on the timber industry at the end of June 1929 proposed a massive rise in output to be achieved by applying NKRKI RSFSR's recommendations.[86]

On 28 June 1929 Gosplan and NKRKI presented reports to STO on the timber industry; the matter was referred to a special STO commission, headed by S.I. Syrtsov, chairman of Sovnarkom RSFSR.[87] The Politburo on 22 August approved a perspective plan for the development of the industry.[88] On 27 August STO increased the procurement timber target for 1932/3 from 125 million cubic metres to 180 million cubic metres, an increase of 45 per cent in line with NKRKI's targets. STO also adopted NKRKI's recommendation for the rationalization and reorganization of the industry.[89]

STO on 12 July 1929, on NKRKI's initiative, adopted a resolution demarcating the responsibilities of the respective procuring agencies of NKPS, NKZem and Vesenkha.[90]

The oil industry

Oil production which in 1927/8 stood at 11.7 million tons was set in the optimal variant of the plan to rise to 21.7 million tons in 1932/3. Radical revision of the targets for tractors and motor vehicles dramatically increased demand for fuel. In August 1929 the 1932/3 output target for oil was raised to 26 million tons.[91] Demand quickly outstripped all previous forecasts; the Oil Syndicate in October 1929 calculated demand for kerosene in 1932/3 at 12 million tons, to produce which 65 million tons of crude oil would be required.

NKRKI in the autumn of 1929 investigated the industry. Its report castigated the industry and alleged that wrecking activity was rife. NKRKI backed a scheme, advanced by a minority of oil industry specialists, for the transfer of the industry from kerosene to benzine production. It was calculated that with this more efficient refining process 12 million tons of benzine could be produced, sufficient to meet expected demand, from only 40 million tons of crude oil.[92]

The production of benzine required the introduction of a new and complex refining technique – the cracking process – well developed in the USA and Germany. The number of cracking plants would have to be increased from 3 to 120 at an estimated cost of 1 milliard roubles. This massive reconstruction was to be undertaken at a time when supplies of materials and equipment were desperately short.

The Oil Syndicate and the trusts opposed the benzine scheme on economic and technical grounds. Prominent specialists such as Ramzin and Larichev of Goelro spoke against it. STO in October 1929 raised the 1932/3 output target for crude oil to 40 million tons and approved the transfer of the industry from kerosene to benzine production. NKRKI claimed responsibility for this policy change.[93]

In November–December 1929 a conference of geologists and oil industry experts, chaired by I.M. Gubkin, declared the project feasible. In 1932/3 25–26 million tons were to be extracted from existing deposits and the remainder from new deposits yet to be located. STO in January 1930 approved NKRKI's proposals to ensure the maximum utilization of existing wells and to speed up drilling and prospecting work.[94]

Tight control was enforced over the policy's implementation. NKRKI spokesmen reported continued opposition to the scheme in 1930. In the summer of 1930 the prospects of realizing the target were still optimistically assessed. Nevertheless, evidence of difficulties in the industry became increasingly evident.[95]

The iron ore industry
Output of iron ore in 1927/8 stood at 5.7 million tons, and in the optimal variant of the plan was set at 19.4 million tons in 1932/3.[96] As the targets for the metallurgical industry were raised so desperate measures were taken to boost ore production.

Early in 1930 an NKRKI commission, headed by A.I. Izrailovich, investigated the Southern Ore Trust which administered the Krivoi Rog complex. All aspects of the trust's work were subject to critical scrutiny. The output target of 12.5 million tons, said to be influenced by wreckers, underestimated the real potential of the complex. NKRKI's report formed the basis for the Central Committee critical resolution, 'Concerning the work of the Southern Ore Trust', of 15 April 1930. It approved developing the complex, and raised the output target for ore for 1932/3 to 16 million tons.[97]

NKRKI also investigated the development of the iron ore industry in the Urals. Its report condemned the lack of leadership provided by Uralmet and Vesenkha, criticized the passivity of the trade unions and party cells, and alleged that 'wrecking' was widespread.[98] Izrailovich's report was discussed by NKRKI on 5 May 1930. NKRKI's criticisms of the Urals iron ore industry were incorporated into the Central Committees resolution, 'Concerning the work of Uralmet', of 15 May 1930.[99] The resolution set no specific target either for metal or ore production for the Urals region.

In the summer of 1930, Izrailovich suggested an output target for iron ore for 1932/3 of 33 million tons. Gipromez proposed a target of 44 million tons.[100] Precise targets yielded to general indicators.

The coal industry

Coal production under the plan was to double from 38.4 million tons in 1927/8 to 75 million tons in 1932/3.[101] This was approved by the party despite strong opposition from the coal industry.

In 1929 an NKRKI commission, headed by Izrailovich, investigated the main Donugol trust to examine the work done to realize its target of 31 million tons in 1932/3. The report savaged the trust's shortcomings in developing prospecting work, in approving new projects and in supervising new construction. It censured Vesenkha and Glavgortop's failure to provide leadership for the trust.[102] The trust disavowed the report's criticisms. STO on 13 August 1929 approved a resolution on capital construction in the trust based on NKRKI's report; this called for the compilation of a five-year plan for mine construction, the setting up of a specialized construction trust (*Shakhtstroi*), and the concentration of equipment production.[103]

In March 1930 the all-union fuel conference estimated demand in 1932/3 at 140 million tons. Estimates in Vesenkha and Gosplan varied between 125 million and 150 million tons.[104] NKRKI spokesmen, Izrailovich and Dedkov, proposed that development should be based on an estimated demand in 1932/3 of 125–150 million tons. Exaggeration of demand, they argued, represented a lesser danger than its underestimation. The output target for the Donbass field in 1932/3, they proposed, should be increased from 40 million to 80 million tons.[105]

In 1930 NKRKI carried out a second investigation of Donugol's work in implementing the five-year plan. NKRKI's report advocated a series of extremely ambitious measures to ensure maximum utilization of existing mines. It proposed also urgent measures to develop coalfields outside the Donbass. NKRKI proposed that Glavgortop's plan for the construction of a large number of small and medium-sized mines should be scrapped and investment concentrated in a limited number of giant mines.[106] Ordzhonikidze at the XVI Party Congress stressed NKRKI's positive contribution to the development of Donbass.[107]

The shipbuilding industry

In 1929–30 an NKRKI commission, headed by A.E. Bliznichenko and assisted by two German consultants (Paul and Weisman), investigated the principal Soviet shipyards at Leningrad, the Black Sea and Vladivostok. The investigation highlighted the high cost of Soviet foreign trade, and the small size of the Soviet merchant fleet, which was still only 30–40 per cent of the pre-war fleet. It voiced concern at the USSR's dependency on foreign shipping, with only 11 per cent of Soviet trade being carried in Soviet vessels. NKRKI's investigations contrasted the serious inefficiency of the Soviet industry with German yards, and proposed a huge increase in the shipbuilding programme.[108]

At the Leningrad yards, managed by Glavmashstroi and Sudotrest, NKRKI proposed to increase the output target of 93 vessels (265,000 tons) to 119 vessels (379,000 tons), to raise output of trawlers from 28 to 178, whilst cutting production costs by 38 per cent, yielding a saving of 150 million roubles, and reducing the investment programme from 45 million to 28 million roubles.[109] The proposals were strongly resisted by the glavk and trust, but were approved by the Politburo on 25 July and confirmed by STO's resolution of 2 August. The revised plan was welcomed by Kuibyshev as a model for all industries of what could be achieved.[110]

NKRKI proposed that at the Nikolaev and Sevastopol yards on the Black Sea the output target should be raised from 69 vessels (260,000 tons) to 264 vessels (540,000 tons), production costs should be slashed, the investment programme cut and unutilized dry-dock facilities brought back into operation. At the Vladivostok yard it proposed increasing output from 251 to 374 vessels, and from 299 to 470 wooden vessels. The Politburo on 25 February 1930 approved these recommendations.[111]

In the course of its investigations NKRKI clashed bitterly with the officials of the industry and claimed to have uncovered a wrecking conspiracy connecting the Nikolaev and Leningrad yards. In October 1929 several officials of Sudotrest were dismissed from their posts.[112] On NKRKI prompting also, Vesenkha in December 1929 presented a plan for an all-union shipbuilding trust to improve the leadership of the industry.[113]

Other industries

Vesenkha's plan for the locomotive and railway wagon industry involved a massive reconstruction programme, estimated to cost 300 million roubles and representing 35 per cent of all investment in engineering.[114] NKRKI in December 1929 categorically denounced the

Vesenkha scheme for exaggerating the need for reconstruction and failing to produce an integrated scheme for the long-term development of the industry. STO on 21 January approved a resolution on the industry's development based on NKRKI's proposals. The proposal to build a new locomotive works and reconstruct two others was rejected. It approved the reconstruction of the wagon industry on American lines, concentrating production in one giant works and slashing the reconstruction programme.[115]

In the summer of 1929 NKRKI completed a detailed study of the Soviet machine tool industry and began a sustained campaign to radically revise the targets and to restructure the industry on American lines. The agency's campaign encountered strong opposition from Vesenkha and Glavmashstroi. The campaign culminated at the XVI Party Congress at which M.M. Kaganovich of NKRKI denounced Kuibyshev's failure to pay sufficient attention to the industry's development. The output target was doubled.[116]

NKRKI also played an active role in reformulating the five-year plans of other key industries – peat extraction, textile machinery, tractors and agricultural implements, chemicals, motor vehicles, mechanical engineering, and construction materials.[117]

NKRKI in addition supervised the construction of new industrial projects. In the summer of 1929 NKRKI examined construction work at the Dneprostroi project and proposed a cut of 10.5 million roubles in the estimate of 212.8 million roubles. This proposal was strenuously resisted by Dneprostroi and Gosplan but was approved by Sovnarkom.[118]

NKRKI also examined major railway building projects including the Turk–Sib line which was estimated to cost 280 million roubles. NKRKI proposed a cut of 46 million roubles whilst NKPS advanced a cut of 23 million roubles. NKRKI's proposal was approved by Sovnarkom, despite strong opposition from NKPS.[119] Desperate measures were taken to cut the investment programmes. NKRKI also supervised construction work in the main engineering works.[120]

In 1929–30, NKRKI increasingly assumed the role of a special *tolkach* or pusher, procuring supplies, coping with emergencies in the enterprises, forcing enterprises to release stocks, combating hoarding, etc. It attempted to deal with the most serious problems arising from an excessively taut plan. The pressure placed on industry resulted in a dramatic increase in waste and deterioration of quality of goods produced. NKRKI in October 1929 proposed measures to tighten control and to establish greater accountability of the managers and officials concerned.[121] STO on 25 December 1929 approved measures to improve the quality of industrial production.[122]

The deterioration in the terms of trade prompted the Central Committee in 1930 to set up a special imports commission. Ordzhonikidze at the XVI Party Congress criticized the preoccupation of industry with securing foreign equipment.[123] NKRKI participated in the commission's work in developing this policy of import substitution.

Recasting the Five-year Plan

The revision of the five-year plan in 1929–30 reflected the adoption by the Politburo of a new conception of the state of industry as promoted by NKRKI and by the radicals in Vesenkha and Gosplan. Vesenkha's estimates allegedly were seriously distorted by departmentalism, localism, managerial and specialist conservatism, sabotage, bureaucratic inertia and trade union resistance. NKRKI emphasized the enormous potential in industry for expansion – through rationalization, the mobilization of stocks, the exploitation of raw material reserves, through reductions in production and construction costs, by the incorporation of new technology and by increasing labour productivity.

The forced development of industry was intended to facilitate the modernization of agriculture, and in turn the forced development of agriculture was to assist rapid industrialization. NKRKI's revision of the plan for agriculture in 1928 was the prelude to its efforts in 1929–30 fundamentally to recast the plan for industry. Its proposals far outdid even the wildest and most optimistic plans developed by Vesenkha and Gosplan, which, inspired by the concept of teleological planning, had sought a fundamental restructuring of the economy. NKRKI's plans accommodated the growing pressures for expansion from the powerful industrial lobby by making industry itself increasingly responsible for financing new investment. These plans fuelled the reckless optimism of the Politburo once the restraining influence of the Right had been removed.

As the Politburo endorsed industry's claim, Rykov's position in Sovnarkom and STO was fatally weakened. In October 1929 he was relieved of responsibility for presenting the 1929/30 control figures and the task was assigned to Kuibyshev and Krzhizhanovskii.[124] The control figures were drafted under the influence of the radical planners in Vesenkha and Gosplan. The successes achieved in 1928/9 further encouraged the radicals.[125]

The Central Committee plenum in November 1929 approved the 1929/30 control figures with an investment target of 3,267 million roubles, and confirmed cuts in production and construction costs of 11 and 14 per cent respectively.[126] Rozengol'ts (for NKRKI) supported the high investment in heavy industry.[127] The incorporation of the revised targets for individual industries into the 1929/30 control figures, however, proved difficult: 'in as much as these directives were not always coordinated it proved impossible to integrate them into one single economic programme'.[128] The coherence of the plan rapidly disintegrated.

The revision of targets for individual industries necessitated a reappraisal of the entire five-year plan. Ordzhonikidze, the Politburo's chief advocate of all-out industrialization, in September 1929 proposed that the '*pyatiletka*' should be completed in its entirety in four years, with some sectors to be finished in three.[129] S.G. Strumilin of Gosplan in September 1929 at the VI All-Union Planners' Congress warned that such a decision would be 'premature' and 'hasty'. Kuibyshev at the Vesenkha plenum in October 1929 criticized the concealed opposition of certain comrades to the high targets but 'categorically' opposed proposals to speed up the tempos.[130] Nevertheless, the slogan 'the five-year plan in four years' was officially launched in February 1930, strengthening the hand of the super-industrialists within Vesenkha and Gosplan.[131]

Stalin at the XVI Party Congress claimed that the plan would be fulfilled in four years and in some sectors of industry in three or even two-and-a-half years. In place of the 'descending Trotskyist curve' of industrial investment, the party had substituted an 'ascending Bolshevik curve'. The colossal strides made by industry confirmed the superiority of the socialist system. The Central Committee, jointly with TsKK, had revised and improved the original five-year plan in accordance with experience.[132]

NKRKI's impact on the five-year plan's industrial targets cannot be quantified precisely. The revisions of targets for key industries in which NKRKI was involved and the actual output of those industries in 1932/3 is given in Table 7.1.[133] For the industries cited, output in 1932/3 failed in all cases (with the exception of oil) to attain even the optimum plan, let alone the revised targets. In some sectors it appears that the new targets had by 1930 assumed a largely programmatic and propaganda role.

NKRKI radically transformed the plan for industry. Not only were targets dramatically raised but the pattern of development was also modified. The restructuring of industry was modelled on the experience of the most advanced capitalist countries. Emphasis was placed on the concentration of production in giant enterprises based on the most modern technology.[134] Great stress was laid on the attainment of western levels of efficiency. Ideologically this was seen as a means whereby the

Table 7.1   Targets and output of key industries (1932/3)

	Output (1927/8)	Optimum plan (1932/3)	Revised plan (1932/3)	Output (1932/3)
Pig iron (million tons)	3.3	10.0	17.0	6.2
Iron ore (million tons)	5.7	19.4	33.0–34	12.1
Oil (million tons)	11.7	21.7	40.0	21.4
Coal (million tons)	38.4	75.0	120.0–150.0	64.0
Timber (million cubic metres)	41.1	125.0	180.0	99.4
Raw cotton (thousand tons)	215.0	606.0	800.0	395.0

USSR could outstrip the west, establishing socialism on a higher technological base. The policy of economic autarky, Ordzhonikidze argued, would transform the USSR into 'a mighty instrument of workers' revolutions in all countries, colonies and semi-colonial lands'.[135]

NKRKI took its proposals for industry seriously. Its reports were lengthy, and based on detailed comparisons of Soviet and western industries. Its criticisms of Soviet mismanagement, inefficiency and waste were no doubt partly justified. These problems were widespread and placed Kuibyshev and his deputies in Vesenkha in a delicate position, unable to defend their subordinates from the controllers without appearing to condone these defects, and defending narrow departmental interests. Kuibyshev's hesitancy and silence on these issues encouraged TsKK–NKRKI's onslaught, and left enterprise directors and specialists in a vulnerable and exposed position.

Many of NKRKI's proposals for individual industries were boldly imaginative and sensible, but it underestimated the huge organizational, economic and technical problems faced by Soviet industry in the throes of this gigantic industrialization drive. The shortage of time, resources and technical personnel inevitably led to serious errors and disorganiza- tion, and made comparisons with western industries misleading. Whilst NKRKI's recommendations for individual industries taken in isolation might have made sense, where the supply of resources from other sectors was assumed, taken collectively they placed an impossible burden on the economy as a whole. The unity and balance of the plan was destroyed as resources in short supply were commandeered for priority heavy industries and key construction projects.[136]

TsKK–NKRKI, fired by political zeal and entranced by the inherent potentialities of a socialist, planned economy for rapid industrialization, undermined the authority of Vesenkha. In the process, it also displaced Gosplan, assuming a role in economic management for which it was neither qualified nor suited. At the XVI Party Congress Kiselev noted critically that 'TsKK–NKRKI has recently become more a punitive planning organ [*bichuyushchii planovyi organ*] than a Rabkrin'.[137]

RABKRIN'S RELATIONS WITH THE ECONOMIC INSTITUTIONS

In 1929–30, NKRKI attained the apex of its influence over industrial policy. NKRKI's relations with the industrial organs were placed on a new, conflict-ridden footing.

The XVI Party Conference Row Over Control

The row at the XVI Party Conference concerning the reconstruction of Yugostal raised fundamental questions. S.P. Birman forthrightly denounced the control-dominated system of administration which NKRKI had nurtured. NKRKI inspectors often adopted a 'scarcely veiled sadistic approach' to the managers. They harassed officials and took a delight in uncovering abuses. Birman himself had been made to feel like 'an idiot or a criminal' by the controllers. Although this was not the official line of NKRKI, it was the attitude adopted by many of its officials:

> This five-year plan requires an incredible tempo, a furious tempo, a savage tempo of work from every worker. It requires courage, demands initiative, flexibility so that workers who are placed in leading positions, at any given moment are able to resolve immediately the questions as they arise, proceeding from the totality of all factors of a huge and complex economy in every given moment. One does not even always have the possibility to think out every problem to the end, because sometimes it is better to decide not quite rightly than not to decide or to delay a decision. And what happens? At the end of the year the examiner of accounts or the RKI inspectors or some other investigative organisation arrive and they pick out one fact, one instance, or one plan from the incredibly large and complicated complex of our economy, they begin investigating outside of time and space, not considering in what circumstances, in

what conditions or why precisely the manager acted in such a way and not another.[138]

Excess control corroded managerial responsibility, initiative and morale. He appealed for relations between NKRKI and industry to be placed on a footing of mutual respect and confidence. Figatner, head of the trade union of soviet employees, echoed Birman's plea.

Birman's speech drew strong fire from NKRKI. V.P. Zatonskii (narkom NKRKI UkSSR) accused Birman of exaggerating the problem. His opposition to control was typical of a bureaucrat and synonymous with the views expressed by Trotsky and Krasin in 1923, aimed at the destruction of party control. Rykov and Kalinin interjected to absolve Birman of the charge. Rozengol'ts, Zemlyachka and Roizenman for NKRKI accused Birman of wishing to dismantle the system of control. Zemlyachka noted sourly that NKRKI was engaged in a 'ceaseless battle with the institutions'. These heated exchanges prompted N.A. Skrypnik from the Ukrainian delegation to accuse NKRKI's spokesmen of waging a vendetta against Yugostal.[139]

Yakovlev stressed the need for effective control over production while untrustworthy elements still occupied key posts in industry. This would continue so long as 'we do not have our own specialists, while they [the old specialists] deceive us at every step'. Birman's plea for improved relations between managers and controllers was curtly dismissed:

I believe that the party cannot and must not allow the establishment of such an alliance because if those who carry out control work conclude an alliance with those whom they control then such an alliance would, without doubt, be a compact concluded with the aim of concealing errors.[140]

Rabkrin and the Collectivization of Agriculture

NKRKI's work in 1929–30 was mainly concerned with industry, but it also helped prepare the ground for the collectivization of agriculture. The party's agricultural policy hinged on NKRKI's plan to increase grain yields by 30–35 per cent over five years, adopted in December 1928. TsSU and Gosplan continued resolutely to resist the target. In his report to Sovnarkom–STO in April 1929 Yakovlev insisted that the five-year plan should be constructed in line with the law passed in December 1928 on the increasing of grain yields. Targets for tractors, implements and fertilizers were to be adjusted to ensure that this increase was attained.[141]

The five-year plan's success depended critically on these wildly optimistic projections for agriculture. In evaluating the 1929 harvest an intense controversy developed. The prospects for the harvest were optimistically assessed by NKZem. NKTorg also anticipated a good harvest and increased its procurement target for 1929/30 by 50.7 per cent above the previous year. TsSU's Expert Council, headed by V.G. Groman, took a much more sceptical view, as did Gosplan in compiling the 1929/30 control figures.[142]

Ordzhonikidze on 18 September, two days before Sovnarkom was to discuss the control figures, bitterly denounced TsSU's statisticians for political bias and their attempt to interfere in policy-making. Groman, head of TsSU's Expert Council, was singled out for criticism: 'He is incorruptible, *but it is his ideology which is most harmful for us*'.[143] The reluctance of TsSU officials to carry out official policy, Ordzhonikidze argued, underlined the need to purge the apparatus.

The attack on Groman was continued by Molotov, Mikoyan and other official spokesmen. On 7 October 1929 Groman was sacked as chairman of the TsSU Expert Council and replaced by V.P. Milyutin. The council was reorganized and two key NKRKI specialists appointed to it.[144]

In December 1929 Sovnarkom and STO approved an increase in the grain output target for the 1930 harvest of 16.6 per cent to make up the shortfall in the 1929 harvest and to maintain the plan's coherence. The problem of grain procurement necessitated recourse to the 'exceptional measures' against the kulaks which Stalin had threatened from the spring of 1929 onwards.

NKRKI pressed its proposals for extending the socialized sector in agriculture. In January 1929 A. Yakovlev, an agricultural specialist in NKRKI, spoke of the 'mass impetus of the *batrak*–middle peasant masses into the kolkhozy'.[145] At the XVI Party Conference in April 1929 Z.M. Belen'kii (for NKRKI) advocated comprehensive collectivization of whole villages, both to bring the kolkhozy under firm control, avoiding the dangers of capitalist degeneration, and to facilitate basic technological improvements.[146]

NKRKI also argued strongly for creating the technical preconditions for socialization and became the most forceful advocate of industrial expansion for this very reason.[147] Its report on the tractorization of Soviet agriculture formed the basis of the Ekoso RSFSR resolution in January 1930, which argued that tractorization not only facilitated but also necessitated mass collectivization.[148]

In dealing with the grain crisis NKRKI adopted a critical attitude to the policy of the Right. Ordzhonikidze in September 1929 caustically attacked Bukharin's policy to 'create kulak co-operative nests which will grow into a socialist state system'. He stressed the need to force industrial development and extend state control over agriculture.[149]

As the problem of the 1929 harvest became clearer, collectivization was increasingly pushed as a solution. In November 1929 NKRKI and Zernotrust presented a report to Sovnarkom which recommended establishing giant grain sovkhozy to overcome the difficulties of grain supply. This policy commanded Stalin's enthusiastic support.[150]

The co-ordination and direction of this policy required the establishment of an agency with all-union powers able to supervise agriculture. At a meeting of Sovnarkom, chaired by Rudzutak, on 11 June 1929, NKRKI argued the need for such a co-ordinating body.[151] It was decided, however, that NKRKI itself was unsuited for such a role and that an all-union NKZem should be established.

At the Central Committee plenum in November 1929 the scheme was strongly resisted by representatives of the Ukraine, which since 1927 had gained considerable autonomy. The opposition was led by N.A. Skrypnik, narkom of NKPros in the Ukraine, an old Ukrainian Bolshevik, one of the main political leaders in the republic, the leading advocate of Ukrainianization, and one of the foremost defenders of the rights of the republics against the centre.[152]

NKZem USSR was established in December 1929. NKRKI claimed the credit and immediately captured the new commissariat.[153] Ya.A. Yakovlev was appointed narkom. M.I. Kalmanovich (formerly of NKRKI) became one of the five deputy narkoms of NKZem. F.A. Tsil'ko, chief architect of NKRKI's agricultural policy, was also transferred to NKZem.[154]

The decision to collectivize agriculture was taken suddenly by the Politburo in response to mounting difficulties with grain procurement. A Politburo commission, chaired by Yakovlev, worked out the details of the policy of collectivization and dekulakization.[155] Yakovlev became the strong man of Soviet agriculture. The same man, Trotsky bitterly reflected, had in 1925 juggled TsSU's statistics to disprove the kulak threat and in 1928 had envisaged collectivization as a long-term objective.[156]

NKRKI staunchly supported the policies of NKZem, but continued to monitor events closely; I.A. Akulov took over as head of NKRKI's agricultural sector. The local KK–RKI in the countryside were reinforced. With the retreat on collectivization forced on the Politburo in the spring of 1930, control assumed growing importance. K.Ya. Kindeev (head of NKRKI RSFSR's agricultural sector) continued to argue the technical superiority of collectivized agriculture. A major NKRKI report was circulated to the delegates at the XVI Party Congress which defended the policies of NKZem.[157]

Tightening of Control in Industry

In December 1929 the Central Committee approved a fundamental reorganization of industrial administration worked out by Vesenkha and NKRKI. NKRKI in 1929 sent a high-powered commission to Germany to study the system of industrial administration. The decree abolished the powerful trusts. The scheme sought to forge closer administrative links between the glavki and the enterprises and to ensure central direction not only over the financial affairs of the works but also over their technical work. It involved the reorganization of industrial administration on functionalist lines.[158]

NKRKI attempted to establish a centralized, hierarchical, control-dominated administrative system. Planning and administrative controls superseded the discipline of the market; rational and considered policy debate became impossible.[159] Strict control, and the insecurity associated with it, sapped independent thinking, initiative, responsibility and creativity amongst administrators. Preoccupation with the observance of formal directives inhibited the work of the industrial organs.[160] Managers were compelled to adopt covert methods, to conceal the capacity of their works, to stockpile materials and secure supplies, in order to circumvent unrealistic directives.

In April 1929 Stalin and Yakovlev argued that wrecking was manifested in attempts to conceal the real capacity of works, to hide stocks, to exaggerate the need for capital construction, in creating bottlenecks and deliberately disorganizing construction and production.[161] NKRKI claimed to have uncovered cases of 'wrecking' in various industries, but its report on the cotton industry voiced a certain perplexity in differentiating between wrecking and genuine error. Elsewhere inspectors were less judicious and automatically interpreted resistance to NKRKI's proposals as proof of sabotage.[162] Ordzhonikidze in September 1929 paid tribute to OGPU's work in uncovering wrecking organizations in industry.[163]

The revision of the plan coincided with the purging of the older generation of specialists and managers. Ordzhonikidze (who had a reputation as a moderate in his dealings with the specialists) in September 1929 noted that there was still 'all kinds of filth' amongst this group and demanded a thorough purge of industry.[164] TsKK–NKRKI through the Purge Commission played a key role in undermining opposition to the new plan targets. NKRKI also became the patron of the younger generation of specialists and managers, many of whom, fired by political zeal, enthusiastically supported the inspectorate's targets for industry and were rewarded with rapid promotion.

Vesenkha's leadership failed to resist NKRKI's seizure of the initiative in policy-making. Only rarely did Kuibyshev give vent to his disquiet concerning the feasibility of these targets.[165]

XVI Party Congress

Ordzhonikidze's report to the XVI Party Congress in July 1930 marked the height of TsKK–NKRKI's power. The report recounted in detail NKRKI's triumphal achievements in revising the targets for all major industries. As such, it was an undisguised indictment of Vesenkha's record. Thanks to the work of NKRKI Soviet industry was proceeding at tempos 'unseen in the history of man'.[166] The huge revisions of the plan, he argued, had been possible not because NKRKI had any 'special forces' at its disposal but because the inspectorate was not contaminated by 'wreckers'. After 'desperate arguments' with industry, matters were referred to the Central Committee which invariably had found NKRKI's proposals to be sound and justified.[167]

As a supplement to the main TsKK–NKRKI report a special OGPU report, '*Materiali k otchety TsKK VKP(b)*', was circulated to the congress delegates. This report, extensively quoted by Ordzhonikidze, underlined the close co-operation between the control agencies. Industrial sabotage, it alleged, was rife, citing the 'confessions' of specialists and managers who had been interrogated. These revealed the retention by engineers and other bourgeois specialists of their own *esprit de corps* and communications networks, demonstrated their contempt for the technical imcompetence of party managers and their scepticism of targets set for industry. Two deputy chairmen of Vesenkha (V.I. Mezhlauk and I.V. Kosior) were criticized, as were the directors of several major trusts. Ordzhonikidze noted that 'some people do not like this OGPU pamphlet, some comrades mentioned in this pamphlet are offended'.[168]

Ordzhonikidze's report stressed the importance of renewing the leading stratum of managers and specialists. He inveighed against the 'malicious bureaucrats' who obstructed and distorted official policies. 'Resolute measures' were needed to expel them from their posts. Mass control was essential to break managerial conservatism and departmentalism. He stressed the need to stimulate the initiative of the workers through the trade union organs and the party cells.[169]

Kuibyshev was shaken by this virulent attack, and in an emotional letter to his subordinates at the congress exhorted them not to retaliate. Ordzhonikidze's speech, he argued, reflected the party 'general line' against which there could be no opposition. Instead managers should critically review their work, reject any notion of caste identity, purge their ranks and strengthen their links with the party. Vesenkha's newspaper, *Za industrializatsiyu*, was instructed to publish an editorial in similar conciliatory vein.[170]

Vesenkha's leaders at the congress adopted the penitent's role. V.I Mezhlauk praised TsKK–NKRKI's work in revising the plan. TsKK–NKRKI had transformed itself into the 'real general staff [*shtab*] of the Central Committee' in enforcing the 'general line' and developing policy.[171] S.S. Lobov applauded the work of the controllers and urged the industrial managers to take Ordzhonikidze's criticisms to heart, but asked NKRKI to work in harmony with the managers rather than set out simply to catch wrongdoers.[172] Kuibyshev also tactfully paid tribute to TsKK–NKRKI's work in assisting the Central Committee in raising the tempos.[173]

TsKK–NKRKI's strictures were not confined to Vesenkha. Ordzhonikidze severely criticized mismanagement in railway construction. In 1929 a joint NKPS–NKRKI commission had visited Japan to study the organization of the railways. NKPS's failure, under Rudzutak, to deal with these problems was strongly condemned. P.S. Shushkov, head of NKRKI's transport inspection, also denounced the influence of wreckers in NKPS in preparing exaggerated plans for railway construction.[174]

Ordzhonikidze also upbraided shortcomings in the work of Mikoyan's NKTorg, especially in the foreign trade network where corruption was allegedly rampant. Other TsKK–NKRKI speakers (Z.M. Belen'kii and B.A. Roizenman) demanded a fundamental reorganization of the trading apparatus.[175] Defects in the food industry, administered by NKTorg, were also criticized.

TsKK–NKRKI drew significant support from trade union spokesmen. N.M. Antselovich denounced the administration of the timber industry and was barracked by delegates who accused him of cynical opportunism. NKRKI's criticism of railway construction were echoed by A.M. Amosov of the railway workers' union. Evreinov of the textile workers' union backed NKRKI's condemnation of the plan to reconstruct the textile industry. Shvernik and Veinberg advocated closer links between the unions and NKRKI and repudiated the policies of VTsSPS under Tomskii.[176]

The transformation in TsKK–NKRKI's role in the first two years of the five-year plan was remarked upon by speaker after speaker. The previously despised '*erkaisty*' now enjoyed authority and status. Bogdanov of Leningrad noted there had been a 'colossal leap' in the work of TsKK–NKRKI although it still encountered 'great opposition'. Roizenman declared that the work of TsKK–NKRKI over the past two-and-a-half years had been 'one of the greatest achievements of the Leninist party', and added that the time when RKI concerned itself with 'trifles' was past. Nazaretyan of the Urals noted that TsKK–NKRKI had become 'the most useful assistant of the party Central Committee'. Tension between controllers and managers, however, persisted. The weakness of the local KK–RKI remained a nagging problem.[177]

Vesenkha's authority was further weakened in the summer of 1930 as industry failed to reach its output targets, allowing NKRKI to execute a spectacular organizational coup. In November Ordzhonikidze replaced Kuibyshev as the chairman of Vesenkha.[178] Kuibyshev took over the chairmanship of Gosplan. Ordzhonikidze immediately announced twelve senior appointments – one vice-chairman and eleven presidium members – of whom eight were from TsKK or NKRKI, two from the party Secretariat and one from OGPU.[179] In 1931, nine out of eighteen positions as Vesenkha sector heads were filled by ex-TsKK–NKRKI personnel.[180] Of NKRKI's fifteen heads of operational groups in 1930 six were working in Vesenkha in 1931 and another two worked there briefly in 1930–1 before moving elsewhere.[181]

Other commissariats criticized by Ordzhonikidze and his subordinates at the congress were reorganized and their leadership changed. In October 1930 A.P. Rozengol'ts from NKRKI took over the new People's Commissariat for Foreign Trade. In January 1931 P.S. Shushkov, head of NKRKI's transport section, was appointed first deputy narkom of NKPS. NKPS was broken up and a new People's Commissariat for Water Transport was established, headed by N.M. Yanson. In 1930 D.Z. Lebed' (deputy narkom NKRKI) was appointed vice-chairman of Sovnarkom RSFSR.[182] By 1931, former NKRKI officials headed Vesenkha, NKZem, Gosplan, TsSU, NK VneshTorg, NK Vod Trans as well as VTsSPS.

CONCLUSION

TsKK–NKRKI in 1929–30 emerged as a major institutional component of the ruling Stalin bloc, exerting enormous influence on policy-making. The aggressive posture adopted by the agency in its dealings with Vesenkha and the other economic commissariats stemmed from a number of factors. Primarily it arose from a radically new conception of the state of the Soviet economy formulated by NKRKI's officials and specialists, shocked by the disorder they encountered, entranced by the possibilities for development, and fired by political zeal. In addition the institutional self-interest of TsKK–NKRKI, thrown into perpetual conflict with the commissariats, and the personal ambitions of Ordzhonikidze and his lieutenants played a large part. TsKK–NKRKI was undoubtedly encouraged in its work by Stalin. Ordzhonikidze, however, was his own man and more than simply 'the conscious instrument of Stalin's Machiavellianism'.[183] Major policy initiatives emanated from TsKK–NKRKI, although the Politburo always retained the final say.

TsKK–NKRKI in 1929–30 played a vital role in defeating the Right opposition, in restructuring the apparatus, and in reformulating the five-year plan for industry and agriculture. This control-dominated system of administration seriously distorted the process of policy formation. The intellectual climate created by the anti-Rightist campaign and the rhetoric of the 'revolution from above' made reasoned and informed debate on these immensely complex economic problems all but impossible. The political objectives of forced development overrode all technical arguments. In the process, the Politburo became the victim of NKRKI's policy advice. The unrealistic targets set had no political or economic advantage but introduced serious distortion in policy and created difficulties which were quick to manifest themselves. Forced development also carried with it unanticipated economic and political costs. It intensified intersectoral and interregional rivalries, and created serious political strains in the party and between the centre and the regions.[184]

At the XVI Party Congress Ordzhonikidze exulted in TsKK–NKRKI's triumph and eulogized Stalin:

> We Bolsheviks have always gone and will continue to go with those who correctly follow the Leninist line, with those who correctly develop the struggle against the enemies of the working class . . . Today we invest our confidence in comrade Stalin, boldly we go with him, knowing that he is leading the party along the Leninist line and however much the rights and lefts cry, however much they persecute comrade Stalin, from this comrade Stalin's stature only grows greater.[185]

In 1929–30 on all the major questions of policy, Stalin and TsKK–NKRKI's leadership were at one.

200

Society for Cultural Relations with the USSR
Plate IX   A.A. Andreev (1895–1971): Chairman of TsKK and narkom RKI
(November 1930–October 1931)

S.N. Ikonnikov, Sozdanie i deyatel'nost' ob''edinennykh organov TsKK–RKI v 1923–1934gg. *(Moscow, 1971)*
Plate X   Ya. E. Rudzutak (1887–1937) : Chairman of TsKK and narkom RKI (October 1931–February 1934)

8 Rabkrin: Decline and Abolition (1931–4)

The massive revision of industrial targets in 1929–30 and the forced collectivization of agriculture set the agenda for economic policy in the remaining period of the first five-year plan. To realize the 'revolution from above' the party–state apparatus was expanded and radically transformed. The relative pluralism of the NEP gave way to a far more centralized, hierarchical, statist system. The alliance of forces which constituted the Stalinist bloc was increasingly strained. TsKK–NKRKI, which had played such a central role in the process of transformation, lost many eminent leaders and specialists. In the dramatically changed circumstances of the early 1930s NKRKI was compelled to redefine its role, and to justify its continuing usefulness to the Politburo.

TsKK–NKRKI AND THE CENTRAL PARTY–GOVERNMENT APPARATUS

In December 1930 Andrei Andreevich Andreev became head of TsKK–NKRKI. A former trade union official, he became a candidate member of the Politburo in 1926. A junior party leader, he was closely connected with Stalin and in 1924–5 worked in the Secretariat. From 1927 until 1930 Andreev was party secretary of the North Caucasus krai committee, one of the critical areas during collectivization. He was rumoured to have wavered in the direction of the Rightists in 1928 and during collectivization adopted a moderate attitude towards the kulaks.[1] An efficient administrator, he lacked a distinct political persona, unlike his two eminent predecessors at TsKK–NKRKI – Kuibyshev and Ordzhonikidze. In NKRKI he was assisted by three deputies – I.A. Akulov, A.I. Krinitskii and N.K. Antipov.[2]

In October 1931 Yan Ernestovich Rudzutak replaced Andreev as head of TsKK–NKRKI. He too was a former trade union official and had served in the Secretariat under Stalin. He became a full member of the Politburo in 1926 and from 1924 until 1930 was narkom of NKPS. It was rumoured that Kamenev and Zinoviev in 1925 had canvassed his name as a replacement for Stalin as General Secretary. He may also have wavered in the direction of the Right in 1928.[3] His personal life was surrounded by tales of scandal though he appears to have been a politician of some independence and courage. He was assisted by newly appointed deputy narkoms G.E. Prokof'ev, former head of OGPU's Special Department and N.M. Antselovich, the latter rewarded for his support for NKRKI at the XVI party congress.[4]

TsKK–NKRKI in this period retained its close links with the Politburo and Sovnarkom. Under Molotov's chairmanship Sovnarkom was revitalized. Andreev on his appointment to NKRKI was made vice-chairman of Sovnarkom and STO in line with established practice. Rudzutak since 1926 had served as a vice-chairman of Sovnarkom and STO, and retained these posts as narkom of NKRKI.[5]

NKRKI's work was sharply reorientated in response to the grave economic difficulties facing the regime. The joint Central Committee–TsKK plenum in December 1930 placed central priority on NKRKI's work in enforcing and checking the correct and timely implementation of party policy.[6] In the next two years this aspect of NKRKI's work was repeatedly stressed, especially in connection with the harvest crisis of 1932.[7]

TsIK and Sovnarkom on 24 December 1930 established a new Executive Commission, attached to Sovnarkom and chaired by Molotov, responsible for enforcing and evaluating government policy.[8] Andreev and Rudzutak, as narkoms of NKRKI, also served as vice chairmen of the Commission.[9] The Commission's board also included P.P. Postyshev from the party Secretariat, N.M. Shvernik (head of VTsSPS) and T.A. Yurkin (from Kolkhoztsentr).[10] For most issues examined by the Commission, reports were submitted by the responsible commissariats with co-reports from NKRKI. In the next three years the Commission carried out extensive investigations of the economy.[11]

Molotov stressed that the Executive Commission should ensure 'stricter contact' between NKRKI and Sovnarkom and STO, and facilitate closer ties between NKRKI and the party, the trade unions, and the collective farm organizations.[12] However, V.P. Zatonskii (head of TsKK–NKRKI UkSSR), saw the establishment of the Executive Commission as a direct warning to NKRKI to tighten policy enforcement. Sovnarkom and the party Secretariat, he noted, were increasingly intervening to check policy implementation.[13]

In this period, the system of 'responsible enforcers' of internal department control, established in 1929, was strengthened. In April 1931 Sovnarkom instructed the departments and institutions to establish sectors and groups to check implementation.[14]

RABKRIN AND ECONOMIC POLICY

After the organizational and policy upheavals of 1929–30 the management of the economy became more settled. Under a strengthened Sovnarkom and STO the operative commissariats reasserted themselves. Gosplan (under V.V. Kuibyshev's chairmanship) assumed a central role in regulating the economy. In industry Vesenkha, led by G.K. Ordzhonikidze, increasingly became an independent administrative empire, capable of resisting interference from outside controllers.

The Central Committee plenum in June 1931 approved three major resolutions on agriculture, the railways and on the urban economy.[15] The TsKK plenum in July took as the major task of NKRKI the enforcement of these resolutions. Andreev and Akulov, in their speeches to the TsKK plenum, outlined as the main responsibilities of NKRKI control over agriculture, transport, food supply and the improvement of the economic and state administration.[16] Control over the work of NKZem, NKPS and NKSnab was to be tightened up.[17] Significantly, NKRKI's work in controlling industry under Vesenkha was passed over.

NKRKI, previously absorbed in policy-making, was to concentrate on policy implementation, especially at local level. This, Andreev noted, meant that its work would become more complex and comprehensive. It required the strengthening of the local control organs and increasing mass involvement in mobilizing all resources. Akulov, however, warned that NKRKI's work might lose its focus and impact, and dissipate its energies.[18]

In 1931 NKRKI monitored NKFin's and Gosbank's role in implementing the credit reform introduced the previous year on the inspectorate's initiative. The reform inaugurated a switch from commercial to bank credit and sought to concentrate the credit function exclusively in the banks. The collapse of the reform's main provisions in 1931 served to further weaken NKRKI's prestige.[19]

Industry

The realization of the heavy industry targets became the main priority. Akulov in December 1930 stressed the central importance of NKRKI's role in ensuring that the target of 17 million tons of pig iron was attained by 1932/3 and that the scheme to develop a second metallurgical base in the Urals, concentrating on special steels, was realized.[20] In line with the resolution of the XVI Party Congress, NKRKI supervised construction work at the new giant plants.[21]

In May 1931 TsKK set up an inter-krai meeting of KKs from the Urals, western Siberia, Kazakhstan and Bashkir to discuss the Urals–Kuznetsk (UKK) project, to exchange information, to co-ordinate their work, to develop a planned approach to control work. The meeting highlighted the need to speed up construction work on the project. The oblast KK–RKI organs supervised the work in Magnitogorsk, the Urals heavy engineering industry and the Kuznetsk works.[22]

The Central Committee plenum in October 1932 discussed the situation in the ferrous metallurgical industry. A report was presented by Ordzhonikidze and a co-report submitted by Rudzutak for NKRKI. TsKK–NKRKI criticized industry's work in supplying the new construction projects. Local KK–RKI's were involved in this work, and mass involvement organized through the control agencies to speed up supplies.[23] The plenum approved a resolution to improve construction work in the ferrous metal industry.[24]

Much of NKRKI's work after 1930 was absorbed in supervising construction work on behalf of the Executive Commission. NKRKI investigated the new tractor and agricultural machinery works under construction and the supply of parts to the newly completed plants.[25] NKRKI also investigated the construction of electrical power stations.[26]

Mass control became the means to mobilize resources, uncover concealed stocks and capacity, intensify labour discipline and expose defects. In April 1931 TsKK–NKRKI, VTsSPS, the Komsomol and the Communist Academy initiated a mass campaign to mobilize reserves of metal in industry.[27] Attention was focused on ferrous, non-ferrous and scrap metal. In June 1931 TsKK–NKRKI assigned several senior officials to lead the campaign in the localities. In the autumn of 1931 NKRKI announced that substantial quantities of metal had been mobilized.[28]

The XVII Party Conference in January 1932 reviewed the progress of industry. Rudzutak strongly criticized the inefficiency of the metallurgical, coal and chemical industries. He condemned low labour productivity, poor technical leadership, overmanning, wage equalization, holdups in supply, failure to maximize capacity, and the irresponsibility of managers.[29] This speech was part of a broader campaign by NKRKI to reassert its control over industry and to recover ground lost since 1930.

Vesenkha in January 1932 was broken up into three more manageable commissariats – the People's Commissariat of Heavy Industry (NKTyazhProm) headed by Ordzhonikidze; the People's Commissariat of Light Industry (NKLegProm) headed by I.E. Lyubimov: and the People's Commissariat for the Timber Industry (NKLes) headed by S.S. Lobov. Although NKRKI was responsible for overseeing the work of these commissariats it failed to establish an effective presence in these fields.

The TsKK plenum in February 1932, on Rudzutak's report, urged the KK–RKI to concentrate their attention on the coal, metallurgical, engineering and chemical industries.[30] In a speech to the IX Trade Union Congress in April 1932, Rudzutak again highlighted the problem of low labour productivity in industry, and the inadequate food supplies for workers. NKRKI's attempts to strengthen its control in industry through closer co-operation with the trade unions provoked leading managers to protest to VTsSPS.[31]

In the summer of 1932 TsKK–NKRKI reported critically on the failure of the industrial and trading organizations to provide sufficient industrial goods for the rural areas in connection with the harvest failure and the anticipated problems of grain collection;[32] it prepared reports on the production of goods for mass consumption for the Executive Commission.[33] In 1932 and 1933, NKRKI supervised NKLes's work in the timber collection programme and investigated the timber industry on the Executive Commission's behalf.[34]

NKRKI's attempts to recapture its lost position in industry failed. At the joint Central Committee–TsKK plenum in January 1933, which discussed the results of the first five-year plan, Rudzutak had no achievements to report for NKRKI.[35] The plenum approved the huge expansion in industry since 1928 but ignored the discrepancies between the targets attained and those advanced by NKRKI in 1929–30. The second five-year plan, drafted under the moderating influence of Ordzhonikidze and Kuibyshev, set more realistic targets.

Railway Transport

The deployment of NKRKI in crisis management was well illustrated by its role on the railways. Dislocation of the transport system threatened the succes of the five-year plan. In January 1931 NKPS's leadership was fundamentally reorganized. M.L. Rukhimovich (narkom of NKPS) campaigned strongly for new investment to deal with the crisis. The Politburo issued a series of directives to deal with the situation.

TsKK–NKRKI on 13 January 1931 instructed the chairmen of republican, krai and local KK–RKI organs to enforce party directives concerning the railways, and to inform TsKK–NKRKI about the state of local lines. TsKK–NKRKI strengthened the transport groups attached to the local KK–RKI, allocating to them the most qualified controllers.[36]

The Central Committee plenum in June 1931 heard a report from Rukhimovich and a co-report from Andreev of NKRKI on the state of the railways, and outlined wide ranging proposals to resolve the crisis.[37] At the TsKK plenum in July 1931 Andreev vehemently attacked NKPS and attributed the shortcomings of the railways to poor leadership and organization, rather than to the lack of resources stressed by Rukhimovich.[38]

In 1931 a Politburo special commission (chaired by Andreev) investigated NKPS and the individual line administrations.[39] NKPS's work was discussed by the Politburo and Sovnarkom on 1 October. Rukhimovich was replaced as narkom of NKPS by Andreev and the leadership of NKPS was transformed.[40] The takeover of NKPS followed the pattern already established by the takeover of NKZem by Yakovlev and of Vesenkha by Ordzhonikidze in 1929 and 1930. The Central Committee plenum in October 1931 outlined the tasks of the new leadership.[41]

Andreev remained narkom of NKPS until February 1935. His term of office coincided with the grave transport crisis of 1932–35, which severely constrained economic development, and stemmed directly from the failure to invest adequate funds in the railways during the first five-year plan.

Agriculture

With the inauguration of the collectivization and dekulakization drive, agriculture became the Politburo's major field of concern. NKZem (headed by Yakovlev) strove to break peasant resistance and to introduce order into the newly-created collective farm sector. NKRKI (under its deputy narkom A.I. Krinitskii) tightened supervision over agriculture, and in 1931 established raion KK-RKI organs to strengthen control in the countryside. In this period also control by the party – through worker detachments dispatched to the countryside, and through the OGPU and the militia – increased in scope.

In June 1931 NKRKI reported to the Central Committee on the spring sowing campaign and preparation for the harvest.[42] The newly-established raion KK–RKI organs were assigned a key role in monitoring policies on the spot.[43] NKRKI examined the state of livestock-rearing sovkhozy which were to make up for the heavy losses suffered as a result of collectivization. It also investigated the dairy farm sector, and poultry and pig rearing, on behalf of Sovnarkom's Executive Commission.[44] The organization of the new collective farm sector also came under scrutiny with highly critical reports on the very high administrative costs of the new kolkhozy and on the disorganized state of the new Machine Tractor Stations (MTS).[45]

In 1932 TsKK–NKRKI endeavoured to strengthen the rural raion KK–RKI. The TsKK plenum in February stressed the KK–RKI's work in supervising the spring sowing campaign.[46] In July TsKK–NKRKI issued instructions to the raion KK–RKI concerning supervision of the harvest and grain collection campaign. TsKK–NKRKI assigned forty leading workers to the localities to assist in this work.[47] NKRKI on behalf of Sovnarkom's Executive Commission checked on the supply of tractors, implements and spare parts to the countryside.[48]

In spite of these efforts, the 1932 harvest fell far below expectations and severe difficulties were encountered in realizing the grain collection campaign. The relatively moderate policies pursued in the spring of 1932 were cast aside as Stalin and the hardliners in the Politburo resolved to take determined action. Draconian laws and administrative measures were employed to break peasant resistance. In August 1932 the death penalty was introduced for the theft of collective farm grain. At the end of the year, entire villages were deported. The internal passport system was reintroduced to control the flight of peasants off the land.

The situation alarmed the rural party and soviet organs. The system of control through the raion KK–RKI broke down. Local KK–RKI organs were accused of failing to report breaches of the party line to TsKK–NKRKI, of ignoring the role of the kulaks in the kolkhozy, failing to defend collective farm property, stifling criticism and failing to respond to peasant complaints against official abuses.[49] *Pravda* in January 1933 condemned the impotence of the rural KK–RKI, their failure to report breaches of policy, and their indulgent attitude towards the kulak and his agents.[50]

The extraction of grain from the drought-hit producer areas to feed the towns exacerbated the famine. Stalin in his speech 'Work in the Countryside' in January 1933 insisted on strengthening party control in the countryside and intensifying the class struggle as a means of enforcing policy and fighting the counter-revolutionary elements.[51] The joint Central Committee–TsKK plenum the same month approved the establishment of political departments (politotdely) in all MTS and sovkhozy as a means of tightening control.[52] The politotdely were staffed with party activists, recruited from the urban centres. They were supervised by the party Secretariat with Kaganovich and Ezhov overseeing this work.[53]

As a result, TsKK–NKRKI was by-passed. Already in December 1932 A.I. Krinitskii was transferred from NKRKI and appointed deputy head of the Central Committee's agricultural sector and deputy narkom of NKZem; as head of NKZem's MTS political administration he had direct responsibility for the MTS politotdely.[54] In April 1933 TsKK–NKRKI instructed the local KK–RKI to assist the politotdely.[55] The rivalry between these bodies became intense. In *Pravda* Krinitskii lauded the successes of the politotdely. The MTS in 1932–3 became the real instrument of control in Soviet agriculture.[56]

The central party organs increasingly assumed responsibility for agriculture. The Central Committee and Sovnarkom in January 1933 issued detailed instructions concerning the spring sowing campaign. Party secretary P.P. Postyshev, led the campaign.[57] The raion KK–RKI supervised the sowing, harvesting and grain collection campaigns but were increasingly isolated.[58] In April 1933, as part of the new purge, TsKK–NKRKI instructed the raion KK–RKI to purge the kolkhoz administration. Three months later Rudzutak noted serious defects in the conduct of the purge.[59]

In the spring of 1933 the party decided to set up politotdely in industry and transport, similar to those in agriculture, further weakening the power of NKRKI.[60]

Trade

After 1930 NKRKI closely monitored the work of the People's Commissariat of Supply (NKSnab) and the main consumer co-operative organization (Tsentrosoyuz) to improve food supplies for the main urban centres. NKSnab, headed by A.I. Mikoyan, was one of the few economic commissariats not to have been colonized by NKRKI personnel. In December 1930 NKRKI reported to the joint Central Committee–TsKK plenum on the work of NKSnab and Tsentrosoyuz.[61] At the TsKK plenum in July 1931 Andreev criticized NKSnab's failure to ensure adequate food supplies to the industrial centres.[62] In October 1931 NKRKI again reported to the Central Committee on the work of the two main supply organizations.[63]

In April 1932 the Politburo, on Stalin's initiative, instructed TsKK–NKRKI to tighten control over trade and supply.[64] NKRKI campaigned to ensure supplies of goods of mass consumption to the countryside to stimulate urban–rural trade. It sought also to improve the supply of agricultural produce to workers in industry.[65] In October 1932 NKRKI again reported to the Central Committee on the work of NKSnab and Tsentrosoyuz.[66] As the situation deteriorated in the winter of 1932/3, control was tightened with TsKK in 1933 leading the purge of the trading apparatus.[67]

THE DECLINE OF RABKRIN

The loss of NKRKI's leading officials and specialists to the operative commissariats in 1929–30 fatally weakened its power and authority. By 1931 former NKRKI officials headed most of the economic commissariats, excepting NKFin and NKSnab. Thereafter NKRKI's role declined, and it increasingly faced a crisis of purpose and identity. This resulted also in a serious deterioration in the quality of its work, which was clearly reflected in its publications and reports.

NKRKI's decline was manifest in the loss of its powers, growing dissatisfaction with its work, and continuing strains in its relations with the economic institutions. In the spring of 1931 TsKK–NKRKI was instructed to ensure proper co-ordination of control work, and to combat the persistent problem of excessive investigations in the economic and administrative organs.[68]

Appeasing the Industrial Managers

NKRKI's decline was most evident in industry. Ordzhonikidze's transfer to Vesenkha placed at the head of industry a powerful figure capable of defending his subordinates and managerial interests generally. After 1930 the flow of weighty reports from NKRKI on industry quickly dried up. After 1930 NKRKI's journals on industrial rationalization, *Za ratsionalizatsiyu* and *Proizvodstvennyi zhurnal*, ceased publication.

The Industrial Party trial of November–December 1930 and the Menshevik trial of March 1931 ominously confirmed OGPU's growing role in fighting subversion and sabotage.[69] However, in a speech to a conference of industrial managers in June 1931 Stalin signalled a major change in relations between the party and the managers. He proposed the creation of a new working class industrial and technical intelligentsia, the adoption of a more conciliatory attitude to the older technical personnel and the adoption of new methods of work.[70]

The intense pressure placed on industrial managers since the Shakhty trial of 1928 was relaxed. The role of OGPU, the procurator and the courts in exposing sabotage in industry was curtailed. Trials of managers and specialists on charges of wrecking diminished. This new understanding remained the party's policy until 1935.[71]

This abrupt change of policy directly affected NKRKI's work in industry. At the TsKK plenum in July 1931 Andreev admitted NKRKI's impotence in industry, which, he argued, was now under the control of former *erkaisty* and no longer needed external control.[72] Stalin's speech on the need to 'work in a new way' had to be applied to NKRKI. A new relationship was needed with the managers and specialists. It was essential, he argued, to create an environment of trust in which specialists could take risks, show initiative, work unsupervised, without fear of being branded as wreckers.[73] This effectively cut the ground from under much of NKRKI's work and was linked also to a return to more sober industrial planning.

The Repudiation of 'NOT'

Yakovlev's report on 'bureaucracy' to the XVI Party Conference in April 1929 constituted a veiled attack on the rationalizers in NKRKI. Thereafter, the advocates of the scientific study of labour organization and administration (NOT) were subject to mounting pressures from the controllers.

E.F. Rozmirovich, director of the State Institute of Scientific Management (ITU), the leader of the rationalizers, strenuously sought to fend off mounting criticism. In the foreword to a book reviewing the institute's work, published in 1930, Rozmirovich insisted that its work was firmly based on Marxist–Leninist principles. The three basic tenets of Marxism on administration – the transition under socialism from the administration of people to the administration of things, the progressive simplification of administration, the development of mass participation in administration – remained valid.[74]

The institute, Rozmirovich argued, should resist non-Marxist influences, particularly Fayolism which stressed the growing complexity and specialization of administration. Many ITU specialists remained ardent disciples of the French theorist on administration Henri Fayol.[75] Eminent Soviet theorists, such as Bogdanov and Ermanskii, were accused of disseminating 'non-Marxist' ideas.[76] Rozmirovich stressed that there was still much to learn from the advanced capitalist countries, but avoided the delicate issue of class struggle in the apparatus.

The attack on the 'Right' was extended to embrace the rationalizers of NKRKI. In September 1930 Rozmirovich was sacked as editor of the journal *Tekhnika upravleniya*, which she had edited since 1925. In March 1931 she was transferred from NKRKI to NKPT.[77] *Tekhnika upravleniya* was renamed *Organizatsiya upravleniya* to emphasize its change of role from concern with technical questions to more organizational and political aspects of administrative work.[78]

In January 1931 an all-union conference on rationalization, reflecting the views of a younger generation of Marxist rationalizers, severely criticized ITU and its journal, denounced the apolitical, non-Marxist stance of many of ITU's workers and demanded a Marxist–Leninist methodology in the science of rationalization which would emphasize class struggle, *partiinost'* and mass involvement in administration. It demanded a purge of ITU and a reorientation of its work. Rationalization could no longer be limited to narrow technical questions but had to address the major political problems confronting the regime.[79]

Under its new editor *Organizatsiya upravleniya* critically reviewed ITU's past work. M.P. Fuks denounced the prevalence of 'bourgeois ideological garbage and theoretical rubbish' in ITU's work.[80] M. Shulgin accused ITU's specialists of 'fruitless scholastic exercises', 'games in abstraction', 'superficial all-knowingness' and 'futile bustle'. The experts allegedly were entranced by western ideas and failed to address the practical problems of socialist rationalization.[81] This contempt for abstract intellectualizing divorced from practical concerns echoed a theme that was always close to Stalin's heart.

The transformation of NKRKI's rationalization work reflected a broad leftward ideological trend. The Central Committee in March 1931, based on the Communist Academy's report, called for ideological struggle against bourgeois and social democratic ideas in the social sciences.[82] The Communist Academy (until its abolition in 1936) gained powerful influence over state organization. In 1931 P.M. Kerzhentsev, a long-standing critic of NKRKI's rationalizers, was appointed vice-president of the Communist Academy and head of the Sovnarkom-STO chancellory.[83] E.B. Pashukanis, the eminent jurist, became the director of the Academy's Institute of Soviet Construction and Law. Through its journal *Sovetskoe gosudarstvo* the role of the state in the transition to socialism was extensively discussed.

Stalin's letter to *Proletarskaya revolutsiya* in the autumn of 1931 intensified the campaign against the rationalizers.[84] An editorial in *Organizatsiya upravleniya* denounced the approach of ITU as a 'bouquet of anti-Marxist theories', which emasculated the political essence of administration, led to the denial of the class struggle and the rejection of Lenin's teachings on the importance of cadre selection.[85] Rozmirovich was criticized for advocating a purely technical view of administration. Leading experts of ITU were condemned for their uncritical advocacy of western rationalization ideas. Mass participation in control work was enthusiastically promoted. The production–technical interpretation of administration, Isakov argued, was directly linked to the Right deviation in the party. It aimed to increase the influence of the technical intelligentsia over economic construction and represented a capitulation to 'counter-revolutionary' ideology.[86] The party's central task, as outlined by Yakovlev to the XVI Party Conference, was to strengthen the proletarian dictatorship.

These attacks heralded a fundamental change of course. The XVII Party Conference in February 1932 inaugurated a new phase in the development of the Soviet state in the transition to socialism. In July 1932 the publication of *Organizatsiya upravleniya* was transferred from NKRKI to Ordzhonikidze's NKTyazhProm.[87] ITU and its affiliates were closed down.

NKRKI's responsibilities for improving accounting and bookkeeping work in the state and economic apparatus declined quickly in this period. Already on 1 June 1930 Sovnarkom had abolished the Institute of State Bookkeeping Experts attached to NKRKI. On 31 August 1931 TsIK and Sovnarkom abolished NKRKI's right to issue compulsory orders to the state and economic institutions on accounting and bookkeeping work.[88]

NKRKI retained its responsibility for restructuring the apparatus. In November 1932 a new campaign to reduce the size and cost of the state apparatus was initiated.[89] Antipov (deputy narkom of NKRKI) assumed responsibility for its conduct.[90]

The shortcomings of the state administration were increasingly analysed from a juridical standpoint. Law and administration lost their limited areas of autonomy and were subject to tight political control. The juridical approach to state organization remained dominant for the next thirty years. Only in the 1960s was scientific rationalization and the NOT movement of the 1920s rediscovered and its advocates rehabilitated.

Development of Popular Control

With the repudiation of NKRKI's rationalization function, renewed attention was paid to developing popular or mass control inaugurated in

1928. This system of direct, participatory democracy was manipulated
by the party, a populistic device, developed as part of the 'cultural
revolution'. It was intended to involve the people in administration, to
shake up and proletarianize the apparatus, mobilize popular support for
official policies and create a new socialist system of administration.[91]

The policy reflected a sharp switch of emphasis in NKRKI's work
from grand policy questions to the minutiae of policy enforcement at
local level. In the enterprises and institutions NKRKI assistant cells
were re-established, particularly in the Urals. RKI sections were formed,
attached to the city soviets, the volost and raion ispolkoms. NKRKI
also worked closely with the Komsomol 'light cavalry' units, the trade
union temporary control commissions (VKK) and the enlarged party
cells in industry.[92] Mass participation in investigations, and the discussion of shortcomings in enterprises before mass audiences of workers,
became common practice.

In June 1931 NKRKI commenced publication of a new fortnightly
journal '*For tempo, quality and checking*' (*Za tempy, kachestvo,
proverku*), edited by E.M. Yaroslavskii, to co-ordinate and publicize this
movement. The slogan 'for tempo and quality' was taken up in the
autumn of 1931.[93] This new journal styled itself as an 'organ of mass
proletarian control' and publicized popular initiatives in correcting
defects in administration. In marked contrast to earlier NKRKI
journals, which were weighty, highly technical and strongly internationalist in outlook, the new journal was populistic, parochial and greatly
inferior in quality.

The mass control movement was also publicized through NKRKI's
regular supplement, *Listok RKI*, published in *Pravda*. Efforts were made
to strengthen NKRKI's links with local worker and peasant press
correspondents (rabselkors) and particularly to improve links between
the KK–RKI and the local press.[94] From 1930 onwards several
important oblast and krai KK–RKI organs published their own
journals which publicized the progress of the popular control
movement.[95]

The movement threw up novel forms for involving workers in
administration. The patronage (*sheftsvo*) movement grew out of the
purge campaign of 1929–30. Enterprises adopted state institutions and
commissariats to assist them in exposing and correcting defects in their
work. Worker brigades were sent from the factories into these institutions to investigate their work, to assist in purging officials, and to
prepare workers promoted for administrative positions (*vydvizhentsy*)
as part of a policy to proletarianize the apparatus.

The patronage movement was directed by TsKK–NKRKI's organization–instruction department. Forty-five TsKK members were attached to thirty-two Moscow factories which exercised patronage over the all-union institutions. By April 1931 there were over 1,000 enterprises and 50,000 workers involved in the campaign.[96] This was part of a wider development of mass control.[97] The RKI assistant cells in the enterprises, institutions and collective farms grew rapidly and by the end of 1933 numbered between 20,000 and 30,000. Non-staff inspectors were also attached to NKRKI's operational groups.[98]

Another aspect of mass control which received much attention in this period were the NKRKI Complaints Bureaux. In April 1932 TsKK–NKRKI reviewed the work of the bureaux. Stalin in *Pravda* urged strengthening these bodies to involve the populace in signalling and correcting defects in the administration.[99] In July 1933 R.S. Zemlyachka took over NKRKI's Complaints Bureau. In the summer months *Pravda* carried numerous articles by NKRKI leaders stressing the need to strengthen and develop the bureau's work in the centre and localities.[100]

In the winter of 1932–3 the movement was further expanded in connection with the new campaign to reduce the state administration, and the new party purge announced in January 1933.[101]

The scale of popular involvement in mass control remains uncertain. One Soviet scholar estimates that from April 1923 until January 1934 there were 5.4 million people involved as activists with TsKK–NKRKI. The great majority (4.7 million) were participants in mass investigations of particular institutions and enterprises. A quarter of a million participated in the Komsomol's 'light cavalry'. The numbers who worked in RKI sections, assistant groups, complaints bureaux and operated as non-staff inspectors were estimated at 140,000.[102]

The movement was intensely disliked by managers and administrators. It reached its peak in the years between 1928 and 1932, but then declined as the leftist phase of the 'cultural revolution' was brought to a close. Mass control, however, was not repudiated and during the purges of 1937–8 was again revitalized.

KK–RKI Organs in Disarray

Throughout the 1920s the local KK–RKI organs remained the Achilles' heel of TsKK–NKRKI. With the reorientation of control work after 1930 a determined effort was made to strengthen control and policy enforcement in the localities. The creation of the raion administrative unit raised the question of the feasibility of establishing raion KK–RKI organs. The presidium of TsKK, aware of the problem of finding suitable cadres, was sceptical.[103] Nevertheless, Andreev at the TsKK plenum in July 1931 announced the decision to establish raion KK–RKI organs.[104] *Pravda* heralded the decision as an important step in strengthening control in the countryside.[105]

In 1931 the shortcomings of the local KK–RKI drew much criticism.[106] In 1932 in connection with the crisis in agriculture the KK–RKI came under a hail of fire. The KK–RKI organs, elected by the local party and soviet organs, lacked backbone and were turned into 'institutions running errands' for the raikom and rai ispolkom.[107]

In February 1932 Shkiryatov warned the TsKK plenum that if the KKs failed to expose disorders they would not be worth a 'brass farthing'.[108] The TsKK plenum approved a resolution to strengthen the raion KK–RKI, which one senior TsKK official complained had become 'homes for invalids'.[109]

In 1931, 15 per cent of raion KK chairmen were dismissed for various offences – incompetence, deviations from the class line and compromising actions. In the first nine months of 1933 the figure leapt to 30 per cent.[110] Attempts by KK–RKI to restrain the local party organs were also denounced as Right opportunism, their officials dismissed and disciplined.

Early in 1933 Rudzutak discussed with Stalin the problems of TsKK–NKRKI. He was instructed to concentrate the agency's forces on agriculture, the weakest link in its work. The weakness of the raion KK–RKI made it 'unable to speak against the raikom, unable to inform TsKK'. Without a fundamental improvement, Rudzutak warned, TsKK–NKRKI would forfeit the party's trust. TsKK–NKRKI established a system of authorized agents dispatched to the localities to strengthen control work.[111]

In the autumn of 1933 *Pravda* repeatedly criticized KK–RKI's work during the harvest campaign.[112] In October it carried a major exposé of the KK–RKI organs in the Stanovaya raion of the Central Black Earth oblast which had been uncovered by the local MTS politotdel. The work of the KK–RKI was influenced by 'family circles' of mutual protection in collaboration with local party and soviet organs. The agencies were poorly staffed and starved of resources. Abuses in economic management were concealed, 'self-criticism' was stifled, the masses were excluded from control work. The KK–RKI were inattentive to peasant complaints and had failed to assist in the purge campaign.[113]

The situation in Stanovaya, it alleged, was widespread. The priority was to strengthen the raion KK–RKI and transform them into the party's 'vigilant eyes' in the countryside. TsKK–NKRKI through its journal vigorously promoted this campaign in the final months of 1933.[114]

TsKK–NKRKI AND THE INTERNAL PARTY STRUGGLE

Much of TsKK's work in dealing with the internal party opposition in the period 1931–4 remains uncertain.[115] With the defeat of the Right, opposition was driven underground and continued as secret conspiracies. The tensions within the party intensified in the face of the growing crisis. The role of OGPU in rooting out opposition grew apace.

In the summer of 1930 the Syrtsov–Lominadze affair revealed for the first time dissension over policy within the Stalin bloc. The group demanded a slackening in the pace of industrialization and collectivization, decentralization of power and freer debate in the party.[116] A joint Central Committee–TsKK resolution in December 1930 expelled Syrtsov and Lominadze from the Central Committee on the charge of forming a 'Left–Right' bloc on a 'common platform, coinciding in all fundamental respects with the platform of the right-wing opportunists'.[117]

In the spring of 1931, TsKK sought to strengthen the hand of the KKs in enforcing party discipline in the localities where the crises of collectivization had severely strained party loyalties. Yaroslavskii at the TsKK plenum in July 1931 delivered a major report on strengthening the party collegiums in the local KKs.[118] The crisis in agriculture and the famine of 1932–3 stoked up bitter animosity against Stalin's leadership.

The Ryutin platform of 1932 attempted to forge an alliance between the Right and the Trotskyist opposition, demanding a slowdown in the pace of industrialization, an end to enforced collectivization, the revitalization of internal party democracy and Stalin's dismissal. TsKK on 9 October 1932 expelled Ryutin and his associates from the party for 'having attempted to set up a bourgeois, kulak organisation to re-establish capitalism, and in particular the kulak system in the USSR, by means of underground activity and under the fraudulent banner of "Marxism–Leninism"'.[119]

According to one account, some TsKK leaders with Politburo support blocked Stalin's demand for the execution of Ryutin and other leaders of the group. They also, temporarily at least, thwarted his demands for the OGPU to be unleashed against party dissentients. Within TsKK there may have been a split between the more moderate

Rudzutak and hardliners such as Shkiryatov, Yaroslavskii and Peters, although this is a matter of conjecture.

The same concerns were voiced by another underground group led by V.V. Eismont, G.G. Tolmachev and A.P. Smirnov. The TsKK presidium in November 1932 expelled Eismont and Tolmachev from the party. The Central Committee–TsKK joint plenum in January 1933, based on Rudzutak's report, confirmed these expulsions and removed Smirnov from the Central Committee.[121]

The insecurity of TsKK's position was underlined by its role in purging the party. In 1929 TsKK was assigned responsibility for purging the party ranks through the Purge Commission, headed by Ya.Kh. Peters. In the following four years the commission and its local *troiki* investigated all party members. At the TsKK plenum in July 1931 Andreev warned that it would be wrong to end the purge of the state apparatus which still harboured hostile elements.[122] In spite of this, many local control organs began to do just that. The indecisiveness of the local purge commissions and the willingness of TsKK to readmit expelled Communists back into the party drew strong criticism.[123]

In January 1933 the Central Committee–TsKK joint plenum authorized a new party purge.[124] Whereas in 1929 the conduct of the purge had been assigned to TsKK, in 1933 a special party Central Purge Commission was set up. This was chaired by Rudzutak and included other prominent TsKK officials. Kirov represented the Politburo, and Stasova and Pyatnitskii represented the 'old Bolsheviks'. In addition L.M. Kaganovich and N.I. Ezhov, both from the party Secretariat and noted hardliners, joined the commission. Rudzutak's leadership of the purge appears to have been nominal.[125] In the oblasty and krai the purge commissions were headed by senior TsKK leaders.[126] Shkiryatov and Yaroslavskii for TsKK played the most prominent role in directing the 1933 party purge.[127]

The Secretariat–Orgburo increasingly became the effective directing centre of the party–state apparatus. Under Stalin's control, this apparatus was staffed by powerful party secretaries such as Kaganovich, Ezhov and Postyshev, who took responsibility for directing policy. After 1931 the Orgburo began usurping TsKK–NKRKI's role as general staff office for the Politburo.[128] Economic institutions were required to submit reports to Orgburo on assigned topics on a planned basis. The Orgburo's structure and staff was expanded to cope with this new function.[129] Party commissions and brigades, directed by the Politburo and Central Committee, were increasingly employed in resolving economic problems.[130]

ABOLITION OF TsKK–NKRKI

By 1932 TsKK–NKRKI's position was badly weakened. The last individual TsKK plenum was held in February 1932,[131] after which it lost influence not only to the party but also to the burgeoning power of OGPU. In July 1931 Akulov was transferred from NKRKI to OGPU and in 1933 he took over the Procuracy. In November 1932 G.E. Prokof'ev was transferred from NKRKI to OGPU, and took charge of the militia.[132] Rudzutak fell from favour and out of prominence.[133] TsKK–NKRKI's tenth anniversary passed almost unnoticed in the national press in marked contrast to the prominence given to OGPU's fifteenth anniversary.[134]

To commemorate NKRKI's anniversary *Sovetskoe gosudarstvo i pravo* carried two articles which sought to fend off NKRKI's critics. N. Speranskii in an article entitled 'Ten Years of Rabkrin', emphasized Lenin's part in establishing TsKK–NKRKI. Whilst its role had to be adapted to new circumstances, only an 'open opportunist' would claim it had lost its function. Lenin, he argued, had envisaged NKRKI as a long-term project, the success of which could not be measured in five or even ten years.[135] S. Bertinskii in a study of NKRKI's early history insisted that the agency still had a 'huge' role to play.[136]

The famine of 1932–3 gravely strained relations between the central and republican governments. In the Ukraine the crisis was acute, with the dispatch in the spring of 1933 of Postyshev to take charge. In April and May the Central Committee and Sovnarkom criticized the state of industry and argriculture in the republic; prominent Ukrainian leaders like Kosior, Chubar' and Skrypnik were compromized. Leading agricultural officials were executed in the 'Postyshev terror', and a major onslaught was initiated against Ukrainian nationalism.[137]

V.P. Zatonskii (head of TsKK–NKRKI UkSSR since 1927) was replaced early in 1933 by K.V. Sukhomlin.[138] In June 1933 TsKK severely censured TsKK–NKRKI UkSSR's work in agriculture, and particularly criticized the ineffectiveness of the Ukrainian KK–RKI organs.[139] At this time also A.Ya. Kalnin (head of TsKK–NKRKI of the Belorussian SSR since 1927) was also sacked. The leadership of the TsKK–NKRKI organs in the Central Asian republics of Tadzhikstan, Turkmenistan and Uzbekistan was also changed, although N.I. Il'in (head of TsKK–NKRKI RSFSR) and A.I. Dogadov (head of TsKK–NKRKI of the Transcaucasus) retained their posts.[140]

At the end of 1933 the Politburo, attended by members of the TsKK presidium, approved a resolution on 'organisational measures in the field of strengthening party–state control', for the abolition of TsKK–NKRKI.[141]

The decision was broken by Rudzutak to a special session of TsKK's presidium. A Soviet scholar provides the following account:

> The extraordinary session of the TsKK presidium opened in deathly silence. The majority of those present did not understand the meaning of the impending reorganisation. The outward appearance of the chairman who was always calm and steady was unusual. Yan Ernestovich [Rudzutak] looked terribly downcast and even perplexed. Having read the decision of the Politburo, he just sat there. There was in fact no debate. The participants at the meeting knew that the proposal by several members of TsKK to discuss in detail the question of the reorganisation at a plenum of TsKK had been categorically refused by Stalin.[142]

The decision came as a bombshell for the workers of TsKK–NKRKI.[143]

On the eve of the XVII Party Congress the press carried a thesis by L.M. Kaganovich on the liquidation of TsKK–NKRKI and its replacement by two separate organs – the Commission of Party Control (KPK) and the Commission of Soviet Control (KSK). The thesis had ben approved 'in the main' by the Politburo and TsKK's presidium.[144] At the Moscow party conference in January 1934 Kaganovich cited the failure of the KK–RKI in agriculture as the central reason.[145] Rudzutak welcomed Kaganovich's scheme as a means of making control 'more concrete and operative'.[146]

The reform had far-reaching implications. It intended to abolish the republican TsKK–NKRKI, the oblast and raion KK–RKI. Within all institutions and enterprises the special sectors of control established on NKRKI's initiative from 1929 onwards, as part of the functional reorganization of the apparatus, were to be liquidated. The heads of institutions were to be responsible for control, thus reuniting control with administrative work.[147]

The XVII Party Congress, 'the congress of victors', convened in January 1934 and, outwardly at least, celebrated the triumph of the 'general line'. Stalin in the keynote Central Committee report stressed the need to improve the organizational leadership in the party, soviet and economic organs. The selection of personnel had to be improved and policy implementation tightened up. TsKK–NKRKI no longer suited the regime's needs. The danger of a party split had passed. The growing complexity of the economy required a new control strategy. The task of the new KPK and KSK lay not in rationalization nor in policy formation but in control, the implementation of party and government directives, and the enforcement of discipline.[148]

Rudzutak in TsKK–NKRKI's report to the congress gave no hint of dissension with the proposals and voiced fulsome praise of Stalin.[149] Other senior TsKK–NKRKI leaders (including E.M. Yaroslavskii, M.F. Shkiryatov, M.I. Ulyanova and M.K. Sukhomlin) endorsed the reorganization as a means of strengthening control, but urged the retention of mass control.[150]

In his report to the congress on the 'organisational question' L.M. Kaganovich, Stalin's most trusted lieutenant, noted the need to 'refashion the levers of the proletarian dictatorship . . . overhaul and sharpen our weapons for the great battles that lie ahead'.[151] Since 1930, he noted, the Central Committee, the Politburo and Stalin personally had assumed a major role in directing the economic organs, supervising policy implementation and resolving disputes. TsKK–NKRKI had proved inadequate and had been by-passed.

Central Committee commissions, headed by Politburo members, had intervened in industry, agriculture, trade and railway transport. Reviewing this trend, Kaganovich declared:

> The whole style and method of work of the Central Committee involves the unity of words and deeds, the unity of decision and execution. Our Politburo of the Central Committee is an organ of operational leadership of all branches of socialist construction. Almost daily comrade Stalin convenes business meetings, summons this or that worker in charge of the operational realisation of matters, checks implementation, resolves various questions, which are connected with the demands and needs of the localities.[152]

The Central Committee apparatus and the Secretariat had been enlarged to cope with this expanded role. Many delegates paid tribute to the work of the Politburo, and Stalin himself, in resolving organizational problems in different industries and sectors. The need to bring political and administrative work into closer correspondence was repeatedly stressed.[153]

The XVII Party Congress after a perfunctory debate on TsKK–NKRKI's report declared that 'having heard comrade Rudzutak's report the XVII congress of CPSU wholly approves the activities of TsKK–RKI'.[154] The resolution was adopted unanimously. The congress, nevertheless, approved TsKK–NKRKI's abolition. The resolution was edited by a forty-two-man commission which included Stalin, Kaganovich and other hardliners but excluded Rudzutak.[155]

The congress resolved to replace NKRKI and Sovnarkom's Executive Commission with a new Commission of Soviet Control (KSK), attached to Sovnarkom and headed by a Sovnarkom vice-chairman. Its members were to be elected by the party congress and endorsed by TsIK and Sovnarkom. KSK was to take over NKRKI's central apparatus and was to appoint its own permanent representatives at republican, krai and oblast level in place of the elected RKI organs. Its main responsibility was to ensure strict policy implementation in the state administration and enforce tight discipline. It resolved also to replace TsKK with a new Commission of Party Control (KPK) to be headed by a Central Committee secretary. KPK was to be elected by the party congress and work under the Central Committee. It took over the central apparatus of TsKK, but appointed its own representatives in the republics, krais and oblasty. Its main function was to ensure the implementation of party policy and to enforce party discipline.[156]

The party congress elected sixty-one members to KPK and seventy members to KSK. KPK was placed in the care of noted hardliners. L.M. Kaganovich became its chairman, and its presidium included N.I. Ezhov, M.F. Shkiryatov, E.M. Yaroslavskii, I.A. Akulov, Ya.Kh. Peters and D.A. Bulatov. The new KSK was chaired by the more moderate V.V. Kuibyshev, and its collegium included N.K. Antipov, Z.M. Belen'kii, N.M. Antselovich, A.I. Gaister, G.E. Prokof'ev, G.I. Lomov, A.M. Tsikhon, R.S. Zemlyachka, I.M. Moskvin and B.A. Roizenman.[157] The two new agencies were recruited mainly from the leadership of the old TsKK–NKRKI.[158] Although there was continuity in personnel, in terms of organization and function the KPK and KSK differed fundamentally from TsKK–NKRKI.

TsKK–NKRKI's abolition carried momentous implications. The separation of party and state control functions created in KSK and KPK two agencies, subject to much tighter central direction. Lacking the authority of TsKK–NKRKI their responsibilities were much more restricted, and confined to control work. TsKK–NKRKI's rationalization work was abandoned. Its responsibility in policy formation was assumed by the Secretariat, which in 1934 was reorganized on the 'production-branch principle', extending its control over every sector of the economy. The republican and local control agencies were replaced by centrally-appointed control plenipotentiaries as part of the drive to streamline and tighten control.[159]

TsKK–NKRKI's abolition transformed the organization of mass control. In July 1933 VTsSPS, headed by N.M. Shvernik, took over NKTrud, completing the transformation of the unions into state instruments of labour management.[160] The XVII Party Congress transferred NKRKI's control functions in the institutions and enterprises, and its role as an organizer of mass control, to the trade unions.[161] In February 1934 NKRKI's Bureau of Complaints and Applications was transferred to the new KSK.[162] To increase responsibility in the institutions and enterprises and to stimulate initiative internal departmental controls were strengthened.[163] As part of a general tightening up of control, OGPU in July 1934 was merged into the People's Commissariat of Internal Affairs (NKVD).

TsKK–NKRKI's abolition was a humiliating defeat for Rudzutak. In 1934 he was re-elected only as candidate member of the Politburo, not as a full member, the position he surrendered on becoming head of TsKK in 1931. He retained his position as vice-chairman of Sovnarkom and STO but received no new appointment.[164] In the following three years Rudzutak appears to have sided with a moderate faction in the Politburo comprising Ordzhonikidze, Kosior, Chubar' and Antipov.[165] In May 1937 he was arrested and charged with affiliation to a 'Rightist bloc'. He signed a confession under torture which he retracted at his trial. He was executed in 1938.[166] In the purges of 1937–8 the former officials of TsKK–NKRKI enjoyed no special immunity and evidently suffered as badly as other categories.

CONCLUSION

TsKK–NKRKI after a lingering decline was finally abolished in 1934. Having attained the height of its power in redrafting the five-year plan in 1929–30 it thereafter struggled to enforce those policies. NKRKI, especially its local organs, failed to cope with these new responsibilities. The agency's role in policy formulation declined as the power of the economic commissariats was reasserted. Its role in rationalization no longer met the needs of the Politburo, and was increasingly suspect ideologically. In the area of policy-making TsKK–NKRKI was supplanted by the leading party and government organs.

The abolition of TsKK–NKRKI left a vacuum in the field of party–state control which other agencies, including the NKVD, were swift to occupy. In 1934, the Politburo hardliners were still not fully in control. At the XVII Party Congress there appear to have been moves behind the scenes to limit Stalin's power and to moderate the Politburo's policies. Those who favoured resolute measures against the opposition still trod warily. TsKK–NKRKI's abolition removed an important check on the party leadership.[167] It cleared the ground for a more centralized, less accountable, more implacable system of control. However, it was not until 1936 that Stalin and his allies had assembled the machinery for an all-out assault on their opponents in all reaches of the party–state apparatus.

Conclusion

The Bolshevik government, as a revolutionary, modernizing regime encountered grave problems in managing and controlling the state. As a Marxist party, influenced by the Russian administrative tradition and by Bolshevik organizational practices, it repudiated the western liberal conception of the state. It sought to create a new state administration which would embody the 'dictatorship of the proletariat' and provide a vehicle for the transition to socialism. The party's relations with the state, and the relations of both with the society, assumed critical importance. A plethora of organizational structures were created to link these units together. At the centre of the problem of state building lay the issue of state control.

NKRKI in 1920 became the dominant instrument of state control and one of the major Bolshevik innovations in state building. From the outset it was a curious hybrid, created from the forced marriage of the antiquated tsarist agency of State Control and the revolutionary workers' control movement which had sprung up in 1917. From the former NKRKI took over the functions of financial control and auditing of the state institutions. From the latter it took over the function of mass popular control over the state machine, through a system of direct participatory democracy.

The inspectorate, led by Stalin, was closely linked to the Politburo and Sovnarkom and exercised oversight over almost the entire state administration. This system of state control was intended to ensure effective political direction over the remnants of the old tsarist state apparatus which the regime had taken over. It was intended also as a means of combating the centrifugal forces in the trades unions and local soviets. It was also to provide a channel for popular involvement in government, to broaden the regime's base of support and to anchor it more firmly in the society.

The question of the organization of the state, state control and accountability, deeply split the party. The debate brought to the fore fundamentally different conceptions of socialism. The left in the party (strongly supported by the trade unions and local soviets) sought a decentralized system of administration, which would reflect the aspirations of the proletariat, and would allow direct popular participation in government. This was seen as a check on state bureaucracy and a means to harness revolutionary *élan* and to stimulate the initiative of the people.

The party leadership clung to a predominantly statist conception of socialism. They feared that decentralization would lead to fragmentation, that it would foster sectional interest, and would impede efficien direction and co-ordination of the state apparatus. They sought instead to restructure the central state machine, to proletarianize its ranks, and through tight party control harness it for the purpose of socialis construction. The trade unions and local soviets were to serve as auxiliary institutions assisting the state machine.

The regime embraced a statist conception of socialist construction Early experiments in workers' management of industry in 1918 were abandoned. During the civil war industry was nationalized, and subjec to tight central control; the role of the trade unions and the local soviet was curtailed. In 1921 this trend was confirmed with the establishment of the Soviet one-party state. Under NEP the scope of state activity was constrained and controls were relaxed. The state, however, remained the guarantor of the regime's survival and the instrument through which the party maintained its dominance.

In 1923 Lenin advanced his famous plan to unify NKRKI with TsKK, thus combining in one immensely powerful body the functions of state, party and popular control. He wished to set up a self-regulating mechanism within the party–state apparatus. It was intended as a democratic check on the central party organs, establishing new mechan isms of control and accountability; it was also to enable the party more effectively to direct the state machine. TsKK–NKRKI was to assist the party in policy-making, ensuring that it avoided excesses and other pitfalls. It was also to preserve the regime's link with the populace.

TsKK–NKRKI never became, as Lenin intended, an instrument for democratising the party, a watchdog to check the work of the leading party organs, or an educative institution to teach the party it. responsibilities and duties. TsKK–NKRKI instead aided the concentra tion of power in the party. Through TsKK party discipline wa tightened up, and through NKRKI party control over the state administration was strengthened.

The reorganized NKRKI of 1923 differed radically from its predeces sor. A small, specialized, prestigious agency, highly centralized and disciplined, it also became a highly politicized body, staffed by party officials and sympathetic specialists. NKRKI's role in financial contro was abandoned, its task was to restructure the administrative and economic institutions on scientific principles. It became part of an international movement for scientific rationalization, scientific man agement and labour organization.

For the Politburo and Sovnarkom the new TsKK–NKRKI became a formidable and indispensable instrument. NKRKI's tentacles penetrated the whole apparatus. It provided a new channel of information and advice on policy. It gave the leadership an instrument by which to insert orders and instruction into the apparatus. NKRKI wielded a panoply of powers – checking, control, exposing criminal activity, rationalizing and supervising, removing and promoting officials. It cultivated close links with the secret police and judicial organs and also with the mass organizations.

Lenin's reorganization of TsKK–NKRKI in 1923 was intended to meet the problem of how to regulate the party and state institutions effectively by linking the leading party organs directly with this new agency of party–state control. Immediately it became one of the central links in the Soviet party and governmental apparatus, closely tied to the Politburo, the Central Committee, and Sovnarkom. The agency's links with the party organs were co-ordinated by the party Secretariat.

The new TsKK–NKRKI in 1923 was closely tied to the Politburo and Sovnarkom as a combined agency of party–state control. TsKK quickly dominated NKRKI. Under Kuibyshev, one of Stalin's most loyal protégés, TsKK–NKRKI was ruthlessly adapted to the Politburo's needs. TsKK worked closely with the leading party organs and sent its representatives to the Politburo and Orgburo and enjoyed an especially close relationship with Stalin's Secretariat. TsKK's party collegium enforced party discipline, and ensured observance of the party statutes, including the ban on factions.

NKRKI was given three principal tasks – to rationalize the state administration, to control the work of the apparatus, and to assist in policy-making. The agency faced a constant problem of reconciling these various facets of its work, and its role as an independent rationalization agency was constantly undermined by the need to adjust its work to meet the needs of the Politburo and Sovnarkom. Increasingly the agency's independence was compromised as it sought to transform itself into an administrative arm and ally of the Politburo.

Through TsKK–NKRKI the Politburo and Stalin's Secretariat were provided with a powerful instrument to control the entire party–state apparatus. As a result, decision-making in the party was centralized and the power of Sovnarkom slowly eroded. TsKK–NKRKI's establishment (as Osinskii had prophesied in 1923) gave impetus to the fusion of the party and state apparatus. This trend became especially pronounced after 1925 when TsKK–NKRKI's links with the leading party and government organs were reinforced and put on a formal footing.

NKRKI's task was to ensure that the state administration operated effectively and responsively to central directions. In the field of policy-making it provided an alternative channel of advice and information as a rival to the operative commissariats, reducing the Politburo's dependency on these agencies, and thereby strengthening its hand in the field of policy-making.

After 1923 NKRKI was placed in a unique position, closely connected to Sovnarkom and (via TsKK) with the leading party organs. Its relations with the administrative and economic institutions were more problematical. NKRKI, like most control agencies, was small in size, its resources limited, its time restricted and it was isolated from the work of the operative commissariats. In these circumstances NKRKI required some co-operation from the operative agencies, who could inhibit control through their access to expertise and resources.

The relations between control and operative agencies assume various forms. Weak control agencies exercise only token control, and are subordinate to the operative agencies, and depend on the latter for whatever information they can obtain. Strong control agencies can establish a working relationship with the operative agencies, and ensure a measure of co-operation and mutual accommodation. Over-strong control agencies can overwhelm the operative agencies and may even usurp their functions.

NKRKI's relations with the administrative and economic institutions exhibited some of these characteristics in different periods. The agency's power derived not only from its own resources but also from the backing it received from the leading party and government organs. In periods of crisis NKRKI's hand was strengthened. In periods of calm the operative commissariats assumed a dominant role. In 1920–3 and again in 1925–6 NKRKI struggled desperately to define a role for itself. Its ineffectiveness reduced its leadership to near despair. After 1928 the balance was tilted dramatically in favour of the controllers, with TsKK–NKRKI emerging as a powerful institutional interest group.

In 1923 L.B. Krasin denounced Lenin's plan for TsKK–NKRKI and warned of the dangers associated with control-dominated administrative systems, anticipating the later work of V.A. Thompson. Excess control breeds 'bureaupathology', erodes responsibility and authority, fosters passivity and departmentalism. Such systems carry important implications for policy-making, creating powerful and irresponsible control lobbies, fostering conflict between controllers and operatives, which can undermine the basis for rational policy-making.

Through TsKK's party collegium, internal party control and discipline were tightened. In each successive party struggle after Lenin's death TsKK–NKRKI associated itself with Stalin. TsKK–NKRKI and the party Secretariat formed a formidable alliance which increasingly dominated the party. In the ensuing battle for the succession TsKK–NKRKI (led by a core of committed Stalinists) assumed critical importance. It played a key role in defeating Trotsky in 1923, Zinoviev and Kamenev in 1925, the united opposition in 1927 and the 'Right' opposition in 1929.

In each crisis TsKK's work in enforcing party discipline was complemented by NKRKI's role in the government sphere. The inspectorate played a critical role during the 'scissors crisis' of 1923, the conflict over agricultural policy in 1925, the debate over the regime of economy campaign in 1926–7, and, most important of all, NKRKI emerged after 1928 as one of the chief architects of the policy of agricultural collectivization and forced industrialization. NKRKI's role was not only to defend, enforce and develop official policies but also to discredit those of the opposition.

The party and governmental aspects of TsKK–NKRKI's work became inseparable. Through TsKK's dominance over NKRKI, political considerations increasingly coloured the inspectorate's work. TsKK–NKRKI developed as a policy directorate of the Politburo, providing information, formulating policies, identifying problems. TsKK–NKRKI also provided the administrative means to enforce and monitor policies once adopted. Although closely tied to Stalin, TsKK–NKRKI, especially under the leadership of Ordzhonikidze, retained a capacity for independent initiative.

TsKK–NKRKI's role as a policy directorate was developed in opposition to Sovnarkom and the operative commissariats. In the face of growing opposition to official policies after 1928 a new approach to the state apparatus was adopted. A wholesale assault against 'bureaucratism' was launched, controls over policy enforcement were tightened, OGPU and the courts led a witch hunt against saboteurs, the apparatus was purged, attempts were made to proletarianize its ranks and to stimulate mass involvement in administration. Yakovlev's report to the XVI Party Conference in 1929 underlined the party's commitment to a control-centred administrative system. The managerial lobby, represented by the forceful Birman, and the trade unions doggedly resisted this trend, but were finally overwhelmed.

The first five-year plan necessitated a new system of administrative discipline. The industrialization and collectivization drive created a new imperative for checking economic performance. Given the political character of the 'second revolution' and the methods required to enforce these policies, TsKK–NKRKI, led by the powerful Ordzhonikidze, forced itself into the centre of economic administration. Although working closely with the Politburo, TsKK–NKRKI displayed all the characteristics of a powerful institutional interest group and policy initiator.

In 1928 TsKK–NKRKI, forcefully encouraged by Stalin, became a major power. The 'left turn' appealed to a strong fundamentalist current in the party. TsKK–NKRKI emerged as the principal architect of the party's economic policy, elbowing Gosplan and Vesenkha aside. The operative commissariats lost the capacity to check the controllers. NKRKI provided the rallying point for radicals in the economic apparatus whilst TsKK provided the muscle which ensured the defeat of the 'Right'. NKRKI, together with OGPU, was instrumental in breaking managerial and trade union opposition to the new 'general line'.

This 'revolution from above' coincided with the leftist phase of the 'cultural revolution' which sought to whip up popular support behind official policies, and repudiated the compromises of the NEP era. The industrialization and collectivization drive created the centralized Stalinist command economy, which enormously extended the state's power. The grave policy errors of this period did incalculable damage to the modernization drive and rebounded back directly on the political system itself, which menacingly developed its full repressive potential.

This turning point was reflected in the re-adoption of the administrative measures employed to deal with problems under war communism. The repudiation of NEP saw the replacement of financial control by planning and administrative levers. The balance of power in the apparatus was shifted in favour of the controllers. TsKK–NKRKI in 1929–30 became the Politburo's 'general staff' office directing policy. The economic policy of the Politburo was fundamentally recast. NKRKI's takeover of the main economic commissariats in 1929–30 underlined the dominance of the controllers.

TsKK–NKRKI profoundly influenced the Politburo's perception, both technical and political, of what was feasible in economic policy. It introduced serious distortions into policy-making. The capacity of the operative commissariats to resist NKRKI's proposals was undermined. This adversarial style of policy-making impeded the rational evaluation of policy options. The Politburo committed itself to a policy of forced development wherein economic and technical considerations were subordinated to a political decision to break the NEP consensus and launch a new phase of socialist construction.

Stalin's Politburo created this system of policy-making and was also its unwitting victim. TsKK–NKRKI fed a mood of wild, reckless optimism in the Politburo regarding the prospects of development, resulting in serious errors in estimating growth targets, which resulted in a wasteful and unbalanced pattern of economic development, and which exacerbated the acute social strains associated with the modernization drive. Agricultural collectivization and forced industrialization created unforeseen difficulties, to cope with which the regime resorted to still more draconian methods of political control.

TsKK–NKRKI, under Ordzhonikidze in 1929–30 reached the apogee of its power. Thereafter, under Andreev and Rudzutak, it declined precipitately. Its rationalization function was repudiated and its influence in policy-making waned. The grave economic problems encountered by the regime and the mounting tension in the party threw TsKK–NKRKI into turmoil. Its failure to deal forcefully with the agricultural crisis in 1932/3 severely strained its relations with the Politburo. The Politburo hardliners led the attack on TsKK–NKRKI.

The XVII Party Congress in 1934 abolished TsKK–NKRKI and paved the way for a stricter system of party and state control. The agency which had been conceived by Lenin as a check on the leading party organs was finally cast aside. The party's commitment to popular control was abandoned. A more repressive era in the organization of party–state control was inaugurated. The party Secretariat and Orgburo increasingly directed and co-ordinated control work. The NKVD, Procuracy and the judicial organs were also swift to occupy the vacuum left by TsKK–NKRKI.

The new Commission of Party Control (KPK) and Commission of Soviet Control (KSK), under the direction respectively of the Politburo and Sovnarkom, provided a system of tight central control, directed mainly at ensuring effective policy enforcement and tightening discipline. They did not match TsKK–NKRKI in either their power or status. In 1940 a new more powerful People's Commissariat of State Control (narkom L.Z. Mekhlis) was set up as part of a fundamental reorganization of control after the bloodletting and terror of 1937–8.

Soviet historians in the Stalin era paid scant attention to TsKK–NKRKI. At the XX Party Congress in 1956 Khrushchev rehabilitated Ya.E. Rudzutak, the last head of TsKK–NKRKI. At the Central Committee plenum in November 1962 he outlined Lenin's role in establishing TsKK–NKRKI. He praised its commitment to the principle of popular control, as an expression of direct participatory soviet democracy, and a valuable tool in the struggle against bureaucracy, and a vital link binding the regime to the society.

In 1934 Stalin, Khrushchev argued, repudiated the 'Leninist principles' of party–state control, rejected the need for an unified agency of control, and flouted the commitment to popular control. He established in its place a system of 'bureaucratic control by the apparatus, isolated from the masses'. The NKVD assumed many of TsKK–NKRKI's functions, and its leaders attempted to place themselves above the party. Moreover, this decision opened the way for the Stalin dictatorship: 'The idea of control in its Leninist conception proved incompatible with the ideology of the personality cult'.[1]

Khrushchev's account clearly indicates the importance of powerful institutional lobbies in shaping the Soviet regime's development at this critical juncture. Stalin's power derived largely from his ability to manipulate, control and check these institutional forces.

This incomplete and partial explanation was shaped by immediate political considerations. In 1962 Khrushchev established a new unified Committee of Party–State Control, chaired by A.N. Shelepin. Like TsKK–NKRKI it combined the functions of party and state control, operated on the principle of popular participation, and stimulated the rediscovery of the rationalization movement of the 1920s.

Khrushchev's speech initiated a flood of historical works on TsKK–NKRKI.[2] Most followed Khrushchev's authorized version of the agency's dissolution – that TsKK–NKRKI's existence prevented Stalin from consolidating his power.[3] A full explanation, however, never materialized. Khrushchev's removal in 1964 halted further research into the genesis of the Stalin system. In 1966 the Committee of Party–State Control was abolished and replaced by separate party and state control agencies.

Soviet historians writing about TsKK–NKRKI since 1964 have either ignored the reasons for its abolition or have simply repeated the formula given in 1934 that the agency had outlived its usefulness.[4] The decision of the XVII Party Congress to abolish TsKK–NKRKI brought to a close a major experiment in the organization of party–state control in the USSR, which had played a vital role in shaping the regime's development. The problem of party–state control persisted and remains an enduring preoccupation of the Soviet political system.

Appendix A   Organs of State Control

LEADERSHIP OF THE ORGANS OF STATE CONTROL (1918–34)[1]

Chairman of the Central Control Collegium
E.E. Essen   January 1918–March 1918

People's Commissars (*narkom*) of NKGosKontrol RSFSR 1918–20
K.I. Lander   March 1918–March 1919
I.V. Stalin   March 1919–February 1920

People's Commissars (*narkom*) of NKRKI RSFSR 1920–3
I.V. Stalin   February 1920–April 1922
A.D. Tsyurupa   April 1922–May 1923

People's Commissars (*narkom*) of NKRKI USSR and Chairmen of TsKK USSR 1923–34
V.V. Kuibyshev   May 1923–August 1926
G.K. Ordzhonikidze November 1926–November 1930
A.A. Andreev   November 1930–October 1931
Ya.E. Rudzutak   October 1931–February 1934

LEADERSHIP OF THE REPUBLICAN ORGANS OF STATE CONTROL (1923–34)[2]

People's Commissars (*narkom*) of NKRKI and Chairmen of TsKK of the union republics

TsKK–NKRKI RSFSR	N.M. Shvernick (1923–5); N.I. Il'in (1925–34)
TsKK–NKRKI Ukrainian SSR	D.Z. Lebed' (1924–7); V.P. Zatonskii (1927–33); K.V. Sukhomlin (1933–4)
TsKK–NKRKI Belorussian SSR	V.P. Gruzel' (1925–7); A.Ya. Kalnin (1927–33); I.A. Lychev (1933–4)
TsKK–NKRKI Transcaucasian SSR	A.M. Nazaretyan (1924–30); A.I. Dogadov (1931–4)
TsKK–NKRKI Turkmen SSR	K. Kuliev (1926–9); A. Moukhamedov (1932); B. Ataiev (1933–4)
TsKK–NKRKI Uzbek SSR	A. Mavlyanbekov (1926–7); A. Karimov (1929); K. Baltabaiev (1932); D. Turabekov (1933–4)
TsKK–NKRKI Tadzhik SSR	A.I. Larichev (1932); S. Abdoullaiev (1933–4)

Appendix B Leadership of NKRKI (1920–34)

NKRKI RSFSR COLLEGIA (1920–3)

1921 (December)
narkom   I.V. Stalin
deputy   V.A. Avanesov
members   M.K. Vetoshkin, A.A. Korostelev, N.A. Reske, N.N. Baranskii[1]

1922 (May)
narkom   A.D. Tsyurupa
deputy   V.A. Avanesov
members   A.I. Sviderskii, L.I. Ruzer, N.N. Baranskii, M.A. Levenson, N.A. Reseke, E.F. Rozmirovich, A.M. Tamarin[2]

NKRKI USSR COLLEGIA (1923–34)

1923 (August)
narkom   V.V. Kuibyshev
deputies   V.A. Avanesov, A.S. Kiselev
members   N.N. Baranskii, N.I. Il'in, V.N. Mantsev, E.F. Rozmirovich, S.E. Chutskaev, N.M. Shvernik[3]

1924 (June)
narkom   V.V. Kuibyshev
deputies   N.M. Yanson, S.E. Chutskaev
members   S.I. Gusev, N.M. Shvernik, N.I. Il'in, E.F. Rozmirovich, V.P. Milyutin, F.V. Lengnik, D.Z. Lebed', A.M. Nazaretyan[4]

1925 (January)
narkom   V.V. Kuibyshev
deputies   N.M. Yanson, S.E. Chutskaev
members   S.I. Gusev, N.M. Shvernik, V.P. Milyutin, F.V. Lengnik, V.P. Gruzel', D.Z. Lebed', A.M. Nazaretyan, E.F. Rozmirovich, N.I. Il'in[5]

1926 (March)
narkom   V.V. Kuibyshev
deputies   S.E. Chutskaev (first), D.Z. Lebed' (second)

members   V.P. Gruzel', N.I. Il'in, A.Z. Gol'tsman, F.V. Lengnik, V.P.
              Milyutin, A.M. Nazaretyan, Ya.Kh. Peters, E.F. Rozmirovich,
              B.A. Roizenman[6]

1927 (May)
narkom   G.K. Ordzhonikidze
deputies   N.M. Yanson (first), D.Z. Lebed', Ya.A. Yakovlev
members   N.I. Il'in, V.P. Milyutin, B.A. Roizenman, Ya.Kh. Peters, A.Z.
              Gol'tsman, E.F. Rozmirovich, F.V. Lengnik, M.F. Shkiryatov,
              E.M. Yaroslavskii[7]

1928 (March)
narkom   G.K. Ordzhonikidze
deputies   D.Z. Lebed', Ya.A. Yakovlev
members   N.I. Il'in, V.P. Milyutin, A.P. Rozengol'ts, B.A. Roizenman,
              M.I. Kalmanovich, Ya.Kh. Peters, I.P. Pavlunovskii, A.Z.
              Gol'tsman, P.S. Shushkov, E.F. Rozmirovich, M.M. Kaga-
              novich, F.V. Lengnik, Z.M. Belen'kii, M.F. Shkiryatov, A.S.
              Svanidze, E.M. Yaroslavskii[8]

1929 (February)
narkom   G.K. Ordzhonikidze
deputies   D.Z. Lebed', Ya.A. Yakovlev, A.P. Rozengol'ts
members   N.I. Il'in, Z.M. Belen'kii, A.Z. Gol'tsman, M.M. Kaganovich,
              A.Ya. Kalnin, F.V. Lengnik, I.P. Pavlunovskii, Ya.Kh. Peters,
              E.F. Rozmirovich, B.A. Roizenman, A.M. Fushman, M.F.
              Shkiryatov, P.S. Shushkov, E.M. Yaroslavskii[9]

1930 (July)
narkom   G.K. Ordzhonikidze
deputies   A.P. Rozengol'ts, I.P. Pavlunovskii, I.A. Akulov
members   N.I. Il'in, Z.M. Belen'kii, P.S. Shushkov, A.Z. Gol'tsman, A.V.
              Ozerskii, M.M. Kaganovich, F.V. Lengnik, Ya.Kh. Peters, E.F.
              Rozmirovich, B.A. Roizenman, M.F. Shkiryatov, E.M.
              Yaroslavskii[10]

1931 (August)
narkom   A.A. Andreev
deputies   A.I. Krinitskii, N.K. Antipov
members   N.I. Il'in, Z.M. Belen'kii, A.Z. Gol'tsman, N.V. Kuibyshev,
              V.Z. Karpov, F.V. Lengnik, Ya.Kh. Peters, B.A. Roizenman,
              M.F. Shkiryatov, E.M. Yaroslavskii[11]

1931 (December)
narkom   Ya.E. Rudzutak
deputies   G.E. Prokof'ev, N.M. Antselovich, Z.M. Belen'kii, N.K.
              Antipov
members   N.I. Il'in, A.Z. Gol'tsman, F.V. Lengnik, Ya.Kh. Peters, B.A.
              Roizenman, M.F. Shkiryatov, N.V. Kuibyshev, V.Z. Karpov,
              V.G. Feigin, E.M. Yaroslavskii[12]

1932 (December)
narkom   Ya.E. Rudzutak
deputies   N.M. Antselovich, Z.M. Belen'kii, N.K. Antipov, I.D. Vermen-
            ichev
members   N.I. Il'in, A.Z. Gol'tsman, F.V. Lengnik, Ya.Kh. Peters, A.A.
            Bukhanov, V.G. Volodin, S.T. Kovylkin, S.I. Komissarov,
            E.M. Ravinkovich, A.G. Remeiko, N.V. Kuibyshev, V.Z.
            Karpov, E.M. Yaroslavskii[13]

1933 (December)
narkom   Ya.E. Rudzutak
deputies   N.M. Antselovich, Z.M. Belen'kii, I.D. Vermenichev, N.K.
            Antipov
members   N.I. Il'in, F.V. Lengnik, Ya.Kh. Peters, B.A. Roizenman, M.F.
            Shkiryatov, E.M. Yaroslavskii, N.V. Kuibyshev, V.Z. Karpov,
            A.A. Bukhanov, V.G. Volodin, S.I. Komissarov, A.G.
            Remeiko, R.S. Zemlyachka[14]

This listing of NKRKI collegia members is not definitive. There is no official listing available, and there is no precise way of checking on transfers and removals, and hence some errors may have crept in.

Appendix C NKRKI USSR

NKRKI USSR: DEPARTMENTAL HEADS (1925)[1]

General administration	Ya.Kh. Peters
Legal department	A.A. Sol'ts
Administration for improving the state apparatus	E.F. Rozmirovich
Administration for accounting and bookkeeping	P.N. Amosov
Inspectorates	
metal working	S.O. Viksin
mining	S.A. Novoselov
textiles	V.M. Kosarev
chemicals	G.L. Shklovskii
foreign trade	A.I. Stetskii
domestic trade	V.F. Larin
finance	Z.G. Zangvil'
labour	I.I. Korotkov
agriculture	Ya.A. Yakovlev
military and naval	S.I. Gusev
transport and communications	N.I. Il'in
unplanned assignments	B.A. Roizenman
Council for the Scientific Organization of Labour (SovNOT)	V.V. Kuibyshev (chairman) A.K. Gastev (vice-chairman)
Central Bureau for Standardization	Z.A. Panerov
Accounting Council	S.E. Chutskaev

NKRKI USSR: DEPARTMENTAL HEADS (1928)[2]

Management of affairs (*upravlenie delami*)	S.F. Redens
Organisation–instruction department	M.F. Shkiryatov
Legal department	A.A. Sol'ts
Sector of control and checking	B.A. Roizenman
Inspectorates and investigating groups	
Centralized inspectorates	
military and naval	I.P. Pavlunovskii
transport and communications	F.V. Lengnik
Operative groups	
staff of the state institutions	N.G. Tsvetkov
supply of building materials	S.O. Viksin
raising of grain yields	F.A. Tsil'ko

accounting in the economic organs	B.A. Bor'yan
accounting and bookkeeping techniques	E.A. Kravtsov
examination of the state budget	Z.G. Zangvil'

Short-term assignments

B.A. Azarkh, Ya.M. Bineman, G.V. Gvakhariya, N.K. Goncharov, V.Ya. Grossman, M.B. Grossman, R.S. Zemlyachka, S.I. Ignat, M.M. Kaganovich, M.N. Kokovikhin, V.F. Larin, S.I. Nazarov, V.A. Radus-Zen'kovich, A.P. Rozengol'ts, D.I. Savostin, V.P. Staranikov, Sheboldaev

Central Bureau of Complaints	S.M. Semkov
Institute of Bookkeeping Experts	B.A. Bor'yan
Accounting Council	D.Z. Lebed'

Appendix D Organisational Structure of Central Apparatus

NOVEMBER 1923[1]

DECEMBER 1926[2]

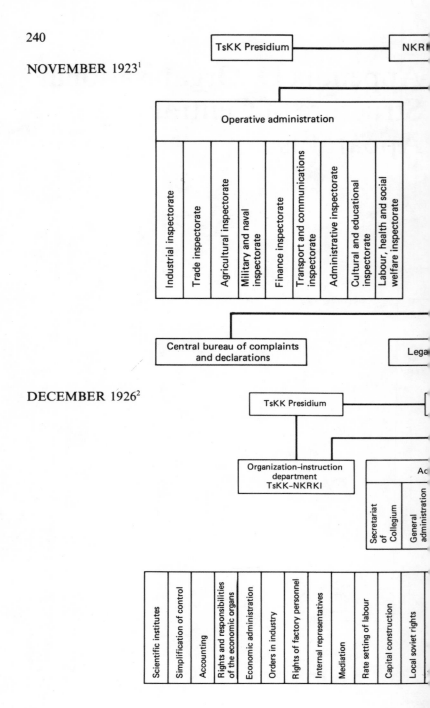

TsKK Presidium

NKR

Operative administration

- Industrial inspectorate
- Trade inspectorate
- Agricultural inspectorate
- Military and naval inspectorate
- Finance inspectorate
- Transport and communications inspectorate
- Administrative inspectorate
- Cultural and educational inspectorate
- Labour, health and social welfare inspectorate

Central bureau of complaints and declarations

Lega

TsKK Presidium

Organization–instruction department TsKK–NKRKI

Ad

- Secretariat of Collegium
- General administration

- Scientific institutes
- Simplification of control
- Accounting
- Rights and responsibilities of the economic organs
- Economic administration
- Orders in industry
- Rights of factory personnel
- Internal representatives
- Mediation
- Rate setting of labour
- Capital construction
- Local soviet rights

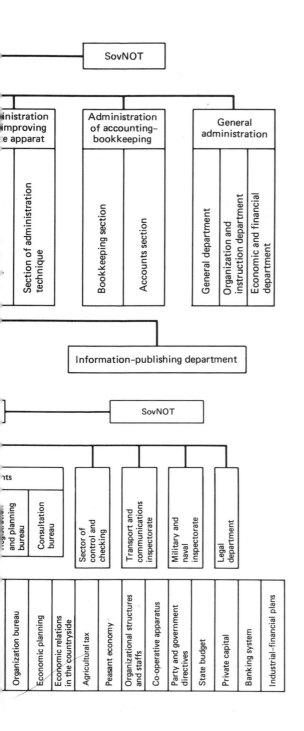

SovNOT

inistration improving e apparat	Administration of accounting-bookkeeping	General administration
Section of administration technique	Bookkeeping section / Accounts section	General department / Organization and instruction department / Economic and financial department

Information-publishing department

SovNOT

hts		
and planning bureau / Consultation bureau	Sector of control and checking / Transport and communications inspectorate / Military and naval inspectorate / Legal department	

Organization bureau
Economic planning
Economic relations in the countryside
Agricultural tax
Peasant economy
Organizational structures and staffs
Co-operative apparatus
Party and government directives
State budget
Private capital
Banking system
Industrial-financial plans

Appendix E TsKK

MEMBERSHIP OF TsKK (1921–30)

Party Congresses	Members	*TsKK* *Candidates*	Total
X Congress March 1921	7	3	10
XI Congress April 1922	5	2	7
XII Congress April 1923	50	10	60
XIII Congress May 1924	150	—	150
XIV Congress December 1925	163	—	163
XV Congress December 1927	195	—	195
XVI Congress July 1930	187	—	187

MEMBERSHIP OF TsKK PRESIDIUM (1921–30)

Party Congresses	Members	*TsKK presidium* *Candidates*	Total
X Congress March 1921	7	3	10
XI Congress April 1922	5	2	7
XII Congress April 1923	9	5	14
XIII Congress May 1924	15	6	21
XIV Congress December 1925	21	9	30
XV Congress December 1927	22	10	32
XVI Congress July 1930	25	6	31

TURNOVER OF TsKK MEMBERS AT EACH PARTY CONGRESS[1]

Party Congress	TsKK members elected	Number re-elected at subsequent Congress	% re-elected
XII	60	43	71.6
XIII	150	70	46.6
XIV	163	80	49.0
XV	195	85	43.5
XVI	187	—	—

TURNOVER OF TsKK MEMBERS BETWEEN XIV AND XV PARTY CONGRESSES[2]

After the XIV party congress 163 TsKK members were elected, divided into three categories: (i) those assigned to work in the central apparatus of TsKK–NKRKI; (ii) those working on local assignments; (iii) workers and peasants who remained in their existing jobs.

Categories of members	Elected at XIV Congress	Re-elected at XV Congress	% re-elected
Central assignments	73	49	67.2
Local assignments	35	21	60.0
Workers and peasants	55	10	18.2
Total	163	80	49.0

Appendix F TsKK Presidium (1920 – 34)[1]

Prior to X Party Congress

F.E. Dzerzhinskii, M.K. Muranov, E.A. Preobrazhenskii, A.A. Sol'ts, N.O. Kuchmenko, D.I. Sorokhov, M.I. Chelishev[2]

X Party Congress (March 1921)
members: T.S. Krivov, N.O. Kuchmenko, Z.Ya. Litvin (Sedoi), P.G. Smidovich, A.A. Sol'ts, I.I. Shvarts, M.I. Chelishev
candidates: I.G. Batishev, A.I. Dogadov, K.A. Ozol[3]

XI Party Congress (April 1922)
members: A.A. Sol'ts, O.A. Varentsova, A.A. Korostelev, I.D. Chentsov, M.F. Shkiryatov
candidates: M.K. Muranov, F.N. Somoilov[4]

XII Party Congress (April 1923)
chairman: V.V. Kuibyshev
members: S.I. Gusev, A.S. Kiselev, N.I. Il'in, A.A. Sol'ts, M.F. Shkiryatov, S.A. Shvarts, N.M. Yanson, E.M. Yaroslavskii
candidates: T.S. Krivov, A.A. Korostelev, E.P. Pozern, N.M. Shvernik, S.E. Chutskaev[5]

XIII Party Congress (May 1924)
chairman: V.V. Kuibyshev
members: S.I. Gusev, N.I. Il'in, A.S. Kiselev, G.A. Korostelev, I.I. Korotkov, N.K. Krupskaya, N.V. Lisitsin, B.A. Roizenman, A.A. Sol'ts, S.E. Chutskaev, N.M. Shvernik
candidates: T.S. Krivov, M.D. Pastykhov, A.V. Shotman, V.I. Ivanov, D.Z. Lebed', A.M. Nazaretyan[6]

XIV Party Congress (December 1925)
chairman: V.V. Kuibyshev
members: M.F. Vladimirskii, S.I. Gusev, N.I. Il'in, M.N. Kokovikhin, S.I. Komissarov, G.A. Korostelev, I.I. Korotkov, V.M. Kosarev, T.S. Krivov, D.Z. Lebed', F.V. Lengnik, N.V. Lisitsin, A.M. Nazaretyan, M.D. Pastykhov, B.A. Roizenman, A.A. Sol'ts, S.E. Chutskaev, M.F. Shkiryatov, N.M. Yanson, E.M. Yaroslavskii
candidates: P.F. Sakharova, Ya.A. Yakovlev, A.V. Shotman, A.S. Enukidze, N.M. Os'mov, P.N. Avdeev, V.A. Radus-Zen'kovich, V.S. Kalashnikov, D.I. Mandzhara[7]

XV Party Congress (December 1927)
chairman: G.K. Ordzhonikidze
members: G.A. Desov, A.S. Enukidze, V.P. Zatonskii, N.I. Il'in, N.N.
Kokovikhin, G.A. Korostelev, I.I. Korotkov, T.S. Krivov, D.Z.
Lebed', F.V. Lengnik, N.V. Lisitsin, A.M. Nazaretyan, N.M.
Os'mov, M.D. Pastykhov, B.A. Roizenman, A.A. Sol'ts, Yu.P.
Figatner, M.F. Shkiryatov, Ya.A. Yakovlev, N.M. Yanson, E.M.
Yaroslavskii
candidates: Ya.Kh. Peters, E.F. Rozmirovich, A.Z. Gol'tsman, V.A. Rudus-
Zen'kovich, M.M. Kaganovich, I.P. Pavlunovskii, N.K. Gon-
charov, S.M. Semkov, P.N. Karavaev, A.P. Rozengol'ts[8]

XVI Party Congress (July 1930)
chairman: G.K. Ordzhonikidze
members: I.A. Akulov, Z.M. Belen'kii, A.Z. Gol'tsman, I.A. Gurevich, A.S.
Enukidze, V.P. Zatonskii, R.S. Zemlyachka, N.I. Il'in, M.M.
Kaganovich, I.I. Korotkov, T.S. Krivov, A.M. Nazaretyan, N.M.
Os'mov, I.P. Pavlunovskii, Ya.Kh. Peters, M.N. Pokrovskii
candidates: A.I. Yakovlev, P.F. Sakharova, K.O. Kirkizh, P.N. Karavaev, A.V.
Artyukhina, P.S. Shushkov[9]

Glossary of Russian Terms and Abbreviations used in Text

ASSR	*Avtonomaya Sovetskaya Sotsialisticheskaya Respublika* (Autonomous Soviet Socialist Republic)
batrak	rural labourer, landless peasant
bednyak	poor peasant
Cheka	*Chrezvychainaya Komissiya* (Extraordinary Commission, political police), later GPU or OGPU
CPSU(b)	Communist Party of the Soviet Union (Bolsheviks)
edinonachalie	one-man management
erkaisty	familiar name for NKRKI officials
Gipromez	*Gosudarstvennyi Institut po Proektirovaniyu Metallicheskikh Zavodov* (State Institute for Projects of Metal Works)
glavk	chief administration of Vesenkha–Glavchermet (ferrous metals); Glavelektro (electrical industry); Glavgortop (mining); Glavmetall (metal industry); Glavkhlopkom (cotton); Glavmashstroi (engineering)
Goelro	*Gosudarstvennaya Komissiya po Elektrifikatsii Rossii* (State Commission for the Electrification of Russia)
Gosbank	*Gosudarstvennyi Bank* (State Bank)
Gosplan	*Gosudarstvennaya Planovaya Komissiya* (State Planning Commission)
ispolkom	*ispolnitel'nyi komitet* (executive committee)
ITU	*Institut Tekhniki Upravleniya* (Institute for Scientific Management)
khozraschet	commercial profit-and-loss accounting
KK–RKI	*kontrol'naya komissiya–raboche–krest'yanskoi inspektsii* (control commission–workers' and peasants' inspectorate) local organs of TsKK–NKRKI
kolkhoz	*kollektivnoe khozyaistvo* (collective farm)
Kolkhoztsentr	*Vserossiskii Sel'sokhozyaistvennykh Kollektivov* (All-Russian Union of Agricultural Collectives)
Komsomol	*Kommunisticheskiya Soyuz Molodezhi* (Communist League of Youth)
KomIspol	*Komissiya Ispolneniya* (Executive Commission of Sovnarkom)
kopek	1/100 rouble
KPK	Commission of Party Control
krai	territory
KSK	Commision of Soviet Control
kulak	rich peasant
MTS	*Mashinno-traktornaya stantsiya* (Machine Tractor Station)

narkom	Narodnyi Komissar (People's Commissar)
NEP	*Novaya ekonomicheskaya politika* (New Economic Policy)
NKFin	*Narodnyi Komissariat Finansov* (People's Commissariat of Finance)
NKGosKon	*Narodnyi Komissariat Gosudarstvennogo Kontrolya* (People's Commissariat of State Control)
NKInDel	*Narodnyi Komissariat po Inostrannym Delam* (People's Commissariat of Foreign Affairs)
NKLegProm	*Narodnyi Komissariat Legkoi Promyshlennosti* (People's Commissariat of Light Industry)
NKLes	*Narodnyi Komissariat Lesnoi Promyshlennosti* (People's Commissariat for the Timber Industry)
NKNats	*Narodnyi Komissariat po Delam Natsional'nostei* (People's Commissariat of Nationalities)
NKProd	*Narodnyi Komissariat Prodovol'stviya* (People's Commissariat for Procurement)
NKPros	*Narodnyi Komissariat Prosveshcheniya* (People's Commissariat of Education)
NKPS	*Narodnyi Komissariat Putei Soobshcheniya* (People's Commissariat of Ways of Communication, i.e. Transport)
NKP&T	*Narodnyi Komissariat Pocht i Telegrafov* (People's Commissariat of Posts and Telegraphs)
NKRKI	*Narodnyi Komissariat Raboche-Krest'yanskoi Inspektsii* (People's Commissariat of Workers' and Peasants' Inspection – known also as Rabkrin)
NKSnab	*Narodnyi Komissariat Snabzheniya* (People's Commissariat of Supply)
NKSotsObes	*Narodnyi Komissariat Sotsial'nogo Obespecheniya* (People's Commissariat for Social Security)
NKTorg	*Narodnyi Komissariat Vneshnei i Vnutrennoi Torgovli* (People's Commissariat of External and Internal Trade)
NKTyazhProm	*Narodnyi Komissariat Tyazheloi Promyshlennosti* (People's Commissariat of Heavy Industry)
NKTrud	*Narodnyi Komissariat Truda* (People's Commissariat of Labour)
NKVneshTorg	*Narodnyi Komissariat Vneshnei Torgovli* (People's Commissariat for External Trade)
NKVMDel	*Narodnyi Komissariat po Voennym i Morskim Delam* (People's Commissariat for War and Naval Affairs)
NKVD	*Narodnyi Komissariat Vnutrennykh Del* (People's Commissariat of Internal Affairs)
NKYust	*Narodnyi Komissariat Yustitsii* (People's Commissariat of Justice)
NKZdrav	*Narodnyi Komissariat Zdravookhraneniya* (People's Commissariat of Health)
NKZem	*Narodnyi Komissariat Zemledeliya* (People's Commissariat of Agriculture (of RSFSR up to December 1929, then of USSR)
nomenklatura	appointment list controlled directly or indirectly by the party

NOT	*Nauchnaya organizatsiya truda* (the scientific study of labour organization)
oblast	province
OGPU (GPU)	*Ob"edinennoe Gosudarstvennoe Politicheskoe Upravlenie* (Unified State Political Administration, Political Police)
okrug	administrative region between region and district
politotdel	political department
Proletkult	*Organizatsiya Predstavitelei Proletarskogo Iskusstva* (Organization of Representatives of Proletarian Art)
pud	measure of weight equalling 36.1 British pounds
pyatiletka	the five-year plan
Rabkrin	see NKRKI
raion	district, administrative unit
RSFSR	*Rossiiskaya Sovetskaya Federativnaya Sotsialisticheskaya Respublika* (Russian Soviet Federative Socialist Republic)
rouble	unit of currency
serednyak	middle peasant
sovkhoz	*sovetskoe khozyaistvo* (Soviet state farm)
Sovnarkom	*Sovet Narodnykh Komissarov* (Council of People's Commissars)
SovNOT	Council for the Scientific Organization of Labour
SSR	*Sovetskaya Sotsialisticheskaya Respublika* (Soviet Socialist Republic)
STO	*Sovet Truda i Oborony* (Council of Labour and Defence Economic sub-committee of Sovnarkom)
tolkach	pusher, individual responsible for procuring goods
Tsentrosoyuz	*Vsesoyuznyi tsentral'nyi soyuz potrebitel'skikh obshchestv* (All-Union Central Union of Consumers' Societies)
TsIK	*Tsentral'nyi Ispolnitel'nyi Komitet* (Central Executive Committee of Soviets of USSR)
TsKK	*Tsentral'naya kontrol'naya komissiya* (Central Control Commission of the party)
TsKK–NKRKI	*Tsentral'naya kontrol'naya komissiya-Narodnyi Komissariat Raboche-Krest'yanskoi Inspektsii* (the Central Control Commission – People's Commissariat of Workers' and Peasants' Inspection – the unified organs of party–state control 1923–34)
TsSU	*Tsentral'noe Statisticheskoe Upravlenie* (Central Statistical Administration)
Vesenkha	*Vysshii Sovet Narodnogo Khozyaistva* (Supreme Council of the National Economy)
VTsIK	*Vserossiskii Tsentral'nyi Ispolnitel'nyi Komitet* (All-Russian Central Executive Committee of Soviets)
VTsSPS	*Vsesoyuznyi Tsentral'nyi Sovet Profsoyuzov* (All-Union Central Council of the Trade Unions)
Zernotrest	*Vsesoyuznyi trest zernovykh sovkhozov* (All-Union Trust of Grain Sovkhozy)

Notes and References

Abbreviations of titles of books and periodical publications used:

ASQ	*Administrative Science Quarterly*
Byulleten' TsKK	*Byulleten' TsKK VKP(b) i NKRKI SSSR i RSFSR*
Carr, *Interregnum*	E.H. Carr, *The Interregnum 1923–1924*
Carr, *SOC 1 and 2*	E.H. Carr, *Socialism in One Country, vols 1 and 2*
Carr, Davies, *FPE* 1	E.H. Carr and R.W. Davies, *Foundations of a Planned Economy 1*
Carr, *FPE* 2	E.H. Carr, *Foundations of a Planned Economy 2*
EZh	*Ekonomicheskaya zhizn'*
Iz	*Izvestiya*
IzRKI	*Izvestiya raboche-krest'yanskoi inspektsii*
KPSS v rez	*KPSS v rezolyutsiyakh i resheniyakh s"ezdov, konferentsii i plenumov TsK*
KhU	*Khozyaistvo i upravlenie*
LS	*Leninskii sbornik*
OU	*Organizatsiya upravleniya*
P	*Pravda*
SR (Ord), ii	*G.K. Ordzhonikidze, Stat'i i rechi*, vol. 2, M., 1957
SR	*Slavic Review*
SS	*Soviet Studies*
SU	*Sobranie uzakonenii*
SZ	*Sobranie zakonov*
TPG	*Torgovo-promyshlennaya gazeta*
ZTKP	*Za tempy, kachestvo, proverku*

Places of publication: Moscow is given as M. and Leningrad as L.

Introduction: Aspects of State Control

1. D. Christian, 'The Supervisory Function in Russian and Soviet History', *SR*, vol. 41, no. 1, Spring 1982, pp. 91–103.
2. M. Weber, *The Theory of Social and Economic Organization* (ed. Talcott Parsons) (New York, 1964) pp. 329–40.
3. J.F. Hough, *The Soviet Prefects* (Cambridge, Mass., 1969), ch. XIV.
4. See B. Chapman, *The Profession of Government* (London, 1959), P. Self, *Administrative Theories and Politics* (London, 1972); M. Crozier, *The Bureaucratic Phenomenon* (London, 1964); H. Simon, D.W. Smithburg and V.A. Thompson, *Public Administration* (New York, 1958). See also recent literature on policy-making: A.G. McGrew and M.J. Wilson, *Decision Making* (Manchester, 1984); B.W. Hogwood and L. Gunn, *Policy Analysis in the Real World* (Oxford, 1984).

5. J. Blondel, *An Introduction to Comparative Government* (London, 1969) p. 396.
6. A. Downs, *Inside Bureaucracy* (Boston, 1967) pp. 148–53.
7. Simon *et al.*, *Public Administration*, p. 534.
8. A. Kassof, 'The Administered Society: Totalitarianism without Terror', *World Politics*, Vol. 16, July 1964; A.G. Meyer, *The Soviet Political System* (New York, 1965), ch. 22; T.H. Rigby, 'Traditional, Market and Organisational Societies and the USSR', *World Politics*, vol. 16, July 1964; A.G. Meyer, *et al.*, 'The Comparative Study of Communist Political Systems', *SR*, March 1967 symposium, P. Hollander, 'Observations on Bureaucracy, Totalitarianism and the Comparative Study of Communism', *SR*, June 1967.
9. D. Granick, *The Red Executive* (New York, 1960); J.S. Berliner, *Factory and Manager in the USSR* (Cambridge, Mass., 1957) chs. 13–16; Hough, *The Soviet Prefects* (Cambridge, Mass., 1969); T.H. Rigby, *Lenin's Government: Sovnarkom 1917–1922* (Cambridge, 1979).
10. H.G. Skilling and F. Griffiths (eds), *Interest Groups in Soviet Politics* (Princeton, 1973); S.G. Solomon (ed.), *Pluralism in the Soviet Union* (London, 1983).
11. See. J. La Palombara, *Bureaucracy and Political Development* (Princeton, 1963).
12. V.A. Thompson, 'Administrative Objectives for Development Administration', *ASQ*, 1964, vol. 19, pp. 91–108; Thompson, 'Bureaucracy and Innovation', *ASQ*, 1965, vol. 10, pp. 1–20; Thompson, 'Hierarchy, Specialisation and Organisational Conflict', *ASQ*, 1961, vol. 5, pp. 485–521.
13. Thompson, 'Administrative Objectives for Development Administration', *ASQ*, 1964, vol. 19.
14. Thompson, *ASQ*, 1964, p. 100.
15. Thompson, *ASQ*, 1964, p. 93.
16. See ch. 2, pp. 52–54.
17. M. Fainsod, 'Bureaucracy and Modernisation: The Russian and Soviet Case', in La Palombara (ed.), *Bureaucracy and Political Development* (Princeton, 1963) p. 235; E. Strauss, *The Ruling Servants* (London, 1961) ch. 8. See also the discussion on the relationship between economic planning and totalitarianism in F.A. Hayek, *The Road to Serfdom* (London, 1976).
18. V.I. Lenin, *The State and Revolution* (M., 1969).
19. See the interesting attempts by two Hungarian Marxist scholars to theorize the problem of state control: L. Torok, *The Socialist System of State Control* (Budapest, 1974); A. Hegedus, *Socialism and Bureaucracy* (London, 1976).
20. M. Fainsod, *How Russia is Ruled* (Cambridge, Mass., 1961) ch. 12; J.S. Reshetar, *The Soviet Polity* (Toronto, 1971) ch. 7.
21. Paul Maupin Cocks, *Politics of Party Control: The Historical and Institutional Role of Party Control Organs in the CPSU* (unpublished Ph.D. dissertation (Harvard University, 1968).
22. Glenn G. Morgan, *Soviet Administrative Legality: The Role of the Attorney General's Office* (Stanford, 1962); Gordon B. Smith, *The Soviet*

Procuracy and the Supervision of Administration (Alphen aan den Rijn, 1978). G. Leggett, *The Cheka* (Oxford, 1981).

23. R.W. Davies, *The Development of the Soviet Budgetary System* (Cambridge, 1958).

24. Jan S. Adams, *Citizen Inspectors in the Soviet Union: The People's Control Committee* (New York, 1977).

25. The question of workers' control in Russia in 1917–18 has generated its own literature – see S. Smith, *Red Petrograd* (Cambridge, 1985); C. Sirianni, *Workers Control and Socialist Democracy* (London, 1982).

26. On the growth of the Soviet state see: T.H. Rigby, *Lenin's Government: Sovnarkom 1917–1922* (Cambridge, 1979); W.R. Batsell, *Soviet Rule in Russia* (New York, 1929); S. Webb and B. Webb, *Soviet Communism: A New Civilization?* (London, 1935); J. Towster, *Political Power in the USSR* (New York, 1948); B.W. Maxwell, *The Soviet State* (London, 1935); O.A. Narkiewicz, *The Making of the Soviet State Apparatus* (Manchester, 1970). On the problem of bureaucracy see: E.H. Carr, *Foundations of a Planned Economy*, vol. 2 (Harmondsworth, 1976) ch. 51; R. Pethybridge, *The Social Prelude to Stalinism* (London, 1977) ch. 6.

1 The Institutionalization of State Control (1919–22)

1. A short history of the establishment of NKRKI is provided by Thomas Remington, 'Institution Building in Bolshevik Russia: The Case of State Kontrol', in *SR*, vol. 41, no. 1, Spring 1982, pp. 91–103.

2. *PSS*, vol. 33, pp. 45–50.

3. T.H. Rigby, *Lenin's Government: Sovnarkom 1917–1922* (Cambridge, 1979) ch. 4.

4. *Bol'shaya Sovetskaya Entsiklopediya* (M., 1930) vol. 18, pp. 463–9, and *Entsiklopedicheskyi Slovar'* (St Petersburg, 1893) vol. 17, pp. 408–11.

5. *PSS*, vol. 35, pp. 199–204.

6. N.A. Voskresenskaya, *V.I. Lenin – organizator sotsialisticheskogo kontrolya* (M., 1970) p. 96. *Obrazovanie i razvitie organov sotsialisticheskogo kontrolya v SSSR* (M., 1975) pp. 42–3.

7. *SU*, 1917, art. 91, 92.

8. *SU*, 1918, art. 264.

9. *Dekrety Sovetskoi vlasti*, vol. 1 (M., 1957) pp. 83–5; *PSS*, vol. 35, pp. 30–1.

10. L. Schapiro, *The Origin of the Communist Autocracy* (London, 1977) ch. VIII.

11. S.N. Ikonnikov, *Organizatsiya i deyatel'nost' RKI v 1920–1925 gg* (M., 1960) p. 14; *Obrazovanie i razvitie*, pp. 44–51.

12. I.G. Ryabtsev (ed.), *Leninskaya sistema partiino-gosudarstvennogo kontrolya i ego rol' v stroitel'stve sotsializma* (M., 1965) pp. 30–1. See *SU*, 1918, art. 898. *Dekrety Sovetskoi vlasti*, vol. 4 (M., 1968) pp. 59–67.

13. Ikonnikov, *Organizatsiya i deyatel'nost'*, pp. 15–16.

14. *LS*, vol. xviii, pp. 240–1, 244, 251–5.

15. Ikonnikov, *Organizatsiya i deyatel'nost'*, pp. 14–16. D.A. Baevskii, *Rabochyi klass v pervye gody sovetskoi vlasti (1917–1921 gg)* (M., 1974) pp. 309–11. On the Workers' Food Supply Inspectorate, see *PSS*, vol. 37, pp. 536–7; *LS*, vol. xviii, pp. 249–50.
16. This point was made in the VTsIK decree of April 1919: *SU*, 1919, art. 122.
17. Ikonnikov, *Organizatsiya i deyatel'nost'*, p. 16.
18. J.V. Stalin, *Works* (M., 1953) vol. 4, p. 231.
19. Ikonnikov, *Organizatsiya i deyatel'nost'*, p. 17.
20. Voskresenskaya, *V.I. Lenin*, p. 124, cites *Rezolyutsii Vtorogo Vserossiiskogo s''ezda professional'nykh soyuzov* (M., 1919) p. 15.
21. See the article by N. Glebov, 'Rabochii kontrol'', *Professional'nyi vestnik*, 1919, no. 1.
22. *Otchet VTsSPS za 1919 god* (M., 1920) pp. 131–2.
23. Voskresenskaya, *V.I. Lenin*, pp. 129–31.
24. Voskresenskaya, pp. 129–30; 145: Pressure from the Moscow Soviet succeeded in changing the rules governing preliminary and financial control exercised by NKGosKon.
25. *PSS*, vol. 37, p. 541.
26. *Vos'moi s''ezd RKP(b)* (M., 1933) p. 251.
27. *Vos'moi s''ezd RKP(b)*, p. 210.
28. *KPSS v rez*, vol. 2, p. 76.
29. *KPSS v rez*, vol. 2, p. 51.
30. Voskresenskaya, *V.I. Lenin*, p. 153. V.A. Avanesov became deputy *narkom* NKGosKon, and M.M. Litvinov and M.K. Vetoshkin were assigned to the commissariat.
31. *Otchet VTsSPS za 1919 god*, p. 131.
32. Voskresenskaya, *V.I. Lenin*, p. 175.
33. Stalin, *Works*, vol. 4, p. 260; *Iz*, 10 April 1919.
34. *SU*, 1919, art. 122; *Iz*, 12 April 1919.
35. *SU*, 1919, art 122.
36. In May 1919 a Bureau of Complaints was established attached to NKGosKon to ensure that the regime was able to keep in touch with popular opinion and as a check on bureaucracy: see *SU*, 1919, art. 271, 272.
37. *PSS*, vol. 37, p. 633.
38. Voskresenskaya, *V.I. Lenin*, pp. 175–6, cites *TsGAOR i SS*, f. 4390, op. 2, d. 281, 1. 242. See also the attack on NKGosKon by the future leader of the Democratic Centralists T.V. Sapronov, 'Kontrol' kak nadstroika nad sovetami ili organ sovetov?', *Sotsialisticheskoe stroitel'stvo*, 1919, no. 6, pp. 3–5.
39. Ryabtsev (ed.), *Leninskaya sistema*, pp. 46–7; *Obrazovanie i razvitie*, pp. 78–80.
40. Schapiro, *The Origin of the Communist Autocracy*, pp. 221–4.
41. Schapiro, p. 261.
42. A.I. Chugunov, *Organy sotsialisticheskogo kontrolya RSFSR 1923–1934 gg* (M., 1972) p. 25. The Moscow Workers' Inspectorate at this time claimed a membership of 60,000 with cells organized in 300 enterprises in the Moscow area.

43. *Vos'maya konferentsiya RKP(b)* (M., 1961) pp. 120–1.
44. *KPSS v rez*, vol. 2, pp. 139, 142.
45. *VII Vserossiiskii s"ezd sovetov rabochikh, kres'yanskikh, krasnoarmeiskikh, kazach'ikh deputatov* (M., 1920) pp. 209–12.
46. Ryabtsev (ed.), *Leninskaya sistema*, p. 48.
47. *VII Vserossiiskii s"ezd sovetov*, pp. 210–11.
48. *LS*, vol. viii, p. 24.
49. *P*, 6 January 1920; *Iz*, 22 January 1920, *Izvestiya gosudarstvennogo kontrolya*, 1920, no. 1, p. 1–2.
50. Ikonnikov, *Organizatsiya i deyatel'nost'*, pp. 22.
51. *Iz*, 22 January 1920.
52. *Otchet VTsSPS za 1919 god*, p. 132.
53. Baevskii, *Rabochyi klass*, p. 313.
54. *P*, 6 January 1920.
55. *LS*, vol. viii, p. 24: *PSS*, vol. 40, p. 64.
56. *LS*, vol. viii, pp. 25–6: *PSS*, vol. 40, pp. 65–6.
57. *LS*, vol. viii, p. 24: *Baevskii, Rabochyi klass*, p. 314.
58. *SU*, 1920, art. 94: *Iz. RKI*, no. 2. pp. 1–2.
59. *PSS*, vol. 40, p. 127, p. 101.
60. *PSS*, vol. 40, p. 201.
61. *KPSS v rez*, vol. 2, pp. 164–9.
62. *Iz.RKI*, 1920, no. 4, p. 19; *P.* 19 March 1920.
63. *Iz.RKI*, 1920, no. 3, p. 16.
64. G.A. Dorokhova, *Raboche-krest'yanskaya inspektsiya v 1920–1923 gg* (M., 1959), p. 75, cites *TsGAOR*, f. 374, op. 365, d.239–b, 1.445.
65. I. Deutscher, *Stalin* (Harmondsworth, 1968), pp. 233–4.
66. S. Liberman, *Building Lenin's Russia* (Chicago, 1945) pp. 82–3. From 1917 to 1919 Avanesov was a member of the VTsIK presidium and served as its secretary. As deputy in NKRKI he retained his post on the VTsIK presidium.
67. Ikonnikov, *Organizatsiya i deyatel'nost'*, pp. 54, 102.
68. *Bol'shaya Sovetskaya Entsiklopaediya* (M., 1970) vol. 1, p. 47.
69. G. Leggett, *The Cheka* (Oxford, 1981) pp. 156–7.
70. P.S. Spoerry, *The Central Rabkrin Apparatus 1917–1925*, unpublished Ph.D thesis (Harvard University, 1967) pp. 121–34.
71. *Obrazovanie i razvitie* pp. 112–13; *SU*, 1920, art. 212.
72. Spoerry, *The Central Rabkrin Apparatus*, pp. 135–48.
73. *Iz*, 20 March 1920; *Iz. RKI*, 1920, no. 4, pp. 25–7.
74. R.W. Davies, *The Development of the Soviet Budgetary System* (Cambridge, 1958) p. 35. See also *Izvestiya gosudarstvennogo kontrolya*, 1920, no. 1, p. 13.
75. Dorokhova, *Raboche-krest'yanskaya inspektsiya*, pp. 60–73.
76. A. Hegedus, *Socialism and Bureaucracy* (London, 1976) p. 85.
77. Stalin, *Works*, vol. 4, pp. 379–80.
78. Stalin, *Works*, vol. 4, pp. 379–81.
79. *PSS*, vol. 42, p. 34. and pp. 35, 37, 49, 260. See also Lenin's letter to Avanesov – *LS*, vol. xxxviii, pp. 336–9.
80. For a detailed discussion of NKRKI's work during 1920, see Dorokhova, *Raboche-krest'yanskaya inspektsiya*, pp. 73–84; Ikonnikov, pp. 43–56.

81. Ikonnikov, *Organizatsiya i deyatel'nost'*, pp. 55–6 cites 'Otchet o deyatel'-nosti NKRKI za vremya c I yanvarya po I noyabrya 1920'.
82. Dorokhova, *Raboche-krest'yanskaya inspektsiya*, pp. 173–5. Voskresenskaya, *V.I. Lenin*, p. 193.
83. L.D. Trotsky, *Sochineniya*, M., 1925–7, vol. XV, *Put' ko edinomu khozyaistvennomu planu*, pp. 222–3. See *Byulleten' NKPS*, 1920, no. 158–66. See also I. Deutscher, *The Prophet Unarmed* (Oxford, 1970) pp. 47–8.
84. Trotsky, *Sochineniya*, p. 225.
85. *P*, 11 March 1921.
86. *P*, 9 March 1921 and *Iz*, 8 March 1921.
87. A. Kollontai, *The Workers' Opposition* (Solidarity, London, 1968).
88. I am indebted for this reference to Professor Getzler of the Hebrew University of Jerusalem – reference to *Pravda o Kronshtadte* (Prague, 1921) pp. 85, 97, 107, 132, 145, 148, 150, 177.
89. B.M. Shekhvatov, *Lenin i sovetskoe gosudarstvo* (M., 1960) p. 228. M.K. Vetoshkin, *Chto delaet Raboche-Krestyanskaiya Inspektsiya (Delegatam X s"ezda RKP(b))* (M., 1921) pp. 5–8.
90. *KPSS v rez*, vol. 2, p. 236.
91. Rigby, *Lenin's Government*, ch. 13.
92. *PSS*, vol. 43, p. 381.
93. *PSS*, vol. 43, p. 410.
94. Ikonnikov, *Organizatsiya i deyatel'nost'*, p. 57.
95. *PSS*, vol. 44, p. 131. See also Lenin's letters to Avanesov and Gorbunov *PSS*, vol. 52, pp. 241; 158.
96. *PSS*, vol. 42, p. 260. See also *PSS*, vol. 43, p. 32.
97. Voskresenskaya, *V.I. Lenin*, p. 196. Cites *TsGAOR*, f. 374, op. 432, d. 22, l. 197–8.
98. Voskresenskaya, p. 196.
99. Voskresenskaya, p. 201, cites *Izvestiya* TsK RKP(b), 1921, no. 28, p. 36.
100. *LS*, vol. xxxvi, p. 228.
101. *PSS*, vol. 44, pp. 127–9. See also *PSS*, vol. 44, pp. 548–9.
102. V.I. Lenin, *Sochineniya* (M., 1957) vol. 33, p. 464.
103. *Iz. RKI*, 1921, no. 7, pp. 1–3.
104. Voskresenskaya, *V.I. Lenin*, p. 205.
105. *SU*, 1921, art. 424. VTsIK on 4 August 1921 also approved a resolution to strengthen the *guberniya* and *uezd* RKI: *Iz*, 9 August 1921.
106. *Iz.RKI*, 1921, no. 7, pp. 1–2.
107. NKRKI'S responsibility for preliminary financial control was abrogated in various areas: *SU*, 1921, art. 169 (wages of workers and employees); art. 274 (co-operatives); art. 403 and art. 458 (on industrial enterprises); art. 554 (on monetary and material turnover).
108. *SU*, 1921, art. 511.
109. *SU*, 1922, art. 384.
110. Ikonnikov, *Organizatsiya i deyatel'nost'*, pp. 60–2. Voskresenskaya, *V.I. Lenin*, pp. 214–19.
111. *SU*, 1922, art. 385. On Lenin's role in drafting this decree see *PSS*, vol. 44, pp. 413–14.
112. For a detailed account of NKRKI's work in 1921–2, see Dorokhova, *Raboche-krest'yanskaya inspektsiya*, pp. 138–59; Ikonnikov, *Organizat-*

siya i deyatel'nost', pp. 74–104.
113. Ikonnikov, *Organizatsiya i deyatel'nost"* pp. 65–8; Voskresenskaya, *V.I. Lenin*, pp. 219–22.
114. Ikonnikov, *Organizatsiya i deyatel'nost'*, p. 81, cites 'Nasha trestirovannaya promyshlennost' (M., 1922).
115. Ikonnikov, *Organizatsiya i deyatel'nost'*, pp. 95–6.
116, Ikonnikov, *Organizatsiya i deyatel'nost'*, p. 89, p. 78 cites *RKI v novykh usloviyakh* (M., 1921) p. 56.
117. Lenin, *Sochineniya*, vol. 35, p. 444.
118. Ikonnikov, *Organizatsiya i deyatel'nost'*, p. 98. *Iz*, 11 January 1922. Lenin, *Sochineniya*, vol. 36, p. 666. *Iz*, 24 February 1922.
119. Lenin, *Sochineniya*, vol. 36, pp. 512–15.
120. *PSS*, vol. 42, p. 253.
121. Ikonnikov, *Organizatsiya i deyatel'nost'*, p. 103:

Year	Delegated members	Assistant cell membership	Mass investigations	Total
1920	18,000	36,000	6,600	60,600
1921	24,000	65,000	35,000	124,000
1922	2,500	18,000	4,500	25,000

122. *Iz*, 17 January 1922 (Vetoshkin).
123. *Iz.RKI*, 1921, no. 3–4, pp. 10–11.
124. *SU*, 1922, art. 675. See Dorokhova, *Raboche-krest'yanskaya inspektsiya*, pp. 123–4.
125. *PSS*, vol. 44, pp. 354–5, pp. 578, 700.
126. *Iz*, 9, 12, 14 and 15 March 1922. See also A. Solzhenitsyn, *The Gulag Archipelago 1918–1956* (1974, Collins/Fontana edn) pp. 336–41, which cites N.V. Krylenko, *Za Pyat' Let* (1918–1922) (M., 1923).
127. *PSS*, vol. 45, p. 180.
128. V.V. Kuibyshev, *Zadachi TsKK i RKI* (M., 1925) pp. 29–30.
129. *Iz*, 17 January 1922.
130. Voskresenskaya, *V.I. Lenin*, p. 207.
131. *PSS*, vol. 45, p. 122.
132. *PSS*, vol. 45, pp. 114–15.
133. A.J. Polan, *Lenin and the End of Politics* (London, 1984).

2 Lenin's Plan for the Reorganization of Rabkrin (1922–3)

1. M. Lewin, *Lenin's Last Struggle* (London, 1973) ch. 1.
2. *PSS*, vol. 45, pp. 80–95.
3. *PSS*, vol. 45, p. 114.
4. *KPSS v rez*, vol. 2, p. 315.

5. See especially Lenin's speech to the Comintern Congress in November 1922 in *PSS*, vol. 45, p. 290.
6. *PSS*, vol. 42, pp. 339–47; vol. 52, p. 280. Lenin's involvement in the case of Larin provides one illustration of his general concern with this question.
7. *PSS*, vol. 44, pp. 364–70, and *PSS*, vol. 45, pp. 55–6; 510.
8. *PSS*, vol. 45, pp. 152–7.
9. *The Trotsky Papers* (The Hague, 1971) vol. II, p. 731–3.
10. *PSS*, vol. 45, pp. 180–1.
11. I. Deutscher, *The Prophet Unarmed* (Oxford, 1970) pp. 35–7; 48–9.
12. *PSS*, vol. 45, pp. 127–8.
13. M. Davydov, *A.D. Tsyurupa* (M., 1961) pp. 76–82. Stalin took with him some control workers from NKRKI to the Secretariat including L.Z. Mekhlis. See *Who Was Who in the USSR* (Metuchen, N.J., 1972) p. 378.
14. *PSS*, vol. 45, p. 274.
15. *PSS*, vol. 45, p. 278; 653.
16. N.V. Kuznetsov, K.E. Kuznetsova and P.F. Petrochenko, 'Osushchestvlenie Leninskikh idei nauchnoi organizatsii truda v pervye gody sovetskoi vlasti', *Voprosy Istorii KPSS*, 1965, no. 8, pp. 3–14.
17. S.N. Ikonnikov, *Sozdanie i deyatel'nost' ob''edinennykh organov TsKK-RKI v 1923–1934 gg.* (M., 1971) p. 54; N.A. Voskresenskaya, *V.I. Lenin – organizator sotsialisticheskogo kontrolya* (M., 1970) p. 232–40.
18. *PSS*, vol. 45, pp. 275, 653, 683, 689, 692, 700.
19. *PSS*, vol. 45, pp. 249–51; 310.
20. *PSS*, vol. 45, p. 323; 328–9.
21. L.D. Trotsky. *The Real Situation in Russia* (London, n.d.) pp. 304–5, Trotsky, *My Life* (New York, 1970), pp. 478–9. Deutscher, *The Prophet Unarmed*, pp. 48–9.
22. *The Trotsky Papers*, vol. II, pp. 783–5.
23. *Iz*, 29 September 1922; see also *Iz*, 6 October, 1922 (reply article by E.F. Rozmirovich) and *IzRKI*, 1922, no. 20, pp. 2–3.
24. On the origin and history of TsKK, see: I.M. Moskalenko, *TsKK v bor'be za edinstvo i chistotu partinnykh ryadov* (M., 1973). In English see P.M. Cocks, *Politics of Party Control: The Historical and Institutional Role of Party Control Organs in the CPSU*, unpublished Ph.D. thesis (Harvard University, 1968). See also M. Neuveld, 'The Origin of the Communist Control Commission', *The American Slavic and East European Review*, vol. xviii, no. 3 (October 1959), pp. 315–33.
25. *PSS*, vol. 45, pp. 90–1.
26. *P*, 9 December 1922.
27. *PSS*, vol. 45, pp. 343–55.
28. *PSS*, vol. 45, p. 347.
29. This was a recurrent theme in Lenin's writings and shaped his ideas on the reorganization of NKRKI: see *PSS*, vol. 43, p. 378; *PSS*, vol. 45, p. 20.
30. L.A. Fotieva, 'Iz vospominanii o V.I. Lenine', *Voprosy Istorii KPSS*, 1957, no. 4, pp. 159–67.
31. *PSS*, vol. 45, p. 383.
32. *PSS*, vol. 45, p. 385.
33. *PSS*, vol. 45, p. 384.

34. PSS, vol. 45, p. 384.
35. *PSS*, vol. 45, p. 386.
36. *PSS*, vol. 45, p. 387; also p. 396: 'The members of TsKK, under the leadership of their presidium, should systematically examine all the papers and documents of the Politburo'.
37. *PSS*, vol. 45, p. 387.
38. *PSS*, vol. 45, p. 387.
39. For an interesting discussion of Lenin's thinking on these questions see V. Ya. Zevin, 'K 50-letiyu raboty V.I. Lenina "Luchshe men'she, da luchshe" ', *Voprosy Istorii KPSS*, 1973, no. 4, pp. 1–18.
40. *PSS*, vol. 45, p. 389. For Lenin's earlier clashes with Proletkult on the question of the 'cultural revolution', see C. Claudin-Urondo, *Lenin and the Cultural Revolution* (Brighton, 1977).
41. *PSS*, vol. 45, pp. 393–4.
42. *PSS*, vol. 45, p. 394.
43. *PSS*, vol. 45, p. 405.
44. *PSS*, vol. 45, p. 399.
45. *PSS*, vol. 45, pp. 405–6.
46. L.D. Trotsky, *The Challenge of the Left Opposition 1923–1925* (New York, 1975) pp. 61–2. Trotsky, *The Real Situation in Russia*, pp. 301–2. Trotsky, *The Stalin School of Falsification* (New York, 1972) pp. 72–3; 75.
47. R.V. Daniels, *The Conscience of the Revolution* (Cambridge, Mass., 1960) pp. 190–1; 473–4. Other historians mistakenly argue that it was Lenin's second article 'Better fewer, but better', which the Politburo tried to suppress. Deutscher, *The Prophet Unarmed*, p. 88, Lewin, *Lenin's Last Struggle*, p. 120; Carr, *Interregnum*, p. 273.
48. *P*, 2 March 1923.
49. *P*, 24 March 1923.
50. *Dvenadtsatyi s"ezd RKP(b)* (M., 1968) p. 105.
51. Trotsky, *The Real Situation in Russia*, p. 303.
52. Carr, *Interregnum* pp. 272–3 and Deutscher, *The Prophet Unarmed*, p. 88.
53. Trotsky, *The Real Situation in Russia*, p. 306.
54. Compare the versions in *P*, 25 January 1923 and that in *PSS*, vol. 45, p. 387. This reference was excluded from all editions of Lenin's collected works until the fifth edition in 1964.
55. Daniels, *The Conscience of the Revolution*, p. 191, cites Trotsky Archives T776. See aslo *PSS*, vol. 45, p. 600.
56. Daniels, p. 192.
57. Deutscher, *The Prophet Unarmed*, pp. 88–9. See also *PPS*, vol. 45, p. 600.
58. Trotsky, *The Real Situation in Russia*, p. 306.
59. Trotsky, p. 306.
60. Cocks, *Politics of Party Control*, p. 91, n. 3, cites Trotsky Archives, T2963.
61. Ikonnikov, *Sozdanie i deyatel'nost'*, pp. 50–1. The commission included Stalin, Frunze, Rudzutak, Molotov, Sol'ts and three others unnamed.
62. *PPS*, vol. 45, pp. 559–600. See *P*, 13 April 1923.
63. Ikonnikov, *Sozdanie i deyatel'nost'*, p. 53. The commission included F.E. Dzerzhinskii, G.E. Zinoviev, A.A. Sol'ts, A.D. Tsyurupa and M.F. Shkiryatov.

64. L.D. Trotsky, *Zadachi XII s"ezda RKP(b)* (M., 1923) pp. 26–36; 54–55. See S. Lovell (ed.), *Leon Trotsky Speaks* (New York, 1972) pp. 155–8; 166.
65. The pre-congress discussion sheets dealing with Lenin's plan were published in *P*, I, 24 March 1923, and 5, 15, 20 April 1923.
66. *P*, 24 March 1923.
67. *P*, 24 March 1923.
68. *P*, 15 April 1923.
69. *P*, 15 April 1923.
70. *P*, 24 March 1923.
71. *P*, 24 March 1923.
72. *P*, 5 April 1923.
73. *P*, 24 March 1923.
74. Carr, *Interregnum*, pp. 90–1.
75. *P*, 4 April 1923.
76. *P*, 24 March 1923.
77. *P*, 20 April 1923.
78. Voskresenskaya, *V.I. Lenin*, p. 261: Cocks, *Politics of Party Control*, p. 97.
79. *PSS*, vol. 45, pp. 477–8 and Ikonnikov, *Sozdanie i deyatel'nost'*, pp. 54–7.
80. E.F. Rozmirovich, *V chem sushchnost' reformy Rabkrina* (M., 1923) p. 15.
81. L.A. Fotieva, 'Iz vospominanii o V.I. Lenine', *Voprosy Istorii KPSS*, 1957, no. 4, p. 165.
82. Trotsky, *The Real Situation in Russia*, p. 302.
83. Ikonnikov, *Sozdanie i deyatel'nost'*, p. 53.
84. *Dvenadtsatyi s"ezd RKP(b)*, p. 61.
85. *Dvenadtsatyi s"ezd RKP(b)*, pp. 206, 237 and 352.
86. Ikonnikov, *Sozdanie i deyatel'nost'*, p. 62 cites the unpublished thesis by F.I. Potashev, *Obsuzhdenie predlozhenii V.I. Lenina ob ob"edinenii TsKK i RKI v period podgotovki i na XII s"ezde partii-Tezisy dokladov k nauchnoi konferentsii Rostovskoi vysshei partiinoi shkoly Oktyabr' 1965 g*, 1965, p. 51. See also *Dvenadtsatyi s"ezd RKP(b)*, p. 886.
87. *Dvenadtsatyi s"ezd RKP(b)*, p. 227.
88. *Dvenadtsatyi s"ezd RKP(b)*, p. 105.
89. *Dvenadtsatyi s"ezd RKP(b)*, pp. 47–8; 224–6.
90. *Dvenadtsatyi s"ezd RKP(b)*, pp. 152–9.
91. *Dvenadtsatyi s"ezd RKP(b)*, pp. 190–3.
92. *Dvenadtsatyi s"ezd RKP(b)*, pp. 119–20.
93. *Dvenadtsatyi s"ezd RKP(b)*, p. 161.
94. *Dvenadtsatyi s"ezd RKP(b)*, pp. 142–4.
95. *Dvenadtsatyi s"ezd RKP(b)*, pp. 106–7, 150–1, 182–4.
96. *Dvenadtsatyi s"ezd RKP(b)*, pp. 124–30.
97. *Dvenadtsatyi s"ezd RKP(b)*, pp. 329, 338.
98. Carr, *Interregnum*, p. 278.
99. *Dvenadtsatyi s"ezd RKP(b)*, p. 247
100. *Dvenadtsatyi s"ezd RKP(b)*, pp. 760–4. See also *P*, 28 April 1923.
101. *Dvenadtsatyi s"ezd RKP(b)*, p. 673.

102. *Dvenadtsatyi s"ezd RKP(b)*, p. 672–3.
103. *Dvenadtsatyi s"ezd RKP(b)*, p. 702.
104. *Dvenadtsatyi s"ezd RKP(b)*, pp. 644–9.
105. *P*, 13 April 1923.
106. *Dvenadtsatyi s"ezd RKP(b)*, p. 702.
107. *Dvenadtsatyi s"ezd RKP(b)*, p. 702.
108. *Dvenadtsatyi s"ezd RKP(b)*, p. 703.
109. Ikonnikov, *Sozdanie i deyatel'nost'*, p. 75.
110. G.V. Kuibysheva *et al.*, *V.V. Kuibyshev* (M., 1966) pp. 194–5; this commission included V.V. Kuibyshev, E.M. Yaroslavskii and N.M. Shvernik.
111. *KPSS v rez*, vol. 2, pp. 447–8.
112. Ikonnikov, *Sozdanie i deyatel'nost'*, p. 51.
113. V.V. Kuibyshev, *Zadachi TsKK i RKI* (M., 1925) pp. 46–7.
114. *Dvenadtsatyi s"ezd RKP(b)*, pp. 662–3.
115. Carr, *Interregnum*, p. 284.
116. Ikonnikov, *Sozdanie i deyatel'nost'*, p. 67; *P*, 27 April 1923.
117. *Dvenadtsatyi s"ezd RKP(b)*, pp. 45–6 (Zinoviev), pp. 329, 348, 350, 352 (Trotsky).
118. Ikonnikov, *Sozdanie i deyatel'nost'*, p. 67. For the composition of the NKRKI collegium and TsKK presidium see Appendixes B and F. Kuibyshev and Yaroslavskii were former Left Communists. Kiselev was a former leader of the Workers' Opposition.
119. Ikonnikov, *Sozdanie i deyatel'nost'*, p. 68.
120. Lewin, *Lenin's Last Struggle*, pp. 117–32.
121. Carr, *Interregnum*, p. 308.
122. A.I. Mirkin, 'Bor'ba Bol'shevistskoi partii za reorganizatsiyu Raboche-Krest'yanskoi Inspektsii v 1923–1925 gg' p. 78, unpublished dissertation (Leningrad State University, 1950) cited by Cocks, *Politics of Party Control*, p. 106.

3 Rabkrin and the Organization of State Control (1923–30)

1. S.N. Ikonnikov, *Sozdanie i deyatel'nost' ob"edinennykh organov TsKK–RKI v 1923–1934 gg* (M., 1971) pp. 66–144; *P*, 27 May 1923; 22, 26 June 1923.
2. *Dvenadtsatyi s"ezd RKP(b)* (M., 1966) p. 700.
3. *SU*, 1923, art. 983, 984.
4. *SU*, 1923, art. 1042.
5. T. Dzhaembaev, *Vozniknovenie i razvitie vnutrivedomstvennogo kontrolya* (Alma Ata, 1957) pp. 57–61. See also *SU*, 1923, art. 983.
6. *SU*, 1924, art. 54. *SU*, 1923, art. 1038.
7. *Dvenadtsatyi s"ezd RKP(b)*, p. 703.
8. The TsKK Secretariat was abolished by the XV Party Congress; see *Pyatnadtsatyi s"ezd VKP(b)*, vol. 2 (M., 1961) pp. 1412–13.
9. *Otchet TsKK XIII s"ezdu partii* (M., 1924) p. 12.

10. For a full list of TsKK plenums see I.M. Moskalenko, *Organy partiinogo kontrolya v period stroitel'stva sotsializma* (M., 1981) pp. 160–8.
11. Ikonnikov, *Sozdanie i deyatel'nost'*, pp. 70–1 cites 'Spravochnik dlya kontrol'nykh komissii RKP(b)" (Moscow, 1923) p. 37. By 1924 Kuibyshev was considering the possibility that all TsKK members should be employed in NKRKI; see V.V. Kuibyshev, *Zadachi TsKK i RKI* (M. 1925 pp. 24–5.
12. V.V. Kuibyshev, *Zadachi TsKK i RKI*, p. 25; *P*, 26 June 1923.
13. Ikonnikov, *Sozdanie i deyatel'nost'*, p. 75 cites 'Otchet TsKK RKP(b) XIII s"ezdu partii' (M., 1924) p. 38. See also the comments by S.I. Komissarov in F.I. Potashev, *Reorganizatsiya Rabkrina i TsKK* (Rostov, 1974) p. 96.
14. V.V. Kuibyshev, 'Pervyi god raboty', *Voprosy sovetskogo khozyaistva i upravleniya*, 1924, no. 4–5, p. 6.
15. *Plenum TsKK RKP(b), mart 1924* (M., 1924) pp. 31–4.
16. Potashev, *Reorganizatsiya Rabkrina*, p. 172.
17. These offices have been the home of successive Soviet control agencies including the present People's Control Committee.
18. *Trinadtsatyi s"ezd RKP(b)* (M., 1961) pp. 118–19.
19. *KPSS v rez*, vol. 3, pp. 58–9; these criteria were revised at the XIV Party Congress; see *KPSS v rez*, p. 306.
20. *Chetyrnadtsatyi s"ezd VKP(b)* (M., 1926) p. 81.
21. For the turnover rate of TsKK members each party congress see Appendix C.
22. For the turnover rate for the three categories of TsKK members from the XIV to XV Party Congresses see Appendix C.
23. *Iz*, 3 February 1924.
24. *Iz*, 19 July 1923; *Iz*, 5 March 1924.
25. For NKRKI's plans of work see *EZh*, 30 March 1924, *EZh*, 8 October 1924, *P*, 11 December 1925; *P*, 3 December 1926; *P*, 17 November 1927; *P*, 27 November 1928.
26. Potashev, *Reorganizatsiya Rabkrina*, p. 71.
27. *SZ*, 1926, ii, art. 12.
28. *SZ*, 1926, ii, art. 13, 23.
29. *KPSS v rez*, vol. 2, p. 449.
30. P.M. Cocks, *Politics of Party Control: The Historical and Institutional Role of Party Control Organs in the CPSU*, unpublished Ph.D. thesis (Harvard University, 1968), p. 105.
31. Ikonnikov, *Sozdanie i deyatel'nost'*, p. 67.
32. Potashev, *Reorganizatsiya Rabkrina*, p. 75.
33. *KPSS v rez*, vol. 4, p. 73.
34. *P*, 14 July 1930. The nine were Akulov, Il'in, Ordzhonikidze, Pavlunov-skii, Rozengol'ts, Sol'ts, Shkiryatov, Yanson and Yaroslavskii.
35. *KPSS v rez*, vol. 2, p. 450.
36. Ikonnikov, *Sozdanie i deyatel'nost'*, p. 69, notes that Stalin and Molotov attended the TsKK plenum in June 1923 as representatives of the Central Committee.
37. *KPSS v rez*, vol. 3, p. 306.
38. *P*, 14 July 1930. The six were Akulov, Enukidze, Zemlyachka, Krivov,

Roizenman and Shkiryatov.
39. *KPSS v rez*, vol. 2, p. 449.
40. *Voprosy Istorii KPSS*, 1965, no. 10, p. 76.
41. *KPSS v rez*, vol. 3, p. 41.
42. *Chetyrnadtsatyi s''ezd VKP(b)* (M., 1926) pp. 399, 402.
43. *Pyatnadtsatyi s''ezd VKP(b)*, vol. 1, p. 69. See also M. Fainsod, *How Russia is Ruled* (Cambridge, Mass., 1963) p. 185.
44. *KPSS v rez*, vol. 2, p. 451.
45. Cocks, *Politics of Party Control*, pp. 188–91.
46. Carr, *FPE 2*, pp. 123–4.
47. *Trinadtsatyi s''ezd RKP(b)*, p. 268.
48. *Trinadtsatyi s''ezd RKP(b)*, pp. 293–4. Ikonnikov, *Sozdanie i deyatel'-nost'*, pp. 179–81.
49. *Trinadtsatyi s''ezd RKP(b)*, pp. 267–8.
50. *Vtoroi plenum TsKK RKP(b) sozyva XIII s''ezda partii* (M., 1924) p. 3; *P*, 3 October 1924.
51. *VI plenum TsKK sozyva XIII s''ezda RKP(b), dekabrya 1925* (M., 1926) p. 63.
52. Ikonnikov, *Sozdanie i deyatel'nost'*, p. 75 cites E.M. Yaroslavskii, *Kak rabotayut TsKK i RKI* (Leningrad, 1926) p. 22.
53. *Chetyrnadtsatyi s''ezd VKP(b)*, p. 625.
54. *Chetyrnadtsatyi s''ezd VKP(b)*, p. 556.
55. *KPSS v rez*, vol. 3, p. 259. On the strengthening of links between the KK–RKI organs and the local party organs, see Moskalenko, *Organy partiinogo kontrolya*, pp. 101–6.
56. *VKP(b) v rezolyutsiyakh i resheniyakh*, vol. 2 (M., 1941) pp. 100–2. See also Potashev, *Reorganisatsiya Rabkrina*, pp. 181–2; *P*, 4 April 1926 and 13 April 1926.
57. *Vtoroi plenum TsKK sozyva XIV s''ezd VKP(b), 2–4 aprilya 1926* (M., 1926) p. 11.
58. *VKP(b) v rezolyutsiyakh i resheniyakh*, vol. 2, pp. 275–6; *P*, 12 April 1928.
59. E.M. Yaroslavskii (ed.), *TsKK–RKI v osnovnykh postanovleniyakh partii* (M.-L., 1927) pp. 6–7.
60. *Protokoly zasedanii kollegii Narodnogo Komissariata Raboche-Krest'yanskoi Inspektsii SSSR* (M., 1924) no. 7–14, 16–20, 22–3, 26, 28, 32–8.
61. *Protokoly TsKK*, 1930, no. 60–8 (in the Smolensk Arc...ives WKP 57).
62. *SU*, 1923, art. 1042.
63. *Deyatel'nost' organov partiino-gosudarstvennogo kontrolya* (M., 1964) pp. 237–9.
64. Ikonnikov, *Sozdanie i deyatel'nost'*, pp. 84–6.
65. *Chetyrnadtsatyi s''ezd VKP(b)*, p. 546.
66. Ikonnikov, *Sozdanie i deyatel'nost'*, pp. 106–7. *Deyatel'nost' organov*, p. 61.
67. Ikonnikov, *Sozdanie i deyatel'nost'*, pp. 88–9.
68. Ya. Bineman and S. Kheinman, *Kadry gosudarstvennogo i kooperativnogo apparata* (M., 1930) p. 86; *Gosudarstvennyi apparat SSSR 1924–1928g* (M., 1929) p. 104.
69. Bineman and Kheinman, *Kadry gosudarstvennogo*, pp. 106–7; 110–11.

70. Bineman and Kheinman, *Kadry gosudarstvennogo*, pp. 106–7; see also Ikonnikov, *Sozdanie i deyatel'nost'*, p. 89.
71. Bineman and Kheinman, *Kadry gosudarstvennogo*, pp. 86–90; 106–7.
72. Bineman and Kheinman, *Kadry gosudarstvennogo*, pp. 86–7; Ikonnikov, *Sozdanie i deyatel'nost'*, p. 89; *RKI v sovetskom stroitel'stvo* (M., 1925) p. 17.
73. Bineman and Kheinman, *Kadry gosudarstvennogo*, pp. 86–7; see also *Gosudarstvennyi apparat SSSR 1924–1928g*, p. 112.
74. *KhU*, 1924, no. 8–9, p. 15; V.V. Kuibyshev, *Rabota TsKK i RKI* (M., 1924) pp. 34–5.
75. *RKI v sovetskom stroitel'stve*, p. 17.
76. *Vtoroi plenum TsKK sozyva XIV s"ezd VKP(b), aprilya 1926* (M., 1926) p. 10.
77. *SR (Ord)*, ii, pp. 39, 45, 99.
78. *KPSS v rez*, vol. 3, p. 491.
79. The leadership of the republican TsKK–NKRKI is given in Appendix A.
80. *KPSS v rez*, vol. 3, pp. 58–9.
81. Ikonnikov, *Sozdanie i deyatel'nost'*, p. 101.
82. *Trinadtsatyi s"ezd RKP(b)*, pp. 276; 662; V.V. Kuibyshev, *Zadachi TsKK i RKI* (M., 1925) pp. 46–7.
83. V.V. Kuibyshev, *Rabota TsKK i RKI* (M., 1924) p. 63; Carr, SOC 2, pp. 237–8.
84. *KPSS v rez*, vol. 3, pp. 306–7.
85. *Pyatnadtsatyi s"ezd VKP(b)*, vol. 1, p. 594 (Shkiryatov), p. 466 (Ordzhonikidze).
86. Ikonnikov, *Sozdanie i deyatel'nost'*, pp. 101–2.
87. *SR(Ord)*, ii, pp. 180–1.
88. *Shestnadtsatyi s"ezd VKP(b)* (M., 1931) pp. 353–4 (Bogdanov), 357 (A. Yakovlev).
89. *SU*, 1923, art. 1042.
90. K.E. Bailes, 'Alexei Gastev and the Soviet Controversy over Taylorism' 1918–1924', *SS*, vol. xxiv, no. 3, July 1977, pp. 373–94. *Carr*, SOC1, pp. 409–10; Z.A. Sochor, 'Soviet Taylorism Revisited', *SS*, vol. xxxiii, no. 2, April 1981, pp. 246–64.
91. P.M. Kerzhentsev, *NOT, Nauchnaya organizatsiya truda i zadachi partii* (M., 1923) pp. 30–1.
92. For the platform of the Central Institute of Labour, see *Trud*, 5 and 6 February 1924.
93. *P*, 13 and 14 February 1924.
94. *TPG*, 16 February 1924.
95. K.E. Bailes, 'Alexei Gastev', pp. 387–8.
96. V.V. Kuibyshev, *Zadachi TsKK i RKI*, pp. 62–73.
97. Ikonnikov, *Sozdanie i deyatel'nost'*, p. 170.
98. P.M. Kerzhentsev, *NOT, Nauchnaya organizatsiya truda* (L., 1925).
99. *RKI v sovetskom stroitel'stve* (M., 1926) pp. 6–7.
100. *Trinadtsatyi s"ezd RKP(b)*, p. 289.
101. *EZh*, 5 February 1924.
102. *Istoricheskii arkhiv*, 1958, no. 3, p. 46. E.F. Rozmirovich, 'RKI na novykh putyakh', *KhU*, 1925, no. 1, pp. 9–20. See also A.K. Gastev, *Ot Nark-*

omata Kontrolya k Narkomata Organizatsii (M., 1925); KhU, 1925, no. 2, pp. 3, 7, 20, 30.
103. NKRKI's publishing house was Tekhnika Upravleniya. For a list of NKRKI publications see Katalog RKI 1924–1925 (M., 1925).
104. Ikonnikov, Sozdanie i deyatel'nost', pp. 87; 112.
105. Byulleten' TsKK, 1925, no. 2–3, p. 2.
106. RKI v sovetskom stroitel'stve, pp. 20–2.
107. Chetyrnadtsatyi s"ezd VKP(b), p. 546.
108. KPSS v rez, vol. 3, p. 258.
109. Vtoroi Plenum TsKK sozyva XIV s"ezd VKP(b), p. 6.
110. Vtoroi Plenum TsKK sozyva XIV s"ezd VKP(b), p. 25.
111. Vtoroi Plenum TsKK sozyva XIV s"ezd VKP(b), p. 43.
112. Vtoroi Plenum TsKK sozyva XIV s"ezd VKP(b), p. 71. See also Potashev, Reorganizatsiya Rabkrina, pp. 139–40.
113. G.V. Kuibyshev et al., Valerian Vladimirovich Kuibyshev: Biografiya (M., 1966) p. 230.
114. Cocks, Politics of Party Control, p. 130 cites a thesis by R.V. Gataullin, 'Voploshchenie Leninskikh printsipov kontrolya i deyatel'nosti organov OKK–RKI Tatarii v vosstanovitel'nyi period' (1921–1926gg), p. 74n.
115. KPSS v rez, vol. 4, pp. 224–5.
116. G.V. Kuibysheva et al., V.V. Kuibyshev, p. 233; Ikonnikov, Sozdanie i deyatel'nost', p. 110.
117. P, 4 May 1927.
118. SZ, 1927, art. 247. The approval of Sovnarkom and STO was still required where changes in the law and government directives were involved. See also Carr, FPE 2, p. 301.
119. Deyatel'nost' organov, pp. 74–8.
120. SU, 1923, art. 1042.
121. Deyatel'nost' organov, p. 74.
122. Kuibyshev, Zadachi TsKK i RKI, p. 79.
123. L.D. Trotsky, The Challenge of the Left Opposition 1923–1925 (New York, 1975) p. 411.
124. KPSS v rez, vol. 2, p. 504.
125. EZh, 1 February 1924 (G. Lakin); EZh, 13 February 1924 (Zaitsev).
126. TPG, 10 April 1924. Plenum TsKK RKP(b), mart 1924, p. 123.
127. Plenum TsKK RKP(b), mart 1924, p. 138: TPG, 10 April 1924.
128. Plenum TsKK RKP(b), pp. 135–8.
129. Plenum TsKK RKP(b), p. 180.
130. EZh, 6 and 10 April 1924.
131. EZh, 2 April 1924. See also P, 4 April 1924 (Yaroslavskii).
132. EZh, 21 May 1924, P, 21 May 1924. Trinadtsatyi s"ezd RKP(b), pp. 174; 838.
133. Trinadtsatyi s"ezd RKP(b), p. 278.
134. Trinadtsatyi s"ezd RKP(b), p. 619.
135. V.V. Kuibyshev, 'Pervyi god raboty', Voprosy sovetskogo khozyaistva i upravleniya, 1924, no. 4–5, p. 13.
136. Ikonnikov, Sozdanie i deyatel'nost', pp. 124; 173.
137. Carr, SOC 1, p. 427.
138. Ikonnikov, Sozdanie i deyatel'nost', p. 260; see also SU, 1923, arts. 106;

480.
139. *SU*, 1923, art. 1042.
140. Carr, *SOC*2, pp. 466–7; 501.
141. *Bol'shaya Sovetskaya Entsiklopaediya*, vol. 15, p 343.
142. *Bol'shaya Sovetskaya Entsiklopaediya*, vol. 19, p. 471; *SZ*, ii, 1925, art. 108; on Peters see also G. Leggett, *The Cheka* (Oxford, 1981) p. 267.
143. *Bol'shaya Sovetskaya Entsiklopaediya*, vol. 19, p. 70; *SZ*, ii, 1927, art. 37; *SZ*, 1928 art. 38. *Who Was Who in the USSR?* (Metuchen, N.J., 1972) p. 549.
144. S.A. Messing was the second vice-chairman of OGPU; V.A. Balitskii was head of OGPU Ukraine; G.E. Prokof'ev was head of OGPU Special Department.
145. J.R. Westgarth, *Russian Engineer* (London, 1934). The author comments on relations between TsKK–NKRKI and OGPU: 'Members of the dreaded 'Cheka' spy on the spies, watch one another and unknowingly are watched themselves'.

4 Rabkrin and the 'Scissors Crisis' (1923–4)

1. P. Berezov, *Valerian Vladimirovich Kuibyshev 1888–1935* (M., 1958); G.V. Kuibysheva, O.A. Lezhava, N.V. Nelidov, A.F. Khavkin, *V.V. Kuibyshev: biografiya* (M., 1966). In English see R.W. Davies, 'Some Soviet Economic Controllers III – Kuibyshev', *SS*, 1961, vol. xii, pp. 23–36.
2. *Kratkii otchet o deyatel''nosti Narodnogo Komissariata Raboche-Krest-'yanskoi Inspektsii, za period mai-dekabr' 1923 goda* (M., 1924) p. 68.
3. Carr, *Interregnum*, pp. 113, 114, 374–80.
4. *KPSS v rez*, vol. 2, p. 495.
5. *SU*, 1923, art. 984; S.N. Ikonnikov, *Sozdanie i deyatel'nost' ob''edinen-nykh organov TsKK–RKI v 1923–1934 gg* (M., 1971) p. 69. *P*, 29 June 1923.
6. *SU*, 1923, art. 1042.
7. *Iz*, 5 February 1924.
8. *TPG*, 5 April 1924, and *EZh*, 30 April 1924.
9. Carr, *Interregnum*, pp. 101, 112, 140–4.
10. *KPSS v rez*, vol. 3, pp. 22–6.
11. Carr, *Interregnum*, pp. 130, 140–1, 154.
12. *Plenum TsKK RKP(b), mart 1924* (M., 1924) p. 13.
13. *EZh*, 4 March 1924. *TPG*, 4 March 1924.
14. *Trinadtsatyi s''ezd RKP(b)*, p. 291.
15. Carr, *Interregnum*, pp. 114–16, 129, 133–35.
16. *KPSS v rez*, vol. 2, p. 527.
17. Carr, *Interregnum*, pp. 149; 152.
18. See the interview with Kuibyshev in *EZh*, 24 January 1924; the report of speeches by Kuibyshev and Avanesov in *EZh*, 5 February 1924; the article by G. Lakin in *EZh*, 13 February 1924.
19. *Plenum TsKK RKP(b), mart 1924*, p. 8.
20. *EZh*, 30 March 1924.

21. *P*, 25 April 1924.
22. *TPG*, 25 April 1924. See also Carr, *Interregnum*, p. 152.
23. *TPG*, 25 April 1924.
24. M. Davydov, *A.D. Tsyurupa* (M., 1961) p. 84.
25. Carr, *Interregnum*, p. 117.
26. *Trinadtsatyi s"ezd RKP(b)*, p. 295.
27. *Trinadtsatyi s"ezd RKP(b)*, pp. 621–2.
28. Carr, *Interregnum*, pp. 95–6, 105, 113–16, 129, 134–6.
29. *TPG*, 22 January 1924.
30. A. Segal', *Vosstanovlenie Donbassa* (M., 1924) p. 3.
31. *TPG*, 22 January 1924.
32. Segal', *Vosstanovlenie Donbassa*, p. 99.
33. *TPG*, 22 January 1924.
34. *TPG*, 3 February 1924. Davydov, *A.D. Tsyurupa*, p. 80.
35. *TPG*, 10 February 1924; 13 February 1924; 21 March 1924.
36. *Plenum TsKK RKP(b), mart 1924*, p. 10.
37. *Industrializatsiya SSSR 1926–1928* (M., 1969) p. 97.
38. *Yuzhnaya metallurgiya* (M., 1924) pp. i–ii.
39. *Yuzhnaya metallurgiya* p. ix. *TPG*, 2 February 1924.
40. *Yuzhnaya metallurgiya*, p. x., 337.
41. Ikonnikov, *Sozdanie i deyatel'nost'*, pp. 321–2. See also *TPG*, 29 June 1924.
42. V.V. Kuibyshev, *Zadachi TsKK i RKI* (M., 1924) p. 50.
43. *Industrializatsiya SSSR 1926–1928*, p. 97.
44. Kuibyshev, *Zadachi TsKK i RKI*, p. 50, and *Plenum TsKK RKP(b), mart 1924*, p. 10.
45. Ikonnikov, *Sozdanie i deyatel'nost'*, p. 320. See also *EZh*, 29 December 1923.
46. *Trinadtsatyi s"ezd RKP(b)*, p. 291.
47. *Plenum TsKK RKP(b), mart 1924*, p. 11.
48. Ikonnikov, *Sozdanie i deyatel'nost'*, pp. 323–4. See also Kuibyshev, *Zadachi TsKK i RKI*, p. 51.
49. *Industrializatsiya SSSR 1926–1928*, p. 97.
50. A.I. Segal', *Ekonomika neftyanykh khozyaistv* (M., 1925). The commission's preliminary findings were published in *Neftyanoe i slantsevoe khozyaistvo*, 1924, no. 9.
51. *EZh*, 29 November 1924.
52. *EZh*, 6 December 1924.
53. *TPG*, 6 December 1924.
54. *EZh*, 17 December 1924. A. Segal', *Ekonomika neftyanykh khozyaistv*, pp. 115–20.
55. *TPG*, 11 February 1925.
56. Ikonnikov, *Sozdanie i deyatel'nost'*, p. 328.
57. *Industrializatsiya SSSR 1926–1928*, p. 97.
58. Ikonnikov, *Sozdanie i deyatel'nost'*, pp. 321–2.
59. *RKI v sovetskom stroitel'stve* (M., 1926) pp. 46–7.
60. Ikonnikov, *Sozdanie i deyatel'nost'*, p. 329.
61. *RKI v sovetskom stroitel'stve*, p. 48.
62. Ikonnikov, *Sozdanie i deyatel'nost'*, p. 320.

63. Carr, *Interregnum*, p. 129.
64. *P*, 4 December 1924; Carr, *SOC* 1, p. 466.
65. Carr, *Interregnum*, pp. 86–7, 102–5, 137–9, 145–7.
66. *Trinadtsatyi s"ezd RKP(b)*, p. 837.
67. *Izvestiya TsK VKP(b)*, 1923, no. 9–10, p. 10.
68. Carr, *Interregnum*, pp. 116–17.
69. *Trinadtsatyi s"ezd RKP(b)*, p. 841; *EZh*, 23 November 1923.
70. *KPSS v rez.*, vol. 2, pp. 521–2.
71. *SU*, 1924, art. 214. Carr, *Interregnum*, p. 133.
72. *P*, 12 January 1924.
73. S.N. Ikonnikov, *Organizatsiya i deyatel'nost' RKI v 1920–1925 gg* (M., 1960) p. 155.
74. *Plenum TsKK RKP(b), mart 1924*, p. 12.
75. Ikonnikov, *Sozdanie i deyatel'nost'*, p. 262, cites *Voprosy sovetskogo khozyaistva i upravleniya*, 1924, no. 2–3, p. 241.
76. *EZh*, 23 November 1923, and *EZh*, 3 April 1924.
77. *TPG*, 20 January 1924 and 2 March 1924 (articles by A.A. Troyanovskii, head of the industrial inspectorate of NKRKI).
78. *EZh*, 1 July 1924.
79. *Trinadtsatyi s"ezd RKP(b)*, pp. 283–4.
80. Ikonnikov, *Sozdanie i deyatel'nost'*, p. 262.
81. *KPSS v rez*, vol. 3, pp. 131–4.
82. *EZh*, 23 September 1924: Carr, *SOC 1*, p. 414.
83. Carr, *Interregnum*, pp. 21–2.
84. Ikonnikov, *Sozdanie i deyatel'nost'*, pp. 400–2. See also *Trinadtsatyi s"ezd RKP(b)*, p. 295.
85. Carr, *Interregnum*, pp. 24–8.
86. Ikonnikov, *Sozdanie i deyatel'nost'*, p. 416.
87. *Trinadtsatyi s"ezd RKP(b)*, p. 294.
88. Ikonnikov, *Sozdanie i deyatel'nost'*, p. 416.
89. Carr, *Interregnum*, pp. 155–8.
90. V.V. Kuibyshev, *Krest'yanskoe khoziastvo za vremya revolyutsiyi* (M., 1923).
91. Ya. A. Yakovlev, *Nasha derevnya* (M., 1963) p. 388.
92. *Trinadtsatyi s"ezd VKP(b)*, p. 388.
93. *KPSS v rez*, vol. 3, p. 75.
94. *Vtoroi plenum TsKK RKP(b), sozyva XIII s"ezda partii, 3–5 oktyabr 1924 g.* (M., 1924) pp. 28–9, 32.
95. *Vtoroi plenum TsKK RKP(b)*, pp. 47; 12–13.
96. Ikonnikov, *Sozdanie i deyatel'nost'*, p. 264.
97. *Trinadtsatyi s"ezd RKP(b)*, pp. 289–90.
98. *Trinadtsatyi s"ezd RKP(b)*, p. 295; 268.
99. *Plenum TsKK RKP(b), mart 1924*, p. 9.
100. Ikonnikov, *Sozdanie i deyatel'nost'*, p. 170.
101. *Plenum TsKK RKP(b), mart 1924*, pp. 6–7. *EZh*, 30 March 1924.
102. Kuibyshev, *Zadachi TsKK i RKI*, pp. 35–6, see also above ch. 1, p. 00.
103. Carr, *Interregnum*, pp. 298–9.
104. L.D. Trotsky, *The Real Situation in Russia* (London, n.d.) pp. 302–3. Carr, *Interregnum*, p. 307.

105. Carr, *Interregnum*, p. 304.
106. L.D. Trotsky, *My Life* (New York, 1970) p. 500.
107. F.I. Potashev, *Reorganizatsiya Rabkrina i TsKK* (Rostov, 1974) p. 77.
108. *Trinadtsatyi s"ezd RKP(b)*, p. 264.
109. *Trinadtsatyi s"ezd RKP(b)*, p. 264. See also Kuibyshev, *Zadachi TsKK i RKI*, p. 26.
110. Berezov, *V.V. Kuibyshev*, p. 232.
111. *KPSS v rez*, vol. 2, p. 496.
112. Carr, *Interregnum*, pp. 330, 308, 337–8, 363–4.
113. *Trinadtsatyi s"ezd RKP(b)*, p. 279.
114. *Trinadtsatyi s"ezd RKP(b)*, p. 279.
115. *Trinadtsatyi s"ezd RKP(b)*, p. 290.
116. *Trinadtsatyi s"ezd RKP(b)*, p. 296.
117. *Trinadtsatyi s"ezd RKP(b)*, p. 297. Note the comments of Uglanov for the congress presidium. Stalin explained that this procedure was due to the lack of time and the heavy congress agenda; Stalin, *Works.*, vol. vi, pp. 250; 260–1.
118. *Trinadtsatyi s"ezd RKP(b)*, pp. 297–9.
119. *Trinadtsatyi s"ezd RKP(b)*, p. 621.
120. *Trinadtsatyi s"ezd RKP(b)*, p. 621.
121. *TPG*, 20 May 1924.

5 Rabkrin at the High Point of NEP (1925–6)

1. See ch. 3, pp. 87–90.
2. S.N. Ikonnikov, *Sozdanie i deyatel'nost' ob"edinennykh organov TsKK-RKI v 1923–1934 gg* (M., 1971)p. 282.
3. *Vtoroi plenum TsKK RKP(b) sozyva XIII s"ezda partii* (M., 1924) p. 7.
4. Carr, *SOC 1*, pp. 491–2.
5. *EZh*, 25 February 1925.
6. P. Berezov, *V.V. Kuibyshev* (M., 1958) pp. 235–6.
7. *Vtoroi plenum TsKK RKP(b) sozyva XIII s"ezda partii*, p. 5.
8. *Vtoroi plenum TsKK RKP(b) sozyva XIII s"ezda partii*, p. 11
9. *EZh*, 27 January 1925.
10. *EZh*, 22 January 1925; V.V. Kuibyshev, *Rabota TsKK i RKI* (M., 1925) pp. 22–4; *Vtoroi plenum TsKK RKP(b) sozyva XIII s"ezda partii*, pp. 13–14.
11. *Dostizheniya i nedochety tekstil'noi promyshlennosti* (M., 1926).
12. *KhU*, 1925, no. 4, pp. 1–12; *EZh*, 8 May 1925.
13. *EZh*, 5 November 1925.
14. See ch. 3, pp. 88–9.
15. *KhU*, 1925, no. 5, pp. 40–3 (A. Segal').
16. *Vtoroi plenum TsKK RKP(b), sozyva XIII s"ezda partii*, pp. 14–15.
17. *EZh*, 28 January 1925.
18. *TPG*, 6 May 1925.
19. Ikonnikov, *Sozdanie i deyatel'nost'*, p. 262.
20. *Itogi raboty TsKK i Rabkrina Ukraina za 1924–1925 gg.* (Kharkov, 1925).

268   *Notes and References to pp. 123–7*

This report is notable less for its length (362 pages) than the paucity of achievements recorded.

21. This account is drawn in part from S.G. Wheatcroft, *Views on Grain Ouput, Agricultural Reality and Planning in the Soviet Union in the 1920s*, unpublished M.Soc. Sci. thesis (CREES, Birmingham University, 1974).
22. *TPG*, 5 October 1924. See also Ikonnikov, *Sozdanie i deyatel'nost'*, pp. 412–13.
23. *EZh*, 8 October 1924 and *TPG*, 4 October 1924; Carr, *SOC 1*, p. 206.
24. *Edinyi sel'sko-khozyaistvennyi nalog v 1924–1925 godu* (M., 1925).
25. Ikonnikov, *Sozdanie i deyatel'nost'*, pp. 416–17.
26. *RKI v sovetskom stroitel'stve* (M., 1926) p. 28.
27. *Selskoe khozyaistvo na putyakh vosstanovleniya* (M., 1925). See also Ya. A. Yakovlev, *Rassloenie derevni* (M.-L., 1925).
28. Yu. Larin, *Sovetskaya derevnya* (M., 1925).
29. *Ekonomicheskoe obozrenie*, 1925, no. 8–9.
30. Carr, *SOC 1*, pp. 320–2, 323, 328–32.
31. Carr, *SOC 1*, pp. 329.
32. *KPSS v rez*, vol. 3, p. 232.
33. Ikonnikov, *Sozdanie i deyatel'nost'*, p. 418.
34. *EZh*, 12 December 1925.
35. Ya. A. Yakovlev, *Ob oshibkakh khlebo-furazhnogo balansa TsSU i ego istolkovatelei* (M., 1926) p. 6: the commission included F.A. Tsil'ko, D. Rozit, prof. A. Rybnikov, A. Chelintsev. It was assisted by Pashkovskii (TsSU), Lositskii (TsSU), Shmemon (TsSU), Lifshits (NKFin), Vishnevskii (Gosplan), Groman (Gosplan), Strumilin (Gosplan).
36. Yakovlev, *Ob oshibkakh khlebo-furazhnogo balansa TsSU i ego istolkovatelei*, pp. 74–86.
37. *EZh*, 12 December 1925, *P*, 11 December 1925. See also *RKI v sovetskom stroitel'stve*, pp. 30–2.
38. *EZh*, 12 December 1925.
39. *EZh*, 12 December 1925.
40. *Chetyrnadtsatyi s"ezd VKP(b)* (M., 1926) p. 44.
41. *VI plenum TsKK sozyva XIII s"ezd RKP(b), dekabriya 1925* (M., 1926) p. 63.
42. *RKI v sovetskom stroitel'stve*, pp. 32–3.
43. *Chetyrnadtsatyi s"ezd VKP(b)*, p. 118.
44. *Chetyrnadtsatyi s"ezd VKP(b)*, p. 44.
45. *Chetyrnadtsatyi s"ezd VKP(b)*, pp. 46–8.
46. *Chetyrnadtsatyi s"ezd VKP(b)*, p. 265.
47. *Chetyrnadtsatyi s"ezd VKP(b)*, p. 118.
48. *Chetyrnadtsatyi s"ezd VKP(b)*, p. 547.
49. *SZ*, ii, 1926, art. 19; 32.
50. Trotsky, *The Challenge of the Left Opposition; 1926–1927*, p. 99. See also B. Souvarine, *Stalin* (London, 1949) p. 402.
51. Ya.A. Yakovlev, *Sel'skoe khozyaistvo i industrializatsiya* (M., 1927) pp. 3–5.
52. Carr, *SOC 2*, p. 238.
53. M. Eastman, *Since Lenin Died* (London, 1925) pp. 24–6.
54. Trotsky, *The Challenge of the Left Opposition 1923–1925*, pp. 312–13.

Notes and References to pp. 128–33   269

55. F.I. Potashev, *Reorganizatsiya Rabkrina i TsKK* (Rostov, 1974) p. 151.
56. *Politicheskii dnevnik 1964–1970* (Amsterdam, 1972) pp. 238–41.
57. Carr, *SOC 2*, pp. 121–5.
58. *Chetyrnadtsatyi s"ezd VKP(b)*, p. 340.
59. Carr, *SOC 2*, pp. 125–7.
60. *Vl plenum TsKK sozyva XIII s"ezd RKP(b)*, p. 59.
61. *Chetyrnadtsatyi s"ezd VKP(b)*, p. 529. Out of 110 members of TsKK who attended the plenum only seven voted against this resolution.
62. *Chetyrnadtsatyi s"ezd VKP(b)*, p. 533. Kuibyshev at the XIV Party Congress pointedly exposed Rozmirovich's vacillation.
63. Carr, *SOC 2*, p. 144 cites *Novaya oppozitsiya*, 1926, pp. 62–7.
64. Carr, *SOC 2*, pp. 243–4.
65. *Chetyrnadtsatyi s"ezd VKP(b)*, p. 603 (S.I. Gusev). See Potashev, *Reorganizatsiya Rabkrina*, pp. 153; 211
66. *Chetyrnadtsatyi s"ezd VKP(b)*, p. 268–9.
67. *Chetyrnadtsatyi s"ezd VKP(b)*, p. 274.
68. *Chetyrnadtsatyi s"ezd VKP(b)*, p. 335.
69. *Chetyrnadtsatyi s"ezd VKP(b)*, p. 468.
70. *Chetyrnadtsatyi s"ezd VKP(b)*, p. 484.
71. *Chetyrnadtsatyi s"ezd VKP(b)*, p. 601.
72. *Chetyrnadtsatyi s"ezd VKP(b)*, pp. 628–9.
73. *Chetyrnadtsatyi s"ezd VKP(b)*, p. 573.
74. *Chetyrnadtsatyi s"ezd VKP(b)*, pp. 566–8 (I.P. Bakaev), pp. 580–3 (S.K. Minin).
75. *Chetyrnadtsatyi s"ezd VKP(b)*, pp. 597; 598.
76. *Chetyrnadtsatyi s"ezd VKP(b)*, p. 603.
77. *Chetyrnadtsatyi s"ezd VKP(b)*, p. 575.
78. *Chetyrnadtsatyi s"ezd VKP(b)*, p. 622; 575 (Yaroslavskii).
79. *Chetyrnadtsatyi s"ezd VKP(b)*, p. 628.
80. *Chetyrnadtsatyi s"ezd VKP(b)*, p. 533.
81. *Chetyrnadtsatyi s"ezd VKP(b)*, p. 548.
82. *KPSS v rez*, vol. 3, pp. 256–7.
83. *KPSS v rez*, p. 256.
84. See ch. 3, pp. 000–000.
85. The XIV Party Congress elected 163 members to TsKK. Of the 150 TsKK members elected by the XIII Party Congress only 59 were re-elected. Two prominent oppositionists were dropped from the TsKK presidium – N.K. Krupskaya and A.S. Kiselev.
86. *KPSS v rez*, vol. 3, p. 306.
87. *SZ*, 1926, art. 12, 13.
88. *SZ*, 1926, art. 13, 23. In October 1926 the administrative staffs of Sovnarkom and STO were unified: *SZ*, 1926, art. 235, 236, 238.
89. *SZ*, 1926, ii, art. 36.
90. *SZ*, 1926, ii, art. 159.
91. Carr, Davies, *FPE 1*, pp. 894–905.
92. *KPSS v rez*, vol. 3, p. 245.
93. I.M. Moskalenko, *TsKK v bor'be za edinstvo i chistotu partinnykh ryadov* (M., 1973) p. 126.
94. *Deyatel'nost' organov partiino-gosudarstvennogo kontrolya* (M., 1964)

pp. 266–7.
95. Carr, Davies, *FPE 1*, p. 358.
96. Trotsky, *The Challenge 1926–27*, pp. 47–55.
97. *KPSS v rez*, vol. 3, pp. 312–21.
98. *Vtoroi plenum TsKK, sozyva XIV s"ezd VKP(b), 2–4 aprilya 1926* (M., 1926) pp. 4–7, *P*, 4 April 1926.
99. *Direktivy KPSS i sovetskogo pravitel'stva po khozyaistvennymom voprosam*, vol. 1 (M., 1957) pp. 578–83.
100. *SZ*, 1926, art. 262.
101. *Direktivy KPSS*, vol. 1, pp. 585–90. See also G.V. Kuibysheva *et al.*, *V.V. Kuibyshev* (M., 1966) p. 232.
102. *Deyatel'nost' organov*, pp. 100–4.
103. *Deyatel'nost' organov*, pp. 186–8.
104. See NKRKI's investigation of the Southern Machine Building trust: *KhU*, 1926, no. 6, p. 41, *SZ*, 1926, art. 377. See also NKRKI's investigation of Krasnoe Sormovo; *EZh*, 12 May 1926.
105. *P*, 14 July 1926.
106. Trotsky, *The Challenge 1926–27*, pp. 78; 84.
107. Carr, Davies, *FPE 1*, p. 520.
108. Ikonnikov, *Sozdanie i deyatel'nost'*, p. 188.
109. *P*, 1 August 1926 (Ya. Bineman).
110. *Direktivy KPSS*, vol. 1, pp. 590–6. See also Carr, *FPE 2*, p. 138.
111. *Direktivy KPSS*, vol. 1, p. 594.
112. *Chetyrnadtsatyi s"ezd VKP(b)*, p. 539.
113. *EZh*, 18 August 1926.
114. Carr, Davies, *FPE 1*, p. 556.
115. Carr, *SOC 1*, p. 408; *SZ*, 1926, art. 514.
116. *P*, 23 October 1926; 24 October 1926.
117. *P*, 22, 24, 25 September 1926.
118. *P*, 24 October 1926 (Vladimirskii).
119. *P*, 26 October 1926.
120. F.E. Dzerzhinskii, *Izbrannye proizvedeniya* (M., 1957) vol. 2, pp. 329–41.
121. G.V. Kuibysheva *et al.*, *V.V. Kuibyshev*, p. 232. Kuibyshev's biographers nevertheless stress that he enjoyed warm personal relations with Dzerzhinskii: *V.V. Kuibyshev*, pp. 194–5, 231–2, 246, 250–1.
122. *SZ*, 1926, art. 144. I.M. Moskalenko, *Organy partiinogo kontrolya v period stroitel'stva sotsializma* (M., 1981), p. 140. N.M. Yanson, Secretary of TsKK, took over as acting chairman of TsKK until November 1926.
123. N. Valentinov, *Novaya ekonomicheskaya politika i krizis partii posle smerti Lenina* (Stanford, Calif., 1971) pp. 139–40; 249–50.
124. X.J. Eudin, N.D. Fisher and H.H. Fisher (eds), *The Life of a Chemist: memoirs of Vladimir N. Ipatieff* (London, 1946) p. 426.
125. *KhU*, 1926, no. 7–8, pp. 29–32; *EZh*, 28 August 1926.
126. *P*, 24 July 1926.
127. *Stenograficheskyi otchet IV Plenum TsKK VKP(b), oktyabr' 1926* (M., 1926) p. 92; *P*, 24 October 1926.
128. Kuibysheva *et al.*, *V.V. Kuibyshev*, p. 253.
129. R.W. Davies and S.G. Wheatcroft, 'Further Thoughts on the First Soviet Five Year Plan', *SR*, 1975, vol. 34, no. 4, p. 794.

130. *Vtoroi plenum TsKK sozyva XIV s"ezd VKP(b)*, pp. 14–15.
131. Carr, *FPE 2*, p. 5.
132. Trotsky, *The Challenge 1926–27*, pp. 75, 87.
133. Carr, *FPE 2*, p. 8.
134. See the editorial 'Kuda napravlen ogon' oppozitsii?', in *Bol'shevik*, 1926, no. 15–16, p. 9.
135. Carr, *FPE 2*, pp. 15, 19, 20.

6 Rabkrin and the 'Left Turn' (1927–9)

1. *SZ*, 1926, art. 202, 203; *P*, 5 November 1926.
2. I. Dubinskii-Mukhadze, *G.K. Ordzhonikidze* (M. 1967); Z. Ordzhonikidze, *Put' Bolshevika, Stranitsy iz zhizni G.K. Ordzhonikidze* (M., 1956); V.S. Kirillov and A.Ya Sverdlov, *G.K. Ordzhonikidze (Sergo)* (M., 1962); *O Sergo Ordzhonikidze* (M., 1980). In English see R.W. Davies, 'Some Soviet Economic Controllers – III – Ordzhonikidze', *SS*, 1961, vol. XII, pp. 36–52. On Lenin's proposal to suspend Ordzhonikidze from the party, see L.D. Trotsky, *My Life* (New York, 1970) pp. 483–4; 486–7.
3. *O Sergo Ordzhonikidze*, p. 114. A. Mikoyan reports that in the joint Central Committee–TsKK plenum in November 1926 only one individual voted against Ordzhonikidze's appointment as chairman of TsKK and six abstained: *SR(Ord)*, ii, p. 809.
4. For Bukharin's views on the regime of economy, see S.F. Cohen, *Bukharin and the Bolshevik Revolution* (Oxford, 1980) p. 246.
5. *SR(Ord)*, ii, p. 1.
6. *SR(Ord)*, ii, pp. 13–14, 29–30, 48. *Pyatnadtsatyi s"ezd VKP(b)*, vol. 1 (M., 1961) p. 495 (Desov).
7. See *Deyatel'nost' organov partiino-gosudarstvennogo kontrolya* (M., 1964) p. 297. For NKRKI's proposals to reduce investigations, see *TPG*, 23 August 1927.
8. *SZ*, 1926, art. 395–6.
9. *Direktivy KPSS i sovetskogo pravitel'stva po khozyaistvennym voprosam*, p. 593.
10. *P*, 9 December 1926; see also NKRKI's plan of work for 1926–7. *P*, 3 December 1926.
11. *SZ*, 1927, art. 106.
12. I.G. Ryabtsev *et al.*, *Leninskaya sistema partiino-gosudarstvennogo kontrolya* (M., 1965) pp. 168–9.
13. *P*, 16 April 1927.
14. *P*, 4 May 1927.
15. *SZ*, 1927, art. 247; see also p. 89 above.
16. Trotsky, *The Challenge of the Left Opposition 1926–27*, p. 232.
17. *Deyatel'nost' organov*, p. 201.
18. S.N. Ikonnikov, *Sozdanie i deyatel'nost' ob"edinennykh organov TsKK–RKI v 1923–1934 gg* (M., 1971) p. 190, cites TsPA IML, f. 85, op 27, d. 356, 1.5.
19. *KPSS v rez*, vol. 3, p. 489.

272   Notes and References to pp. 146–50

20. *SZ*, 1927, art. 542.
21. Trotsky, *The Challenge 1926–27*, pp. 338; 320. *SR(Ord)*, ii,'p. 69.
22. Ya.A. Yakovlev, *Partiya v bor'be s byurokratizmom* (M., 1928).
23. Ikonnikov, *Sozdanie i deyatel'nost'*, p. 193. *Deyatel'nost organov*, pp. 202–3 cites a resolution passed at one meeting of managers endorsing the campaign.
24. A. Samarin, *Za udeshevlenie gosapparata* (M., 1929) p. 22.
25. *SR(Ord)*, ii, p. 94.
26. *Pyatnadtsatyi s"ezd VKP(b)*, vol. 1, pp. 470–1 (Zatonskii), p. 495 (Desov).
27. *Pyatnadtsatyi s"ezd VKP(b)*, vol. 1, p. 525.
28. *KPSS v rez*, vol. 4, p. 23.
29. *EZh*, 16 February 1928. For institutions on the all-union budget savings of 19.5 per cent were claimed, yielding 55 million roubles, and in union republics savings of 10–13 per cent yielding 6.6. million roubles.
30. Ikonnikov, *Sozdanie i deyatel'nost'*, p. 191 cites TsGAOR SSSR, f. 374, op. 4, d. 178, 1.80.
31. *P*, 22 August 1928 (A. Samarin)
32. Samarin, *Za udeshevlenie gosapparata*, p. 24. See also Ikonnikov, *Sozdanie i deyatel'nost'*, p. 194.
33. *SR(Ord)*, ii, p. 127, pp. 130–1.
34. Samarin, *Za udeshevlenie gosapparata*, pp. 28–9.
35. Ikonnikov, *Sozdanie i deyatel'nost'*, pp. 178–9; see also NKRKI's detailed studies of the Soviet state apparatus: Ya. Bineman and S. Kheinman, *Kadry gosudarstvennogo i kooperativnogo apparata* (M., 1930); *Gosudarstvennyi apparat SSSR 1924–1928 g* (M., 1929).
36. *SZ*, 1928, art. 257.
37. *SR(Ord)*, ii, p. 151.
38. *KPSS v rez*, vol. 4, p. 223.
39. R.W. Davies and S.G. Wheatcroft, 'Further Thoughts on the First Soviet Five Year Plan', *SR*, vol. 34, no. 4, December 1975, pp. 794–5.
40. Carr, Davies, *FPE 1*, p. 905.
41. See *EZh*, 1 July 1926 and 9 January 1927.
42. *Deyatelnost' organov*, pp. 190–5.
43. *SZ*, 1927, art. 373.
44. Carr, Davies, *FPE 1*, pp. 853–4.
45. Carr, Davies, *FPE 1*, pp. 264–5.
46. *P*, 5 February 1927.
47. *KPSS v rez*, vol. 3, pp. 454–61.
48. Ryabtsev *et al.*, *Leninskaya sistema*, p. 172.
49. *EZh*, 1 October 1927.
50. *SZ*, 1927, art. 564.
51. TPG, 5 October 1927.
52. *SR(Ord)*, ii, p. 96.
53. *KPSS v rez*, vol. 4, p. 39.
54. *EZh*, 22 January 1928. See also *EZh*, 28 January 1928.
55. *EZh*, 5 February 1928. *Byulleten' TsKK*, 1928, no. 2–3, pp. 5–8.
56. *Za ratsionalizatsiyu*, 1928, no. 1, p. 1.
57. *SR(Ord)*, ii, p. 121.

58. See the Politburo plan of work for 1928 in *VKP(b) v rezolyutsiyakh i resheniyakh*, vol. 2 (M., 1941) p. 275.
59. *III Plenym TsKK sozyva XV s"ezda VKP(b), 25–29 avgusta 1928* (M., 1928); see also *EZh*, 30 August 1928.
60. *EZh*, 30 August 1928.
61. *P*, 11 September 1928.
62. Stalin, *Works*, vol. 11, p. 229.
63. *EZh*, 6 May 1928; see also the Sovnarkom decree of 7 August 1928 *Resheniya partii i pravitel'stva po khozyaistvennym voprosam*, vol. 1 (M., 1967) pp. 750–5.
64. *P*, 15 October 1928.
65. Carr, Davies, *FPE 1*, pp. 400–3.
66. Carr, Davies, *FPE 1*, p. 370.
67. *SR (Ord)*, ii, p. 137.
68. Carr, Davies, *FPE 1*, p. 1009.
69. *P*, 8 April 1926.
70. Ikonnikov, *Sozdanie i deyatel'nost'*, p. 333.
71. G. Gvakhariya, 'Stroitel'stvo novykh metallozavodov', *KhU*, 1927, no. 4–5, p. 97. *EZh*, 30 April 1927.
72. *TPG*, 7 May 1927. *TPG*, 11 May 1927.
73. *Resheniya partii*, vol. 1, pp. 648–9.
74. *SR(Ord)*, ii, pp. 88–9. See also *Byulleten' TsKK*, 1927, no. 8, p. 9.
75. G. Gvakhariya, 'Rekonstruktsiya metallopromyshlennosti', *KhU*, 1927, no. 7–8, p. 120 and *EZh*, 27 August 1927.
76. Gvakhariya, 'Stroitel'stvo novykh metallozavodov', *KhU*, 1927, no. 4–5, p. 93.
77. *SZ*, 1927, art. 678 and *EZh*, 28 December 1927.
78. *KPSS v rez*, vol. 3, p. 480.
79. *EZh*, 26 August 1927; see also *SZ*, 1927, art. 679.
80. *SZ*, 1928, art. 62; see also *EZh*, 20 January 1928.
81. *Byulleten' TsKK*, 1928, no. 2–3, pp. 10–15.
82. *TPG*, 22 July 1927; *EZh*, 24 February 1928, 22 May 1928. See also *TPG*, 7 June 1928.
83. *SR(Ord)*, ii, pp. 134–5.
84. *Industrializatsiya SSSR, 1926–1928* (M., 1969) p. 517.
85. For NKRKI's work in the chemical industry, see *TPG*, 9 February 1928, *TPG*, 2 March 1928; rubber: *EZh*, 10 March 1928, *SZ*, 1928, art. 259, glass: *TPG*, 29 April 1928, *SZ*, 1928, art. 250.
86. Ikonnikov, *Sozdanie i deyatel'nost'*, p. 352. *Shestnadtsataya konferentsiya VKP(b)* (M., 1962) pp. 506–7; 492–6.
87. *Industrializatsiya SSSR 1926–1928*, p. 516.
88. *Byulleten' TsKK*, 1929, no. 1, p. 37.
89. Ikonnikov, *Sozdanie i deyatel'nost'*, p. 352; see also *EZh* 7 April 1928. *TPG*, 29 June 1928.
90. *TPG*, 28 February 1928. See also Ikonnikov, *Sozdanie i deyatel'nost'*, p. 350. See also the report of A.P. Rozengol'ts to the Council of the Congress of State Industry and Trade: *TPG*, 18 April 1928.
91. *Resheniya partii*, vol. 1, pp. 724–42. *EZh*, 9 June 1928. *SZ*, 1928, art. 292.
92. *TPG*, 8 October 1928. *EZh*, 14 October 1928.

93. *SR(Ord)*, ii, p. 135.
94. *P*, 30 September 1928. See also *Economy and Society*, vol. 8, no. 4, November 1979, p. 473.
95. Carr, Davies, *FPE 1*, pp. 338; 344–9.
96. *EZh*, 28 October 1928 (Ya.A. Yakovlev).
97. Carr, Davies, *FPE 1*, p. 372.
98. *EZh*, 11 October 1928. See also *EZh*, 27 July 1928 and 30 September 1928.
99. *EZh*, 28 October 1928.
100. *KPSS v rez*, vol. 4, pp. 132; 134.
101. E. Zaleski, *Planning for Economic Growth in the Soviet Union 1919–1932* (Chapel Hill, 1971) p. 77.
102. G.B. Kuibysheva *et al.*, *V.V. Kuibyshev* (M., 1966) p. 287.
103. *EZh*, 27 January 1929. *EZh*, 25 July 1929.
104. *EZh*, 11 October 1928; *EZh* 14 October 1928. See also I. Belen'kii, 'Voprosy kapital'nogo stroitel'stva promyshlennosti', *Byulleten' TsKK*, 1929, no. 1, p. 3.
105. *KPSS v rez*, vol. 4, p. 13; *SZ*, 1929, art. 34; *EZh* 3, January 1929.
106. *SR(Ord)*, ii, p. 137.
107. *EZh*, 3 January 1929 and 1 March 1929.
108. *P*, 30 September 1928.
109. A.P. Rozengol'ts (ed.), *Promyshlennost*, (M., 1930) p. 224; *EZh*, 10 October 1928. *SR(Ord)*, ii, p. 174.
110. *EZh*, 12 April 1928. For the background to this debate see Carr, Davies, *FPE 1*, p. 479.
111. *SZ*, 1928, art. 374.
112. *SR(Ord)*, ii, p. 174.
113. This account is based partly on the work of S.G. Wheatcroft, *Views on Grain Output, Agricultural Reality and Planning in the Soviet Union in the 1920s*, M.Soc.Sci. thesis (CREES, Birmingham University, 1974).
114. In 1926 NKRKI viewed the situation in agriculture very cautiously: see Yakovlev's articles, *EZh*, 26, 27 October 1926.
115. *EZh*, 19 November 1927. F.A. Tsil'ko in 1927 headed NKRKI's operative group on the 'socialist reconstruction of agriculture' and in 1928 NKRKI's operative group on raising grain yields. See *Vsya Moskva 1927* (M., 1927) p. 74 and *Vsya Moskva 1928* (M., 1928) p. 101.
116. *EZh*, 9 December 1927.
117. *Pyatnadtsatyi s"ezd VKP(b)*, vol. 2, pp. 1358–9.
118. Stalin, *Works*, vol. 10, pp. 312–16.
119. *KPSS v rez*, vol. 4, pp. 65–6.
120. S.F. Cohen, *Bukharin and the Bolshevik Revolution* (Oxford, 1980), pp. 250–1.
121. Stalin, *Works*, vol. 11, p. 10.
122. A. Erlich, 'Stalin's Views on Soviet Economic Development', in E. Simmons (ed.) *Continuity and Change in Russian and Soviet Thought* (Cambridge, Mass., 1955) pp. 81–99.
123. *SZ*, 1928, ii, art. 43.
124. *EZh*, 30 March 1928.
125. *EZh*, 24 June 1928.
126. Ya.A. Yakovlev (ed.), *K voprosu o sotsialisticheskom pereustroistve*

sel'skogo khozyaistva (M.-L., 1928). The report's authors were B.Ya. Baevskii, S.I. Ignat, V.V. Matyukhin, S.G. Uzhanskii, F.A. Tsil'ko and Ya.A. Yakovlev.
127. P, 2 June 1928.
128. EZh, 13 June 1928.
129. EZh, 3 July 1928; 8 July 1928.
130. Yakovlev (ed.), K voprosu, p. xxxvii; EZh, 3 June 1928.
131. P, 5 April 1928.
132. Ikonnikov, Sozdanie i deyatel'nost', p. 437.
133. Ya.A. Yakovlev, Za kolkhozy; kollektivnoe ili kulatskoe khozyaistvo (M.-L., 1928)
134. EZh, 17 May 1928; 19 May 1928.
135. EZh, 13 July 1928.
136. EZh, 17 July 1928; 18 July 1928.
137. EZh, 3 July 1928. This article and other writings by Yakovlev, was published in Yakovlev, Za kolkhozy, pp. 166–75.
138. Stalin, Works, vol. 11, pp. 164–96.
139. KPSS v rez, vol. 4, pp. 110–11.
140. SZ, 1928, art. 421.
141. M. Lewin, Russian Peasants and Soviet Power (London, 1968) p. 277.
142. Wheatcroft, Views on Grain Output, p. 138.
143. EZh, 5 August 1928.
144. EZh, 14 August 1928.
145. EZh, 26 August 1928.
146. Stalin, Works, vol. 11, pp. 267–79.
147. KPSS v rez, vol. 4, p. 126.
148. EZh, 24 November 1928.
149. Wheatcroft, Views on Grain Output, pp. 144–5.
150. EZh, 15 December 1928.
151. EZh, 9 March 1929.
152. Carr, Davies, FPE 1, p. 258.
153. SR(Ord), ii, p. 138.
154. KPSS v rez, vol. 3, pp. 486–92.
155. SR(Ord), ii, pp. 105–6; see also p. 86.
156. Pyatnadtsatyi s"ezd VKP(b), vol. 1, pp. 494–7 (Desov); p. 468 (Zatonskii); p. 455 (Il'in); p. 482 (Ordzhonikidze); p. 572 (Lobachev).
157. Pyatnadtsatyi s"ezd VKP(b), p. 465.
158. Pyatnadtsatyi s"ezd VKP(b), pp. 482–6 (Il'in); p. 569 (Yakovlev).
159. Pyatnadtsatyi s"ezd VKP(b), pp. 452, 465, 613. For the background to this debate see Carr, SOC 2, pp. 466–7; 501, and Carr, FPE 2, pp. 361–4; 381–9.
160. Pyatnadtsatyi s"ezd VKP(b), p. 527 (Yanson); pp. 591–3 (Sol'ts); pp. 603–4 (Shkiryatov).
161. Pyatnadtsatyi s"ezd VKP(b), pp. 570, 614, 604–5.
162. Pyatnadtsatyi s"ezd VKP(b), pp. 577–8; 582–3.
163. SZ, 1928, art. 23.
164. KPSS v rez, vol. 4, pp. 21–7.
165. SZ, 1928, ii, art. 56. The seven were A.P. Rozengol'ts, M.I. Kalmanovich, I.P. Pavlunovskii, P.S. Shushkov, M.M. Kaganovich, Z.M. Belen'kii and

A.C. Svanidze.
166. See K.E. Bailes, *Technology and Society under Lenin and Stalin* (New Jersey, 1978) ch. 3 and N. Lampert, *The Technical Intelligentsia and the Soviet State* (London, 1979).
167. *P*, 10 March 1928.
168. M. Reiman, *La Nascita Dello Stalinismo* (Rome, 1980) pp. 249–51.
169. *KPSS v rez*, vol. 4, pp. 84–93.
170. *SR(Ord)*, ii, pp. 116–23.
171. *SR(Ord)*, ii, pp. 147, 151, 168.
172. Ikonnikov, *Sozdanie i deyatel'nost'*, pp. 267–70.
173. *Obrazovanie i razvitie organov sotsialisticheskogo kontrolya v SSSR* (M., 1975) pp. 232–6, 251–5, 261–2.
174. Stalin, *Works*, vol. 11, pp. 35, 376.
175. Ikonnikov, *Sozdanie i deyatel'nost'*, pp. 140–4.
176. *KPSS v rez*, vol. 4, pp. 94–8; see also J.V. Stalin, *Works*, vol. 11, pp. 31–42.
177. *P*, 16 May 1928.
178. Stalin, *Works*, vol. 11, pp. 71–8.
179. *P*, 3 June 1928.
180. Stalin, *Works*, vol. 11, pp. 102–4, 119–20, 133–44.
181. *OP*, 1 September 1928.
182. *P*, 9 September 1928.
183. *SR(Ord)*, ii, p. 244.
184. *SR(Ord)*, ii, p. 123.
185. *KPSS v rez*, vol. 4, pp. 111–17.
186. S. Fitzpatrick, 'Stalin and the Making of a New Elite 1928–1939', *SR*, vol. 38, no. 3, September 1979, pp. 377–402.
187. *SR(Ord)*, ii, p. 231.
188. *Pyatnadtsatyi s"ezd VKP(b)*, vol. 1, p. 70.
189. *SR(Ord)*, ii, pp. 144, 147–9.
190. *Deyatel'nost' organov*, pp. 279–81.
191. *EZh*, 14 January 1928; *SZ*, 1928, art. 224.
192. *SR(Ord)*, ii, pp. 148–9. See also *Obrazovanie i razvitie*, pp. 256–60.
193. Ikonnikov, *Sozdanie i deyatel'nost'*, p. 130.
194. *SR(Ord)*, ii, pp. 149, 157–8, 162. See also *Deyatel'nost' organov*, pp. 138–9.
195. B. Souvarine, *Stalin* (London, 1940) pp. 452–3.
196. Carr, *FPE 2*, pp. 26; 29–32.
197. Trotsky, *The Challenge 1926–27*, p. 361.
198. Trotsky, *The Real Situation in Russia* (London, n.d.) pp. 14–15; Deutscher, *The Prophet Unarmed, Trotsky 1921–1929* (Oxford, 1970) pp. 366–7.
199. Carr, *FPE 2*, p. 40.
200. *SR(Ord)*, ii, p. 58; see also p. 63.
201. V. Serge, *Memoirs of a Revolutionary* (Oxford, 1975) pp. 177, 257.
202. See Trotsky's disparaging comments on Yaroslavskii: L.D. Trotsky, *Stalin* (London, 1969) pp. 157, 209, 247; L.D. Trotsky, *The Stalin School of Falsification* (New York, 1972) pp. 21–3, 46, 150.
203. Carr, *FPE 2*, pp. 50–1.

204. *SR(Ord)*, ii, pp. 109–15.
205. Carr, *FPE 2*, pp. 37, 40–1, 44–5, 56, 1411.
206. *Pyatnadtsatyi s"ezd VKP(b)*, vol. 1, pp. 551–2.
207. *O Sergo Ordzhonikidze* (M., 1980) pp. 78–80; 114.
208. Souvarine, *Stalin*, p. 484.
209. Carr, *FPE 2*, pp. 83–4; *P*, 29 November 1928.
210. Carr, *FPE 2*, pp. 92–6.
211. A. Avtorkhanov, *Stalin and the Soviet Communist Party* (London, 1958) p. 114 claims that at least half of the 195 members of TsKK were supporters of the right and that the right also had a majority in the TsKK presidium. The leadership of the Moscow KK–RKI in the autumn of 1928 supported Uglanov and the rightist leadership in the Moscow party apparatus: I.M. Moskalenko, *TsKK v bor'be za edinstvo i chistotu partiinykh ryadov* (M., 1973) pp. 150–1.
212. *SR(Ord)*, ii, pp. 162–4.
213. Avtorkhanov, *Stalin and the Soviet Communist Party*, pp. 114–15. This manoeuvre was made possible, Avtorkhanov asserts, because the XV Party Congress had failed to specify that the TsKK members attending the Politburo should exercise only non-voting rights as in the past.
214. *KPSS v rez.*, vol. 4, p. 187.

7 Rabkrin and the 'Revolution from Above' (1929–30)

1. Bukharin in April 1929 was sacked as editor of *Pravda* and Tomskii lost his post as chairman of VTsSPS, *KPSS v rez*, vol. 4, p. 187.
2. In 1929 five major Politburo commissions were set up to deal with particular questions – the right opposition; Rykov's two-year plan for agriculture; the metallurgical industry; the railways; collectivization. See Stalin, *Works*, vol. 12, pp. 7, 84; *SR (Ord)*, ii, pp. 190, 237; R.W. Davies, *The Socialist Offensive* (London, 1980) p. 185.
3. On the work of the joint TsKK presidium-NKRKI collegium sessions from November 1929 to June 1930 see *Protokoly TsKK*, no. 60–8, in the Smolensk Archives, WKP 57, T-87.
4. In 1929 a number of articles appeared in the Soviet press on NKRKI's role in organizing the work of the foreign specialists: see *EZh*, 24 May 1929; 14 July 1929; 3, 18, 19 August 1929; 27, 29 December 1929; 4 January 1930; *TPG*, 4 May 1929; 22 February 1930. The experiences of one foreign specialist who worked for NKRKI is recounted in J.N. Westergarth, *Russian Engineer* (London, 1934).
5. *Istoriya SSSR*, no. 1 (M., 1966) p. 87; *Byulleten' TsKK*, 1929, no. 4–5, pp. 44–5.
6. A. Avtorkhanov, *Stalin and the Communist Party* (London, 1959) p. 92. This author asserts that from the autumn of 1928 onwards Ordzhonikidze was assigned the task of shadowing Rykov in Sovnarkom and STO.
7. R.W. Davies, 'The Syrtsov-Lominadze Affair', *SS*, vol. xxxiii, no. 1, January 1980, p. 30.

8. In the RSFSR strong support for the Stalinist line was provided by N.I. Il'in (narkom NKRKI RSFSR), and by N.M. Yanson (narkom NKYust RSFSR, formerly of TsKK−NKRKI). In the Ukraine V.Ya. Chubar', chairman of Sovnarkom UkSSR, a firm supporter of the 'general line' was strongly supported by V.P. Zatonskii, head of TsKK−NKRKI UkSSR: see T.N. Kol'yak, *Vlas Yakovlevich Chubar'* (Kiev, 1981) pp. 182−5.
9. Stalin, *Works*, vol. 12, pp. 29−30.
10. Stalin, *Works*, vol. 12, p. 17. At the XVI Party Congress Stalin again stressed the need to give a 'sharp edge' to all organizations: *Works*, vol. 12, p. 321.
11. *Shestnadtsataya konferentsiya VKP(b)* (M., 1961) p. 446.
12. *Shestnadtsataya konferentsiya VKP(b)* (M., 1961) p. 469.
13. *Shestnadtsataya konferentsiya VKP(b)* (M., 1961) pp. 446, 634−6. On the work of the sector of control from the XV to XVI Party Congress see A. Landau, *Protiv byurokratizma, beskhozyaistvennosti, besplanovosti* (M., 1930).
14. *Shestnadtsataya konferentsiya VKP(b)* (M., 1961) p. 646.
15. *SZ*, 1929, art. 313.
16. *Iz*, 8 July 1929. S.N. Ikonnikov, *Sozdanie i deyatel'nost' ob''edinennykh organov TsKK−RKI v 1923−1934 gg* (M., 1971) pp. 285−6.
17. *P*, 10 January 1930. The purge of Vesenkha was welcomed by Kuibyshev as a means of 'proletarianizing' its apparatus.
18. *SR(Ord)*, ii, p. 223.
19. Ikonnikov, *Sozdanie i deyatel'nost'*, pp. 281−319.
20. *Deyatel'nost' organov partiinogo-gosudarstvennogo kontrolya po sovershenstvovaniyu gosudarstvennogo apparata* (M., 1964) pp. 75, 156−7.
21. *P*, 16 March 1920.
22. *Deyatel'nost' organov*, pp. 162−9. The first shots in the campaign against the right in the trade unions were fired at the VIII VTsSPS Congress in December 1928. In his speech to the Congress Ordzhonikidze demanded closer co-operation between the unions and NKRKI. See also A.I. Gurevich, *Raboche-krest'yanskaya inspektsiya i profsoyuzy* (M., 1929).
23. Stalin, *Works*, vol. 12, p. 232; see also pp. 114−17, 125−6, 323−4.
24. *SR(Ord)*, ii, p. 174.
25. *Voprosy Istorii KPSS*, no. 4, 1962, p. 58.
26. S.F. Cohen, *Bukharin and the Bolshevik Revolution* (Oxford, 1980) p. 452.
27. *Shestnadtsayti s''ezd VKP (b)* (M., 1931) p. 326; see also the attacks on the Right by other TsKK-NKRKI spokesmen: *Shestnadtsatyi s''ezd VKP(b)*, pp. 199−210 (Shkiryatov); pp. 253−5 (Yaroslavskii).
28. *Ordzhonikidze (Sergo), Biografia* (M., 1962) p. 226.
29. R.W. Davies and S.G. Wheatcroft, 'Further Thoughts on the First Soviet Five Year Plan', *SR*, vol. 34, no. 4, December 1975, pp. 790−802.
30. *EZh*, 28 October 1928 (Ya.A. Yakovlev).
31. Carr, Davies, *FPE 1*, p. 941.
32. *P*, 9 April 1929.
33. Stalin, *Works*, vol. 12, p. 64.
34. V.I. Kuz'min, *V bor'be za sotsialisticheskuyu rekonstruktsiyu 1926−1937* (M., 1976) p. 91.

35. *SR(Ord)*, ii, pp. 155–6. See also the letter issued by NKRKI to the republican NKRKI on the need to tighten control over stockpiling: *EZh*, 16 February 1929. See also *EZh*, 26 April 1929.
36. A.Z. Gol'tsman, *Rezervy v narodnom khozyaistve* (M., 1929). See also *EZh*, 10 March 1929.
37. *Resheniya partii i pravitel'stva po khozyaisvennym voprosam*, vol. 2 (M., 1967) pp. 14–16.
38. *Nedochety kapital'nogo stroitel'stva v promyshlennosti v 1927–28, 1928–29 g.* (M., 1929).
39. Z.M. Belen'kii, *Resul'taty obsledovaniya NKRKI kapital'nogo stroitel'stva VSNKh SSSR* (M., 1929).
40. S. Fitzpatrick, 'Ordzhonikidze's Takeover of Vesenkha: A Case Study in Soviet Bureaucratic Politics', *SS*, vol. xxxvii, no. 2, April 1985.
41. Carr, Davies, *FPE 1*, p. 939.
42. *TPG*, 6 April 1929. See also *Shestnadtsataya konferentsiya*, p. 459.
43. *EZh*, 4 January 1929. NKRKI's concern was deepened by its investigation into the building of the Kerch metallurgical project in October 1928. At this one project the costs, originally estimated at 22 million roubles, had tripled: see *TPG*, 15 October 1928 and *SR(Ord)*, ii, p. 135.
44. *P*, 2 February 1929. See also Carr, Davies, *FPE 1*, p. 463.
45. *O rekonstruktsii zavodov Yugostali* (M., 1929) p. 70.
46. Belen'kii, *Resul'taty obsledovaniya NKRKI*, pp. 16–17.
47. *TPG*, 6 April 1929.
48. *TPG*, 27 April 1929. See also *Shestnadtsataya konferentsiya VKP(b)*, pp. 459; 815. Birman was probably the author of a letter complaining about excessive investigation by NKRKI cited in an article by Iosif Kosior (a former chairman of Yugostal, to whom Birman had been deputy, now a deputy chairman of Vesenkha), 'On the working conditions of economic cadres', in *P*, 7 April 1928, p. 1.
49. *Shestnadtsataya konferentsiya VKP(b)*, p. 61.
50. *Shestnadtsataya konferentsiya VKP(b)*, pp. 459–61.
51. *Shestnadtsataya konferentsiya VKP(b)*, p. 460. Other Ukrainian spokesmen, Skrypnik (Ukrainian Commissar of Education), Lyubchenko and Postyshev (from the Ukrainian party organization), interjected repeatedly in support of Birman and in opposition to the NKRKI speakers (*Shestnadtsataya konferentsiya*, pp. 492, 500, 528, 532, 551, 556, 557, 558, 597).
52. *Shestnadtsataya konferentsiya VKP(b)*, p. 499.
53. *Shestnadtsataya konferentsiya VKP(b)*, p. 508 (Yakovlev); pp. 554–60 (Rozengol'ts). The wider implications of this debate are examined below, p. 140–1.
54. *O rekonstruktsii zavodov Yugostali*, p. 4. NKRKI's report on Yugostal was published in *EZh*, 12 May 1929 and *TPG*, 15 May 1929. See also A.P. Rozengol'ts (ed.), *Promyshlennost'* (M., 1930) (article by I. Gokhman).
55. Birman had articles on the question in *Metall*, 1929, no. 2; *Puti industrializatsii*, 31 May 1929, no. 10 and 15 June 1929, no. 11.
56. *TPG*, 24 July 1929.
57. *SR(Ord)*, ii, p. 190.

58. *KPSS v rez.*, vol. 4, pp. 284–94; *P*, 13 August 1929.
59. *SR(Ord)*, ii, p. 191.
60. *XI z'izd komunistichnoi partii (bil'shovikiv) Ukraini (5–15 chervnia 1930 roku) Stenografichnii zvit* (Kharkov, 1930) pp. 199–232 (A.P. Rozengol'ts), pp. 469–76 (S. Kosior). Cited by S. Fitzpatrick, 'Ordzhonikidze's Takeover'.
61. *SR(Ord)*, ii, pp. 188; 192.
62. *Obsledovanie deyatel'nosti tresta Uralmet* (Sverdlovsk, 1929).
63. Ikonnikov, *Sozdanie i deyatel'nost'*, p. 345; *SR(Ord)*, ii, p. 193; *Obsledovanie deyatel'nosti tresta Uralmet*, pp. i–ii. In the foreword to the report the director of Uralmet criticized NKRKI's concern with the uncovering of defects in its work, its neglect of positive achievements and its failure to take account of the difficulties which beset the trust.
64. A.V. Krasnov, *TsKK-RKI v bor'be za sotsializm 1923–1934 gg* (Irkutsk, 1973) p. 384; *SR(Ord)*, ii, p. 193; *KPSS v rez*, vol. 4, pp. 398–404.
65. *Rabota NKRKI SSSR ot V k VI Vsesoyuznomu s"ezdu Sovetov* (M., 1931) p. 6.
66. *Za industrializatsiyu*, 11 May 1930.
67. E. Zaleski, *Planning for Economic Growth in the Soviet Union, 1919–1932* (Chapel Hill, 1971) p. 119; *Za industrializatsiyu*, 11 May 1930.
68. Stalin, *Works*, vol. 12, pp. 281, 335, 341, 355.
69. *SR(Ord)*, ii, p. 193.
70. *KPSS v rez*, vol. 4, p. 441.
71. A. Khavin, *U rulya industrii (Dokumental'nye ocherki)* (M., 1968) p. 78.
72. Zaleski, *Planning for Economic Growth*, p. 309.
73. *Resheniya partii*, vol. 2, pp. 45–53.
74. *NKRKI v bor'be za khlopkovyio nezavisimost'* (M., 1930) p. 10. See also A.M. Kaktyn (ed.), *Sotsialisticheskaya rekonstruktsiya khlopkovodstva* (M., 1934).
75. *Resheniya partii*, vol. 2, pp. 85–93. See also *EZh*, 28 July 1929; *SR(Ord)*, ii, p. 198.
76. *NKRKI v bor'be za khlopkovuyu nezavisimost'*, pp. 12–14. See also Rozengol'ts (ed.), *Promyshlennost'*, pp. 256–73; *SR(Ord)*, ii, p. 197.
77. G.V. Kuibysheva *et al.*, *V.V. Kuibyshev* (M., 1966) p. 303.
78. *EZh*, 8 September 1929; 16 October 1929.
79. *NKRKI v bor'be za khlopkovuyu nezavisimost'*, p. 16.
80. *SR(Ord)*, ii, p. 198.
81. *EZh*, 11 July 1930.
82. Zaleski, *Planning for Economic Growth*, p. 308.
83. K.I. Albrekht, *Rekonstruktsiya i ratsionalizatsiya lesnogo khozyaistva, po materialam NKRKI SSSR v 1928–1929 gg.* (M., 1930) p. 20.
84. *EZh*, 16 April 1929; *Rekonstruktsiya lesnogo dela, materialy k 16 s"ezdu VKP(b)* (M.-L., 1930) p. 3.
85. *Industrializatsiya SSSR 1928–1932* (M., 1970) p. 584.
86. *EZh*, 30 June 1929.
87. I.V. Leder, *Sotsialisticheskaya ratsionalizatsiya v bor'be s poteryami* (M., 1930) pp. 242–5; 274.
88. *Industrialisatsiya SSSR 1929–1932*, p. 585.
89. *Byulleten' finansov i khozyaistvennogo zakonodatel'stva*, no. 42, 1929,

pp. 17–22; Zaleski, *Planning for Economic Growth*, p. 95; Leder, *Sotsialis-ticheskaya ratsionalizatsiya*, p. 274; *SR(Ord)*, ii, p. 200.
90. *EZh*, 18 July 1929.
91. Zaleski, *Planning for Economic Growth*, p. 306; *SR(Ord)*, ii, p. 199;
92. Rozengol'ts (ed.) *Promyshlennost'*, pp. 124–5 (article by Bulushev and Izrailovich).
93. G. Krzhizhanovskii, 'Vreditelstvo v energetike', *Planovoe khozyaistvo*, no. 10–11, 1930, cited in Zaleski, *Planning for Economic Growth*, p. 118. A vivid account of this dispute is given in the short story 'Neft', Isaac Babel, *Izbrannoe* (M., 1966) p. 281; *SR(Ord)*, ii, p. 199.
94. Rozengol'ts (ed.), *Promyshlennost'*, pp. 117–19; 129. See also *Protokoly TsKK*, no. 54, 1930, pp. 12–15.
95. Rozengol'ts (ed.), *Promyshlennost'*, p. 124; *Shestnadtsatyi s"ezd VKP(b)*, p. 356 (A. Yakovlev).
96. Zaleski, *Planning for Economic Growth*, p. 307.
97. Rozengol'ts (ed.), *Promyshlennost'*, pp. 74, 91–4 (article by Izrailovich).
98. Rozengol'ts (ed.), *Promyshlennost'*, p. 84. See also *Protokol TsKK*, no. 65, 1930, pp. 1–5.
99. *KPSS v rez*, vol. 4, pp. 398–404.
100. Rozengol'ts (ed.), *Promyshlennost'*, p. 67 (article by Izrailovich).
101. Zaleski, *Planning for Economic Growth*, p. 306.
102. *EZh*, 4 August 1929. See also *EZh*, 21 July 1929.
103. *EZh*, 21 August 1929; *SZ*, 1929, art. 487.
104. Zaleski, *Planning for Economic Growth*, p. 119.
105. Rozengol'ts *Promyshlennost'*, p. 97 (article by Dedkov and Izrailovich).
106. Rozengol'ts (ed.), *Promyshlennost'*, p. 97.
107. *Protokol TsKK*, no. 68, 1930, pp. 3–4; *SR(Ord)*, ii, p. 200.
108. Leder, *Sotsialisticheskaya ratsionalizatsiya*, pp. 222, 227–8; *SR(Ord)*, ii, pp. 194–5.
109. *EZh*, 23 June 1929.
110. Leder, *Sotsialisticheskaya ratsionalizatsiya*, p. 241; *Industrializatsiya SSSR 1929–1932*, p. 584.
111. Leder, *Sotsialisticheskaya ratsionalizatsiya*, pp. 228–30; *EZh*, 5 November 1929; *Protokol TsKK*, 1930, no. 56, p. 8; *Industrializatsiya SSSR 1929–1932*, p. 589.
112. Leder, *Sotsialisticheskaya ratsionalizatsiya*, pp. 236–8; *EZh*, 17 October 1929; *TPG*, 25 October 1929.
113. Leder, *Sotsialisticheskaya ratsionalizatsiya*, p. 241; *EZh*, 5 November 1929.
114. Rozengol'ts (ed.), *Promyshlennost'*, pp. 181–97.
115. *EZh*, 24 December 1929. See also *Protokoly TsKK*, 1929, no. 53. Rozengol'ts (ed.), *Promyshlennost'*, pp. 196–7. See also NKRKI's role in revising the plan for the reconstruction of the Lugansk works: *SR(Ord)*, ii, p. 204.
116. J.M. Cooper, *The Development of the Soviet Machine Tool Industry 1917–1941*, unpublished Ph.D. (Birmingham University, 1975) pp. 47–63. See also V. Leder, *Sotsialisticheskaya ratsionalizatsiya*, pp. 146–78. *Shestnadtsatyi s"ezd VKP(b)*, pp. 519–21.
117. Rozengol'ts, *Promyshlennost'*, pp. 224–6.

118. Rozengol'ts, *Promyshlennost'*, pp. 239–55 (article by N. Uskov and P. Shinder). See also S.N. Ikonnikov, *Sozdanie i deyatel'nost'*, pp. 357–8, and Krasnov, *TsKK–RKI*, pp. 395–6; Carr, Davies, *FPE 1*, p. 962.
119. Ikonnikov, *Sozdanie i deyatel'nost'*, pp. 359–60, and Krasnov, *TsKK–RKI*, pp. 403–4. See also *EZh*, 1 January 1929; 1 February 1929.
120. *EZh*, 26 November 1929, report of NKRKI's investigation of the Stalingrad tractor works, the Rostov agricultural implements works, and other engineering works – Urals, Kerch, Mariupol, Korsapaiskii.
121. *EZh*, 24 October 1929. Carr, Davies, *FPE 1*, p. 373, n. 5.
122. *EZh*, 27 December 1929. See also Stalin, *Works*, vol. 12, p. 342.
123. *SR(Ord)*, ii, pp. 205, 210. See also Zaleski, *Planning for Economic Growth*, pp. 104–6.
124. *Industrializatsiya SSSR 1929–1932*, p. 586.
125. *SR(Ord)*, ii, pp. 170–4.
126. Zaleski, *Planning for Economic Growth*, p. 94.
127. *EZh*, 11 November 1929.
128. Zaleski, *Planning for Economic Growth*, p. 117 cites *Planovoe khozyaistvo*, no. 2, 1930.
129. *SR(Ord)*, ii, p. 183. See also p. 243.
130. Kuz'min, *V bor'be za sotsialisticheskuyu rekonstruktsiyu*, p. 92.
131. Zaleski, *Planning for Economic Growth*, p. 117.
132. Stalin, *Works*, vol. 12, pp. 278, 330, 333, 349, 351, 360.
133. Zaleski, *Planning for Economic Growth*, p. 119.
134. *SR(Ord)*, ii, p. 204; see also p. 380.
135. *SR(Ord)*, ii, pp. 207–10.
136. Zaleski, *Planning for Economic Growth*, pp. 120–3.
137. *Shestnadtsatayi s"ezd VKP(b)*, p. 653.
138. *Shestnadtsataya konferentsiya VKP(b)*, pp. 496–7.
139. *Shestnadtsataya konferentsiya VKP(b)*, p. 568 (Figatner); p. 528 (Zatonskii); p. 568 (Zemlyachka); p. 567 (Rozengol'ts). During the speech of Rozengol'ts, Skrypnik interjected: 'What is the reason that a fourth prominent representative of Rabkrin is speaking against Yugostal? Isn't it because Birman criticized Rabkrin in his speech?'
140. *Shestnadtsataya konferentsiya VKP(b)*, p. 574.
141. *P*, 9 April 1929.
142. Wheatcroft, *Views on Grain Output, Agricultural Reality and Planning in The Soviet Union in the 1920s*, M. Soc. Sci. thesis (CREES, Birmingham University, 1974), pp. 163–4.
143. *SR(Ord)*, ii, p. 177.
144. *SZ*, 1929, ii, art. 230; *EZh*, 8 October 1929. The two NKRKI specialists were F.A. Tsil'ko and S.G. Uzhanskii.
145. R.W. Davies, *The Socialist Offensive* (London, 1980) p. 115 cites *Derevenskii kommunist*, no. 2, 22 January 1930.
146. *Shestnadtsataya konferentsiya VKP(b)*, pp. 404–5.
147. *P*, 9 April 1929.
148. *Traktorizatsiya sel'skogo khozyaistva RSFSR* (M., 1930) foreword by N.I. Il'in, narkom NKRKI RSFSR.
149. *SR(Ord)*, ii, p. 175.
150. Ikonnikov, *Sozdanie i deyatel'nost'*, pp. 437–8; Stalin, *Works*, vol. 12,

p. 135.
151. S.I. Yakubovskaya, *Razvitie SSSR kak soyuznogo gosudarstva 1922–1936 gg.* (M., 1972) p. 64 cites TsGAOR SSSR, f. 5446, op. 1, d. 47, 1.175.
152. S.I. Yakubovskaya, 'K voprosy o razvitii soyuznykh organov vlasti v 1924–1932 gg.', in E.N. Gorodetskii *et al.* (eds), *Stroitel'stvo sovetskogo gosudarstva* (M., 1972) p. 58 cites TsPA IML, f. 17, op. 2, ed. khr. 411, 1. 90–92. On the role of Skrypnik in the Ukraine see J.E. Mace, 'Famine and Nationalism in Soviet Ukraine', *Problems of Communism*, vol. xxxiii, May–June 1984, pp. 37–50.
153. *Bor'ba za sotsialisticheskuyu rekonstruktsiyu sel'skogo khozyaistva* (M.-L., 1930) p. 3.
154. *SZ*, 1929, ii, art. 278, 292; *SZ*, 1930, ii, art. 258.
155. Davies, *The Socialist Offensive*, p. 185.
156. L.D. Trotsky, *The Writings of Leon Trotsky 1930* (New York, 1975) pp. 109, 114, 271–3, 311–12, 318.
157. *Bor'ba za sotsialisticheskuyu rekonstruktsiyu sel'skogo khozyaistva* (M.-L., 1930): materials supplied by the NKRKI agricultural sector to the XVI Party Congress. See also *Iz*, 15 July 1930. For Kindeev's views see *Planovoe khozyaistvo*, no. 7–8, 1930, p. 98. Ordzhonikidze at the XVI Party Congress endorsed Yakovlev's policy stance: *SR(Ord)*, ii, p. 211.
158. Carr, Davies, *FPE 1*, pp. 400–2, 404, 409, 677. Ikonnikov, *Sozdanie i deyatel'nost'*, pp. 378–9.
159. Carr, *FPE 2*, pp. 325–6.
160. N. Lampert, *The Technical Intelligentsia and the Soviet State* (London, 1979), p. 967.
161. *Shestnadtsataya konferentsiya VKP(b)*, pp. 454–9.
162. *NKRKI v bor'be za khlopkovuyu nezavisimost'*, p. 10. See also Leder, *Sotsialisticheskaya ratsionalizatsiya*, p. 15.
163. *SR(Ord)*, ii, p. 176.
164. *SR(Ord)*, ii, p. 177.
165. G.V. Kuibysheva *et al.*, *V.V. Kuibyshev* (M., 1966) p. 291.
166. *SR(Ord)*, ii, pp. 253–4.
167. *SR(Ord)*, ii, p. 200.
168. *SR(Ord)*, ii, p. 231. See also S. Fitzpatrick, 'Stalin and the Making of a New Elite, 1928–1939', *SR*, vol. 38, no. 3, September 1979, pp. 288–9.
169. *SR(Ord)*, ii, p. 239.
170. *SR(Ord)*, ii, pp. 300–2; see also A. Khavin, *U rulia industrii*, p. 82.
171. *Shestnadtsatyi s''ezd VKP(b)*, p. 329. One western scholar describes TsKK–NKRKI in this period as 'an unofficial Economic Bureau of the Party alongside the Politburo and Orgburo', P.M. Cocks, *Politics of Party Control: The Historical and Institutional Role of Party Control Organs in the CPSO*, unpublished Ph.D. thesis (Harvard University, 1968), p. 150.
172. *Shestnadtsatyi s''ezd VKP(b)*, pp. 361–3 (Lobov).
173. *Shestnadtsatyi s''ezd VKP(b)*, p. 503.
174. *Shestnadtsatyi s''ezd VKP(b)*, pp. 306–7, 322 (Ordzhonikidze); pp. 381–3 (Shushkov).
175. *Shestnadtsatyi s''ezd VKP(b)*, pp. 315–16 (Ordzhonikidze); pp. 370–1 (Belen'kii); pp. 400–2 (Roizenman).
176. *Shestnadtsatyi s''ezd VKP(b)*, pp. 384–8 (Antselovich); pp. 273–5 (A.M.

Amosov); p. 391 (Evreinov); p. 191 (Veinberg); p. 661 (Shvernik).
177. *Shestnadtsatyi s"ezd VKP(b)*, p. 357 (Yakovlev); p. 379 (Bogdanov); p. 402 (Roizenman); p. 403 (Nazaretyan).
178. *SZ*, 1930, ii, art. 355, 356; *P*, 16 December 1930.
179. *SZ*, 1930, ii, art. 398, 399. The eight were I.P. Pavlunovskii (deputy commissar), F.R. Martinovich, Z.G. Zangvil', M.M. Kaganovich, A.I. Izrailovich, and A.I. Gurevich, together with S.Z. Ginzburg and A.E. Bliznichenko who were TsKK members but not ranking NKRKI officials. Two members were appointed from the Central Committee Secretariat – I.M. Moskvin and Ya.D. Rozental' – and one from OGPU, G.E. Prokof'ev.
180. The nine sectors were Planning (A.I. Gurevich), Labour (Yu.P. Figatner – a TsKK member elected in July 1930, though also listed in *Vsya Moskva*, 1930 as head of Vesenkha's Chief Inspectorate), Organization, Rationalization of production and administration of industry (V.Ya. Grossman), Finance (Z.G. Zangvil'), Supply and distribution (M.A. Fushman), Machine building (M.M. Kaganovich), Fuel and energy (A.I. Izrailovich) and Building and timber (S.Z. Ginzburg): data from *Vsya Moskva*, 1930 (Rabkrin listing), *Vsya Moskva*, 1931 (Vesenkha listing) and *P*, 14 July 1930 (TsKK listing).
181. The six were V.Ya. Grossman, Z.G. Zangvil', A.I. Izrailovich, M.M. Kaganovich, S.I. Ignat, and F.G. Ego, A.V. Ozerskii and M.B. Grossman also worked briefly in Vesenkha. Ozerskii was transferred to NKVneshTorg and then back to NKRKI as head of its precious metals group: data from *Vsya Moskva*, 1930 and 1931. I.Z. Gokhman (a member of the NKRKI team which investigated Yugostal in 1929–30) was moved to the Vesenkha planning sector in November 1930, and subsequently headed the ferrous metal group of the metallurgical sector.
182. *SZ*, 1930, ii, art. 360. A.V. Ozerskii was briefly transferred from NKRKI as deputy *narkom* in NKVneshTorg; *SZ*, 1930, ii, art. 388; *SZ*, 1931, ii, art. 3; *SZ*, 1931, ii, art. 8. On D.Z. Lebed', see *Who Was Who in the USSR* (Metuchen, N.J., 1972) p. 340.
183. B. Souvarine, *Stalin* (London, 1940), pp. 489–90.
184. Stalin, *Works*, vol. 12, pp. 372–5.
185. *SR(Ord)*, ii, p. 246.

8   Rabkrin: Decline and Abolition (1931–4)

1. *SZ*, 1930, ii, art. 432. See also B. Souvarine, *Stalin* (London, 1940) pp. 270, 430, 434; R.W. Davies, *The Socialist Offensive* (London, 1980) pp. 131, 160–1, 177, 316, 408.
2. *SZ*, 1929, ii, art. 289; *SZ*, 1930, ii, art. 254, 257. Krinitskii was the secretary of the Transcaucasian *kraikom* in 1929–30 and must have been closely acquainted with Andreev: *SZ*, 1931, ii, art. 84. Antipov was transferred to NKRKI from NKPT where he made way as *narkom* for the demoted Kamenev.
3. *SZ*, 1931, ii, art. 223, 224; *P*, 10 October 1931; see also B. Souvarine, *Stalin*, pp. 386, 480.

4. *SZ*, 1931, ii, art. 235; *P*, 17 October 1931. Prokof'ev was transferred from Vesenkha, and Antselovich from trade union work.
5. *SZ*, 1930, ii, art. 431; *SZ*, 1926, ii, art. 13, 23.
6. *P*, 22 December 1930.
7. *P*, 27 July 1932 (Roizenman).
8. *SZ*, 1931, ii, art. 18, 100.
9. *SZ*, 1931, ii, art. 18, 234.
10. *Sovetskoe stroitel'stvo*, 1931, no. 1, p. 139.
11. *Industrializatsiya SSSR 1929–1932 gg.* (M., 1970), pp. 598–614, and *Industrializatsiya SSSR 1933–1937 gg.* (M., 1971), pp. 612–16. The commission was also given responsibility for financial control – R.W. Davies, *The Development of the Soviet Budgetary System* (Cambridge, 1958) p. 242.
12. *Dva goda raboty, materialy k otcheta pravitel'stva RSFSR na pyatnadtsatom vserossiskom s''ezd sovetov* (D.Z. Lebed', ed) (M., 1931) p. 137.
13. V.P. Zatonskii, *Organizatsiya ispolneniya i kachestvo raboty* (Kharkov, 1931) pp. 8–12.
14. T. Dzhambaev, *Vozniknovenie i razvitie vnutrivedomstvennogo kontrolya* (Alma Ata, 1957) pp. 68–71; *SZ*, 1931, art. 215; *SZ*, 1932, art. 301.
15. *KPSS v rez*, vol. 4, pp. 525–53.
16. *III Plenum TsKK, iyulya 1931* (M., 1931), pp. 8–33 (Andreev); pp. 35–53 (Akulov).
17. *III Plenum TsKK*, pp. 87–96, TsKK plenum resolution on agriculture, transport and the urban economy.
18. *III Plenum TsKK*, p. 28 (Andreev); pp. 39–40 (Akulov).
19. R.W. Davies, *The Development of the Soviet Budgetary System*, pp. 229–31; A.V. Krasnov, *TsKK–RKI v bor'be za sotsializm 1923–1934 gg.* (Irkutsk, 1973) pp. 360–2.
20. *Iz*, 16 December 1930.
21. Krasnov, *TsKK–RKI*, pp. 385–6.
22. *I-e mezhkraevoe soveshchanie obl KK-RKI Urala, Sibiri, Bashkiri i Kazakhstana po Uralo-Kuzbassu* (Sverdlovsk-Moscow, 1931).
23. *Za tempy, kachestvo, proverku (ZTKP)*, 1932, no. 13–14, pp. 21–3.
24. *KPSS v rez*, vol. 5, pp. 46, 58–63; *P*, 3 October 1932.
25. *P*, 4 May 1931; 8 May 1931, 13 June 1931, 20 October 1931; 13 November 1931.
26. *P*, 27 May 1931, 23 July 1931; 24 February 1933; 30 May 1933.
27. *P*, 6 April 1931; 27 April 1931 (Roizenman); 28 May 1931.
28. *P*, 2 June 1931; 13 August 1931; 6 October 1931; 23 November 1931; Krasnov, *TsKK–RKI*, p. 368; *Industrializatsiya SSSR 1929–1932*, p. 605.
29. *Semnadtsataya konferentsiya VKP(b)* (M., 1932) pp. 71–5; Ya.E. Rudzutak, *Metall, Ugol', Khimiya* (M., 1932).
30. Ya.E. Rudzutak, *Narodnokhozyaistvennyi plan 1932 g i zadachi KK–RKI* (M., 1932).
31. Ya.E. Rudzutak, *Za povyshenie proizvoditel'nosti truda i ulushenie rabochego snabzheniya* (M., 1932) pp. 17–18.
32. *P*, 12 July 1932; 21, 28 August 1932; 2, 3 October 1932.
33. *P*, 2 December 1932 (Shakhnovskaya); 3 January 1933 (Roizenman); 6 January 1933; 16 April 1933; 20 June 1933 (Belen'kii).

34. *P*, 12 July 1932; 7 January 1933; 15 March 1933; 14 April 1933.
35. Ya.E. Rudzutak, *Za novuyu rabotu na novoi technicheskoi baze* (M., 1933).
36. *ZTKP*, 1931, no. 9–10, pp. 91, 100–1.
37. *KPSS v rez*, vol. 4, p. 531; *P*, 17 June 1931; 19 July 1931.
38. *III Plenum TsKK, iyulya 1931*, pp. 13–15 (Andreev); p. 46 (Akulov).
39. Krasnov, *TsKK–RKI*, p. 404.
40. *SZ*, 1931, art. 408; *SZ*, 1931, ii, art. 216–23; 237–40.
41. *KPSS v rez*, vol. 5, p. 12.
42. *KPSS v rez*, vol. 4, p. 525.
43. *III Plenum TsKK, iyulya 1931*, pp. 38–42 (Akulov), pp. 87–90 (resolution).
44. *P*, 20 January 1931 (Uzhanskii); 7 June 1931; 3 August 1931; 10 October 1931.
45. *P*, 16 July 1931; *ZTKP*, 1931, no. 3, p. 26.
46. *P*, 27 February 1932.
47. *P*, 11 July 1932.
48. *P*, 17 August 1932.
49. *ZTKP*, 1932, no. 1, pp. 77–8; *P*, 11, 18 August 1932.
50. *P*, 8 January 1933.
51. *P*, 17 January 1933; Stalin, *Works*, vol. 13, pp. 220–39.
52. *KPSS v rez*, vol. 5, pp. 78–89.
53. *P*, 24 March 1933.
54. *P*, 21 February 1933.
55. *ZTKP*, 1933, no. 13, pp. 9–12; no. 14, pp. 71–3.
56. See the articles by Krinitskii in *P*, 20 June 1933; 10 December 1933. On the role of the MTS see R. Millar, *One Hundred Thousand Tractors: the MTS and the Development of Controls in Soviet Agriculture* (Cambridge, Mass., 1970).
57. *P*, 30 January 1933; 6 February 1933.
58. *P*, 1 February 1933; 1, 12, 13, 31 March 1933; see also *ZTKP*, 1933, no. 6, pp. 63–4.
59. *ZTKP*, 1933, no. 7, p. 80.
60. *KPSS v rez*, vol. 5, pp. 108–11, 198–205; *Istoriya KPSS*, vol. 4, book 2 (M., 1971) pp. 242, 249–50.
61. *KPSS v rez*, vol. 4, p. 490.
62. *III Plenum TsKK, iyulya 1931*, pp. 14–15, 26 (Andreev); p. 47 (Akulov).
63. *KPSS v rez*, vol. 5, pp. 16–19; *P*, 20 October 1931; 1, 15 November 1931; 4 December 1931.
64. A.V. Krasnov, *TsKK–RKI*, p. 410.
65. *P*, 24 July 1932; 2 August 1932; 3 October 1932; *KPSS v rez*, vol. 5, p. 46.
66. *P*, 23 July 1932; 15 November 1932; 5, 20 December 1932.
67. *P*, 3, 18, 25, 30 April 1933; 5, 18 June 1933; 28 October 1933.
68. *P*, 14 April 1931; 4 May 1931; 8 June 1931.
69. R. Conquest, *The Great Terror* (Harmondsworth, 1971) pp. 733–4.
70. Stalin, *Works*, vol. 13, pp. 53–82.
71. N. Lampert, *The Technical Intelligentsia and the Soviet State* (London, 1979) pp. 99–101; 105.
72. *III Plenum TsKK, iyulya 1931*, p. 14.
73. *III Plenum TsKK*, p. 20.

74. E.F. Rozmirovich (ed.), *Rekonstruktsiya tekhniki upravleniya, 1926– 1930 gg.* (M., 1930) pp. 3–13.
75. The debate between Marxism and Fayolism was a long-standing one: see E.F. Rozmirovich, 'Faiolizm ili Marksizm', *KhU*, 1925, no. 6, pp. 3–12.
76. *P*, 6 June 1931; see the review attacking Ermanskii's 'Menshevism' and 'anti-Marxist' approach to rationalization.
77. *SZ*, 1931, ii, art. 65.
78. M.I. Fuks took over the editorship of *Organizatsiya upravleniya* (*OU*) in February 1931 but was replaced by Ya.M. Paikin in June.
79. *OU*, 1931, no. 1, p. 57.
80. *OU*, 1931, no. 1, pp. 4–10 (M.P. Fuks); see also *OU*, 1931, no. 2–3, p. 1 (M.P. Fuks).
81. *OU*, 1931, no. 1, p. 1 (M. Shulgin).
82. *OU*, 1931, no. 4–5, p. 12 (N.N. Laskin).
83. On Kerzhentsev's career, see K.E. Bailes, 'Alexei Gastev and the Svoiet Controversy over Taylorism', *SS*, vol. xxiv, no. 3, July 1977, pp. 373–94.
84. J. Barber, 'Stalin's Letter to the Editors of Proletarskaya Revolyutsiya', *SS*, January 1976, vol. xxviii, pp. 21–41. Amongst those censured by Stalin was E.M. Yaroslavskii of TsKK–NKRKI.
85. *OU*, 1932, no. 1, p. 1.
86. *OU*, 1932, no. 1, pp. 3–26 (B. Isakov); see also pp. 27–41 (M. Gribanov).
87. *OU*, 1932, no. 5–6.
88. L.F. Morozov and V.P. Portnov, *Organy TSKK–RKI v bor'be za sovershenstvovanie sovetskogo gosudarstvennogo apparata 1923–1934 gg.* M., 1964) p. 78.
89. *P*, 19, 29 November 1932; 1 December 1932.
90. *P*, 9, 19 December 1932. For NKRKI investigations see *P*, 10 February 1933; 18 March 1933.
91. S. Fitzpatrick, 'Cultural Revolution in Russia 1928–1932', *Journal of Contemporary History*, vol, 9, no. 1, January 1974.
92. *III Plenum TsKK, iyulya 1931*, pp. 17, 28.
93. *P*, 15, 23 November 1931.
94. The importance of NKRKI's links with the *rabselkor* movement was stressed in a series of press articles: *P*, 12, 16, 17, 18 February 1931. On the KK–RKI's links with the press, see *P*, 16 July 1931, 29 October 1931.
95. Local KK–RKI journals published from 1930 onwards included *V razvernutoe sotsialisticheskoe nastuplenie* (Urals *oblast* KK–RKI, 1931); *Kontrol' mass* (Central Black Earth *oblast* KK–RKI, 1930); *Pod kontrol' mass* (Far Eastern *krai* KK–RKI, 1931–2); *Proletarskii kontrol'* (North Caucasus *krai* KK–RKI, 1930).
96. Cocks, *Politics of Party Control: The Historical and Institutional Role of Party Control Organs in the CSPU*, unpublished Ph.D. thesis (Harvard University, 1968), pp. 440–59; S.N. Ikonnikov, *Sozdanie i deyatel'nost' ob"edinennykh organov TsKK–RKI v 1923–1934 gg.* (M., 1971) pp. 155– 60.
97. *P*, 5 April 1933 (Roizenman).
98. Ikonnikov, *Sozdanie i deyatel'nost'*, p. 158.
99. Stalin, *Works*, vol. 3, pp. 137–8; 397–8.
100. *P*, 12 February 1933; 24 June 1933; 26 July 1933; 4 September 1933. See

also *ZTKP*, 1933, no. 13, pp. 13–16; no. 14, pp. 4–38.
101. *P*, 1 December 1932; 10 February 1933.
102. Ikonnikov, *Sozdanie i deyatel'nost'*, pp. 158–9.
103. *Spravochnik rabotnika KK–RKI* (M., 1931) p. 34.
104. *III Plenum TsKK, iyulya 1931*, p. 29 (Andreev); pp. 37–43 (Akulov).
105. *P*, 6, 18 July 1931.
106. *P*, 12 February 1931; 17 April 1931.
107. Cocks, *Politics of Party Control*, pp. 169–71.
108. M. Shkiryatov, *O rabote KK–RKI v raione* (M., 1932) p. 50.
109. S. Khavkin, 'Ukreplenie KK–RKI v raione', *ZTKP*, 1932, no. 7, p. 46.
110. Cocks, *Politics of Party Control*, p. 172.
111. *ZTKP*, 1933, no. 4, pp. 12–13 (Rudzutak).
112. *P*, 14 July 1933; 3 August 1933; 10, 21, 23 September 1933.
113. *P*, 13, 14, 25 October 1933.
114. *ZTKP*, 1933, no. 19–20, pp. 2–5; no. 21, p. 18; no. 22, pp. 41–53; no. 23, pp. 15–31.
115. The main Soviet history of TsKK deals very cursorily with the commission's work between 1930 and 1934: see I.M. Moskalenko, *TsKK v bor'be za edinstvo i chistotu partiinykh ryadov* (M., 1973).
116. R.W. Davies, 'The Syrtsov–Lominadze Affair', *SS*, vol. xxxviii, no. 1, January 1981, pp. 29–50.
117. *P*, 2 December 1930.
118. *III Plenum TsKK, iyulya 1931*, pp. 53–77; see also *P*, 23 April 1931 (report of KK–RKI conference); *P*, 23 May 1931 (Yaroslavskii).
119. *P*, 11 October 1932.
120. B.I. Nicolaevsky, *Power and the Soviet Elite* (London, 1966) p. 72.
121. *P*, 13 January 1933; *KPSS v rez*, vol. 5, p. 90.
122. *ZTKP*, 1931, no. 6–7, p. 13 (Andreev).
123. Cocks, *Politics of Party Control*, pp. 512–13.
124. *KPSS v rez*, vol. 5, pp. 98–103.
125. J. Arch Getty, *Origins of the Great Purges* (Cambridge, 1985) pp. 50–1; L. Schapiro, *The Communist Party of the Soviet Union* (London, 1978) pp. 400–1.
126. *P*, 20 May 1933.
127. *P*, 5 May 1933 (Yaroslavskii); 26 June 1933 (Yaroslavskii); 28 May 1933 (Shkiryatov).
128. Alexandrov, *Kto upravlaet Rossiei?* (Berlin, n.d.) pp. 316–30. N.E. Rosenfeldt, *Knowledge and Power* (Copenhagen, 1978).
129. Schapiro, *The Communist Party*, p. 451. Compare the Orgburo's plans of work for 1928 and 1931 in *P*, 17 May 1928 and *P*, 5 March 1931.
130. *Istoriya KPSS*, vol. 4, book 2 (M., 1971) pp. 242; 244–6.
131. *ZTKP*, 1932, no. 4.
132. *SZ*, 1931, ii, art. 182; *SZ*, 1932, ii, art. 257, 258.
133. Rudzutak's speech to the joint Central Committee–TsKK plenum in January 1933 – his only speech reported in the national press in 1933 – was half-hearted and made no mention of TsKK–NKRKI's work: *P*, 26 January 1933.
134. *P*, 10 February 1933 (commemorative article by E.M. Yaroslavskii). See also Yaroslavskii's article in *ZTKP*, 1933, no. 7–8, pp. 1–7. Compare this

with the commemoration of OGPU's fifteenth anniversary in *P*, 20 December 1932, with lead articles by Stalin and Molotov.

135. N. Speranskii, 'Desyat' let Rabkrina', *Sovetskoe gosudarstvo i pravo*, 1933, no. 1–2, p. 24.
136. S. Bertinskii, 'Leninskii put' razvitiya RKI', *Sovetskoe gosudarstvo i pravo*, 1933, no. 1–2, p. 51.
137. James E. Mace, 'Famine and Nationalism in Soviet Ukraine', *Problems of Communism*, vol. xxxiii, May–June 1984, pp. 37–50.
138. See appendix A. Zatonskii was transferred to NKPros UkSSR, where he replaced N.A. Skrypnik as narkom. Skrypnik, the main advocate of Ukrainianization, shortly afterwards committed suicide.
139. *ZTKP*, 1933, no. 14, pp. 69–71.
140. See Appendix A.
141. I.M. Moskalenko, *Organy partiinogo kontrolya v period stroitel'stva sotsializma* (M., 1981) p. 158.
142. G.A. Trukan, *Yan Rudzutak* (M., 1963) p. 92.
143. A.P. Konstantinov *et al.*, *Leninskie traditsii partiinogo-gosudarstvennogo kontrolya* (L., 1963) p. 130.
144. *P*, 31 December 1933; see also *ZTKP*, 1934, no. 1, pp. 13–16.
145. *P*, 22 January 1934.
146. *ZTKP*, 1934, no. 2, pp. 5–6 (Rudzutak); see also *P*, 16 January 1934.
147. *ZTKP*, 1934, no. 2, pp. 7–13 (A. Kaktyn').
148. *Semnadtsatyi s"ezd VKP(b)* (M., 1934) p. 35.
149. *Semnadtsatyi s"ezd VKP(b)*, pp. 278–83, 290–1.
150. *Semnadtsatyi s"ezd VKP(b)*, pp. 298, 299–302, 600, 294. The importance of mass control was also stressed by Veinberg of VTsSPS, p. 597, and by Salmanov of the Komsomol, pp. 630–1.
151. *Semnadtsatyi s"ezd VKP(b)*, p. 560.
152. *Semnadtsatyi s"ezd VKP(b)*, p. 564.
153. *Semnadtsatyi s"ezd VKP(b)*, p. 576 (Furer on the Donbass coal industry); p. 579 (Ugarov); p. 583 (Kalinin); p. 587 (Andreev on the railways).
154. *Semnadtsatyi s"ezd VKP(b)*, p. 659.
155. *Semnadtsatyi s"ezd VKP(b)*, p. 647.
156. *Semnadtsatyi s"ezd VKP(b)*, pp. 673–4.
157. *SZ*, 1934, ii, art. 34.
158. The Commission of Party Control numbered 61 members of whom 18 (29 per cent) were former members of TsKK; the Commission of Soviet Control numbered 71 members of whom 19 (29 per cent) were former members of TsKK. Out of 187 TsKK members elected in 1930 only 37 (19.7 per cent) were elected in 1934 to either of the two new commissions.
159. The implication of this decision is directly hinted at in some of the histories of republican party organs: see *Ocherki istorii Kommunisticheskoi partii Gruzii* (Tbilisi, 1971) pp. 556–7.
160. *P*, 4 July 1933.
161. *Semnadtsatyi s"ezd VKP(b)*, p. 673.
162. Stalin, *Works*, vol. 13, p. 398.
163. *Iz*, 16 March 1934.
164. Conquest, *The Great Terror* (Harmondsworth, 1971), p. 66.
165. K.E. Bailes, *Technology and Society under Lenin and Stalin* (New Jersey,

1978) p. 276.
166. N.S. Khrushchev, *The Secret Speech* (Zh. A. Medvedev and R.A. Medvedev, eds) (Nottingham, 1976) pp. 42–3.
167. Conquest, *The Great Terror*, pp. 130–1; A. Avtorkhanov, *Stalin and the Soviet Communist Party: A Study in the Technology of Power* (Munich, 1959) pp. 207–8.

Conclusion

1. N.S. Khrushchev, *Razvitie ekonomiki SSSR i partiinoe rukovodstvo narodnym khozyaistvom* (M., 1962) pp. 95–6.
2. For a review of this literature see F.I. Potashev, *Reorganizatsiya Rabkrina i TsKK* (Rostov, 1974) pp. 12, 190.
3. G.A. Trukan, *Yan Rudzutak* (M., 1963) pp. 91–2; L.F. Morozov, V.P. Portnov, *Organy TsKK–RKI v bor'be za sovershenstvovanie sovetskogo gosudarstvennogo apparata 1923–1934 gg.* (M., 1964) pp. 49–50; *Leninskaya sistema partiino-gosudarstvennogo kontroliya i ego rol' v stroitel'stve sotsializma 1917–1932 gg.* (M., 1965) pp. 196–8; D. Sturua, *V bor'be za edinstvo ryadov partii: Deyatel'nosti TsKK–RKI Gruzii 1924–1934 gg.* (Tbilisi, 1972) pp. 4–5; R.A. Medvedev, *Let History Judge* (Nottingham, 1976) pp. 427–8.
4. The conservative approach is exemplified by the official party history: *Istoriya KPSS* (M., 1972) vol. iv, book 2, p. 275.

Appendixes

Appendix A

1. E.L. Crowley (ed.), *Party and Government Officials of the Soviet Union 1917–1967* (Metuchen, N.J., 1969) p. 104.
2. *Ezhegodnik Narodnogo Komissariat po Inostrannym Delam* (M., published annually). Numbers consulted for 1925, 1926, 1927, 1929, 1932, 1933.

Appendix B

1. S.N. Ikonnikov, *Organizatsiya i deyatel'nost' RKI v 1920–1925 gg.* (M., 1960) p. 63.
2. N.A. Voskresenskaya, *V.I. Lenin–organizator sotsialisticheskogo kontrolya* (M., 1970) p. 205.
3. *Iz*, 14 August 1923.
4. *Iz*, 23 March 1924; 5 July 1924.
5. *Ezhegodnik Narodnogo Komissariata po Inostrannym Delam na 1925 god*

(hereafter *Ezhegodnik* and date) (M., 1925) p. 36.
6. *Ezhegodnik* 1926, p. 51; *SZ*, 1926, ii, art. 17, 22, 75.
7. *Ezhegodnik* 1927, p. 51; *SZ*, 1926, ii, art. 202; *SZ*, 1927, ii, art. 13, 73, 124.
8. *SZ*, 1928, ii, art. 23, 56.
9. *Ezhegodnik* 1929, pp. 49–50; *SZ*, 1928, ii, art. 271; *SZ*, 1929, ii, art. 25.
10. *SZ*, 1929, ii, art. 289, 290, 311, 312; *SZ*, 1930, ii, art. 39, 178.
11. *SZ*, 1930, ii, art. 312, 330, 355, 374, 377, 397, 403, 432, 453; *SZ*, 1931, ii, art. 31, 32.
12. *SZ*, 1931, ii, art. 223, 224, 235, 256, 257.
13. *SZ*, 1932, ii, art. 112, 257, 259; *SZ*, 1933, ii, art. 3.
14. *SZ*, 1933, ii, art. 35, 184, 213; *SZ*, 1934, ii, art. 7.

Appendix C

1. Source: *Ezhegodnik Narodnogo Komissariata po Inostrannym Delam na 1925 god* (M., 1925) pp. 36–8.
2. Source: *Vsya Moskva 1928* (M., 1928) pp. 101–2.

Appendix D

1. S.N. Ikonnikov, *Sozdanie i deyatel'nost' ob''edinennykh organov TsKK–RKI v 1923–1934gg.* (M., 1971) p. 85.
2. S.N. Ikonnikov, *Sozdanie i deyatel'nost' ob''edinennykh organov TsKK–RKI v 1923–1934gg.* (M., 1971) p. 108.

Appendix E

1. E.L. Crowley (ed.), *Party and Government Officials of the Soviet Union 1917–1967* (Metuchen, 1969).
2. E.L. Crowley (ed.), *Party and Government officials of the Soviet Union 1917–1967* (Metuchen, 1969) pp. 30–2, 37–9.

Appendix F

1. For full listings of TsKK members see E.L. Crowley (ed.) *Party and Government Officials of the Soviet Union 1917–1967* (Metuchen, 1969).
2. I.M. Moskalenko, *TsKK v bor'be za edinstvo i chistotu partiinykh ryadov* (M., 1973) pp. 13, 15.
3. Moskalenko, *TsKK*, p. 23.
4. Moskalenko, *TsKK*, p. 29.
5. *P*, 27 April 1923.
6. *P*, 4 June 1924.
7. *P*, 3 January 1926.
8. *P*, 21 December 1927.
9. *P*, 14 July 1930.

Bibliography

NEWSPAPERS, JOURNALS AND OTHER PERIODICAL PUBLICATIONS

Ekonomicheskaya zhizn'
Ezhegodnik Narodnogo Komissariata po Inostrannym Delam
Istoricheskii arkhiv
Istoricheskie zapiski
Istoriya SSSR
Izvestiya
Izvestiya Tsentral'nogo Komiteta VKP(b)
Partiinoe stroitel'stvo
Pravda
Slavic Review
Sovetskoe gosudarstvo i pravo
Soviet Studies
Torgovo-promyshlennaya gazeta
Voprosy Istorii
Voprosy Istorii KPSS
Za industrializatsiyu
For TsKK and NKRKI journals see p. 294–5.

RUSSIAN LANGUAGE SOURCES

Stenographic Reports of Party Congresses and Conferences

Vos'moi s''ezd RKP(b) (M., 1933).
Vos'maya konferentsiya RKP(b) (M., 1961).
Devyatyi s''ezd RKP(b) (M., 1961).
Desyatyi s''ezd RKP(b). Stenograficheskii otchet (M., 1963).
Odinnadtsatyi s''ezd RKP(b). Stenograficheskii otchet (M., 1961).
Dvenadtsatyi s''ezd RKP(b). 17–25 aprelya 1923 goda. Stenograficheskii otchet (M., 1968).
Trinadtsatyi s''ezd RKP(b). Mai 1924. Stenograficheskii otchet (M., 1963).
XIV (Chetyrnadtsatyi) s''ezd Vsesoyuznoi Rossiiskoi Kommunisticheskoi partii (b). Stenograficheskii otchet (M.–L., 1926).
Pyatnadtsatyi s''ezd VKP(b). Dekabr' 1927 goda. Stenograficheskii otchet, vol. I and II (M., 1961–2).
Shestnadtsataya konferentsiya VKP(b). Aprel' 1927 goda. Stenograficheskii otchet (M., 1962).
XVI (Shestnadtsatyi) s''ezd Vsesoyuznoi Kommunisticheskoi partii (b). Stenograficheskii otchet (M., 1931).

XVII (Semnadtsataya) konferentsiya Vsesoyuznoi Kommunisticheskoi partii (b). Stenograficheskii otchet (M., 1932).
XVII (Semnadtsatyi) s"ezd Vsesoyuznoi Kommunisticheskoi partii (b). 26 yanvarya – 10 fevralya 1934 g. Stenograficheskii otchet (M., 1934).

Party and Government Resolutions, Directives and Decrees

Direktivy KPSS i sovetskogo pravitel'stva po khozyaistvennym voprosam, vol. 1 and 2 (1917–45) (M., 1957).
Industrializatsiya SSSR 1926–1928 gg.: dokumenty i materialy (M., 1969).
Industrializatsiya SSSR 1929–1932 gg.: dokumenty i materialy (M., 1970).
KPSS v rezolyutsiyakh i resheniyakh s"ezdov, konferentsii i plenumov TsK, vol. 1–5 (1898–1941) (M., 1970–1).
Resheniya partii i pravitel'stva po khozyaistvennym voprosam, vol. I and II (1917–40) (M., 1967).
Sobranie uzakonenii i rasporyazhenii RSFSR.
Sobranie zakonov i rasporyazhenii SSSR.
VKP(b) v rezolyutsiyakh i resheniyakh, vol. I and II (M., 1941).

Books and Articles

Alexandrov, *Kto upravlyaet Rossiei?* (Berlin, 1933).
Berezov, P., *V.V. Kuibyshev, 1888–1935* (M., 1958).
Bineman, Ya. and Kheinman, S., *Kadry gosudarstvennogo i kooperativnogo apparata* (M., 1930).
Chugunov, A.I., *Organy sotsialisticheskogo kontrolya RSFSR 1923–1934 gg.* (M., 1972).
Dorokhova, G.A., *Raboche-krest'yanskaya inspektsiya v 1920–1923 gg.* (M., 1959).
Drobizhev, L.M., *Glavnyi shtab sotsialisticheskoi promyshlennosti (Ocherki istorii VSNKh, 1917–1923 gg.)* (M., 1966).
Dubinskii-Mukhadze, I., *Ordzhonikidze* (M., 1967).
Dzhaembaev, T., *Vozniknovenie i razvitie vnutrivedomstvennogo kontrolya* (Alma Ata, 1957).
Gosudarstvennyi apparat SSSR, 1924–1928 g. (M., 1929).
Ikonnikov, S.N., *Organizatsiya i deyatel'nost' RKI v 1920–1925 gg.* (M., 1960).
Ikonnikov, S.N., *Sozdanie i deyatel'nost' ob"edinennykh organov TsKK–RKI v 1923–1934 gg.* (M., 1971).
Kirillov, V.S., Ivanov, V.M. and Zubarev, V.I., *Leninskie traditsii partiino-gosudarstvennogo kontrolya* (L., 1963).
Krasnov, A.V., *TsKK–RKI v bor'be za sotsializm 1923–1934 gg.* (Irkutsk, 1973).
Kuibysheva, G.V., Lezhava, O.A., Nelidov, N.V. and Khavin, A.F., *V.V. Kuibyshev: biografiya* (M., 1966).
Kuzmin, V.I., *V bor'be za sotsialisticheskuyu rekonstruktsiyu* (M., 1976).
Lenin, V.I., *Polnoe sobranie sochinenii*, 5th edn. 55 vols (M., 1958–65).
Leninskii sbornik, (M.–L.: starting 1924), vol. 1. *et seq.*

Mikheev, M.K., *Organy sotsialisticheskogo kontrolya na evropeiskom severe SSSR 1917–1934 gg.* (L., 1983).

Morozov, L.F. and Portnov, V.P., *Organy TsKK–RKI v bor'be za sovershenstvovanie sovetskogo gosudarstvennogo apparata (1923–1934 gg.)* (M., 1964).

Moskalenko, I.M., *TsKK v bor'be za edinstvo i chistotu partiinykh ryadov* (M., 1973).

Moskalenko, I.M., *Organy partiinogo kontrolya v period stroitel'stva sotsializma* (M., 1981).

Ocherki istorii Kommunisticheskoi partii Ukrainy (Kiev, 1977).

Ocherki istorii Kommunisticheskoi partii Gruzii (Tiblisi, 1971).

Nelidov, A.A., *Istoriya gosudarstvennykh uchrezhdenii SSSR*, Chast' I (*1917–1936*) (M., 1962).

Ordzhonikidze, Z., *Put' bolshevika: stranitsy iz zhizni G.K. Ordzhonikidze* (M., 1967).

Orlov, L., *Deyatel'nost' Moskovskoi kontrol'noi komissii i raboche-krest'yanskoi inspektsii v 1924–1934 gg.* (M., 1972).

O Sergo Ordzhonikidze (M., 1980).

Otchet VTsSPS za 1919 god (M., 1920).

Pashukanis, E., *Proletarskoe gosudarstvo i postroenie besklassovogo obshestva* (M., 1932).

Pashukanis, E., *Za marksovo–leninskuyu teoriyu gosudarstva i prava* (M., 1931).

Potashev, F.I., *Reorganizatsiya Rabkrina i TsKK* (Rostov, 1974).

Sturua, D., *V bor'be za edinstvo ryadov partii: Deyatel'nosti TsKK–RKI Gruzii 1924–1934* (Tbilisi, 1972).

Trukan, G.A., *Yan Rudzutak* (M., 1963).

Ryabtsev, I.G. (ed.), *Leninskaya sistema partiino-gosudarstvennogo kontrolya i ego rol' v stroitel'stve sotsializma* (M., 1965).

VII (Sedmoi) vserosssiskii s"ezd sovetov rabochikh, krest'yanskikh, krasnoarmeiskikh i kazach'ikh deputatov (M., 1920).

SSSR Deyatel'nost' SNK i STO. Svodnye materialy I kvartal 1928–1929, (M., 1929).

SSSR God raboty pravitel'stva: Materialy k otchety za 1926–1927 byudzhetnyi god (M., 1928).

Svodnye materialy o deyatel'nosti Soveta Narodnykh Komissarov i Soveta Truda i Oborony, iyulya-sentyabrya 1924–1925 (M., 1925).

Valentinov, N., *Novaya ekonomicheskaya politika i krizis partii posle smerti Lenina* (Stanford, 1971).

Voskresenskaya, N.A., *V.I. Lenin-organizator sotsialisticheskogo kontrolya* (M., 1970).

Za tri mesyatsa, Deyatel'nost' Soveta Narodnykh Komissarov i Soveta Truda i Oborony, oktyabrya-dekabrya 1929 (M., 1930).

Zlotnik, M.I., *Deyatel'nost' organov partiino-gosudarstvennogo kontrolya BSSR v gosudarstvennom stroitel'stve (1917–1934 gg.)* (Minsk, 1969).

TsKK and NKRKI Publications, Reports and Journals

Journals and periodicals

Izvestiya gosudarstvennogo kontrolya (M., published 1918–20).

Izvestiya raboche-krest'yanskoi inspektsii (M., published 1920–3).

Bylleten' TsKK VKP (b) i NKRKI SSSR i RSFSR (M., published 1924–9).
Tekhnika upravleniya (M., published 1925–30).
Khozyaistvo i upravleniya (M., published 1925–7).
Organizatsiya upravleniya (M., published 1931–4).
Za ratsionalizatsiyu (M., published 1928–30).
Za tempy, kachestvo, proverku (M., published 1931–4).

Stenographic reports of TsKK plenums
Stenografìcheskii otchet Plenuma TsKK RKP (b), 28–30 marta 1924 g. (M., 1924).
Vtoroi Plenum TsKK RKP(b) sozyva XIII s"ezda partii, 3–5 oktyabrya 1924 g. (M., 1924).
VI Plenum TsKK RKP(b) sozyva XIII s"ezda RKP(b), 11–13 dekabrya 1925 g. (M., 1926).
Vtoroi Plenum TsKK sozyva XIV s"ezda VKP(b), 2–4 aprelya 1926 g. (M., 1926).
IV Plenum TsKK sozyva XIV s"ezda VKP(b), 21–22 oktyabrya 1926 g. (M., 1926).
VI Plenum TsKK sozyva XIV s"ezda VKP(b), 26–27 iyulya 1927 g. (M., 1927).
III Plenum TsKK sozyva XV s"ezda VKP(b), 25–29 avgusta 1928 g. (M., 1928).
III Plenum TsKK VKP(b), 6–10 iyulya 1931 g. (M., 1931).

Internal documents of TsKK and NKRKI
Protokoly zasedaniya kollegii Narodnogo Komissariata Raboche-Krest'yanskoi Inspektsii SSSR (M., 1924) nos. 7–14, 16–20, 22, 23, 26, 28, 32–38.
Protokoly TsKK (M., 1930) nos. 60–68. Available in the Smolensk Archives, WKP 57.

Collections of resolutions concerning TsKK and NKRKI
TsKK–RKI v osnovnykh postanovleniyakh partii (M.–L., 1927).
Deyatel'nost' organov partiino-gosudarstvennogo kontrolya po sovershenstvovaniyu gosudarstvennogo apparata (M., 1964).
Lenin, V.I., *O kontrole i proverke ispolneniya* (M., 1980), vol. 1.
Obrazovanie i razvitie organov sotsialisticheskogo kontrolya v SSSR (1917–1975), Sbornik dokumentov i materialov (M., 1975).

TsKK–NKRKI reports
Al'brekht, K.I., *Rekonstruktsiya i ratsionalizatsiya lesnogo khozyaistva* (M.–L., 1930).
Belen'kii, Z.M., *Rezul'taty obsledovaniya NKRKI kapital'nogo stroitel'stva VSNKh SSSR* (M., 1930).
Bor'ba za sotsialisticheskuyu rekonstruktsiyu sel'skogo khozyaistva (M.–L., 1930).
Dostizheniya i nedochety tekstil'noi promyshlennosti (M., 1926).
Edinyi sel'sko-khozyaistvennyi nalog v 1924–1925 gody (M., 1925).
Gastev, A.K., *Kak nado rabotat'* (M., 1926).
Gastev, A.K., *Ot narkomata kontrolya k narkomatu organizatsii* (M., 1925).
Gol'tsman, A.Z., *Reservy v narodnom khozyaistve* (M., 1929).
Gol'tsman, A.Z., *Rezhim ekonomii i stroitel'stvo sotsializma* (M., 1926).

296   *Bibliography*

Gurevich, A.I., *Raboche-krest'yanskaya inspektsiya i profsoyuzy* (M., 1929).
Itogi raboty TsKK i Rabkrina Ukraina za 1924–1925 gg. (Khar'kov, 1925).
Kaktyn', A.M. (ed.), *Sotsialisticheskaya rekonstruktsiya khlopkovodstva* (M.–L., 1934).
Kerzhentsev, P.M., *NOT, Nauchnaya organizatsiya truda i zadachi partii* (M., 1923).
Kerzhentsev, P.M., *NOT, Nauchnaya organizatsiya truda* (L., 1925).
Kratkii otchet o deyatel'nosti Narodnogo Komissariat Raboche-Krest'yanskoi Inspektsii za period mai–dekabr' 1923 g. (M., 1924).
Kuibyshev, V.V., *Rabota TsKK–RKI v svyazi s osnovnymi zadachami partii* (M., 1924).
Kuibyshev, V.V., *Zadachi TsKK i RKI* (M., 1924).
Kuibyshev, V.V., *Zadachi TsKK i RKI po ratsionalizatsii gosapparata* (M., 1925).
Landau, A., *Protiv byurokratizma, beskhozyaistvennosti, besplanovosti* (M., 1930).
Leder, V., *Sotsialisticheskaya ratsionalizatsiya v bor'be s poteryami* (M., 1930).
Nedochety kapital'nogo stroitel'stva (M., 1929).
NKRKI v bor'be za khlopkovuyu nezavisimost' (M., 1930).
Ordzhonikidze, G.K., *Stati'i i rechi*, vol. 2, 1926–1937 gg. (M., 1957).
O rekonstruktsii zavodov Yugostali (M., 1929).
Obsledovanie deyatel'nosti tresta Uralmet (Sverdlovsk, 1929).
Rabota Narodnogo Komissariat Raboche-Krest'yanskoi Inspektsiii SSSR ot V k VI vsesoyuznomy s"ezdy sovetov (M.–L., 1931).
RKI v sovetskom stroitel'stve (M., 1926).
Rekonstruktsiya lesnogo dela, materialy k 16 s"ezdu VKP(b) (M.–L., 1930).
Rozengol'ts, A.P. (ed.), *Promyshlennost'* (M., 1930).
Rozmirovich, E.F. (ed.), *Rekonstruktsiya tekhniki upravleniya 1926–1930 gg.* (M., 1930).
Rozmirovich, E.F., *Printsipy metodologii i organizatsionnoi politiki v tekhnike upravleniya* (M., 1930).
Rozmirovich, E.E., *V chem sushchnost' reformy Rabkrina* (M., 1923).
Rudzutak, Ya. E., *Metall, Ugol', Khimiya* (M., 1932).
Rudzutak, Ya. E., *Narodnokhozyaistvennyi plan 1932 g. i zadachi KK–RKI* (M., 1932).
Rudzutak, Ya. E., *Za novuyu rabotu na novoi tekhnicheskoi baze* (M., 1933).
Rudzutak, Ya. E., *Za povyshenie proizvoditel'nosti truda, za ulushenie rabochego snabzheniya* (M., 1932).
Samarin, A., *Za udeshevlenie gosapparata* (M., 1929).
Segal', A.I., *Ekonomika neftyanykh khozyaistv* (M., 1925).
Segal', A.I., *Vosstanovlenie Donbassa* (M., 1924).
Traktorizatsiya sel'skogo khozyaistva RSFSR (M., 1930).
Yakovlev, Ya. A., *K voprosu o sotsialisticheskom pereustroistve sel'skogo khozyaistva* (M.–L., 1928).
Yakovlev, Ya. A., *Ob oshibkakh khlebo-furazhnogo balansa TsSU i ego istolkovatelei* (M., 1926).
Yakovlev, Ya. A., *Partiya v bor'be s byurokratizmom* (M.–L., 1928).
Yakovlev, Ya. A., *Rassloenie derevni* (M.–L., 1925).
Yakovlev, Ya. A., *Sel'skoe khozyaistvo i industrializatsiya* (M.–L., 1927).

Yakovlev, Ya. A., *Za kolkhozy: kollektivnoe ili kulatskoe khozyaistvo* (M., 1928).
Yuzhnaya metallurgiya (M., 1924).
Zatonskii, V.P., *Industrializatsiya SSSR i rezhim ekonomii* (Khar'kov, 1926).
Zatonskii, V.P., *Organizatsiya ispolneniya i kachestvo raboty* (Khar'kov, 1931).

ENGLISH LANGUAGE SOURCES

Books and Articles

Adams, J.S., *Citizen Inspectors in the Soviet Union: The People's Control Committee* (New York, 1977).
Avtorkhanov, A., *Stalin and the Soviet Communist Party: A Study in the Technology of Power* (Munich, 1959).
Azrael, J., *Managerial Power and Soviet Politics* (Cambridge, Mass., 1966).
Bahro, R., *The Alternative in Eastern Europe* (London, 1987).
Bailes, K.E., *Technology and Society under Lenin and Stalin* (Princeton, 1978).
Batsell, W.R., *Soviet Rule in Russia* (New York, 1929).
Berliner, J.S., *Factory and Manager in the USSR* (Cambridge, Mass., 1957).
Black, C.E. (ed.), *The Transformation of Russian Society* (Cambridge, Mass., 1960).
Blondel, J., *An Introduction to Comparative Government* (London, 1969).
Carr, E.H., *The Bolshevik Revolution, 1917–1923*, vol. 1 and 2 (Harmondsworth, 1966).
Carr, E.H., *The Interregnum, 1923–1924* (Harmondsworth, 1969).
Carr, E.H., *Socialism in One Country, 1924–1926*, vol. 1 and 2 (Harmondsworth, 1970).
Carr, E.H. and Davies, R.W., *Foundations of a Planned Economy, 1926–1929*, vol. 1 (Harmondsworth, 1974).
Carr, E.H., *Foundations of a Planned Economy, 1926–1929*, vol. 2 (Harmondsworth, 1976).
Chapman, B., *The Profession of Government* (London, 1959).
Christian, D., 'The Supervisory Function in Russian and Soviet History', *Slavic Review*, vol. 41, no. 1, Spring 1982, pp. 91–103.
Ciliga, A., *The Russian Enigma* (London, 1979).
Cohen, S.F., *Bukharin and the Bolshevik Revolution* (Oxford, 1980).
Conquest, R., *The Great Terror* (Harmondsworth, 1971).
Conquest, R., *The Harvest of Sorrow: Soviet Collectivisation and the Terror Famine* (London, 1986).
Crowley, E.L. (ed.), *Party and Government Officials of the Soviet Union 1917–1967* (Metuchen, N.J., 1969).
Daniels, R.V., *The Conscience of the Revolution* (Cambridge, Mass., 1960).
Davies, R.W., *The Development of the Soviet Budgetary System* (Cambridge, 1958).
Davies, R.W., *The Socialist Offensive: The Collectivisation of Soviet Agriculture, 1929–1930* (London, 1980).
Davies, R.W., 'Some Soviet Economic Controllers–III–Kuibyshev, Ordzhon-

ikidze', *Soviet Studies*, 1961, vol. xii, pp. 23–52.

Davies, R.W. and Wheatcroft, S.G., 'Further Thoughts on the First Soviet Five Year Plan', *Slavic Review*, 1975, vol. 34, no. 4, pp. 790–802.

Day, R., *Leon Trotsky and the Politics of Economic Isolation* (Cambridge, 1973).

Deutscher, I., *Stalin* (Oxford, 1949).

Deutscher, I., *The Prophet Armed, Trotsky 1879–1921* (Oxford, 1970).

Deutscher, I., *The Prophet Unarmed, Trotsky 1921–1929* (Oxford, 1970).

Deutscher, I., *The Prophet Outcast, Trotsky 1929–1940* (Oxford, 1970).

Dobb, M., *Soviet Economic Development Since 1917* (London, 1948).

Downs, A., *Inside Bureaucracy* (Boston, 1967).

Eastman, M., *Since Lenin Died* (London, 1925).

Erlich, A., *The Soviet Industrialization Debate 1924–1928* (Cambridge, Mass., 1960).

Etzioni, A., *Modern Organizations* (New Jersey, 1964).

Eudin, X.J., Fisher, H.D. and Fisher, H.H., *The Life of a Chemist: memoirs of Vladimir N. Ipatieff* (London, 1946).

Fainsod, M., *How Russia is Ruled* (Cambridge, Mass., 1967).

Fainsod, M., *Smolensk under Soviet Rule* (London, 1958).

Fitzpatrick, S. (ed.), *Cultural Revolution in Russia* (Bloomington, In., 1978).

Fitzpatrick, S., 'Stalin and the Making of a New Elite 1928–1939' *Slavic Review*, vol. 38, no. 3, September 1979, pp. 377–402.

Fitzpatrick, S., 'Ordzhonikidze's Takeover of Vesenkha: A Case Study in Soviet Bureaucratic Politics', *Soviet Studies*, vol. xxxvii, no. 2, pp. 153–72.

Franklin, B. (ed.), *The Essential Stalin* (London, 1973).

Granick, D., *The Red Executive* (New York, 1970).

Harding, N., *Lenin's Political Thought*, vol. 2 (London, 1981).

Hayek, F.A., *The Road to Serfdom* (London, 1976).

Hegedus, A., *Socialism and Bureaucracy* (London, 1976).

History of the Communist Party of the Soviet Union (Bolsheviks): Short Course (Moscow, 1945).

Hough, J.F., *The Soviet Prefects* (Cambridge, Mass., 1969).

Kaplan, F.I., *Bolshevik Ideology and the Ethics of Soviet Labour 1917–1920* (London, 1969).

Khrushchev, N.S., *The Secret Speech* (Zh. A. Medvedev, R.A. Medvedev, eds.) (Nottingham, 1976).

Kollontai, A., *The Workers' Opposition* (Solidarity, London, 1968).

Lampert, N., *The Technical Intelligentsia and the Soviet State 1928–1935* (London, 1979).

La Palombara, J. (ed.), *Bureaucracy and Political Development* (Princeton, 1963).

Lewin, M., *Lenin's Last Struggle* (London, 1973).

Lewin, M., *Russian Peasants and Soviet Power* (London, 1968).

Lewin, M., *The Making of the Soviet System* (London, 1985).

Maxwell, B.W., *The Soviet State* (London, 1935).

Medvedev, R., *Let History Judge* (Nottingham, 1976).

Miller, R., *One Hundred Thousand Tractors: the MTS and the Development of Controls in Soviet Agriculture* (Cambridge, Mass., 1970).

Morgan, G.G., *Soviet Administrative Legality: The Role of the Attorney General's Office* (Stanford, 1962).

Bibliography   299

Narkiewicz, O.A., *The Making of the Soviet State Apparatus* (Manchester, 1970).
Nove, A., *An Economic History of the USSR* (London, 1972).
Perrins, M., 'Rabkrin and Workers' Control in Russia 1917–1934', *European Studies Review*, 1980, vol. 10, pp. 225–46.
Pethybridge, R., *The Social Prelude to Stalinism* (London, 1977).
Polan, A.J., *Lenin and the End of Politics* (London, 1984).
Remington, T., 'Institution Building in Bolshevik Russia: The Case of "State Kontrol"', *Slavic Review*, vol. 41, no. 1, Spring 1982, pp. 91–103.
Reshetar, J.S., *The Soviet Polity* (Toronto, 1971).
Rigby, T.H., *Lenin's Government: Sovnarkom 1917–1922* (Cambridge, 1979).
Self, P., *Administrative Theories and Politics* (London, 1972).
Serge, V., *Memoirs of a Revolutionary, 1901–1941* (London, 1967).
Service, R., *The Bolshevik Party in Revolution, 1917–1923* (London, 1979).
Schapiro, L., *The Origins of the Communist Autocracy* (London, 1977).
Schapiro, L., *The Communist Party of the Soviet Union* (London, 1970).
Simon, H., Smithburg, D.W. and Thompson, V.A., *Public Administration* (New York, 1958).
Sirianni, C., *Workers Control and Socialist Democracy: The Soviet Experience* (London, 1982).
Skilling, H.G. and Griffiths, F. (eds), *Interest Groups in Soviet Politics* (Princeton, N.J., 1973).
Smith, G.B., *The Soviet Procuracy and the Supervision of Administration* (Alphen aan den Rijn, 1978).
Smith, S., *Red Petrograd* (Cambridge, 1985).
Solomon, S.G. (ed.), *Pluralism in the Soviet Union* (London, 1983).
Souvarine, B., *Stalin: A Critical Survey of Bolshevism* (London, 1940).
Stalin, I.V., *Works* (vols 1–13) (Moscow, 1952–5).
Strauss, E., *The Ruling Servants* (London, 1961).
Thompson, V.A., 'Administrative Objectives for Development Administration', *Administrative Science Quarterly*, 1964, vol. 9, pp. 91–108.
Thompson, V.A., 'Bureaucracy and Innovation', *Administrative Science Quarterly*, 1965, vol. 10, pp. 1–20.
Thompson, V.A., 'Hierarchy, Specialisation and Organisational Conflict', *Administrative Science Quarterly*, 1961, vol. 5, pp. 485–521.
Torok, L., *The Socialist System of State Control* (Budapest, 1974).
Towster, J., *Political Power in the USSR 1917–1947* (New York, 1948).
Trotsky, L.D., *The Trotsky Papers*, vol. I and II (The Hague, 1964).
Trotsky, L.D., *The Real Situation in Russia* (London, n.d.) (M. Eastman ed.).
Trotsky, L.D., *My Life* (New York, 1970)
Trotsky, L.D., *The Revolution Betrayed* (London, 1967).
Trotsky, L.D., *The Challenge of the Left Opposition 1923–1925* (New York, 1975).
Trotsky, L.D., *The Challenge of the Left Opposition 1926–1927* (New York, 1980).
Webb, S. and Webb, B., *Soviet Communism: A New Civilisation?* (London, 1935).
Weber, M., *The Theory of Social and Economic Organisation* (Glencoe, 1947).
Weber, M., 'The Essentials of Bureaucratic Organisation: An Ideal-Type

Construction', in R.K. Merton (ed.), *Reader in Bureaucracy* (New York, 1952).

Westgarth, J.R., *Russian Engineer* (London, 1974).

Zaleski, E., *Planning for Economic Growth in the Soviet Union 1918–1932* (Chapel Hill, 1971).

Unpublished Theses

Cocks, P.M., *Politics of Party Control: The Historical and Institutional Role of Party Control Organs in the CPSU*, unpublished Ph.D. thesis (Harvard University, 1968).

Rees, E.A., *Rabkrin and the Soviet System of State Control 1920–1930*, unpublished Ph.D. thesis (Centre for Russian and East European Studies (CREES), University of Birmingham, 1982).

Spoerry, P.S., *The Central Rabkrin Apparatus 1917–1925*, unpublished Ph.D. thesis (Harvard University, 1967).

Wheatcroft, S.G., *Views on Grain Output, Agricultural Reality and Planning in the Soviet Union in the 1920s*, unpublished M.Soc.Sci. thesis (Centre for Russian and East European Studies (CREES), University of Birmingham, 1974).

Name Index

301

Subject Index